THE EUROPEAN PARLIAMENT

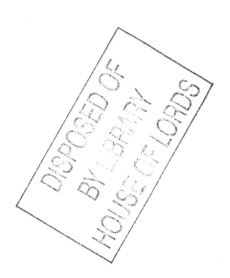

The European Parliament
4th edition

by

RICHARD CORBETT MEP, FRANCIS JACOBS
and
MICHAEL SHACKLETON

The European Parliament
4th edition

Published by John Harper Publishing
27 Palace Gates Road
London N22 7BW, United Kingdom.
Telephone: +44 (0) 20 8881 4774
E-mail: jhpublish@aol.com

First and second editions published by Longman Group UK Limited
First edition 1990
Reprinted 1992
2nd edition 1992
3rd edition Cartermill International Ltd 1995
Reprinted 1995
4th edition 2000
ISBN (Cased) 0–9536278–2–9
ISBN (Paperback) 0–9536278–1–0

© John Harper Publishing 2000

Typeset in 10/11pt Palatino by Fakenham Photosetting

Printed and Bound in Great Britain by Bookcraft (Bath) Ltd.

Dedication

To Anne, Susan and Jan

"On my first visit to Strasbourg in 1979 as a Member of the European Parliament, I went for a walk across the bridge from Strasbourg to Kehl. Strasbourg is in France. Kehl is in Germany. They are very close. I stopped in the middle of the bridge and I meditated. There is Germany – there is France. If I had stood on this bridge 30 years before at the end of the Second World War when 25 million people lay dead across our continent and if I had said: 'Don't worry. In 30 years time we will all be together in a new Europe, our conflicts and wars will be ended and we will be working together in our common parliament', I would have been sent to a psychiatrist. But it has happened and it is now clear that the European Union is the best example in the history of the world of conflict resolution."

John Hume MEP
Acceptance speech upon winning the Nobel Peace Prize
Oslo, 10 December 1998

TABLE OF CONTENTS

Tables and figures xiv
Foreword xvii
About the authors xviii
Acknowledgements xix

I: THE FRAMEWORK

Chapter 1. The Parliament in context 2

From fig-leaf to co-legislature 3
A federal system in the making? 6
The style of Parliament 7

Chapter 2. How it is elected 10

Moving towards direct elections 10
The variety of national systems in force and the main differences
    between them 12
Main issues in drawing up a uniform electoral system 16
   – Specific issues 16
   – (i) The nature of the electoral system 16
   – (ii) Conditions applying to candidates 19
   – (iii) The right to vote 20
   – (iv) Finance 20
   – (v) The number of seats per country 20
Attempts that have been made to draw up a uniform electoral
    system 22
The European elections so far 24

Chapter 3. Where, when and in quale lingua 26

The seat issue: where the Parliament meets 26
   – Historical background 27
When: Parliament's cycle of activities 32
In *quale lingua*: languages within the European Parliament 33

II: THE ACTORS AND WORKING STRUCTURES

Chapter 4: The individual members 40

Rights and obligations of individual members 40
   – Incompatibilities and verification of credentials 40
   – Facilities, salaries and allowances 41
   – Immunities 44
   – Declaration of financial interests 45
   – Steps towards adoption of a members' statute 46
   – Members' assistants 47
Background of the individual members elected in 1999 49
   – Length of service 49
   – Dual mandate MEPs 50
   – Balance between men and women 50
   – National parliamentary and ministerial experience 50
   – Other political experience 52
   – Other experience 52
   – Post-MEP experience 53
The role of individual members within the European Parliamentary
   system 54
The work of an individual MEP: choice of priorities 56

Chapter 5. The Political Groups 59

Historical evolution 59
Composition of the Groups after the 1999 elections 67
   – Group of the European People's Party (Christian Democrats)
     and European Democrats (EPP-ED) 67
   – Group of the Party of European Socialists (PES/PSE) 70
   – European Liberal, Democratic and Reformist Group (ELDR) 71
   – Group of the Greens/European Free Alliance 73
   – Confederal Group of the European United Left/Nordic Green
     Left 75
   – Group of the Europe of Nations 77
   – Europe of Democracies and Diversities 79
   – The non-attached members 79
Changing Groups 81
Support provided by the European Parliament to the Political
   Groups 81
Structures of Groups 82
Political Group staffing 82
Working methods within the Groups 86
Own activities of the Groups 86
National party delegations 87
Group discipline and whipping 89
Power balances and relationship between the Groups 90
European party federations 91

Chapter 6. Leadership structures 94

The President 94
The Vice-Presidents 96
The Quaestors 98
The election of the President, Vice-Presidents and Quaestors 98
The Conference of Presidents, the Bureau and the College of
       Quaestors 102
The Conference of Committee Chairmen and the Conference of
       Delegation Chairmen 103

Chapter 7. The Parliamentary committees 105

The structure and character of committees 105
Membership of committees 106
Office-holders and their selection 108
Group coordinators 110
Staff of committees 111
Place, time and character of meetings 112
Committee business 113
       – Draft reports and opinions 113
       – Volume and distribution of reports 115
       – Nomination of rapporteurs and draftsmen 117
       – Choices facing a rapporteur 118
       – The progress of reports through a committee 120
       – Alternative procedures 122
       – Treatment of confidential documents in committee 123
Subcommittees, working parties and temporary committees 124
       – Subcommittees 124
       – Working parties 124
       – Temporary committees 125

Chapter 8. Interparliamentary delegations 130

Historical development 130
Number and composition of delegations 131
Leadership of the delegations 134
Role of delegations and joint parliamentary committees 134
Relations with the rest of the Parliament 136
The ACP-EU Joint Assembly 137
Other interparliamentary assemblies 139
Ad hoc delegations 139
Overall assessment 140

Chapter 9. Plenary 141

The setting 141
The typical timetable of a part-session 143
How the plenary agenda is drawn up 145
       – Topical and urgent debates 146

The allocation of speaking time in debates 147
Voting procedures 148
   – Voting order 150
Building majorities: bargaining among Groups 152
Common procedural manoeuvres 153
Order in the chamber 154
Record of plenary sittings 155
"Open" Bureau and Conference of Presidents 156
Formal sittings 156

Chapter 10. Intergroups 157

The evolution of intergroups since 1979 157
Advantages and disadvantages 158
Specific intergroups 160
   – European Constitution Intergroup 160
   – Intergroup on the Welfare and Conservation of Animals 161
   – The Sports Intergroup 163

Chapter 11. The Parliament Secretariat 166

Who are the staff of the Parliament? 166
The structure of the Secretariat 168
Issues affecting the Secretariat 171

III: THE POWERS OF THE PARLIAMENT

Chapter 12. The Parliament and legislation 176

The consultation procedure 176
   – Extension of the scope of the procedure 176
   – Improving the quality of the procedure 178
   – Giving teeth to the procedure: the Court ruling of 1980 and its
     repercussions 179
   – Taking advantage of the *Isoglucose* ruling 180
   – The limits of the *Isoglucose* ruling 181
   – The 1975 conciliation procedure 181
   – Consultation after Amsterdam 183
The cooperation procedure 185
The co-decision procedure 188
   – The nature of the procedure 188
   – Scope of the procedure 191
   – The impact of the procedure 193
   – The prospect of conciliation 196
   – The process of conciliation 196
   – Composition of the conciliation committee 198

Developments resulting from the cooperation and co-decision
    procedures 200
  – Determination of the legal basis of proposals 200
  – Reconsultation of Parliament 201
  – Negotiations and dialogue with the Council and Commission ..201
Assent procedure 203
Parliament and the approval of international agreements 204
  – The Luns procedure 205
  – The AETR ruling of the Court 205
  – The Luns-Westerterp procedure 205
  – Improvement of the Luns-Westerterp procedure 206
  – The Stuttgart "Solemn Declaration on European Union" 206
  – The assent procedure introduced by the Single European Act ...207
  – The extension of the assent procedure by the Treaty of
    Maastricht 208
Right to initiate legislation 209
  – Resolutions seeking to initiate legislation 210
Annual legislative programme 211
Overall assessment 212

Chapter 13. The budgetary role 216

The annual budgetary procedure 216
  – Preparing for the preliminary draft budget 218
  – Responding to the draft budget as adopted by the Council 220
  – First reading of the draft budget in Parliament 221
  – From first to second reading 222
  – The option of rejection 223
  – Implementation of the budget 224
Parliament's budgetary objectives 225
  – Developing Non-Compulsory Expenditure 225
  – Using the Maximum Rate of Increase 226
  – Promoting policies through the budget 229
  – Influencing the level of revenue 232

Chapter 14. Appointment and dismissal 233

Introduction 233
The development of the Parliament's formal powers as regards EU
    appointments 233
Parliament and the appointment of the Commission 234
Appointments to the Central Bank and European Monetary
    Institute 238
Appointments to the Court of Auditors 239
Appointments to the Office of Ombudsman 240
European Parliament role in other appointments 241
Possible future changes in appointments to other European Union
    posts 241
The right of censure 243

Chapter 15. Scrutiny and control of the executive 246

Scrutiny through debates, questions and reports 247
    – Debates on statements 247
    – Parliamentary questions 248
    – Reports 250
Control of expenditure 252
Scrutiny of executive decisions and implementing measures:
    the issue of "comitology" 255
    – What is comitology? 255
    – The 1987 comitology decision 256
    – The Plumb-Delors procedure 257
    – The "Modus Vivendi" of December 1994 258
    – Related developments 259
    – The Council decision of 28 June 1999 259
    – Concluding remarks on comitology 260
Committees of inquiry 261
Judicial review 264
    – The right to be consulted 265
    – Institutional autonomy 265
    – Illegal failure to act 266
    – Annulment of parliamentary acts 266
    – Annulment of the acts of other institutions 267
    – Annulment of acts of Council and Parliament acting jointly 268
    – Observations by Parliament on international agreements 268
    – Parliament and the Court: a brief assessment 268
    – Parliament and the application of Community law in the
        Member States 269
Overall assessment 269

Chapter 16. A forum and channel for communication 270

Parliament broadening the agenda 270
    – Debates 270
    – Resolutions adopted at the Parliament's own initiative 271
    – Hearings 272
    – Activities in the field of human rights 273
    – Petitions 275
A network of contacts 278
    – Contact channels to the other EU institutions 278
    – Contacts with individual governments 281
    – Contact channels to national parliaments 283
Openness, transparency and public awareness 287
    – Visibility of proceedings 287
    – Lobbyists 289
    – The media 290
    – Visitors 291
    – Public awareness of the Parliament 293
Overall assessment 294

Chapter 17. Parliament and constitutional change 295

Draft Treaty on European Union and the Single European Act 296
From the Single European Act to Maastricht 299
From Maastricht to Amsterdam 300
The Millennium IGC and enlargement 304
Conclusion 305

IV: APPENDICES

1. European Parliament elections 308
2. Who are the MEPs? 314
3. Contact details of Parliament Offices 330
4. Sources of information on the Parliament 333

INDEX 345

TABLES AND FIGURES

Tables   *Page*

Table   1   Main events in the Parliament's history   9
Table   2   Number of MEPs per country and ratio to population   12
Table   3   Electoral system used for 1999 European elections   13
Table   4   Participation by non-nationals in European elections   14
Table   5   Turnout in European Parliament elections   25
Table   6   Growth of time spent in plenary sittings   33
Table   7   Comparison of salaries and expenses of MPs and MEPs   43
Table   8   Women MEPs (June 1999)   50
Table   9   Previous parliamentary and governmental experience of
              MEPs   52
Table   10   MEPs and parties in the European Parliament   64
Table   11   Leaders of the main Political Groups   83
Table   12   Leaders of the UK Conservative and Labour MEPs   88
Table   13   Presidents of the Parliament   95
Table   14   The Vice-Presidents: 1999–2002 term of office and
              responsibilities   97
Table   15   The Quaestors: 1999–2002 term of office   98
Table   16   Presidential elections since 1979   100
Table   17   Number of reports adopted in plenary, listed by
              committee of origin, during the 1994–99 legislature   116
Table   18   Committee chairmanships in the elected Parliament
              1979–99   126
Table   19   Interparliamentary delegations and delegations to joint
              parliamentary committees   132
Table   20   Indicative list of intergroups at beginning of 1999–2004
              legislature   165
Table   21   Breakdown of permanent officials by category and
              nationality   167
Table   22   Secretaries-General of the European Parliament   168
Table   23   Distribution of legislative procedures and voting
              methods in Council under Amsterdam Treaty provisions   214
Table   24   Votes of confidence on incoming Commissions and
              incoming Commission Presidents   236
Table   25   Motions of censure tabled within the European
              Parliament   245
Table   26   Parliamentary questions tabled during the fourth
              legislature 1994–99   250

Table   27   Sakharov Prize Winners   278
Table   28   Former MEPs in the Commission   280
Table   29   List of specialist committees on European affairs in the
             parliaments of the Member States   286
Table   30   Visitors' Groups (1998)   292
Table   31   Approximate number of MEPs for applicant states under
             current system   304

Figures

Figure 1   Evolution of Political Groups   66
Figure 2   European Parliament Secretariat   169
Figure 3   The consultation procedure   177
Figure 4   The cooperation procedure   186
Figure 5   Presentation of the new co-decision procedure   190
Figure 6   Assent procedure   203

FOREWORD

It is with great pleasure that I welcome this fourth edition of *The European Parliament*. Over ten years this book has proven its worth as an invaluable guide to the workings of the one directly elected institution in the European Union. As we enter a new and crucial phase in the democratisation of the Union, I am confident that it will continue to make an important contribution towards improving the level of knowledge and understanding about the institution of which I have the honour to be President.

C'est avec grand plaisir que je souhaite la bienvenue à cette quatrième édition du livre *Le Parlement européen*. Pendant dix ans ce livre a démontré sa valeur en tant que guide essentiel au fonctionnement de la seule institution élue au suffrage universel au sein de l'Union européenne. Au moment où nous entrons dans une nouvelle phase décisive dans le démocratisation de l'Union, je reste convaincue que cet ouvrage contribuera encore grandement à ameliorer le niveau de connaissance et de compréhension de l'institution que j'ai l'honneur de présider.

Nicole Fontaine
President of the European Parliament

ABOUT THE AUTHORS

Dr. Richard Corbett is a Labour MEP for Yorkshire and the Humber. He is spokesperson on constitutional affairs in the European Parliament both for the Labour MEPs and for the whole Socialist Group. He was first elected to the Parliament in a by-election in 1996, but previously worked there as Deputy Secretary-General of the Socialist Group and, prior to that, as a civil servant. He has written widely on European affairs, including *The Treaty of Maastricht: from conception to ratification* (Longman, 1994) and *The Role of the European Parliament in closer EU Integration* (Macmillan, 1997).

Francis Jacobs is the Head of Division responsible for the Committee on the Environment, Public Health and Consumer Protection within the European Parliament secretariat. He has previously worked on the European Parliament Committees on Constitutional Affairs and on Economic and Monetary Affairs, as well as on its Temporary Committee on German Unification. He was the editor and principal author of *Western European Political Parties: A Comprehensive Guide* (published by Longman), and has contributed various articles and chapters on European Union matters, notably on the work of the European Parliament.

Dr. Michael Shackleton is the Head of the Division responsible for conciliation under the co-decision procedure within the European Parliament Secretariat. He has previously worked in the secretariat of the Committee on Budgets, the division for relations with national parliaments and as head of the unit responsible for the Committee of Inquiry into the Community Transit System. He has published across a diverse range of Community issues, including the budget, interparliamentary relations and the democratic deficit, and has lectured widely on the role of the Parliament, including as a Visiting Fellow at the College of Europe from 1994–99.

ACKNOWLEDGEMENTS

In the five years since the last edition the nature of the Parliament has changed considerably. As a result the authors needed help more than ever from their colleagues in the Parliament and friends outside.

Particular thanks go to Steve Clark, Ben Hagard, Eamonn Noonan and José Luis Rufas Quintana, for helping to prepare revised versions of specific sections of the book, and to Timothy Bainbridge, Helmut Betz, Roger Brawn, Charlotte Burns, Antoine Cahen, Fernando Carbajo, Carlo Chicco, Jeff Coolegem, Alfredo De Feo, Jo Dunne, Paul Dunstan, David Earnshaw, John Fitzmaurice, Roger Glass, Thomas Grunert, Angel Luis Guillén Zanón, Jean Marc Laforest, José Luis Linnzasoro, Gordon Lake, Nikolas Lane, Leena Linnus, Walter Masur, Pekka Nurminen, Una O'Dwyer, Niall O'Neill, Peter Pappamikail, Chris Piening, Janet Pitt, Bryan Rose, Dermot Scott, Saverio Solari, Ralph Spencer, Miguel Tell Cremades, Patrick Twidle, Lord Tomlinson of Walsall, Juan Urbieta Gandiaga, Roger Vanhaeren, David Walker, David Wilkins, Barry Wilson and Roy Worsley for offering helpful comments on draft material and providing additional information. The authors would also like to acknowledge the inclusion on pp. 193–98 of a section of an article by Michael Shackleton entitled "The Politics of Co-decision" from the June 2000 issue of the *Journal of Common Market Studies*.

Any errors remain, as ever, the responsibility of the co-authors alone.

Thanks also go to Anne De Malsche who gave special help in finalising the manuscript and preparing tables and figures and to Philippa Wood, Lorraine Kirkwood, Caroline Costello, Brenda James and Leena Luoma, who gave extra assistance as the final deadline approached.

As in the first three editions, we want to express our appreciation to Michel Beiger and his hospitable staff at the restaurant "La Vignette" in Strasbourg, at which many of the editing sessions took place, with papers and notes strewn among the delicious food and bottles of Pinot Noir.

Finally, the co-authors would like to emphasise that the views expressed in this book are theirs alone, and do not necessarily reflect those of the Parliament.

I: THE FRAMEWORK

1.   The Parliament in context

Every parliament has its own history, culture and powers, and operates within a particular political environment. The European Parliament has its own blend of such features, but it also has additional special characteristics that set it apart.

First, it is the world's most far-reaching experiment in trans-national democracy, where international diplomacy is replaced – or at least complemented by – trans-national democracy.

Second, it forms part of a unique and historically unprecedented institutional system: the European Union (of which more below), with its mixture of supranational legislative powers and intergovernmental cooperation.

Third, its very existence is controversial, with some politicians in some Member States having opposed its creation and further development.

Fourth, it is evolving quickly. Elected for the first time in 1979, the European Parliament is still a young parliament but has developed its role and powers considerably in the 20 years that have passed since then.

Fifth, it is obliged by the Member States to operate in three different locations rather than have a single seat.

Sixth, it is multi-lingual to a degree unknown elsewhere in Europe (only the Indian and South African Parliaments are comparable) with interpretation at meetings and translation of all documents.

Seventh, like the US Congress, but unlike the national parliaments of all the EU Member States, no government emerges directly from a majority in Parliament and elections to it are not therefore about keeping or changing an executive.

For all these reasons and others, the European Parliament defies easy categorisation and explanation. Moreover, its nature and role cannot be understood without reference to the European Union as a whole and the unique characteristics that mark it out from any other international organisation in the world.

The EU continues to be marked by the historical circumstances surrounding its establishment. It was initiated after World War II through the Coal and Steel Community "as a first step to a European Federation" (Schuman Declaration) – a bold attempt to bring together former enemies and to establish a lasting framework of binding cooperation among the states of Europe to ensure peace and stability. This aim is again prominent as the states of Central and Eastern Europe seek accession to the EU.

But there is also a pragmatic driving force behind European integration, namely the practical concern to manage the growing economic interdependence of European countries. The existence of a single European market, with goods and services flowing freely from one country to another, requires a degree of common policy-making. A common market needs common rules and assurance that everyone will apply those rules. It needs a level playing field and some harmonisation of the ways in which public authorities intervene in the market. It generates pressure for European-level rules in areas such as consumer protection, environmental standards, external trade, assistance to less prosperous regions, competition policy, and workplace standards, and for a common policy in areas where all governments intervene, notably transport and agriculture.

From fig-leaf to co-legislature

The recognition of the need for common policies and rules in such matters led national parliaments, when ratifying the founding Treaties, to confer legislative power on the EU in limited but important areas. Initially, these powers were given to the *Council*, composed of ministers representing national governments, acting on a proposal of the *Commission*, a collegial European executive appointed by national governments but charged with acting in the overall European interest. The Council could approve Commission proposals in most matters by a "qualified majority" of about 71 per cent of the votes, each Member State having a weighted vote according to its size (now ten votes each for the largest four States, compared with two for Luxembourg), but unanimity was required to modify Commission proposals. On some issues, unanimity was required to adopt a proposal. Application of European legislation was to be a matter for Member States, but subject to monitoring by the Commission, which could, if necessary, take a Member State to the *Court of Justice*, composed of judges appointed by national governments to rule on disputes concerning the interpretation of the Treaties and European legislation.

Under this initial system, the European Parliament was essentially a forum, composed until 1979 of delegations from national parliaments. It was merely consulted on a small range of legislative proposals prior to their adoption by Council and given the right to dismiss the Commission in a vote of censure by a two-thirds majority.

These powers were, not surprisingly, considered to be too limited, especially by those called upon to serve in the European Parliament, who claimed that a system whereby ministers alone could adopt legislation was suffering from a "democratic deficit". Parliament had to fight to for its powers, and it did so with a degree of success. Over four decades, the Parliament has moved from being a largely consultative assembly to being a genuine co-legislature in a European Union that has itself evolved considerably beyond the original European Communities, both in scope and in powers.

There were seven important steps forward in Parliament's journey:

First, the budget treaties of 1970 and 1975 created what amounts to a bicameral "budgetary authority", composed of Council and Parliament, which jointly thrashes out the annual budget within a fixed revenue limit. The budget procedures are complicated (they are described in Chapter 13), but they allow Parliament to amend – and over the years, reshape – the budget. Parliament has managed, by using its powers, to allocate expenditure in areas other than agriculture and thereby to develop policies in new areas.

Second, in 1975 a conciliation procedure was introduced for adopting legislation with budgetary consequences where there was a need to avoid potential conflict between Council's legislative powers and Parliament's budgetary powers. The procedure was established by a Joint Declaration – a sort of constitutional convention – between the institutions. It laid down that should Council wish to diverge from Parliament's opinion, the matter should first be referred to a conciliation committee composed of the members of Council and an equal number of MEPs, although it would still be up to the Council to adopt the act in question.

Third, in 1979, Parliament was elected by universal suffrage for the first time. This was designed to generate greater democratic legitimacy and more public debate on European issues, but also provided Parliament with full-time members, and more of them. The nominated Parliament had 198 members, the first elected Parliament 410, a figure which has risen to 626, following the successive accession of new Member States and the adjustments made following the unification of Germany.

Fourth, in 1980 the *Isoglucose* ruling of the Court of Justice (cases 138 and 139/79) struck down a piece of Community legislation because Council had adopted it before Parliament gave its opinion. This ruling gave Parliament a *de facto* delaying power, which it could use to bargain for amendments. Clearly, Parliament's bargaining position was stronger when there was pressure for a rapid decision, as was the case, for instance, for much of the 1992 single market programme where all the institutions had to work to a strict timetable.

Fifth, in 1987, the Single European Act came into force, introducing two new procedures for the adoption of Community acts.

One was the *cooperation procedure*. This applied initially to only ten Treaty articles, but they covered most of the legislation necessary for the completion of the internal market as well as individual research programmes and the rules for the structural funds. This procedure in effect added a second reading to the traditional consultation procedure. Council's "common position" is referred back to Parliament, which has three months to approve it, reject it (in which case it falls unless Council then overrules Parliament by unanimity within three months) or press for amendments (which, if supported by the Commission, can only be rejected unanimously in Council, whereas a qualified majority can approve).

The Single Act also gave Parliament equal rights with Council in requiring Parliament's *assent* for the ratification of accession treaties and association agreements. Accession treaties are relatively infrequent events enabling new Member States to join the Union. On the other hand, association agreements arise more frequently, not least because subsequent protocols (e.g. financial protocols) which need renewing also fall under the assent procedure.

The *sixth* step forward for the European Parliament was the Treaty of Maastricht, which came into force on 1 November 1993. This brought in a number of increases in the powers of the European Parliament:

– It introduced a new procedure, known as the *co-decision* procedure, based on the cooperation procedure, but with two important additional provisions: first, the inclusion of a formal conciliation committee with the task of negotiating a compromise between the Council and the Parliament; and second, the option for the Parliament to reject the decision of the Council following conciliation, thus causing the legislation to fall. This procedure applied to most legislation that the Single European Act had subjected to the cooperation procedure plus a number of new areas.

- The cooperation procedure was extended to most of the other areas where Council acts by a qualified majority.
- The assent procedure was extended to a wider category of international agreements and a number of other areas.
- Parliament was given a number of rights enshrined in the Treaties in relation to appointments. It was given a right to vote on the nominations for President of the Commission and President of the European Monetary Institute/Central Bank. This vote was formally consultative but few would disagree that it was politically binding. Parliament was also given a legally watertight right to allow (or not) the Commission as a whole to take office through a vote of confidence and the normal term of office of the Commission was changed to match the five-year term of the Parliament. In addition, the Parliament was given the task of selecting an Ombudsman whose five-year term of office also coincides with that of the Parliament.
- Various powers of scrutiny were enhanced, notably by the provision in the Treaty for parliamentary committees of inquiry.

The *seventh* and latest step was the Treaty of Amsterdam, which came into force on 1 May 1999. This greatly extended the scope of co-decision so that most non-agricultural legislation is now subject to it. It also modified the procedure to Parliament's advantage in ways that are described in chapter 11. At the same time, the Treaty made Parliament's vote on the candidate for Commission President a legally binding one. If a Commission President designated by the European Council fails to gain majority support in the Parliament, he or she cannot take office.

As a result of all these changes, we now have in the EU what has been described as "a classic two chamber legislature: in which the Council represents the states and the European Parliament represents the citizens" (Hix, 1999). Whether it is "classic" or not, the pooled policy making at EU level is not just a matter for governments alone, but for the directly-elected Parliament as well.

The Parliament also has a role in scrutinising the executive in the form of the European Commission. Commissioners are politicians nominated (like national ministers) by Prime Ministers or Presidents. However, the team of Commissioners as a whole requires the approval of a majority in Parliament to take office and, once in office, can be dismissed by (and only by) a vote of no confidence taken in the European Parliament. This latter aspect of Parliament's powers, which it has enjoyed from the beginning, remained rather theoretical until early 1999 when it was illustrated in a spectacular way with the dramatic resignation of the Santer Commission. The watchdog role of the Parliament worked. It was the Parliament that initially unearthed the practices that gave rise to concern. It was Parliament that set up the committee of independent experts (and forced the Commission to accept that it could go through the Commission's books, files and papers to identify exactly who was responsible for what). And it was within two hours of it becoming clear that there was (as a result of the investigation) the necessary majority in Parliament for a vote of no-confidence that the Commission pre-empted this and resigned.

All this makes the EU radically different from a traditional intergovern-mental organisation. Indeed, it is only necessary to imagine what the EU would be like without the Parliament: it would be a system totally domi-nated by bureaucrats and diplomats, loosely supervised by ministers flying periodically into Brussels. The existence of a body of full-time representa-tives in the heart of decision-taking in Brussels, asking questions, knocking on doors, bringing the spotlight to shine in dark corners, in dialogue with their constituents back home, makes the EU system more open, transparent and democratic than would otherwise be the case. MEPs are drawn from governing parties and opposition parties and represent not just capital cities but the regions in their full diversity. In short, the Parliament brings plural-ism into play and brings added value to the scrutiny of EU legislation.

It also takes the edge off national conflict. Council can all too often give the appearance of decision-taking by gladiatorial combat between those rep-resenting "national interests". Reality is more complex and the fact that the Parliament organises itself not in national delegations but in Political Groups shows that the dividing line on most concrete subjects is not between nations but between political viewpoints or between sectoral interests.

A federal system in the making?

Common policy-making through common institutions in such a wide area has led many to conclude that the European Union is, or is becoming, a federal system. This conclusion depends entirely on what is meant by "federal".

Some use the term to mean a centralised super-state. In fact, this has never been the aim of the European Union and it is, indeed, far from becoming such a super-state. The European budget represents a mere 3 per cent of public expenditure, with 97 per cent remaining national or sub-national. European legislation can only be adopted in the areas defined by the Treaties, which can themselves only be amended with the unanimous agree-ment of each and every national parliament. Even within that area, no major legislation or policy can be adopted without the agreement of the Council, composed of national ministers who are members of national governments accountable to national parliaments. Disputes are settled by a Court whose members are appointed by national governments, not by the European Commission. The Commission itself, far from being the gargantuan bureaucracy of tabloid mythology, has fewer employees than Leeds City Council and does not itself decide key policies: it simply proposes and implements.

These structural and legal safeguards against the creation of an over-centralised system are reinforced by the diverse emotional ties and commit-ments of European peoples. There is little danger of a Euro-nationalist hyperbole carrying people away. Furthermore, the key gut issues of political life are national rather than European in character: health service provision, education, housing policy, pensions, social security, law and order, the level of income tax, and so on. All these issues will remain national rather than European in focus.

But although it is not a centralised system, the European Community has always had a number of federal characteristics. In its field of competence, European law prevails over national law. Qualified majority voting, rather than consensual intergovernmental agreements, is the norm for adopting legislation within that field of common policy making. It has an executive, the Commission, that, once appointed, is independent of national governments, has a monopoly on initiating proposals for new legislation and is given the responsibility for managing existing policies and verifying the application of Community law. It has a directly elected supra-national Parliament. It has a common Court to settle differences in interpreting Community law. It has a budget composed of revenues which belong to the Community as of right under the Treaty, not of national subscriptions. Rights are conferred directly on individual citizens by the Treaty. Last but not least the wide scope of the field of competence of the European Union goes far beyond any traditional international organisation. All these are federal characteristics and it would not be distorting the meaning of the word federal to claim that the European Union is already a system of federal type, albeit a decentralised one. In that sense, the European Parliament and the Council together constitute a federal type legislature, with a limited field of responsibility.

Rather than argue about the theology of federalism, most governments and MEPs avoid using the term and focus more on the practicalities: what are the areas in which we need to or want to adopt common policies? What should the content of such common policies be? In those areas, how can we organise a European institutional system that is both efficient and democratic? What legislation is necessary and what should it lay down? This is the stuff of day-to-day discussion and debate in the Parliament.

The style of Parliament

The European Parliament is not a "sexy" Parliament in media terms. Compared to many national parliaments, it lacks the cut and thrust of debate between government and opposition. Like the US Congress, its real work is done in committee. The plurality of languages used makes the debates far from spectacular. For these reasons among others, it gets far less coverage in the media.

But when it comes to the detail of legislative or budgetary work, MEPs shape legislation in a way that members of many national parliaments do not. In the national context, when a government publishes a bill, it is usually clear what will come out of the procedure. It is headline news if the parliament amends it against the will of the government. This is not the case in the European Parliament. A draft directive really is a *draft* – MEPs go through it paragraph by paragraph amending it and rewriting it. So do the ministers in the Council – and ultimately the positions of the two must be reconciled – but the net effect is that every year, thousands of amendments to draft legislation put forward by ordinary back-bench MEPs end up on the statute book and apply in fifteen different countries. In national parliaments, being a back-bencher, or an opposition party MP, often offers very limited power and little job satisfaction other than the prospect of, perhaps, one day wielding ministerial power. MEPs, on the other hand, whilst not having a career path to a ministry (though a surprising number do become ministers in their Member States) can play a significant role in shaping legislation – a classical parliamentary function almost forgotten by some national parliaments.

The nature of day-to-day work is also different. One measure of a good MP in a national context is someone who is a good debater, able to score points over his or her opponents. An effective MEP is someone who is good at explaining, persuading and negotiating with colleagues from 15 different countries. This is done at three levels. First, within Political Groups, as MEPs from different national parties work towards developing a common position as a Group. Second, with other Groups in the Parliament, as no Group has an overall majority and coalitions must be built. Indeed, the type of majority can vary from one issue to another as there is no predetermined coalition, but a general willingness to work by means of achieving substantial majorities on most issues. Third, once Parliament has a position, there is a need to negotiate with Council for the final outcome. Such a parliamentary style leaves ample scope for an active MEP, providing that he or she is good at building the necessary majorities.

Despite the significant and growing role of the European Parliament, turnout in European elections has remained low, and even declined to half the electorate in the 1999 election. Although better than, for example, US congressional elections, it remains below that commonly experienced in EU Member States for national parliamentary elections (although these too have been declining in some countries). This is likely to remain the case, for a number of reasons. First, European elections will remain less significant for day to day issues than national elections, for the reasons alluded to above. Second, there is no government directly at stake in European elections and the bulk of the electorate is used to voting in national elections to keep or throw out a national government. Third, the EU institutions are inevitably more distant than national or local institutions and, as in other federal-type systems, will usually have a lower turnout (e.g. USA, Switzerland). Fourth, the lower media coverage of the European Parliament alluded to earlier. Fifth, the consensus-style decision-making at EU level, which often prevents partisan alternatives from being highlighted to the electorate.

Finally, however, there is the widespread lack of understanding of how the EU institutions actually operate. In some countries, a significant proportion of the press is overtly hostile to the EU, but in all countries there is an abundance of incorrect information, false assumptions and numerous misunderstandings in the media and among national politicians. We hope that this book can help fill the gap by improving understanding of how the European Parliament works and the contribution it makes to ensuring that the EU is open, transparent, accountable and democratic.

Table 1: *Main events in the Parliament's history*

10 September 1952	ECSC Parliamentary Assembly with 78 members holds its first meeting.
1 January 1958	Treaty of Rome enters into force. Assembly (common to ECSC, EEC and EAEC) enlarged to 142 members.
30 March 1962	European Assembly decides to describe itself as European Parliament.
22 April 1970	Treaty changes give the Parliament certain budgetary powers.
16 January 1973	First meeting of enlarged Parliament of 198 members following accession of the UK, Ireland and Denmark.
22 July 1975	Treaty changes giving further budgetary powers to the Parliament.
20 September 1976	Adoption by Council of act providing for direct elections.
7–10 June 1979	First direct elections to the European Parliament. Repeated every 5 years.
17 July 1979	First meeting of directly elected European Parliament of 410 members.
13 December 1979	Parliament rejects budget for the first time.
1 June 1981	Membership increases to 434 after Greek accession.
14 February 1984	European Parliament adopts Spinelli Draft Treaty on European Union.
1 January 1986	Membership increases to 518 following Spanish and Portuguese accession.
1 July 1987	Entry into force of Single European Act allocating new powers to the Parliament and giving Treaty status to the title European Parliament.
1 November 1993	Entry into force of Maastricht Treaty on European Union allocating further new powers to the European Parliament.
July 1994	General adjustment to number of seats per member state following German unification brings parliament to 567 seats.
1 January 1995	Membership increases to 626 following Austrian, Finnish and Swedish accession.
15 March 1999	Commission resigns when faced with probable adoption of a vote of censure by Parliament.
1 May 1999	Entry into force of Amsterdam Treaty extending Parliament's powers. Parliament and Council now effectively a bicameral legislature for most EU legislation.

2.   How it is elected

Nearly all international parliamentary assemblies consist of representatives nominated from members of national parliaments. This was true of the European Parliament itself up to 1979, but since then it has been directly elected. This status is not completely unique – the Central American Parliament is also now directly elected – but the much greater powers of the European Parliament make it different from any other such Parliament in the world.

Although organised trans-nationally, the elections are still not held under a uniform system as foreseen in the Treaties. Member States have been allowed to retain their own national systems until a common one can be devised.

The procedures for drawing up a common system are also unique. Unlike other areas of Community law where it is the Commission that has the right of initiative, in this case it is the European Parliament itself that enjoys this right. Its proposal must then be adopted by the Council by a unanimous vote.

Progress on these issues, first, in moving to direct elections and second, on devising a uniform electoral system, has been very slow. It was not until 1976 that the Council finally agreed on the form of direct elections, 16 years after Parliament had first submitted proposals for such elections. Moreover, 20 years have now gone by since the first elections in 1979 without a uniform electoral system having been adopted. Parliament submitted proposals in 1983, 1992 and 1998, but these remained blocked in the Council, although the chances of agreement on the latest set of proposals are probably greater than ever before.

The present chapter is divided into four sections. The first deals briefly with the period preceding direct elections, and with the Council Decision which finally enacted them. The second examines the variety of national systems in force, and the main differences between them. The third looks at the consequences of the current diversity, and at the main issues that have to be tackled in drawing up a uniform electoral system. The final section examines the efforts that have been made so far to draw up such a system. A brief postscript presents the five sets of elections held so far.

Moving towards direct elections

Direct elections to a European Assembly were envisaged in the original Treaties. Article 138 of the Treaty of Rome, for example, stated that "the Assembly shall draw up proposals for elections by direct universal suffrage in accordance with a uniform procedure in all Member States. The Council shall, acting unanimously, lay down the appropriate procedures which it shall recommend to the Member States for adoption in accordance with their respective constitutional requirements". Parliament first put forward such proposals on 17 May 1961 (Dehousse report), and further resolutions on this subject were adopted in 1963 and 1969, but to no avail (although some national parliaments such as that of Italy considered bills unilaterally to elect their own MEPs by universal suffrage).

In 1973 Parliament decided to prepare new proposals and appointed Dutch Socialist, Schelto Patijn, as rapporteur. The following year, the Paris Summit of Heads of Government decided to institutionalise their meetings in the form of the European Council, and to meet three times per year. To balance this reinforcement of the intergovernmental side of the Community, they also agreed that direct elections to the Parliament "should be achieved as soon as possible" and stated that they awaited Parliament's new proposals, on which they expected Council to act in 1976 with a view to holding direct elections in or after 1978.

Parliament's new proposals were adopted in January 1976. One of the main stumbling blocks had been the Treaty requirement for a *uniform* electoral procedure. Patijn's strategy was to overcome this by allowing each country to use its own procedure for the first elections, and providing for the elected Parliament to make new proposals thereafter.

The draft Convention put forward by Parliament suggested a five-year term of office, for members to vote on an individual and personal basis and not be bound by any instructions or mandate, and for membership to be compatible with membership of the parliament of a Member State, but not membership of a national government or of the European Commission. Parliament would have 355 members, ranging from six from Luxembourg, to 67 from the UK and 71 from West Germany. Elections were to be held in principle on the same day, although individual Member States could have them a day earlier or later than the fixed date or spread them over two consecutive days. Other elements of the electoral system, including the method of filling seats that became vacant, were provisionally left to individual Member States until a uniform electoral system was adopted.

Although Council reached agreement in October 1976, it still took a further three years before the first direct elections were held (they were originally scheduled for May/June 1978, but had to be postponed for a year). The Council Decision 76/787 (OJ 278 of 8.10.1976) was accompanied by an "Act Concerning the Election of the Representatives of the Assembly by Direct Universal Suffrage". It followed the Parliament's proposal in most respects. The most important difference concerned the sensitive issue of the number and distribution of seats between the individual Member States. The Parliament was now to have 410 members. Compared to Parliament's draft, the less populous Member States were generally to be relatively less well represented (although the smallest Member State, Luxembourg, was still given the disproportionate total of six Members), and the more populous Member States were given higher representation. Moreover, the four largest Member States, West Germany, the UK, Italy and France, were given the same total of 81 members each, although the population of West Germany was a bit higher. These figures were revised in 1994 (after German unification) and now stand as indicated in Table 2.

Table 2: *Number of MEPs per country and ratio to population (1999 figures)*

Country	No. MEPs	Inhabitants per MEP
Germany	99	829,000
UK	87	681,000
France	87	678,000
Italy	87	663,000
Spain	64	616,000
Netherlands	31	508,000
Greece	25	422,000
Belgium	25	409,000
Portugal	25	399,000
Sweden	22	402,000
Austria	21	385,000
Denmark	16	332,000
Finland	16	323,000
Ireland	15	249,000
Luxembourg	6	72,000
Total EU	626	600,000

Another difference from Parliament's draft was that the elections would take place over a four-day period, starting on a Thursday morning and ending on the following Sunday.

As in the Parliament's draft, the electoral system, and the method for fill-ing vacancies, was not tackled by the Council's Act pending a uniform system. The Act also added a new clause to the procedures for developing a uniform system when it stated that the Council would take its unanimous decision on a proposal from the Parliament only after "endeavouring to reach agreement with the European Parliament in a Conciliation Committee consisting of the Council and representatives of the European Parliament".

The variety of national systems in force and the main differences between them

The first direct elections in 1979 were thus fought under differing national legislation and this has remained the case ever since. The temporary rules became increasingly entrenched and this was compounded by the fact that six new Member States have joined the Community since 1979 with their own national rules.

The systems used by individual Member States for European elections have not necessarily been identical to those used for national elections. France uses a proportional system for the European elections with the whole country as one constituency and with a 5 per cent threshold, rather than the majority system in two rounds within single member constituencies which has been the traditional system for French domestic elections. Germany, too, created a unitary proportional system for the European elections (although retaining the traditional 5 per cent threshold) rather than the mixed constituency-list system used in national elections. Greece, Spain and Portugal, Denmark, Luxembourg, Austria, Finland and Sweden all maintained a form of proportional representation but also made substantial breaks with national practice by having only one national constituency for the European elections rather than the smaller units used for national elections. Belgium and Italy greatly reduced the number of constituencies for the European elections compared to national elections, as did Ireland and the UK. The last two countries retained, however, their distinctive national electoral systems: the single transferable vote (STV) in the case of Ireland, and the majority "first past the post system" in single member constituencies in the case of Great Britain (after the House of Commons had rejected the 1978 Labour government's alternative proposal for a regional list system). The UK did make an exception to its normal practice by permitting the three Northern Ireland seats to be contested under the much more proportional system of STV. In 1999, however, the UK switched to using proportional representation with regional lists. Finally, the Netherlands made the least change of all, with one national constituency with fully proportional results being the practice for both European and national elections.

All the systems now used are proportional. Nevertheless there still remain considerable differences between them: some countries have one national constituency, whereas others have several regional constituencies. In some countries there are *de jure* electoral thresholds (5 per cent in France and Germany) below which no seats can be won. Some countries' electoral laws provide for closed party lists, whose order cannot be changed by the voter (Germany, Greece, France, Spain, Portugal and the UK), while others provide for preferential voting in which the order of candidates can be modified by the voter. Irish and Luxembourgish voters can even vote for individual candidates from different lists.

Table 3: *Electoral system used for 1999 European elections*

Member State	Constituency	Preference voting for individuals	Voting day	Type of proportional calculation
Austria	National	Yes	Sunday	D'Hondt
Belgium	Regional	Yes, within list	Sunday	D'Hondt
Denmark	National	Yes, within list	Thursday	D'Hondt
Finland	National	Yes	Sunday	D'Hondt
France	National	No, simple list	Sunday	D'Hondt
Germany	Nat. + Reg.	No, simple list	Sunday	Hare-Niemeyer
Greece	National	No, simple list	Sunday	Hagenbach-Bischoff
Ireland	Regional	Yes, STV	Friday	Single Transf. Vote
Italy	Regional	No, simple list	Sunday	Hare-Niemeyer
Luxembourg	National	Yes	Sunday	Hagen-Bischoff
Netherlands	National	Yes, within list	Thursday	D'Hondt
Portugal	National	No, simple list	Sunday	D'Hondt
Spain	National	No, simple list	Sunday	D'Hondt
Sweden	National	Yes	Sunday	Modified St. Lagüe
UK-GB	Regional	No, simple list	Thursday	D'Hondt
UK-NI		Yes, STV	Thursday	Single Transf. Vote

Rules on the **eligibility** to be a candidate have also varied greatly. Originally, candidates usually had to be a national of the Member State in which they wished to stand and in some countries they also had to be domiciled in that country. An early exception was Italy which by 1989 was already permitting candidates from any European Community country, thus allowing former UK Liberal leader David Steel to stand in the Central Italy constituency and Maurice Duverger, the French political scientist, to be elected on the Italian Communist ticket. The UK was also an exception in permitting any Commonwealth or Irish citizen to stand (as in national elections), thus allowing Christine Crawley (Ireland) and Anita Pollack (Australia) to be elected as Labour MEPs in 1984 and 1989 respectively. Council directive 93/109/EC of 6 December 1993 (implementing Article 8B, paragraph 2 of the Maastricht Treaty) now allows any European Union citizen to stand as a candidate in their country of residence under the same conditions as citizens of that country. A temporary derogation was initially permitted for Luxembourg, with its exceptionally high percentage of resident foreigners.

The new law has so far led to five more candidates being elected in countries other than their own. These are the Belgian Olivier Dupuis in Italy in 1994 and in 1999, the Dutch Wilmya Zimmermann in Germany in 1994, the Italian Monica Frassoni and the Luxemburger Frédérique Ries, both in Belgium in 1999 and the German Dany Cohn-Bendit in France in 1999 (although there have been many MEPs with dual or changed nationality who have been elected in their " new" country).

Table 4: *Participation by non-nationals in European elections*

Member State	Registered non-national voters 1994	1999	candidates 1999	Elected 1999
Belgium	23 999	37 345	14	2
Denmark	6 719	12 356	0	0
Germany	+/−80 000	32 578	16	0
Greece	622	1 474	4	0
Spain	24 229	64 904	–	0
France	44 800	74 609	8	1
Ireland	–	27 449	0	0
Italy	2 809	5 874	8	1
Luxembourg	6 907	9 811	7	0
Netherlands			2	0
Austria	7 433	15 169	3	0
Portugal	715	4 084	0	0
Finland	2 514	3 911	0	0
Sweden	36 191	40 707	0	0
UK	7 000	92 000	0	0

N.B. Figures do not include dual nationals. Swedish, Finnish and Austrian figures in the 1994 column refer to the first EP elections held after their accession in 1995, 1995 and 1996 respectively. The Netherlands does not operate a prior electoral registration system. Figures for Ireland (1994) and Spain (1999 candidates) not available. *Source*: ASECA, Paris.

In other respects eligibility rules still vary considerably. Age limits, for example, vary between 18 years (Denmark, Finland, Germany, Netherlands, Portugal, Spain and Sweden), 19 (Austria), 21 (Belgium, Greece, Ireland, Luxembourg and United Kingdom), 23 (France) and 25 (Italy). Eleven countries formally permit the dual mandate of membership of both the national and European parliaments (although it is now informally discouraged or prevented in most of these). One country (Greece) permits it on only the most limited scale (the first two candidates of lists receiving a certain percentage of votes), and three formally forbid it (Belgium, Portugal and Spain). These last three countries are in apparent breach of Article 5 of the 1976 Act (which states that "the office of representative in the European Parliament shall be compatible with membership of the parliament of a Member State"). In some countries candidates must be nominated by political parties, in others independents can also stand. Some countries require deposits, others lists of signatures. There are differing rules on the length of campaign and on election expenses, and on whether public money is available to meet certain party expenses.

Another important set of differences is on **methods of filling vacancies**, for example by the next candidate on the list (Denmark, Greece, Spain, France, Italy, Luxembourg, Netherlands, Portugal, Sweden, Finland, Austria and UK), by designated substitutes (Belgium and, optionally, Germany) or through special by-elections (United Kingdom until 1999). Ireland found itself in particular trouble in this regard, as it had a system of nomination by the party holding the vacant seat, which cut out the voter completely. This has now been replaced by a system of designated substitutes.

Rights to vote also differed until 1994. In some countries it followed the nationality principle without qualifications, so that all citizens of that country could vote in the European elections irrespective of where they live in the world or, for some countries, in the Union. In other countries, such as Ireland, voters lose their rights if they live outside their country. On the other hand, Ireland was quick to give the vote in European elections to resident citizens of other European Union countries. Similar rights were granted in Belgium and the Netherlands, provided that a foreign resident's home country had not given them the right to vote. The UK permitted resident Irish and Commonwealth citizens to vote as well as stand for election.

As a result of the Maastricht Treaty, a major reform was introduced (Council Directive of 6 December 1993, see above). Besides being able to stand as a candidate any European Union citizen is now allowed to vote in his or her country of residence. The conditions for exercising this new right, however, have by no means been uniform. In some countries (Denmark, Ireland, Netherlands), resident EU citizens were automatically entered on the electoral register. In others an EU citizen had to register in person, sometimes on the basis of full and timely information from the national government concerned, and sometimes on the basis of little, no, or even misleading information. In practice, therefore, a certain measure of discrimination still remains in a number of EU countries between local nationals and other EU citizens. Whether for this reason, apathy, or lack of awareness of this new right, or because they could still vote in their own country, relatively few EU citizens resident in other EU countries than their own availed themselves of their new legal rights in the 1994 and 1999 European elections.

Age limits for voting are more uniform: 18 in all countries. In three countries, however, voting is compulsory (Belgium, Greece and Luxembourg), whereas in all others it is not. A final set of differences is over the **polling day** for European elections, currently Sunday in most countries but Thursday in three (UK, Denmark and the Netherlands), and Friday in one (Ireland).

Main issues in drawing up a uniform electoral system

The above survey has indicated the range of issues to be tackled in drawing up a uniform electoral system. Before tackling the specific issues, however, one preliminary set of questions must first be answered. How important is uniformity as an overall objective? What is the meaning of uniformity? And should it mean uniformity of detail or only certain common principles?

Apart from the legal requirement for a uniform system in the Treaties and the 1976 Act, there is a practical case for greater uniformity. Divergent national regulations do not give equal weight to European citizens' votes, and the overall balance within the European Parliament is distorted. On the other hand, some differences in national regulations are less fundamental. While it would be a symbolic gesture, for example, to hold the elections on the same day in every Member State instead of over four days, it is not clear that it is of vital importance. The consensus within the European Parliament, therefore, has been that certain uniform principles must be established, but that full uniformity of the details is not required, at least not at present.

There has, however, been less consensus over which principles should be applied. Examples are the extent to which proportionality in the overall outcome should be balanced against other factors (such as the need for a constituency element or to protect regional or other minorities), and whether voters should have the right to choose between candidates as well as between parties.

Finally, should a uniform electoral system be introduced at one go, or on a step-by-step basis? To what extent should account be taken of special cases and derogations granted? Again there seems to be wide agreement that the main principles need to be established soon, but that a certain amount of flexibility will be required. National political realities and traditions should be taken account of, but not be allowed to block all progress.

Specific issues

(i) The nature of the electoral system

A first and fundamental issue has been whether there should be an obligation to have a system of **proportional representation** in all countries. The main exception in this regard was the majority system used in the UK, which could alone alter the entire political balance in the European Parliament. A small swing in votes can produce a magnified swing in seats in a "first past the post" system. This was all the more so in the large constituencies that were used for European elections with relatively fewer "safe seats". As a result the overall balance in the European Parliament depended on the result in some 20 to 25 marginal seats in Britain. In 1979, the British Conservatives won 60 of the 78 seats available in Britain (excluding Northern Ireland), with 50 per cent of the vote, thus obtaining 21 more seats than they would have obtained by a completely proportional system. In 1984, the European Democratic Group, of which they were the main component, won 50 seats with 6 million votes across Europe compared with the 32 seats obtained by the Liberal Group with 10 million votes (and with the UK Alliance parties unrepresented on 19.5 per cent of the United Kingdom vote, as were the Greens on 14 per cent of the vote in 1989). In 1994, the Socialist Group received the bonus, with the British Labour party obtaining 62 out of the 87 seats on only 44 per cent of the vote, whilst this time the Conservatives only obtained 18 seats. The British electoral system was thus not only a British problem, but also a matter of concern for everyone else in the European Parliament as well.

The Irish system is not inherently proportional in its outcome either. The Labour Party, for example, could be said to have been over-represented in 1979 with four seats (27 per cent of the total seats) on 14.5 per cent of the first preference vote but under-represented in 1984 with none on over 8 per cent. Nevertheless the distorting impact of the Irish electoral system is much less, partly because there are far fewer Irish MEPs but also because the outcome is more closely related to the votes cast.

There is a wide range of electoral systems used in the other countries, but whatever their other shortcomings they are all broadly proportional in their effects, and have had little or no distorting impact on the political balance of the European Parliament.

There has, thus, been broad support within the European Parliament for the principle of proportional representation to be introduced as a central element of a uniform electoral system. A simple majority voting system has been generally felt to be inappropriate for Parliament elections, where the objective is to achieve fair representation of major currents of opinion rather than to form a stable government majority as in national parliaments.

A second important issue has been whether an element of **constituency representation** should be built into a uniform electoral system. There has been considerable (and probably growing) recognition of the advantages of regional rather than national constituency representation in terms, in particular, of strengthening links between the electors and the elected, and of bringing local or regional concerns more to the forefront. However, only a few countries have such systems (the UK, Ireland, Belgium, and Italy, and to a lesser extent, Germany, with its possibility for *Land* lists). In other countries it is implicit in some cases, in that individuals on party lists may well represent particular regions or interest groups, but there is no guarantee of this or any open accountability. The most purely proportional systems, those where the entire country is the electoral area, are those where the constituency element is inevitably weakest. On the other hand, the more constituencies there are, and the smaller the electoral areas, the less proportional is the overall result.

There has been considerable discussion as to possible ways of combining proportional representation with a constituency element. Two main alternatives have been suggested. The first is proportional representation in limited-size constituencies. The second is a mixed system on the lines of that used in German federal elections (and now for the Scottish Parliament and Welsh Assembly), in which a number of members are directly elected in single member constituencies and others are elected on national lists to "top up" the parties and provide a more proportional overall outcome. A third possibility, the single transferable vote system used in Ireland (and Northern Ireland), appears to be too unfamiliar to win widespread support.

Many continue, however, to support national list systems. Certain central governments, for example, such as that of Spain, have been concerned about the advantages more regionally-based constituency systems might have for regional parties such as those in Catalonia and the Basque country, which might be expected to use such systems to further their case for greater regional autonomy or independence. Opposition has also come from certain small national parties able to win, say, 5–10 per cent of the vote, which would give them seats in a national constituency, but not enough to win seats in small regional constituencies. Thus the Green and Communist parties in France were able to help block the proposals of their socialist coalition partners in the Jospin government to move to regional lists for the 1999 elections.

A third contentious issue has been whether **preferential voting** should be allowed. There has been considerable criticism of simple or closed lists (especially those at national level), where the voters have no possibility of altering the order of the lists of candidates put up by the parties or of expressing a preference between individual candidates: in 1998 in the UK the proposal for closed lists became the main reason-or rather excuse! – for the conflict between the Commons and the Lords over the proposed new electoral system. This is felt by some to give too much power to party leaders and/or "apparatchiks", as a candidate placed by a major party at the top of the list is certain to be elected (although no more so than a candidate in a "safe seat" in a single member constituency). There has thus been some support for allowing voters to express a preference for individual candidates within a party list. There has been less support for systems allowing even greater choice among individual candidates, such as STV in Ireland, or the system of *panachage* in Luxembourg, where the voters can express preferences between candidates on several lists. One concern is that such systems could turn the electoral battle into fights within parties instead of between them.

A fourth issue has been that of **minimum legal thresholds**, such as the 5 per cent provisions in Germany and France. The main argument against *de jure* thresholds (there will always be *de facto* thresholds, especially in more regional-based systems) is that they exclude small but significant elements of public opinion. The argument in their favour is that they can help to avoid fragmentation and prevent extremist parties from being given a political platform, though they have not prevented protest parties of the right such as the *Front National* in France from winning seats in the European Parliament.

A final issue has been whether allowances should be made for specific geographical or regional circumstances, such as the seat reserved for the German speaking minority in Belgium.

(ii) Conditions applying to candidates

The issue of whether the nationality or residence principle should apply as regards the eligibility of candidates, has now been settled by the adoption of the Council Directive of 6 December 1993 (see above) permitting practically all EU citizens to stand as candidates on the basis of the residence principle. In the longer term, and to a degree in practice already, there is a strong case for allowing any EU citizen to stand anywhere in the European elections irrespective of nationality or residence (though they will generally be at a practical disadvantage compared to local candidates).

Among the other issues are whether individuals or only parties can stand and whether deposits or only signatures should be called for. As some feel strongly about both issues no consensus has emerged yet to include common rules on these subjects in the first version of a uniform electoral system.

There has been more widespread concern, however, about the *dual mandate*. As mentioned above, the Council's 1976 Act expressly permitted members of national parliaments also to be members of the European Parliament, but a number of Member States have (possibly illegally) forbidden it in their national legislation. Moreover, a large number of political parties, even from countries which permit the dual mandate, either forbid it formally in their statutes or informally in practice.

In 1988 the European Parliament adopted a report by its Committee on Legal Affairs and Citizen Rights (DOC A2–0065/88) prepared by the British Labour MEP, Geoff Hoon. This report came out in favour of prohibiting dual membership of the European Parliament and national parliaments, although not of the European Parliament and regional assemblies, a position Parliament later reiterated when working out proposals on a uniform electoral procedure, and on a members' statute. (Ironically, Hoon himself later became a dual mandate member for two years, after being elected to the UK House of Commons in 1992 and before standing down from the European Parliament at the 1994 elections).

The main argument against the dual mandate is that membership of the European Parliament is now a very demanding full-time job, and cannot be combined with another such job without the member's performance and attendance being undercut in both parliaments. The main arguments in favour are that the dual mandate, if used sparingly, permits a number of very well known national politicians to stand for, and hence give publicity to, the European Parliament, and that it enables stronger links to be maintained between the European Parliament and national parliaments.

Another controversial issue has been that raised by candidates who have given undertakings to their political parties to give up their seats after a certain time so they can be replaced by other candidates on the list. This was first raised on a major scale by the French Gaullist party (the RPR) in 1979: their MEPs were meant to stand down after one year, so that in theory about 70 of their candidates would have entered the European Parliament in the course of the Parliament's five-year term. This so-called "tourniquet" or "turnstile" system was challenged by some MEPs who considered that it violated the terms of the 1976 Act which stipulated that members were elected for five-year terms, and were not to receive any binding instructions from outside.

The issue was twice examined by Parliament's competent committee (Sieglerschmidt reports), which concluded that the system was legally acceptable but politically objectionable. This, and the fact that the system did not work smoothly in practice, with some RPR members refusing to resign, led the RPR to abandon the "tourniquet". Rotation of members has only been very sparingly used by other parties (e.g. the German Greens from 1984 to 1989; the French Greens from 1989 to 1994, who practically all stood down after two-and-a-half years to make way for the next members in their list; and the Italian Greens, who devised a more complicated system of rotation). This practice has now been generally abandoned.

(iii) The right to vote

As we saw above, the main issue has been whether this should be based on the nationality or residence principle. The residence principle has been considered by many to be the more "European" option, and has now been adopted in the above-mentioned Council Directive of 6 December 1993. Some EU citizens, however, still have much more interest in and understanding of the political system of their country of origin than that of their country of residence, and would thus prefer to continue to vote on the basis of their nationality.

(iv) Finance

Another controversial issue is finance, in particular, whether there should be public financing of parties' election campaigns for the Parliament. If so, there are further questions about the extent to which such support should be granted before election day on the basis of a party or group's size, or afterwards on the basis of results actually achieved. This is a matter of great sensitivity, not only because some Union countries provide for public funding of elections, whereas others do not, but also because of the extent to which the system might favour established parties at the expense of new ones.

The above issues came to the fore when the French Greens challenged the Parliament's budgetary allocations for information campaigns (item 3708 of the budget) which were distributed to individual political parties through the Political Groups (see Chapter 5). The sums involved were substantial, and the whole system was felt by many parties with few or no members in the Parliament to discriminate strongly against their interests.

The European Court of Justice eventually found in favour of the French Greens, primarily on the grounds that it was *ultra vires* for Parliament to have developed what amounted to public financial support for parties in the absence of a uniform electoral system. Since then the Parliament's information funds have not been discontinued, but have been modified to conform to the Court's judgment. They now have to stop 30 days before election day.

(v) The number of seats per country

In theory one of the central elements of a uniform electoral system should be approximate equality between the number of people per seat in each European Union country. However, this is balanced by the need to ensure that smaller countries have adequate representation. These two divergent

concerns are often met in bi-cameral systems with one chamber elected proportionally to population and another representing the component states
equally or more equally (e.g. US Congress: House and Senate; German
Bundestag and Bundesrat). In the Union, it is in the Council that the Member
States are represented as such. However, neither is the Council based on full
equality nor the Parliament based on full proportionality. In the Council, the
scale ranges from ten votes each for the "big four" down to two for
Luxembourg. In Parliament, the weighting is more proportional to population, but still with an advantage to small countries. The result is that
Luxembourg has one MEP per 72,000 population, whereas Germany now
has one per 829,000 (though apart from Luxembourg the discrepancies are
not quite so huge, see Table 2 above).

In 1990–91 German unification raised the immediate question of what to
do about representation of the 16 million new citizens of the European
Union from the former East Germany who were not directly represented in
the European Parliament. West German members could hardly resign to
make way for them, since all members had been elected for a five-year term
and they naturally felt that extra seats should be created for the 16 million
new German citizens (and even if they did resign their seat would go to the
next candidate on their party list). But creating new members of the
European Parliament for the former East Germany could not be done
overnight, since it necessitated a controversial treaty change that would
have to be negotiated and then ratified by the Member States.

The *ad hoc* solution that was adopted (on 12 July 1990) was to nominate 18
observers ("*Beobachter*") from the former East Germany, (who came initially
from the former East German Parliament but were later chosen by the
German *Bundestag*). These observers could attend plenaries (where they sat
in special seats at the back) and committees and were also integrated into
their respective Political Groups. They had speaking rights in committee
and in their Groups but not in plenary, and had no voting rights nor the
right to become Parliament office-holders. They could not table questions,
resolutions or amendments, and could only take part in the work of the
interparliamentary delegations in Brussels, Luxembourg or Strasbourg.

This unsatisfactory situation was only intended to be a temporary solution since the case for German membership to be increased was un-
answerable. In 1991 the European Parliament voted by 241 votes in favour
to 62 against (38 of which were French) and 39 abstentions to support an
increase of German membership to 99. However, this solution was not
accepted by the European Council meeting at Maastricht in December 1991,
despite being endorsed by the preparatory meeting of foreign ministers. The
issue was then postponed with a view to taking a decision in 1992.
Parliament then proposed (de Gucht Report, June 1992), a solution that not
only increased the number of German seats but also, to a lesser degree, those
of the other large and medium-sized Member States (especially the
Netherlands, which was curiously under-represented before). Parliament's
new proposal was endorsed without modification by the December 1992
Edinburgh European Council and ratified by the Member States. As a result,
the increase of 18 in the number of German seats was exactly matched by an
increase of six seats each for the three next largest countries, the UK, France
and Italy. Spain was given four more seats, the Netherlands six more and

Belgium, Greece and Portugal one more each. Only Denmark, Ireland and Luxembourg were left with the same number of seats as before. The total number of seats in the European Parliament was thus increased from 518 to 567.

In the context of the enlargement negotiations in 1993–94, Parliament put forward figures for Norway, Sweden, Austria and Finland. Swedish negotiators objected, requesting the same number of MEPs as Belgium, Greece and Portugal (25). Parliament was not willing to go so far (Sweden's population being smaller) but did increase its proposal by one to 22. Parliament's figures were then accepted by all old and new Member States except that an additional seat was given to Austria to keep it only one fewer than Sweden (with 21 seats). Austria is therefore the only Member State of the Union not to have the number of seats in the European Parliament that the Parliament itself proposed. Finland was allocated 16 seats and Norway 15. Norway subsequently decided not to join the EU after a referendum on 27–28 November 1994.

The European Parliament now has 626 members, making it the fifth largest chamber in the EU after the UK House of Lords (over 1000 members in the pre-reform House), the German *Bundestag* (669 members), the UK House of Commons (659 members) and the Italian *Camera dei Deputati* (630 members).With enlargement, especially to Poland, the European Parliament will become easily the largest in Europe (apart from the special case of the UK House of Lords, which has less than 400 active members). The issue of a reform in the existing number of members per country will then be placed squarely on the table. Parliament has itself suggested that an upper limit on its size would be 700, and this was accepted by the Member States and incorporated into the Amsterdam Treaty.

This will now have to be implemented. The accession of Poland (with 64 seats under the existing key) and of Hungary (with 24 seats) alone would bring the EP over this figure of 700, but reducing the number of seats for individual Member States will prove a highly sensitive issue.

Attempts that have been made to draw up a uniform electoral system

In 1979 the first elected Parliament established a special sub-committee of its Political Affairs Committee to deal with the issue, and appointed as rapporteur Jean Seitlinger, a Christian Democrat from Lorraine. He put forward two main options on the key issue of the type of electoral system. Option A attempted to reconcile proportionality with a strong constituency element (and also to win over the then 60-strong British Conservative contingent) by suggesting a mixed system as in elections to the German *Bundestag*. Each voter would have two votes, one cast in single-member constituencies, the other for national lists in order to ensure overall proportional representation of each party. Option B consisted of proportional representation within multi-member constituencies of between three and nine members.

In March 1982 the full Parliament (by 158 votes to 77 with 27 abstentions) opted for proportional representation in multi-member constituencies of between three and 15 seats. There would be the option of preferential voting (within a list). Member States could make exceptions to take account of special geographical or other factors recognised by the Constitution of a Member State. Nationals of a Member State would be able to vote and to stand for election there irrespective of the place of residence. One anomalous feature of the text, however, was that it conferred the right to stand for election to those who had been resident in a country for at least five years, but did not similarly confer the right to vote.

The text was then submitted to the Council, which examined it within a working party for a year, without finding the necessary unanimity, with the British posing the main, but by no means the only, obstacle. Eventually the Council abandoned any attempt to agree on a system for the 1984 European elections, but undertook to continue this work with a view to the 1989 elections.

After the impasse, the 1984–89 Parliament decided to draw up another report and chose Reinhold Bocklet (German CSU) as rapporteur. Bocklet favoured a step-by-step approach towards a uniform electoral system, with agreement on a few essential issues rather than uniformity in the details. He suggested proportionality in small multi-member constituencies or in a single national constituency. Thresholds could be maintained as long as they did not exceed 5 per cent. He even mooted the idea of Member States being granted a temporary exemption from applying the agreed system. The report was adopted in Committee, but only by the unconvincing majority of 16 to 8, with 13 abstentions. This was considered insufficiently strong support to bring the report to the House, and it was referred to a special working party under the chairmanship of the rapporteur. In view of continuing disagreements, however, the 1984–89 Parliament did not adopt any text. The Council was not, therefore, forced to consider any new proposal.

In the 1989–94 Parliament, responsibility was transferred to the Committee on Institutional Affairs, which chose Karel de Gucht (Flemish Liberal) as rapporteur. After first adopting an interim resolution in October 1991, Parliament adopted a new set of proposals on 10 March 1993, by 216 to 79 with 19 abstentions. The basic premise was that uniformity did not require a completely identical electoral procedure but only a harmonisation of its main elements, notably the principle of proportional representation, taking account of the votes cast throughout the territory of the Member State. However, lists could be drawn up either for the whole territory of a Member State or for regional constituencies. A concession was made to the UK electoral system by enabling a Member State to retain single-member constituencies as long as they comprised no more than two-thirds of the total number of seats for that country. The remaining seats would have to be distributed in such a way as to ensure overall proportionality. Preference votes for individuals would be allowed. Member States would also be permitted to institute minimum thresholds of between 3 per cent and 5 per cent for parties to obtain seats. Finally, Member States could also make limited arrangements to take account of special regional features.

The Council did not act on the Parliament's resolution before the 1994 elections. The issue was again considered during the 1994–99 term, by which time the Maastricht Treaty had specified that the Parliament, acting by majority of its component members, had to give its assent to any uniform electoral procedure agreed upon by the Council. Moreover, the Amsterdam

Treaty later made a further and crucial change by providing that any European system need no longer be uniform but only "in accordance with principles common to all Member States."

To take advantage of this new flexibility, a report was drawn up by Parliament's Institutional Affairs Committee, with Giorgios Anastassopoulos (Greek EPP) as rapporteur. His report (A4–0212/98) was adopted in plenary on 15 July 1998, and included a draft act containing the basic principle that all MEPs should be elected by a list system of proportional representation. Otherwise it went into little detail, with only a few articles. On sensitive matters, such as whether there should be electoral thresholds (of not more than 5 per cent), preferential voting and special arrangements to take account of "specific regional characteristics", it suggested that these should be optional rather than mandatory. One controversial requirement, however, was that Member States with more than 20 million inhabitants would have to establish regional constituencies.

The rapporteur also proposed that a certain percentage of seats should be filled on a Europe-wide rather than a national basis, thus encouraging the establishment of trans-national party lists and stimulating a European campaign rather than just a series of national ones. The idea also met with considerable opposition, so the compromise in the report suggested that only 10 per cent of the total number of seats should be allocated to such a Europe-wide constituency and that it should only apply after 2009. The Parliament text as finally adopted further watered down this idea by stating that such a proposal would only have to be "considered" in 2009.

Parliament's new text is as of end 1999 being examined by the Council. There is a greater chance than ever before that a text will be adopted by the Council. The situation in the UK, for example, no longer poses an obstacle. However a few of the more difficult issues, such as the establishment of mandatory regional constituencies for countries with more than 20 million inhabitants, were still unresolved at the time of writing.

The European elections so far

Five sets of European elections have been held so far, in 1979, 1984, 1989, 1994 and 1999. (For a more detailed analysis of results by country, see the tables in Appendix 1.) A few brief general observations can be made.

European elections can still more accurately be characterised as a set of different national elections than as co-ordinated European-wide campaigns. The issues have tended to be primarily domestic, and the elections used to test governments' (and oppositions') popularity or unpopularity. In some countries the European elections have been on the same day as national elections, making it even more difficult to separate the issues, and to provide a distinctly European identity to the European elections.

Nevertheless, European issues have gradually come more to the forefront, be it specific issues such as EU environmental and social legislation and regional policy, or else the EU's general development with some parties or lists opposing, for instance, the Maastricht and Amsterdam Treaties or the Euro. Moreover, certain political families have campaigned on common manifestos throughout Europe, such as the Party of European Socialists, the European People's Party, the European Liberals and the Greens. National party use of these manifestos is still very variable, but they have generally grown in importance from one European election to the next.

The **turnout** in the elections has also varied greatly from country to country, but has in general declined (see Table 5). It is lower than for national elections in Europe, but higher than for congressional elections in the United States. The downward trend (loss of 13 percentage points from 1979 to 1999) mirrors a trend in recent national and local elections in many Member States. Electoral turnout in national elections fell, for instance, by 14.8 points in the Netherlands between the 1977 and the 1998 elections, by 14.4 points in France between the 1978 and 1997 elections, by 13.1 points in West Germany between the 1976 and 1990 elections, and 10.2 points in Ireland between 1979 and 1996.

The decline is therefore not just a problem for the European Parliament, but the lower level is considered by many to be significant. There is no consensus on how to stimulate greater interest in European elections. Like local elections, they are of secondary importance compared to national elections: no government is at stake, merely the political balance in the Parliament. Some have suggested that the composition of the Commission should depend entirely on the majority in Parliament, thus making European elections more like national elections in that an executive with (relatively) known faces would be at stake, and turnout might thus rise. Others argue that the EU is too heterogeneous to permit this kind of majoritarian system comparable to those in Member States. In any event, the issue of electoral participation is a challenge for political parties and for the 1999–2004 Parliament.

Table 5: *Turnout in European Parliament elections (% of electorate)*

	1979	1981	1984	1987	1989	1994	1995	1996	1999
EU	**63.0**	–	**61.0**	–	**58.5**	**56.8**	–	–	**49.4**
Belgium	91.6	–	92.2	–	90.7	90.7	–	–	90.0
Luxembourg	88.9	–	87.0	–	87.4	88.5	–	–	85.8
Italy	85.5	–	83.9	–	81.5	74.8	–	–	70.8
Greece	–	78.6	77.2	–	79.9	71.2	–	–	70.2
Spain	–	–	–	68.9	54.8	59.1	–	–	64.4
Ireland	63.6	–	47.6	–	68.3	44.0	–	–	50.5
Denmark	47.1	–	52.3	–	46.1	52.9	–	–	50.4
Austria	–	–	–	–	–	–	–	67.7	49.0
France	60.7	–	56.7	–	48.7	52.7	–	–	47.0
Germany	65.7	–	56.8	–	62.4	60.0	–	–	45.2
Portugal	–	–	–	72.2	51.1	35.5	–	–	40.4
Sweden	–	–	–	–	–	–	41.6	–	38.3
Finland	–	–	–	–	–	–	–	60.3	30.1
Netherlands	57.8	–	50.5	–	47.2	35.7	–	–	29.9
UK	31.6	–	32.6	–	36.2	36.4	–	–	24.0

3.   Where, when and in *quale lingua*

The seat issue: where the Parliament meets

It is a hazardous business, on the Friday before Strasbourg plenary sessions, to walk in the corridors of the European Parliament's buildings in Luxembourg and Brussels, blocked as they are by large metallic trunks stuffed with files and office equipment about to be transported by the Parliament delivery men to other offices in Strasbourg. This is one of the most visible signs that the European Parliament is nomadic. Often referred to as the Strasbourg Parliament, the reality is in fact much more complex.

Under the Treaties, the decision on the seat belongs not to the Parliament, but to the national governments. The representatives of the governments of the Member States reached a common agreement at Edinburgh in December 1992 "on the location of the institutions and of certain bodies and departments of the European communities" (OJ C-341 23/12/1992), and this was later given additional legal weight with the adoption of a protocol to the Amsterdam Treaty on the same subject. This states in paragraph (a) of its sole article that: "The European Parliament shall have its seat in Strasbourg where the twelve periods of monthly plenary sessions, including the budget session, shall be held. The periods of additional plenary sessions shall be held in Brussels. The committees of the European Parliament shall meet in Brussels. The General Secretariat of the European Parliament and its departments shall remain in Luxembourg."

In practice, the situation is even more confusing. Whilst the majority of plenary sessions are indeed held in Strasbourg, a considerable number of short additional sessions are now held in Brussels. On the other hand, whilst most committee meetings are held in Brussels, committees also often meet during the plenaries in Strasbourg. Finally, although somewhat over half of Parliament staff are based in Luxembourg, not far short of half are now based in Brussels, including most committee and information staff and practically all the Political Group staff.

As a result, Parliament has to maintain extensive facilities in all three cities. There are now two plenary debating chambers (or "hemicycles") in use, one in Strasbourg and one in Brussels (as well as two no longer used in Luxembourg: a small one which housed the Parliament before direct elections in 1979 and a larger one, built by the Luxembourg authorities in the 1980s, which was only used on about four occasions, the last time in 1986). The hemicycle of the Council of Europe in Strasbourg that Parliament used until 1999, is now used only by its owner and the WEU.

The duplication extends still further: MEPs have offices in Strasbourg and Brussels. Members of the secretariat have their own offices in Luxembourg or Brussels, and share a smaller number of offices in Strasbourg. Parliament now spreads over nine main buildings in the three cities, the Paul-Henri Spaak, Altiero Spinelli and Bertha von Suttner buildings in Brussels; the Louise Weiss, Winston Churchill and Salvador de Madariaga buildings in Strasbourg; and the Robert Schuman, Alcide de Gasperi and Konrad Adenauer buildings in Luxembourg. Although Luxembourg is the official home of the secretariat, it contains less than 20 per cent of the total surface area of Parliament's buildings, and 2,000 of the 7,200 offices. (The corresponding figures for Brussels are 50 per cent and just over 3,000 offices, and for Strasbourg 32 per cent and 2,200 offices).

The lack of a single fixed seat is costly not just in terms of buildings, but also in terms of substantial additional travel, with a proportion of the staff "commuting" between the three cities. For part-sessions in Strasbourg, PCs, printers, filing cupboards and a large number of trunks of documents have to be transported from Brussels in four semi-trailers, three other trucks and a van. Similar equipment has to be transported from Luxembourg. Moreover, additional temporary staff and equipment have to be hired. It is not surprising, therefore, that the cost to the Parliament of its geographical dispersion is considerable (about 15 per cent of its budget).

This waste of resources must be put in perspective. The figures involved only constitute a very small proportion (about 0.13 per cent) of the whole EU budget. Whether MEPs travel from their constituency to Brussels or to Strasbourg is not very different in cost. Only a proportion of the staff needs to travel. Such waste is, however, still unnecessary, and difficult, if not impossible, to justify. Parliament undoubtedly loses influence, access to power and effectiveness by being dispersed in three cities, and its public image is also harmed.

Historical background

How did the present situation come about, what has been done to remedy it, and what are the prospects for change in the future? The Treaties laid down that the seat of the institutions should be determined by common accord of the governments of the Member States. Until 1992 no such common accord was reached and the initial working places of the institutions and bodies were only provisional. Most ended up, however, in one city. Only Parliament is split between three cities.

The Common Assembly of the ECSC began to meet in Strasbourg (with only two extraordinary sessions being held elsewhere) as Strasbourg was the seat of the Parliamentary Assembly of the Council of Europe to which most of the initial members belonged and which had the only fully-equipped, multilingual parliamentary hemicycle. The Secretariat, however, was installed at the site of the Council and Commission (High Authority), which was then Luxembourg.

Sessions continued to be held in Strasbourg when the Common Assembly became the European Assembly, with the entry into force of the EEC and Euratom Treaties in 1958. However, its committees began meeting on a regular basis in Brussels where the bulk of the new Community institutions were now based. The staff remained in Luxembourg. The 1965 Merger Treaty, whereby the three separate Communities (ECSC, EEC and Euratom) were given a common Council and Commission, did not come up with a permanent solution for the seat. Instead, an accompanying decision by the governments of the Member States confirmed that Luxembourg, Brussels and Strasbourg would remain the provisional places of work of the Community and that the General Secretariat of the Assembly and its departments would remain in Luxembourg. No mention was made of the Assembly's plenary sittings or committee meetings, and the *status quo* (plenaries in Strasbourg, committee meetings in Brussels) was left untouched.

From 1967 onwards, however, and on its own initiative, Parliament began to hold occasional plenary sittings in Luxembourg as well as in Strasbourg. Only one was held in Luxembourg in 1967 but from 1968 to direct elections in 1979, 58 took place there compared to 77 in Strasbourg. In 1976 and 1977 more were held in Luxembourg than in Strasbourg. One important practical reason for this development was the convenience of holding the sittings at the working place of the secretariat.

The situation changed rapidly after direct elections in 1979. For the first few months after the elections only Strasbourg had a hemicycle large enough to seat the greatly enlarged Parliament, and by the time Luxembourg had completed its own new hemicycle the members had got used to going to Strasbourg. Another important factor was that members were given their own offices in Strasbourg, and these facilities were not available in Luxembourg. By then, furthermore, the majority of members had come around to the belief that it was preferable to have to travel regularly to only two cities, Brussels and Strasbourg, than to three. This evolution was of great concern for the Luxembourg-based staff who went on strike over the issue.

The solution that most wanted was a single seat, and the directly elected members began to call more insistently on national governments to take such a decision. However, in March 1981 the European Council meeting at Maastricht only decided to reiterate the *status quo*. There followed various attempts to revise the situation.

On 7 July 1981, Parliament adopted a resolution (based on a report by an Italian Socialist, Mario Zagari), by 187 votes to 118 with seven abstentions, in which it again called for a decision on a single working place but, pending such a decision, for plenary sessions to be held in Strasbourg and for committee meetings to take place as a general rule in Brussels. The workings of the Parliament's secretariat would have to be reviewed to meet these new requirements, although there was no explicit call for a major transfer of staff. In August 1981 the Luxembourg government challenged this resolution (Case C-230/81) but in February 1983 the Court of Justice found in the Parliament's favour. It stated that Luxembourg could not prevent the Parliament giving up the practice of meeting in Luxembourg, which it had only introduced on its own initiative and was not an integral part of the *status quo*.

In February 1983, Parliament voted by 130 to 99 with 11 abstentions that an additional part-session, which could not be held in Strasbourg, should take place in Brussels (at the Palais des Congrès) rather than in Luxembourg. It took place on 28 April 1983 and was the only sitting in Brussels, apart from one ECSC Assembly meeting in 1956, until the two meetings in early 1991 (described below). The sitting did show, however, that unless held in a properly equipped parliamentary chamber, such sittings were particularly vulnerable to filibusters (e.g. by requests for roll-call votes in the absence of voting machines).

In July 1983, Parliament decided to go a step further by adopting a resolution (by a written declaration of over half its members rather than by a formal vote in plenary) to divide up the secretariat in the most rational manner between the effective places of work, with services concerned with the functioning of part-sessions in Strasbourg and with those of the parliamentary committees in Brussels. This resolution was again challenged by the Luxembourg government (Case C-108/83), on this occasion successfully, when the Court of Justice annulled the Parliament's resolution as a violation of the *status quo*.

On 24 October 1985, a resolution was adopted by the Parliament by 132 votes to 113 with 13 abstentions which called for the construction of a new Parliament building in Brussels, including a chamber with seating for no less than 600 people. The resolution stated that Parliament needed a large meeting room in Brussels for many of its routine meetings (such as those of the larger Political Groups) but also for any supplementary plenary sittings that might be held in Brussels. The resolution's opponents argued that this was the opening step in a process that would lead to the abandonment of Strasbourg in favour of Brussels. The French government called for the resolution to be declared null and void (Case C-258/85). The Advocate-General of the Court found in the French government's favour, but the full Court rejected the request in September 1988, thus acknowledging that Parliament would be within its rights to hold some sittings outside Strasbourg.

In January 1989, Parliament adopted, by 222 to 176 with four abstentions, a new resolution on its working place (based on a report by Derek Prag, a British Conservative) calling for a reduction in the dispersal of its work and staff. It again called for a final decision on a single seat but expressed pessimism that such a decision would be taken after more than 30 years of failure to do so by the national governments. Meanwhile, it provided for staff dealing with certain activities, such as committee and information work, to be based in Brussels and declared that it was now necessary to hold additional plenary sittings during the weeks traditionally set aside for committee or Group meetings. The resolution had particularly strong support from Belgian, British, Dutch and Spanish members, but was contested by French and Luxembourgish members, with the vast majority of EPP members also opposed. Luxembourg again took it to the Court (see below).

In early 1990, controversy again arose over the proposed renting of the new buildings in Brussels, and with a counter-attack by French members, in particular, calling for a guarantee with regard to plenary sessions in Strasbourg, and for negotiations over the construction of a new hemicycle in the city. In March 1990 a compromise on these lines was adopted by Parliament's Bureau, but was challenged by back-bench supporters of Brussels. At the April 1990 plenary a bitter debate culminated in a final vote in which the Parliament supported the Bureau's text.

A further episode stemmed from the decision by the plenary in January 1991 to hold two supplementary sittings in Brussels, so that the Parliament could hear a statement and debate developments in the Gulf War and in the

Baltic States, but without any formal votes being taken on motions for resolution. These sittings were held on 30 January and 6 February 1991, in the presence of the Commission but not of the President of the Council, the Luxembourg Foreign Minister. The Council's refusal to allow its President to attend these sittings was later condemned by the Parliament in a resolution of 14 March 1991. It considered that this absence was a mark of disrespect for the Parliament and that it was the Council's duty to attend Parliament. This controversial precedent of holding debates in Brussels was subsequently pursued, but, until the new buildings were ready, such meetings were not described as plenary sittings. Instead, they were known as meetings of the "open enlarged Bureau" (see Chapter 9).

On 28 November 1991, the Court of Justice (in joined cases C-213/88 and C-39/89) dismissed the Luxembourg Government's challenge to the Parliament resolution of January 1989 (cited above), as well as to other decisions of Parliament's Bureau of June 1988. The Court found, *inter alia*, that the Parliament's objectives as regards its internal organisation justified its building projects in Brussels, and that the transfer of a number of Parliament officials to Brussels was not on such a scale as to be in breach of prior government decisions on the seat.

Shortly afterwards, on 8 January 1992, President Baron signed the lease for the new Parliament buildings in Brussels. Parliament began to plan additional sittings in Brussels and to cut the number in Strasbourg. This prompted a vigorous reaction from the French government, which put pressure on the other governments, leading to the Edinburgh Council Decision of December 1992 and ultimately to the Amsterdam Treaty protocol cited at the beginning of this chapter. This requires Parliament to hold 12 plenary sessions in Strasbourg, but allows additional sittings in Brussels.

Conflict has continued, however, over the implementation of these decisions. In 1993, the French *Assemblée Nationale* delayed the procedures for ratification of the increase in the number of MEPs agreed by the Member States in 1992, until the Parliament's President agreed to sign the lease for the new building and hemicycle built by the French authorities in Strasbourg. The lease was finally signed by President Klepsch, amid some controversy, in the spring of 1994, a signature later questioned by the Court of Auditors. The new building was inaugurated at the July 1999 part-session with further argument about its cost and facilities.

A further source of conflict has been over the number and length of plenary sessions in Strasbourg, in particular whether there should be twelve such sessions per year which, given the August recess, means holding two plenary sessions in one other month. A second session in October had traditionally been held in order to hold Parliament's first reading on the budget, which took up too much time for a normal part session. Streamlined procedures for considering the budget within the Parliament meant that the second session in the same month was no longer necessary, and Parliament held only 11 Strasbourg sessions in 1992, 1993 and 1996 and ten in the election year of 1994, all with only one in October. The French government sought to annul the Parliament's 1996 decision, and the Court of Justice found in its favour (case C-345/95) on 1 October 1997. The Court ruled that Parliament could only hold additional sessions in Brussels if it had first provided for 12 sessions in Strasbourg, and that if it did not hold a session in

August then it would have to hold an extra session during one of the other months of the year. The Court conceded, however, that the Parliament need only hold 11 sessions during election years. Parliament has since had to re-introduce two plenary sessions during the month of October.

In October 1999 these issues were again raised in adopting Parliament's calendar of meetings for the year 2000, with some members calling for Strasbourg plenaries to last only from Monday to Thursday, and others for two plenaries to be held during the same week in February, with one of the two October sessions being deleted in consequence. Amendments to this effect were rejected, but received substantial support, indicating continuing dissatisfaction.

A final outstanding issue has been the location of Parliament's staff. Luxembourg is unlikely to see further plenary sessions, and hosts very few committee meetings, but considers that maintenance of a large part of the secretariat in Luxembourg is a major national interest. Its position has been reinforced by the Amsterdam Treaty Protocol, which talks of the General Secretariat and its departments being based in Luxembourg. At the same time the practical needs of the Parliament have meant that many committee and information staff, in particular, have had to be transferred to Brussels to avoid incessant commuting between the two cities. The increase in Parliament's staff, notably in response to EU enlargement, has given the Parliament some margin in reconciling these different needs. An agreement between the Luxembourg government and then Parliament President, Klaus Hänsch, permitted a limited transfer of staff to Brussels over a certain period of time, in return for a guaranteed minimum number of staff in Luxembourg. Even if further such agreements are negotiated in the future, the likelihood is that Parliament will continue to have to face up to the costs (financial and human) of having staff based in Luxembourg when all the Parliament's meetings are elsewhere. It will also have an increasingly div-ided secretariat, with little job mobility between Brussels and Luxembourg, and with fewer and fewer people in one city knowing their colleagues in the other.

In formal terms the problem of the seat has now been resolved: only con-firmed optimists can expect further Treaty revision. In practice, however, the continuing cost of having three working places for the Parliament, the renting or ownership of three sets of buildings, the unnecessary travel, the relative inaccessibility of Strasbourg and the dispersion of Parliament's secretariat, indicate that the question of the Parliament's seat is likely to continue to prove controversial. The flashpoints are likely to focus on the remaining ambiguities concerning the length of plenary sessions in Strasbourg, on the number and duration of additional plenaries in Brussels and, more generally, on the implications of possible future reform of Parliament's own timetable of activities.

Strasbourg is, for the majority of members, more difficult to travel to than Brussels. Strasbourg has direct air links, outside France, to only six national capitals and three other main EU airports, with about 20 such flights daily. Brussels has direct flights from all EU capitals and 17 other major airports, with over 200 such flights daily. Many members have considerable incon-venience in getting to Strasbourg and back, having to make complicated connections (which, if missed due to a delayed flight, will result in hours wasted in airport lounges or even unplanned stopovers in hotels) and some having to leave home by Sunday afternoon if they are to be in Strasbourg for the start of the session. Many members have a flat or a house in Brussels where they work three weeks out of four, but few do in Strasbourg where they spend only three or four nights a month. Strasbourg will therefore remain unpopular with many members.

When: Parliament's cycle of activities

Parliament's timetable has traditionally followed the same monthly pattern. The plenary week in Strasbourg has been followed by two "committee weeks", during which the individual committees meet in Brussels. The cycle is then completed by the "Group" week when the Political Groups meet, to prepare their stance at the next plenary session and other business. There is a one-month recess in August.

There have been few exceptions to this pattern. There is the extra plenary week in October dealt with above, and in the early 1980s, there was occasionally an extra plenary in March to deal with agricultural prices, but this has not proved necessary in recent years. During election years, the outgoing Parliament winds up its activities by May, and the new one assembles in late July.

The traditional timetable has always been less simple in practice than it looks. The Political Groups have always had to hold additional meetings, and committees extra meetings, during plenary weeks. Committees sometimes meet during Group weeks.

For a variety of reasons, however, the normal timetable above is now being modified in more fundamental ways. It has proved too inflexible, as Parliament's legislative, control and other activities built up, creating conflicting pressures to hold more frequent plenary sittings and more committee meetings, as well as providing time for a growing number of Conciliation Committee meetings with the Council (see chapter 12). The availability from 1993 of the hemicycle in Brussels provided an opportunity for more flexibility, by enabling plenary sittings in Brussels during what were normally committee weeks.

Since such plenary sessions began in Brussels on a regular basis in autumn 1993, the typical pattern has been for them to last two half-days. Six such Brussels plenary sessions are scheduled in 2000. In October 1999 an attempt was made by a number of members to add systematic mini-plenary sessions on Wednesday afternoons in Brussels (besides any already planned) to allow the President of the Commission to report directly to Parliament on the decisions taken by the Commission at its regular meetings. The idea of doing this in the course of such micro-plenaries was rejected by the Parliament, but is being implemented in another form as "meetings of the Conference of Presidents open to all members".

As regards committee meetings, more time has been found by allowing committees to meet on the Monday afternoon and Tuesday morning of Group weeks. More evening meetings or shorter breaks in the middle of the day remain possible options. Indeed, the holding of two afternoon sessions was one of the recommendations of the Bureau's Multilingualism Working Group (see below). Holding committee meetings in Strasbourg remains con-

Table 6: *Growth of time spent in plenary sittings*

	1988	1989	1990	1991	1992	1993	1994	1995	1996	1997	1998
No. of sittings (days)	60	54	60	60	56	61	57	72	71	69	73
No. of hours	394	351	420	435	411	433	366	470	483	472	492

troversial (not least because they can conflict with the plenary or other meetings, and also because they are not envisaged in the Amsterdam Treaty protocol), but in practice has become inevitable, especially in cases of urgency related to the current plenary.

Many members have complained that the rhythm of Brussels and Strasbourg meetings has been such as to give them inadequate time to remain in touch with their home political base or constituency. As a result committee meetings on Friday mornings have become the exception rather than the rule, though more far-reaching attempts to provide for occasional entire weeks free of parliamentary activities have proved extremely hard to implement.

More radical changes to Parliament's cycle of activities, such as holding committee meetings in the mornings with plenary sessions in the afternoons, have fewer prospects since the adoption of the Amsterdam protocol, yet further reforms seem certain.

In *quale lingua*: languages within the European Parliament

The European Parliament is unique amongst parliaments in the number of its working languages, at present 11: Danish, Dutch, English, Finnish, French, German, Greek, Italian, Portuguese, Spanish and Swedish. Why does it have to have more working languages than the six used in the United Nations? Unlike the latter, it is a Parliament, adopting legislation that is binding directly on citizens. Its elected members, unlike career diplomats, cannot automatically be expected to be competent linguists, although many are. The electorate should be free to choose a popular trade unionist from Germany or farmer from Portugal even if he or she cannot speak or understand a foreign language.

There is also another issue of principle involved. Many members, especially from the smaller countries, feel that they must defend their country's culture and language, since it is central to the country's identity. At formal meetings, Danish members, for example, have often insisted on Danish interpretation, even if they are fluent in English or another language.

It is thus difficult to cut back on simultaneous interpretation at any Parliament meeting. Such reductions are only attempted for meetings where few members are involved. Thus informal meetings (such as those of committee co-ordinators) are often conducted in English or French, if all concerned agree.

As regards documents, Parliament's Rules of Procedure state unambiguously (Rule 117.1) that "... all documents of Parliament shall be drawn-up in the official languages." Moreover, in the context of the legislative procedures of cooperation and co-decision the Parliament will only announce receipt of a Commission or Council position when all the necessary documents have been "... duly translated into the official languages " (Rule 74.1). There is very limited scope for flexibility as regards translation: untranslated amendments, for example, may not be put to a vote if at least 12 members object (Rule 139.6).

These strong principles were further underlined in a Parliament resolution of 6 May 1994 "on the right to use one's own language". The resolution stated that it was "undesirable for an institution composed of elected members to introduce restrictions on the use of languages", and reaffirmed that "all of the Union's official languages must be used on a strictly equal basis, whenever necessary, for any meetings of the European Parliament whether they are used actively or passively, orally or in writing".

In committee meetings the practice is more informal. Oral amendments or untranslated written amendments are often put to the vote, with members who do not understand them having to rely on the interpretation into their own language. Even here, however, an oral amendment may not be put to the vote if a single member objects.

Within the Political Groups, a less rigid system applies. Some Groups do not have a membership requiring all languages anyway, but even the Socialist Group, which, with the EPP-ED Group, is the only one with MEPs from all Member States, only uses four languages (English, French, German and Spanish) for most internal documents. English and French are used within the Liberal Group for documents, although English is currently dominant for spoken purposes. This, however, is only feasible in the context of non-public meetings among colleagues of the same political family. Another feature of Groups is that their secretariats often do a lot of their own translation because of time constraints.

Translation requirements are only less stringent for internal documents within the Parliament secretariat. French is not the main internal working language of Parliament's secretariat to the same extent as it is in certain other Community institutions (for example the European Court of Justice). Its *primus inter pares* position is giving way to a dual-language regime of French and English for most purposes. Meetings of Parliament's staff are normally conducted in French or English, although to prevent a native speaker having an advantage an informal rule has been developed for some internal meetings that speakers should use a language other than their own: British officials must speak French, and vice-versa.

In practice French and English language documents now account for an increasingly high share of all original texts sent to the Parliament's translation services. Until recently there were considerably more French than English texts, but English has now caught up, and by 1998 had even slightly overtaken it. Between them, French and English now make up over two-thirds of the original texts sent to translation (and with linguistic quality often suffering as a result of many of these texts being drafted by non-native French or English speakers!). German is a poor third, followed by Spanish, Italian and Dutch texts in that order. The five remaining official languages (Portuguese, Greek, Swedish, Finnish and Danish) currently account together for less than 2 per cent of the total volume of texts needing translation.

These original texts then have to be translated into all the languages. Certain attempts have been made to cut down on the volume of documents requiring translation, for example by trying to eliminate translation of the verbatim debates or to restrict translation of individual members' resolutions, but these have not been successful. One reform has been the imposition of length limits on certain types of document. Motions for a resolution, for example, are not meant to exceed two pages, nor explanatory statements more than ten pages. Documents exceeding these limits have to obtain a special derogation from the Bureau if they are to be translated.

The volume of translation and the resources devoted to it are impressive. By 1998, for example, verbatim report of plenary debates alone added up to 5,092 pages per language. About a quarter of Parliament's staff are in its linguistic services. Since 1989, there has been a separate Directorate General for translation with 466 LA grade translators (1999 figures). Parliament directly employs around 200 interpreters who carry out about 45 per cent of the work, and also relies on a considerable number of freelance interpreters for the remaining 55 per cent.

The constraints on Parliament's working methods are considerable. Certain potentially useful documents cannot be translated at all. Transcripts of US Congressional hearings or House of Lords inquiries are valuable documents, but translation of the full proceedings of all European Parliament hearings would be too costly. This is only done in exceptional cases, such as the hearings of the incoming Commissioners in 1999.

Reaction time by Parliament is affected. As a general rule, a text has to be handed in to translation at least ten working days before the meeting at which it is to be considered if it is to be ready in all languages. Any subsequent modifications add to this. Even when the text is ready in most languages one or two may still be missing. If there is goodwill by the members affected this may not further delay adoption of the report in question, but it can hand a new weapon to a determined filibusterer, who can use translation gaps to delay further progress.

The quality of texts can also suffer, leading to misunderstandings, and frequently to unnecessary amendments. To improve this quality it is best to have a collation of texts between the different language sections, ideally in the presence of the person who drafted the initial text, or who knows best why a text was drafted in a particular way. This is often difficult to put into practice, however, not just because of tight deadlines but also because the translation service is in Luxembourg, whereas the vast majority of texts are now produced in Brussels. In the specific co-decision context, this problem has led to the establishment in Brussels of a small team of lawyer linguists, working closely with their counterparts in the Council to ensure the equivalence of legislation adopted under this procedure in the different language versions.

The constraints imposed by interpretation in meetings are of a different nature. However excellent the interpretation, it is a brake on spontaneity and comprehension. Words can be successfully interpreted but cultural differences may not. The indirect irony or criticism of an Italian member may well be completely lost in interpretation whereas the directness of a Dutch or Danish member may only seem like rudeness to a southern member. A joke told by a member in committee may well result in laughter from some members and perplexed silence from others. As a result, when members wish to direct a point to a specific member they may address them in the latter's language.

One constraint, for which the interpreters are primarily responsible, is regarded as beneficial by many members. This is the limitation on Parliament's working hours, with plenary and committee meetings needing to have special permission to go past certain fixed hours. Committee meetings, for example, cannot exceed seven hours a day (9–12:30 in the morning, 3–6:30 in the afternoon). If the committee wishes to go on longer without prior authorisation it has to do so without interpretation. This is because of agreed limits to interpreters' working hours, with longer meetings requiring costly additional teams of interpreters.

The cost of multilingualism is considerable. In 1999 it amounted to 34.5 per cent of the Parliament's total budget. Together with the percentage due to the geographical dispersion of the Parliament (13.4 per cent), these two cost centres alone amount to not far short of half the Parliament's budget.

Even without further enlargement, the prospects for reduction in the number of working languages are slim. There is even pressure from groups such as the Catalans to have documents translated into their language, which is spoken by more EU citizens than, say, Danish. Parliament meetings in Catalonia have sometimes gone ahead only after a Catalan interpreter's booth was provided!

The situation is gradually getting worse. Every additional language used creates a large number of additional language combinations (the formula is $n \times (n - 1)$ where n equals the number of working languages). This imposes a major new burden on the Parliament. Before Spanish and Portuguese accession there were already 42 such combinations: there are now 110 such combinations with 11 working languages.

The addition of Swedish and Finnish in 1995 required an extra 80 interpreters and 80 translators. The shortage of interpreters capable of direct interpretation from Finnish meant that native Finnish interpreters had to be placed in other language booths, leading to an extension of the relay system, and breaching the general rule that an interpreter should work into his or her own language. Moreover, as regards translation, increasing use is being made of external translators, so that the Finnish and Swedish translation divisions are smaller than the others.

Substantial further new enlargement of the European Union will thus place the existing system under unprecedented strain. An EU with 16 languages implies 240 language combinations, and one of 22 languages 462! Many of these new languages are difficult ones, and some are only used by a relatively small number of people. Even the physical demands on Parliament's facilities would be enormous: with over 20 languages more than 100 interpreters could be required for each meeting if present practices were maintained.

There is widespread agreement that there will need to be substantial changes in working methods. In the last Parliament a Bureau working party drew up a report on the implications of multilingualism in the context of further EU enlargement. It pointed out that, with more than 20 languages, there would be neither enough interpreters to cover individual meetings, nor enough rooms large enough to hold all the interpreters.

The working party's final report put forward a number of possible sol-utions to these problems. These included the provision of more booths in meeting rooms, removing interpreters from the meeting rooms, and having them interpret at longer range while looking at the speakers on screens, and changing the working day, so as to provide three rather than two afternoon sessions for committee meetings. The most radical option proposed would be to give up the present matrix system of interpretation (whereby each lan-guage is interpreted into every other language), and to develop, instead, a radial system, with interpretation from all languages into, and out of, a pilot language or languages. The report recognised, however, that this could only be a longer-term solution, since the new training required for interpreters would take a considerable time. In the shorter term a combination of these various options would have to be adopted.

As regards translation, the report suggested the problems would be less immediately acute. Nevertheless, translation needs would also grow expo-nentially, with more time being needed for documents to be translated, and with the costs of the investments required being disproportionate to the actual demand for some of the lesser-used languages.

As with interpretation, there is no one easy solution to these problems. There will have to be direct recruitment of new translators, increased recourse to external translators and to computer-aided translation, and per-haps also the use of the technique of translation in to, and out of, a relay or pilot language.

As a result of all these factors, the tension between the conflicting criteria of democratic fairness and logistical practicality is likely to become ever more acute as the Union continues to enlarge.

II: THE ACTORS AND WORKING STRUCTURES

4. The individual members

Any examination of Parliament's key "actors" must begin with its 626 individual members. This chapter looks at their rights and obligations, (including the thorny and still to be resolved questions of the members' statute and the status and role of their assistants), the background of the individual members, their role within the Parliament, their capacity for independent action, and the position of back-benchers.

Rights and obligations of individual members

Incompatibilities and verification of credentials

A few common principles were established in the 1976 Act adopted by the Council concerning the election of the representatives of the Assembly by direct universal suffrage. It laid down, for example, a list of posts that were held to be incompatible with the job of MEP. These were: minister in a government of a Member State, European Commissioner, a member or the Registrar of the Court of Justice or an active (i.e. not on leave) official of an EU institution. Member States were permitted to lay down additional incompatibilities, pending the entry into force of a uniform electoral procedure.

The 1976 Act also provided for the Assembly to verify the credentials of representatives. This is done on the election of every new member, is carried out by the Parliament's competent committee, and is usually just a matter of taking note of the results. Pending verification, newly elected members have the same rights as other members, and verification is usually a formality. One exception was the challenge to the credentials of the Irish Labour members nominated in 1981 to replace colleagues who had become ministers: no criteria had been established for the replacement of elected Irish MEPs. In most Member States, either individuals are designated at the elections as substitutes for members in case of their departure, or a departing member is replaced by the next on the party list. In Ireland, however, it had only been provided for the national parliament to choose a replacement and one of the individuals in question was not even a member of the national parliament. Although unsuccessful, the challenge did eventually lead to a change in the Irish system with the introduction of a procedure for replacement candidates. Problems subsequently emerged, however, even with this new system when Proinsias de Rossa of the then Workers' Party, resigned in February 1992. He was replaced only by his fourth replacement candidate, Des Geraghty, after the first three replacement candidates informed their party that they did not want to go to the European Parliament. One of them later changed his mind, but Geraghty's credentials were ratified, although with doubts again being expressed about the replacement system that had been chosen by the Irish government.

Only one member has actually had her election invalidated (in 1979), and had to stand again (successfully) for election, the late Dame Shelagh Roberts: she had been deemed to occupy a post of profit under the Crown, which was incompatible with being an MEP under the relevant UK rules.

Problems have also arisen over the acceptance of resignations from Parliament, on the grounds that the free exercise of certain members' mandates might have been compromised by undertakings made to their political party to stand down from office. In March 1994, Parliament's competent committee ruled that, in circumstances where freedom to exercise the mandate was not guaranteed, Parliament could reserve the right to declare the mandate invalid, even where the member in question had already been involved in Parliament's work. Parliament adopted more systematic rules on the verification of credentials (Rule 7) and on the term of office of members (Rule 8) in May 1994. In 1999 the rules were further reinforced as regards the examination of cases where the appointment of a member is due to the withdrawal of a higher-placed candidate or candidates from the same list.

Facilities, salaries and allowances

Once elected, new members are given an initial background briefing, receive a voting card for use in electronic votes at the plenary sessions, and also a special *laisser-passer*, which allows them to travel freely around the European Union without any other documents. They are also given offices in Brussels and Strasbourg. These offices are broadly equal in size and facilities, with only Parliament's Presidents and Vice-Presidents, former Presidents, Quaestors and Political Group and committee chairs getting larger offices. Members also have working space available to them collectively in the European Parliament's offices in their own national capital.

The issue of individual members' salaries and allowances has become an increasingly controversial one in recent years. The continuing failure of Member States to agree a uniform statute for MEPs, and the consequent continued application of national rules, has led, *inter alia*, to huge differences in the basic remuneration of members from different countries, as well as to the divergent treatment mentioned elsewhere in this chapter as regards regimes for such matters as incompatibilities and immunity requests.

Members' basic salary is still paid from the budgets of the Member States and is the same as the salary paid to national parliamentarians from the member's own country, apart from in the Netherlands where national parliamentarians are now paid considerably more than Dutch MEPs. The difference arose during the last term of office when Dutch national parliamentarians' salaries were raised, but their allowances restrained. The salary rise was not given to the Dutch MEPs when it was realised that their allowances could not be cut back in the same way!

This difference in national treatment results in basic annual salaries varying enormously. The best paid are members from Italy, who receive more than €9600 per month, whereas members from Spain only receive €2800 and those from Sweden and Finland only receive around a third as much as the Italians. This anomaly is a matter of great sensitivity. In those Member States where salaries are lower, a sharp rise in MEPs' salaries aimed at achieving comparable treatment between MEPs could have a negative effect on public opinion at large and on relations with lower paid national parliamentarians. In countries where salaries are higher, there is a natural reluctance to favour too sharp a drop in salary.

MEPs from different countries are treated equally, however, in the size of the five main allowances to which they are entitled. Members receive *daily allowances for attendance* at Parliament to cover accommodation and subsistence. Members have to sign a register to prove their presence. They are also reimbursed for the *travel expenses* to and from their constituencies or places of residence, on the basis, for members who have to fly, of the cost of a" full fare economy ticket", paid as a flat rate lump sum upon presentation of proof that the journey has been made. Members may also claim up to €3,000 per annum for other travel, on the basis of receipts and proof that the travel was undertaken in the performance of their duties, except for travel within the country in which they were elected. Members do not have any special funding for the latter category of travel, which is very high in the case of MEPs whose regional constituencies are large. Members can use, however, their monthly *general expenditure allowance* (amounting to €3,314 per month) for this purpose as well as for its main purpose, namely office, telephone and postage costs. Any member attending on fewer than 50 per cent of the plenary days in the course of a parliamentary year has to reimburse 50 per cent of their general expenditure allowance unless there are valid medical or family reasons or unless the member has been on other official Parliament business. Finally, members receive *staff allowances* for one or more secretaries or assistants (see Table 7).

In addition, members are given insurance cover, are reimbursed for certain medical expenses, have invalidity and retirement pensions and also receive a transitional allowance for three months after the end of their term-of-office. They have access to Parliament cars under certain circumstances (primarily to and from the airport or railway stations in Brussels and Strasbourg), and may also attend language and computer courses.

The common system of allowances and of reimbursements for travel and other expenses has been developed by Parliament itself but it has sometimes been criticised as too generous and too susceptible to abuse. Members' allowances were originally paid, as in many national parliaments, without much in the way of verification, on the basis that members are by definition honourable, unlikely to take the political risks of being caught in an abusive situation, and are subject to spot checks by the Court of Auditors. Nevertheless, partly in response to concerns of members from countries with stricter traditions, including some of the newer Member States, and partly as a result of allegations made in the press about potential abuse, there was increasing recognition that reform was needed to reassure public opinion. Thus the 1994–99 Parliament *inter alia* introduced the requirement to prove that travel had actually been made; froze the value of travel reimbursements; and introduced a rule whereby attendance is defined as participation in more than half of any roll-call votes taking place on Tuesdays, Wednesdays or Thursdays. Further reform is in prospect in the context of

Table 7: *Comparison of salaries and expenses of MPs (UK House of Commons) and MEPs (1999)*

Item	MP	MEP
Salary	£47,000 p.a.	£47,000 p.a.
Hotels or accommodation at seat of Parliament	£13,000 p.a. "additional cost allowance" paid as a monthly lump sum irrespective of actual attendance.	£150 per day attended (approx. £18,000–24,000 p.a.). "Subsistence allowance" paid per day only if member signs in (and participates in Roll Call votes in midweek plenaries)
Normal travel (Constituency to Parliament)	Air and train tickets at cost plus mileage allowance for car of 51 pence per mile up to 20,000 miles and 23 ppm above 20,000 miles.	Lump sum equal to cost of "YY-economy class air fare" plus 31 pence per mile from home to airport and a "distance allowance" for journeys of £65 for journeys of over 500km and £130 for over 1000 km. One journey per week maximum under this rule.
Travel within constituency	Refunded on basis of normal travel mileage above.	Not reimbursed.
Travel to other parliaments	Two return tickets per year to European Parliament or national parliament of any EU member state and subsistence costs.	Not reimbursed.
Family travel	Spouse and children up to 30 single journeys per annum between constituency and parliament (First Class)	Not reimbursed.
Other travel	Within UK as parliamentary business, without limit but must be notified in advance to Fees Office. Cost of ticket or mileage allowance as above.	Within EU but not within own Member state up to €3000 per year (£1890) maximum, at cost of tickets, plus extra midweek returns to own Member State if needed.
Office allowance	£50,000 for office and staff jointly *plus* contributions to staff personal pension funds of up to £5000 (10% of allowance). Temporary secretarial allowances for replacement staff if staff are ill or on maternity leave. Redundancy costs at end of mandate. Administration of payments tax etc. by House of Commons. Staff travel of up to 18 single journeys per year between Constituency and Parliament. Insurance against accidents etc. Employer's liability insurance. Free post for letters sent out as MP.	£25,000 for office and, £78,000 for staff *but* staff pensions, temporary replacement staff, redundancy costs, staff travel (including between Brussels and Strasbourg), insurance and employer's liability must all be paid from these allowances, as well as any Belgium tax and social security (significantly higher than UK) for assistants employed in Brussels. All postage must be paid out of office allowance.
Winding up at end of mandate	Four months of office cost allowances.	Three months of office cost allowances.

agreeing a members' statute (of which more below). On this Parliament has made proposals including the abandonment of the lump sum basis for travel, which allows members to benefit when they can purchase tickets more cheaply than the full economy class air fare. This feature is considered by some to be compensation for the low salaries of MEPs from certain countries where members of the national parliament (to whose salaries those of MEPs are tied) have a system of low salaries but generous expenses. This justification would fall with a common statute giving identical salaries.

Immunities

This is another area where the lack of a uniform statute for members has led to considerable diversity between nationalities. Members' immunity is still covered by the protocol on the privileges and immunities of the European Union. This provides for MEPs to enjoy the same immunities in their own country as national parliamentarians and, while in other countries of the Union, to be immune from any measure of detention and from legal proceedings. Members are in any case immune while travelling to and from the Parliament. Immunity does not apply when caught in the act of committing a criminal offence. Immunity can only be waived by the European Parliament, upon application from the legal authorities in the Member States, thus allowing the MEP in question to appear in Court.

Parliament called in 1983 for the protocol to be amended, and the Commission subsequently tabled a proposal to this effect, which would have provided uniform rules. This has still not been adopted and pressure to develop a distinctive European Parliament system of immunity is again mounting.

Requests by the national authorities of the Member States for members' immunity to be waived are a regular feature at plenary sessions. Such requests are transmitted to the competent committee, which submits its report recommending in favour of or against the waiving of immunity, but without, of course, pronouncing on or even examining the member's guilt, which is a matter for the courts. The committee has traditionally nominated one or two specialist rapporteurs for such requests for a number of years.

In its many reports on requests for the waiving of immunity the Parliament has established a number of basic principles, the most important of which is not to waive immunity if the acts of which a member is accused form part of his or her political activities. In the majority of cases, Parliament has not acceded to requests to waive immunity. Between 1979 and the 1999 elections, around 100 requests for waiving of immunity were made by national authorities. On only 17 occasions was immunity waived. Allegations of corruption or serious criminal activities (e.g., embezzlement or fraud, membership of the Camorra, provision of assistance to criminals, etc.) constituted some of these latter cases, as did more minor and non-political offences such as parking in a prohibited area or failure to report a road accident. A particularly controversial case arose in December 1989, when Jean Marie Le Pen's immunity was waived by a large majority after a long and passionate debate on whether the particularly obnoxious nature of his remarks justified abandonment of Parliament's customary concern to protect members' expression of political opinions. Parliament thus overruled its relevant committee's narrow decision (ten to nine with two abstentions) not to waive Le Pen's immunity. Le Pen's immunity was waived in similar circumstances on another charge at the March 1990 plenary, and yet again on 6 October 1998, on this latter occasion on a request submitted not by the French but by the German authorities.

Declaration of financial interests

Rule 9 of Parliament's Rules of Procedure states that Parliament may lay down a code of conduct for its members. The only implementing provision so far is that contained in Annex I of the Rules providing for a declaration of financial interests. National traditions on this issue vary greatly, with some countries such as the UK and Germany having fairly rigid rules, others much weaker ones, and some none at all.

Parliament first adopted a report in March 1983 on the issues involved, drawn up by Hans Nord (Dutch Liberal, former Parliament Secretary-General). It opted for brief general provisions rather than a set of very detailed rules. Over time, these have been tightened up and Annex I now provides that each member make a detailed declaration of professional activities and list any other paid functions or activities in so far as these are relevant (Article 2). Members are also meant to disclose orally any direct financial interest in a subject under discussion in Parliament or in one of its bodies, and, in a recent reform of the rule, irrespective of whether this interest is obvious from their written declaration (Article 1). Finally members' declarations are to be contained in a register, which is open for public inspection.

For this purpose, members are now given a form on which to declare their financial interests. The register is kept for inspection in an office in Luxembourg, Strasbourg (during plenary sessions) and Brussels, and will now be placed on the Internet.

Over the years certain members have tabled motions for a resolution, complaining about the lack of detailed information provided by many members, and the lack of sanctions against members not in compliance, and also calling for greater public accessibility of the register. As a result of these initiatives the rules have recently been made more rigorous, with sanctions introduced for the first time. If a member persists in not submitting a declaration, the President shall give him or her two months to comply, after which he or she is "named or shamed" in the minutes of the first day of each part-session after expiry of the time limit. If he or she continues not to comply the President is to take action to suspend the member concerned.

Moreover, members must now have duly completed their financial declaration before they may be validly nominated as an office-holder of Parliament or one of its bodies, or as a member of any delegation representing Parliament externally. Indeed one of the first tasks that had to be carried out at the constituent meetings of Parliament's committees in July 1999 was to verify that the various Group nominees for Chairman or Vice-Chairman had filled in such a declaration! The considerable effectiveness of the new measures was shown by the fact that 90 per cent of the 1999 intake of members had already made their declaration by the Thursday of the constituent plenary.

Steps towards adoption of a members' statute

Until recently progress on eliminating the main differences in treatment of MEPs from different Member States was hampered by the lack of any formal legal basis in the Treaty for the adoption of a members' statute. This was finally remedied in the Amsterdam Treaty. Article 190(5) TEC now states that "the European Parliament shall, after seeking an opinion from the Commission and with the approval of the Council acting unanimously lay down the regulations and general conditions governing the performance of the duties of its members."

Following initial discussion in a working party of the Parliament's Bureau, the matter was then referred to the Legal Affairs Committee, which appointed Willi Rothley as rapporteur. His most controversial recommendations concerned the financial entitlements of members. Foremost among these were recommendations calling for a common and transparent salary for all MEPs, based on the weighted average of the existing salaries of the 626 members, and for all MEPs to be subject not to national taxation but to a common Community tax, so that the establishment of a common salary would not be undercut by great differences in tax treatment. He also covered the complex issue of pensions and other benefits, sought to establish a transitional regime and called for a longer-term solution to be drawn up on the basis of an external study by independent experts. Finally he also recognised that the content of the statute should not be restricted to the issue of financial entitlements but should also include common provisions on such issues as the independence of members and references to rules of conduct on their financial interests.

Rothley's report (A4–0426/98) was easily adopted in committee but had a much tougher passage in plenary on 3 December 1998, when his basic approach was supported by the plenary, but with some very close votes on some of his key recommendations. The finally adopted text also included a number of new points on non-financial matters, such as a list of incompatibilities, immunity and verification of credentials, and on the filling of vacant seats.

The Parliament's text was then examined by a Council working party, which met on several occasions with Parliament representatives. The Council was divided between those Member States that wanted to have a statute adopted before the 1999 Parliament elections, and those for which this was a less important objective. The issue of common tax treatment for MEPs was particularly controversial for certain Member States, notably among the Nordic countries. On 26 April 1999, only shortly before the Parliament's final plenary before the elections, the Council adopted its own version of the statute, which followed the Parliament's draft on certain issues but took a different approach on others. It eliminated the proposed transitional arrangements, permitted derogations from a common tax regime for MEPs (so that some but not all members would continue to be subject to national taxation regimes) and proposed a different regime as regards pensions. The Council also sought to include more detailed rules on the reimbursements of MEPs' expenses within the statute.

At the plenary on 5 May 1999 the EP decided, on a vote of 336 to 140 with 31 abstentions, to follow Rothley's recommendation, and not to accept the

Council's text. He argued not just on the substance, but on the procedure: it was not up to Council to make a counter-proposal when the Treaty provided for Parliament to elaborate and adopt a text with the assent of the Council. After all, Parliament does not elaborate counter-proposals when it has to give assent to Council texts! Instead the Parliament sought to pursue negotiations with the Council on the basis of the Parliament's original draft, with a view to a decision "if possible before the end of this parliamentary term" and otherwise "before the end of 1999".

This timetable was not met, and the newly elected Parliament in 1999 is still confronted with the issue. On the one hand, the issue is now somewhat less urgent than it appeared to be in the run-up to the elections; on the other hand there are still strong political reasons for reaching agreement on a common statute as soon as possible. The new Parliament has thus immediately set up a working group to examine the matter, but the issue was still unresolved at the moment of writing.

Members' assistants

As indicated earlier, members are given a secretarial allowance to employ personal assistants. They have to certify that a contract has been concluded with an assistant, and must provide an affidavit on the assistant's behalf. They may choose to have such assistants officially accredited in Brussels (ensuring fewer formalities for the assistant in using Parliament's facilities and also permitting them to receive a special residence permit in Belgium), but this is not mandatory.

Members are allowed considerable freedom in the use of these funds. They may choose to have two better paid full-time assistants or several less well paid or part-time assistants. Some members prefer to have more assistance in Brussels, others in their own constituencies, and a few in their national capital. There are also those who make little use of assistants.

The role of assistants also varies greatly, with some given considerable political responsibilities, and other concentrating more on office tasks, such as typing, booking tickets or running other errands. Typical tasks are to arrange meetings with Commission officials or representatives of trade associations, to draft letters, articles, press releases or parliamentary questions, and to carry out background research. Some assistants help to draft reports when their boss becomes a rapporteur, but this still tends to be the exception. Brussels-based assistants also often attend meetings when the member is elsewhere engaged, and brief the member on what took place. Some help service the intergroups in which their member is active (see Chapter 10).

Assistants based in the member's home country tend to deal with constituents' enquiries, handle mail and have a liaison function with the party, the press, and national or regional interests – all matters of considerable importance in view of the large amount of time spent travelling by the average MEP.

Assistants are less well paid (although there are great variations between them) than Parliament or Political Group staff, and there is a far higher turnover. They tend to be younger (often just out of university), and take on the job for a short period to gain experience. A minority, however, remain assistants for several years, and when they leave the employment of one member may then start working for another. Some even work for two or more members at once. In at least one case assistants have formed a consortium with a number of MEPs on its books, as well as members from the respective national parliament. In other cases several members have pooled some of their resources and run a joint secretariat. The Spanish Socialist Party (PSOE) has insisted upon such an arrangement.

A few assistants have their own successful careers (in consultancy, for example) and have a part-time role as assistants in order primarily to widen their range of contacts. In this context, assistants must declare in writing any additional remuneration from sources outside the Parliament. This is included in a special register on the financial interests of members' assistants, which is available for public consultation. A number of assistants have gone on to political careers in their own right, such as the current Labour MEPs Stephen Hughes (who worked for Roland Boyes), Gary Titley (Terry Pitt and then John Bird) and Simon Murphy (also John Bird), former MEPs such as Anita Pollack (Barbara Castle), or the MPs Oonagh King (Glyn Ford and then Glenys Kinnock), and John Grogan. Others include the German CSU MEP, Bernd Posselt , the Dutch Green MEP Kathalijne Buitenweg, the Italian Radical MEP Gianfranco Dell' Alba and the former German SPD MEP Axel Schaefer.

The working conditions and status of members' assistants remains on a rather *ad hoc* and variable basis. They work from the members' offices in Brussels or the constituency office or even from their own home. A considerable number come regularly to Strasbourg plenary sessions, but many remain in Brussels or in their national base. On the other hand, their access to meetings, which was once a problem in certain committees and Groups, is now normally unrestricted.

There has been lengthy discussion as to whether and how to regulate the status of assistants, by providing them with a proper statute and with guaranteed rights in relation to their employers. The Parliament's secretariat remains unwilling to take over the role of employer from the members. In the meantime, a number of the Brussels-based assistants of British MEPs have joined the GMB (the only British union with a branch in Brussels), which has been active on their behalf and a general Assistants' Association has been set up.

In May 1998 the Commission finally put forward a proposal for a Council Regulation (COM(1998)312.fin.) designed to provide for assistants to be covered by the Conditions of Employment of Other Servants and Auxiliary Staff in the existing Staff Regulations. However, it included an important derogation allowing MEPs to retain autonomy in determining the level of assistants' remuneration. Although Parliament subsequently adopted a report on this proposal by Klaus-Heiner Lehne (A4–0018/99) the issue was still unresolved at the moment of writing, and is unlikely to be before the members' statute is settled.

Background of the individual members elected in 1999

Length of service

One of the more remarkable features of the European Parliament is the high turnover in its membership at each election and, to a lesser extent, even between elections. In 1989, for example, only 266 (51.3%) of the 518 members elected were outgoing MEPs and no less than 73 MEPs (over 14%) were replaced by new members from 1989 to 1993 alone (eight as a result of death and 65 because of resignation). This turnover was even more striking after the 1994 elections, when only 241 (42.5%) of the admittedly higher total figure of 567 MEPs were outgoing members of the Parliament. In 1999, 340 of the 626 members (54.3%) were newly elected and 286 (45.7%) were previous incumbents.

Those with more than five years' experience of the Parliament are even fewer in number. Only 14 of the current MEPs have served continuously since 1979, and, with the departure of Winnie Ewing, none have been members continuously since before 1979. Taking new and former members together, the group of MEPs elected in 1999, as in 1994, had an average of around 3½ years' membership of the Parliament, an unusually low figure by parliamentary standards, even for the start of a new Parliament.

Nevertheless, there are clear variations in length of service between the different national delegations. Ireland now provides the delegation with the longest service, with an average of almost eight years (i.e. likely to be nearly 13 years by the end of the Parliament), and also with the highest percentage of re-elected members at 80%. Of the delegations from the larger countries German MEPs have by far the highest average length of service at six years, with eight of them having been members since 1979. Almost 70% of German members elected in 1999 were previous incumbents. The UK delegation also has a higher than average length of service at 4½ years but this is a sharp decline from the previous figure of six years in 1994, caused by the changes stemming from the new electoral system as well as from the retirement of a number of long-serving incumbents.

At the opposite end of the spectrum, Italy and France continue to be countries with exceptionally low average lengths of service among their MEPs, and with the highest turnover in membership. 55 of the 81 French members elected in 1989 were new to the Parliament, as were 56 of the 87 French members in 1994 and 60 out of 87 in 1999. The average length of service of French MEPs elected in 1999 was under 2½ years.

The figures for Italy are even more striking. 58 of the 81 Italian members elected in 1989 were new, as were 68 of the 87 Italian members in 1994 and 66 of the 87 in 1999. The average length of service of Italian MEPs elected in 1999 was little over two years, and no Italian MEPs have served continuously since 1979, nor even since 1984 (although Marco Pannella was a member from 1979 to 1996, and was again re-elected in 1999). Already MEPs from the new member states of Austria and Sweden have achieved a higher average length of service than their Italian colleagues!

Dual mandate MEPs

The dual mandate is now formally or informally discouraged in most Member States (see chapter 2 above) and after the 1999 elections only 40 of the elected MEPs (6.4% of the total) were also members of a national parliament. Of these no less than 22 were from the one Member State of Italy, where over one quarter of the MEPs thus have dual mandates. Seven others were from the UK, two being the long-standing dual mandate members John Hume and Ian Paisley from Northern Ireland, and the others all coming from the House of Lords (Bethell, Inglewood and Stockton from the Conservatives, Ludford and Nicholson from the Liberal Democrats). Five were from France and two each from Denmark, Ireland and Greece. The other Member States had none.

Balance between men and women

188 women MEPs (around 30% of the total) were elected in 1999. This compares to 69 women (16.8%) in 1979 and 103 (around 20%) in 1989. The current figure is higher than that in most national parliaments within the Member States. Again there is considerable variation in these figures between the different national delegations (see Table 8) and parties (e.g. in the UK, only three of the 36 Conservatives are women, compared to ten out of 29 Labour and five out of ten Liberals).

Table 8: *Women MEPs (June 1999)*

Country	No. Women MEPs	Total No. MEPs	Women as a % of MEPs
Finland	7	16	43.8
Sweden	9	22	40.9
France	35	87	40.2
Austria	8	21	38.1
Denmark	6	16	37.5
Germany	37	99	37.4
Netherlands	11	31	35.5
Ireland	5	15	33.3
Luxembourg	2	6	33.3
Spain	21	63	33.3
Belgium	7	25	28.0
United Kingdom	20	87	23.0
Portugal	5	25	20.0
Greece	4	25	16.0
Italy	10	87	11.5

National parliamentary and ministerial experience

While so many of the current MEPs are newcomers and their average length of service in the European Parliament is limited, many of them have nevertheless had considerable experience in their own national parliaments, and/or as office-holders in their national governments or in their own party.

In all, there were 177 former or current national parliamentarians elected in 1999, just over 28% of the total. This percentage has remained relatively stable since 1989 after dropping sharply from the figure of 45% in the first directly elected Parliament (see Table 9). In 1999, as in 1994, former or current national parliamentarians were in the majority in the Luxembourg (at present five out of six), Portuguese (19 out of 25) and Irish (nine out of 15) delegations. They were also in the majority among Finnish (nine out of 16) and Swedish (12 out of 21) members. Among the larger Member States by far the largest number was in Italy (35 out of 87, largely because of the large number of dual mandate members). The British figure was 20 out of 87, a sharp rise from the 1994 figure of nine and to be explained by the influx of members from the House of Lords, and by the arrival of former Conservative MPs who had been defeated in the 1997 elections. There were lower percentages in Germany (17 out of 99, nine of whose members were former members of the East German *Volkskammer*) and in France (12 out of 87).

No fewer than 64 (over 10%) of the MEPs elected in 1999 have held ministerial office. Among them are six former prime ministers: Michel Rocard from France, Ciriaco de Mita of Italy, Jacques Santer of Luxembourg, Mario Soares of Portugal (who was also President), Hans Modrow of the former East Germany and Silvio Berlusconi of Italy.

This follows on from a distinguished list of former heads of government in earlier European Parliaments. Since direct elections in 1979, there have been one former French president (Valery Giscard d'Estaing) and four former French prime ministers (Pierre Pflimlin, Michel Debré, Jacques Chirac and Laurent Fabius); six former Italian prime ministers (Emilio Colombo, Arnaldo Forlani, Bettino Craxi, Mariano Rumor, Giulio Andreotti and Giovanni Goria); one former German chancellor (Willy Brandt); one former Spanish prime minister (Calvo Sotelo); one former prime minister from Luxembourg (Gaston Thorn), two former Portuguese prime ministers (Francisco Balsemao and Maria de Lourdes Pintasilgo), two former Belgian prime ministers (Leo Tindemans and Wilfried Martens) and one former Danish prime minister (Poul Schluter).

Not all of these former leaders have been particularly active in the European Parliament, but some have held important office (Colombo as President of the European Parliament just before direct elections and Pflimlin from 1984–87; Rumor and later Goria as Chairman of the Political Affairs Committee; Tindemans and Martens as Chairmen of the EPP Group; Giscard d'Estaing as Chairman of the Liberal Group; Schlüter as an EP Vice-President; and Rocard as Chairman first of the Development and now of the Employment Committee).

Among the current MEPs, there are also three former members of the European Commission: Jacques Santer, President of the last Commission; Emma Bonino, a high-profile member of the same Commission; and, from an earlier Commission, Willy de Clercq (who went in 1989 from being Commissioner responsible for External Relations to being Chairman of Parliament's External Relations Committee). Catherine Lalumière of France is a former Secretary-General of the Council of Europe, Michel Hansenne of

Table 9: *Previous parliamentary and governmental experience of MEPs*

	1979	1984	1989	1994	1999
MEPs with national parliamentary experience	45%	35%	26%	30%	28%
MEPs with ministerial experience	16.7%	13%	14.1%	10.5%	10.2%

Belgium a former Director-General of the International Labour Office, and Anders Wijkman of Sweden a former deputy UN Secretary-General. Carlos Westendorp of Spain (also one of several former foreign ministers) is a former UN Mediator in Bosnia, and previously chaired the Reflection Group that prepared the Amsterdam IGC.

Another significant group among the current MEPs are those holding leadership positions in their national parties. There are two UK MEPs in this position (John Hume of the SDLP and the Rev. Ian Paisley of the DUP). Others include Jean-Marie Le Pen of the *Front National* in France and Paolo Portas of the CDS/PP in Portugal, and no less than seven in Italy (Silvio Berlusconi of *Forza Italia*, Fausto Bertinotti of *Rifondazione Comunista*, Armando Cossutta of *Comunisti Italiani*, Umberto Bossi of *Lega Nord*, Gianfranco Fini of *Alleanza Nazionale* , Rocco Buttiglione of the CDU, and Walter Veltroni of the PDS.

Other political experience

A considerable number of current MEPs have held other important posts in their countries. There are over 50 former regional office-holders, notably in Spain, Germany, Italy and France, and several current or former regional presidents, such as Mathieu Grosch (former President of the Council of the German-speaking Community in Belgium), Alfred Gomolka (former Prime Minister of the German Land of Mecklenberg-Vorpommern), Amalia Sartori (former President of the Veneto regional government in Italy), Fiorella Ghilardotti (former President of the Lombardy regional government in Italy), and Fernando Fernandez Marin (former President of the Canaries regional government in Spain).

There are also a considerable number of former or serving mayors. In particular, the Italian delegation includes two serving mayors of major cities (Francesco Rutelli of Rome and Massimo Cacciari of Venice) and several former mayors (notably Marco Formentini of Milan and Renzo Imbeni of Bologna).

Other experience

The MEPs elected in 1999 also include members with a wide range of other experience, including celebrated judges (such as Thierry Jean-Pierre of France and Antonio Di Pietro and Elena Pacciotti of Italy), trade union leaders (such as Franco Marini and Bruno Trentin of Italy), and media personalities (such as Dirk Sterckx and Frédérique Ries among the Belgian delegation).

Among those of other backgrounds are the 1968 student leader Daniel Cohn-Bendit (formerly a German and now French Green MEP); the actor Michael Cashman (British Labour) from TV soap opera "Eastenders"; Eurovision Song Contest winner Dana (Rosemary Scallon, an Irish independent); the French General Philippe Morillon (former Commander of UNPROFOR in Bosnia); the cross country skiing champion Marja Matikainen-Kallstrom of Finland; the Finnish rally driver, former world champion Ari Vatanen; the Italian Olympic champion athlete Pietro Mennea; the Italian mountain climber Reinhold Messner; and the Olympic and world sailing champion from Spain, Teresa Zabell.

Post-MEP Experience

Those MEPs who leave the Parliament to move on to other things frequently remain active in political life. In the UK, for example, of the eight MEPs first elected to Westminster in 1983/84 and the five elected in 1987, every single one of them was later promoted to positions in government or on the opposition front-bench. Furthermore, many have played a prominent part in European affairs, such as by serving on the Commons Select Committee on European legislation or by playing an important role in major European debates (Ann Clywd in the SEA ratification debate in 1987, and Geoff Hoon in the Maastricht ratification procedure, for which he won the parliamentarian of the year award of *The Guardian*). Some have become ministers in roles where their European experience would be likely to be relevant (David Curry – Ministry of Agriculture, and Eric Forth – Department of Trade and Industry). Two others (Joyce Quin and Geoff Hoon) became European affairs ministers in the Labour government after 1997, and Hoon has since become Defence Secretary. In the words of David Curry: "in senior positions in national governments, increasingly the new men are people who have served their apprenticeship in Europe and are formed by a European dimension".

The above comments have been confined to the UK where seepage back to national politics was complicated by the constituency system and by the fact that both major British parties now frown upon MEPs standing for selection as Westminster candidates. In other Member States, the osmosis between the European Parliament and national politics is easier, thanks notably to the list system and, in some Member States, to the fact that ministers do not have to be MPs. In some Member States, a stint as an MEP is a not infrequent part of a political career. In France, for instance, ten of the 16 prime ministers who have held office in the Fifth Republic have, at one stage or another in their careers, been directly elected MEPs (as have four out of the six presidents). Five post-war Belgian prime ministers have similarly been MEPs (though only two since direct elections) and ten Italian prime ministers (six since direct elections). Indeed, the only Member States never to have had a prime minister who has spent part of their political career in the European Parliament are the UK, Ireland and Greece (and the new Member States, Sweden, Finland and Austria).

Others who went on to important responsibilities were Federigo Mayor (to Secretary-General of UNESCO), Elio Di Rupo (former Belgian Deputy Prime Minister, and now Prime Minister of Wallonia as well as being leader of his party), and Bernard Kouchner (current UN Administrator in Kosovo).

Moreover, a number of MEPs who go on to important political posts in their own Member State subsequently return to the European Parliament, like Hanja Maij-Weggen amongst the current Dutch MEPs, and Hedy d'Ancona and Piet Dankert among former Dutch MEPs.

All these factors imply that MEPs are not simply an isolated political group with no links or inter-connections with the rest of the political class. The osmosis with national politics has not eroded its identity, nor the commitment of the majority of MEPs to strengthening the Parliament in its own right, but has given the Parliament the added advantage of being an integral part of Europe's political network. Indeed, it is the place *par excellence* where politicians from different Member States are in regular contact. No other group of politicians in Europe is in such constant contact with colleagues from other Member States.

The role of individual members within the European Parliamentary system

The independence of individual MEPs is emphasised at the very beginning in Rule 2, which states that "they shall not be bound by any instructions and shall not receive a binding mandate". However, as in any Parliament there are significant constraints on the freedom of action of individual members.

Most notable is the discipline required of belonging to a Political Group and the pressure to follow the collective position adopted by the Group. Group whipping and discipline are discussed in the next chapter; suffice to say here that they are less strict than in most national parliaments. Furthermore, individual members can play an important role in defining a Group position in the first place. Group positions are worked out by their coordinators on the relevant committee and/or by the Group's leadership after wide discussion, if necessary in the Group meeting itself. They are not handed down from above by ministers or a party leader. Individual members have real opportunities to shape their Group's position, in the first place, but they can also (and occasionally do) opt out of the position if they are not satisfied. As a result, individual "back-bench" members do play a considerable role in the life of the Parliament.

There are also a number of maverick or "outsider" members who have made a considerable impact within the Parliament by effective use of the relevant Rules of Procedure. Another phenomenon is that of back-bench revolts against Group leaderships, especially when members from different Groups are angered by what they see as a cosy deal cooked up by the Group leaders behind closed doors, though these are more often on procedural or timetable issues.

Parliament's Rules of Procedure provide for numerous rights for individual members, or for several members acting together outside the normal Political Group or committee framework.

A single individual member may put questions to the Commission or Council in the context of question time or, for a written answer, table a motion for resolution or a written declaration. He may table and move amendments to any text in committee, make explanations of vote, ask questions related to the work of Parliament's leadership (Conference of

Presidents, Bureau and Quaestors), table amendments to the Rules of Procedure, raise points of order, or move the inadmissibility of a matter (both of these latter rights entailing a prior claim over other requests to speak). Individual members may also make personal statements, notably when derogatory comments have been made about them by other speakers.

The use of some of these powers is described in greater detail elsewhere in this book. A few comments, however, can be made at this stage, regarding some of these powers and their value for individual members.

The value of question time in plenary, for example, which was initiated before British entry into the Community, but which has been dominated by British members, has often been questioned in the European Parliament context, in that it has little of the cut and thrust of its original model, is often very poorly attended, and yet takes up valuable plenary time. Nevertheless, all attempts to shift it to a time other than that originally planned, or to reduce its duration, are met with strong resistance from certain MEPs (not exclusively British), who claim that it is of great importance for individual MEPs.

Written questions, too, can be of considerable value in enabling an individual member to put down a marker on an issue of constituency or other importance. Certain individual members have made particular use of written questions, such as Henk Vredeling or Lord O'Hagan before direct elections, or Dieter Rogalla (German SPD) in the context of his fierce campaign to remove internal frontiers within the Community. Another prolific questioner in the 1989–94 Parliament was Sotiris Kostopoulos (Greek – PASOK).

Another device for putting down a marker on a specific issue is by tabling individual motions for a resolution. Although they only rarely lead to a committee report, members can, nevertheless, still gain publicity from their initiative, and show their constituents or other groups that they have played an active role on their behalf (thus comparable to "early-day motions" in the UK House of Commons). A similar function is provided by written declarations (see chapter 15).

Another individual right is to make explanations of vote in plenary. They used to precede the final vote on a text and, although limited to one minute per member, cumulatively delayed it by up to half an hour or more. Considerable pressure was often exerted for them not to be made orally, but converted into written explanations (cheers often greeted members' calls of "in writing" and groans when they actually started to speak!). Members often did assert their right to an oral statement, however, and these statements were often more concise and passionate than those made in the preceding debate, and made before a much fuller, if often noisy, house. In 1994, however, a rule change allowed the President to place these explanations of vote after the final vote (when most of the members have left the chamber) in order to speed up voting time.

As in any parliament, points of order and procedural motions are often used (and sometimes abused) by individual members. They are particularly frequent at the beginning of sittings (when they can go on for half an hour or more), or after controversial rulings have been made by the President, or in order to continue a terminated debate by other means. They are also often used to make isolated points of constituency or sectoral concern. The British,

Irish and French members in general have been particularly active in this regard. The most well-known member of all for such activity was Marco Pannella, who made a particular crusade of defending the rights of back-benchers, non-attached members and small Groups, and also of baiting Parliament's leadership. The President of Parliament once pointed out that Pannella had spoken on 31 different occasions during the September 1989 plenary, for a total speaking time of 56 minutes! In order to provide greater discipline as regards points of order the Rules were changed in January 1992, limiting individual points of order to one rather than three minutes, and requiring the members concerned to specify which rule or rules were not being respected.

Besides these rights granted to individual members, Parliament's Rules of Procedure also grant rights to individual members acting together with a certain specified number of other members. This is done wherever the Rules confer such rights on Political Groups, and even in a few cases where Political Groups have no such rights (such as a request for a quorum to be ascertained by 32 or more members). The actual number of members required to assert such rights is usually 32, but in some special cases is 12, one-tenth, one-fifth, one-quarter, or one-third of MEPs. Thirty-two members may, for example, nominate candidates for President, Vice-President, Questor or Ombudsman; table the types of motions for resolution dealt with directly in plenary (to wind up debates on statements or on oral questions or topical and urgent debates); propose to reject or amend legislative "common positions" of the Council or the draft budget; request roll call votes; and oppose the adoption of reports without debate.

The Rules thus give considerable scope for dissident members within a Political Group, or coalitions of individual members across Group divides, to request that certain action be taken.

The work of an individual MEP: choice of priorities

So far this chapter has examined the formal rights and obligations of individual MEPs, their political background and the techniques and procedures that they can use to make an impact as individuals. This final section looks at the wider choices that they must make, namely how best to spend their time.

The pressure on a member's time is great. One week a month is taken up by the plenary session in Strasbourg, and much of the next three weeks by committee, plenary or Group meetings in Brussels (especially if an MEP is on two committees or is an active substitute on another committee), and with occasional meetings in other countries as well.

This is compounded by the time it takes to travel between these various locations and the member's home country. In addition, members are expected to keep in touch with their political base at home. Members with geographical constituencies (such as UK and Irish members) typically spend a couple of days each week dealing with individual constituents, NGOs, local government leaders and staff, businesses, trade unions, development agencies, MPs, party structures, etc. in their areas and taking up invitations to speak at universities, schools, organisations, clubs and, last but not least, local media. These may relate to their work in the Parliament, to the local application of European legislation, to European grants and assistance or to problems encountered by constituents travelling or working in other Member States. Even if members do not have a geographical constituency to nurse, they may have some similar activities or have sectoral (e.g. trade union) or specific responsibilities within their party.

Within Parliament, there are further conflicting pressures. The meeting of their main committee may coincide with a hearing or debate in another committee that is of greater political importance to them. Intergroup meetings (see Chapter 10) may take up time, as does speaking to visitors' groups. MEPs may well be involved in their own national party committees or working groups. Lobbyists wish to meet members, and to invite them to presentations and receptions. The member will also have requests for interviews from the Brussels press corps, or from journalists from home, and will anyway wish to cultivate these contacts on a regular basis.

The pressure is even greater on the President, the leaders of the Political Groups and of national party delegations, committee chairmen and committee co-ordinators, together with rapporteurs on controversial policy issues who have fuller agendas because of their specific role. Members who have established a reputation in a particular field are also in particular demand, especially if they are proficient linguists.

In spite of these pressures, members do not have large personal staffs to help them to respond (in contrast especially with the US Congress).

Being an MEP is an increasingly tough full-time job. Yet there are still a few who have "dual mandates", being also members of their national parliament, or have other important responsibilities within their Member State. Whilst this can lead to such members spending little time in the European Parliament, their other activities may also have benefits, in terms of maintaining links between the European Parliament and national structures.

All this shows that an individual MEP is faced with tough choices. An active member of a committee or of a Political Group may well gain greater influence within the Parliament, with prestigious rapporteurships, and so on. On the other hand, a member can be extremely active within the Parliament and lose touch with his or her own political base at home, and risk not being re-elected. While the choice is not usually as stark as this (members who have built up their reputations within the Parliament may well gain domestically as well), a member must select an appropriate balance of priorities. How much time should they spend in Brussels, Strasbourg and at home? Should they remain generalists or seek to become policy specialists? What activities should they concentrate on?

A number of factors condition these choices. Geographical proximity to Brussels or Strasbourg makes it easy for certain members to come and go frequently, whereas this is more difficult for other members, such as those from Ireland, Southern Italy, Spain, Portugal, Greece or Finland.

Secondly, a constituency-based electoral system may put more pressure on a member to spend a lengthy period of time at his or her home base than a list system would do, at least if the latter is nationally rather than regionally based, and if there is no preferential element. Nevertheless, list systems do not preclude regional or local responsibilities being put on a member, and list members must also spend time cultivating their base if they want to ensure that they remain on the list the next time around.

Another factor is the nature of a member's interests and responsibilities. Moreover, whilst individual members cannot be mandated, some of them retain close links with particular sectors or interest groups which will help to condition their choice of priorities.

Degree of access to positions of responsibility within the European Parliament is yet another factor. Members from small Groups, or non-attached members, may well find it easier, for example, to make an impact in plenary where they can make a well publicized speech, than in committee where they will find it hard to get major rapporteurships.

Differences in national culture also play a role, with different emphasis being put on different aspects of a parliamentarian's role, and even on the importance attached to attendance at meetings. Examples of such differences in national culture abound. Members from Northern European countries have generally been more prepared to spend time, for example, on the details of technical legislation than many members from Southern Europe; British members have traditionally put more of an emphasis on question time in plenary, and so on.

As a result of all these factors, the priorities of individual members are very different, as are their profiles within the European Parliament. Some become known as men or women of the House, and are constantly present in plenary. Others are more effective within committee, or in their Group or their national party delegation; others concentrate more on their national or regional political image. Some members remain generalists, whereas others become specialists, and are always allocated reports or opinions within a particular policy area. Some even develop functional rather than policy specialities (e.g. the Rules of Procedure). Some only pay short visits to Brussels or Strasbourg, whereas others are always present. Many but by no means all, have even bought accommodation in Brussels and some make that their family home rather than have their family compete for the member's precious time in the constituency.

MEPs thus enjoy considerable freedom to choose their priorities yet there are certain constraints on this freedom, not least the internal rules and priorities of the Political Groups to which they belong. It is to these that we now turn.

5. The Political Groups

Rule 29 of the Parliament's Rules states that members "may form themselves into groups according to their political affinities". When a Group is established it has to make a statement specifying its name, its members and its Bureau (main office-holders). The minimum number of members required to form a Group is 23 if they come from two Member States, 18 from three, and 14 from four or more Member States. Since the EP Rules revision in 1999 a Group must comprise members from more than one Member State. Before this revision a Group could be set up by 29 members from one country. After the 1994 elections for example, *Forza Italia* set up a Group, *Forza Europa*, on its own. In spite of the recent change the current thresholds to set up a Group within the Parliament are still relatively low by national parliamentary standards within Europe, but any further attempts to raise these thresholds would meet with strong resistance from the smaller Groups.

The Groups are of central importance in the work of the Parliament. It is the Groups that play the decisive role in choosing the President, Vice-Presidents and committee chairmen. They set the parliamentary agenda, choose the rapporteurs and decide on the allocation of speaking time. They have their own staff, receive considerable funds from the Parliament and often influence the choice of the Parliament's top officials. The power of the Groups is also shown by the powerlessness of those non-attached members who are not in Political Groups, who are highly unlikely, for example, ever to hold a powerful post within the Parliament, or be a major rapporteur.

There are now seven Political Groups within the Parliament, some with familiar names, others whose titles do not immediately indicate the nature of their membership or even their position in the ideological spectrum.

This chapter examines the historical evolution and current position of the Groups. It surveys their structures and working methods, assesses their cohesion and examines the balance of power between them.

Historical evolution

The evolution of the Groups has blended continuity and change. Since direct elections, the Socialists and the EPP have been the two large Groups with a constantly changing pattern of smaller Groups, some of which have been absorbed by them, particularly by the EPP.

Groups were first formally established in 1953 by the Common Assembly of the European Coal and Steel Community, which set the minimum membership for a Group at nine (out of 78). This was the first international assembly whose members sat according to political affiliation.

The first three Groups to be founded, all in June 1953, were those representing the Socialists, the Liberals and the Christian Democrats. From 1953
to 1965 these remained the only three Political Groups, and they are the only
ones with continuous existence until today, when they are again the three
largest Groups. Until 1975 the largest was the Christian Democrats, often
close to an absolute majority (38 out of 77 in 1953, 39 out of 78 in 1955 and
1956, 67 out of 142 after the Assembly was enlarged in 1958). The Socialists
were generally the second largest Group, and the Liberals the third, apart
from the years 1959/60 to 1961/62 when the Liberals overtook the Socialists
(43 Liberals to 33 Socialists in 1961/62).

After the **enlargement of the Assembly in 1958** the rules for forming
Groups were also changed, with the minimum membership raised to 17,
though this was again lowered to 14 in 1965, to enable the French Gaullists
to break away from the Liberals and form the European Democratic Union.
From 1965 to 1973 the Christian Democrats remained by far the largest
Group, with the Socialists in second place, the Liberals third and the
European Democratic Union fourth.

British, Irish and Danish entry into the Community in 1973 led to the creation by British and Danish Conservatives of a completely new Group, the
European Conservatives, with 20 members. The European Democratic
Union was joined by members from the Irish party, *Fianna Fáil*, and the
name of the Group was changed to that of the European Progressive
Democrats. The Socialist Group was reinforced and would have become the
largest Group if the British Labour Party had not refused to nominate the
members to which it was entitled until after the 1975 referendum on
whether the UK should remain a member of the Community. After British
Labour members did join in 1975, the Socialist Group became by far the
largest Group, and it remained so until 1999.

In 1973 there was another rule change. A Group could now be formed by
as few as ten members, if they were from three or more Member States. The
last Group to be created in the old nominated Parliament was, in October
1973, the Communist Group. This began with only 14 members, and
remained the smallest of the six Groups in existence before direct elections.

With direct elections in 1979, the number of members more than doubled
from 198 to 410. An attempt was immediately made to adapt proportionally
the minimum threshold for the creation of Groups. This would have prevented the formation of a proposed Group for the Technical Co-ordination
and Defence of Independent Groups and Members. This comprised a heterogeneous mixture of small parties and individuals (the Italian Radicals
and two small Italian parties of the left, the Belgian Regionalists, the Danish
anti-marketeers and an Irish independent, Neil Blaney), who had no
common platform but recognised that it was much more advantageous to be
in a Group than to be non-attached. Filibustering techniques (notably by
Marco Pannella of the Italian Radicals) were then successfully used to stop
any rule change. The Technical Group was able to survive. Unlike the other
Groups it did not have one leader but three co-presidents who took turns to
represent the Group.

While no other new Groups were created immediately after direct elections there was a change in the balance between the Groups. The Christian
Democrats (who changed their name to the Group of the European People's

Party, EPP) won seats but remained narrowly second to the Socialists. The European Conservatives moved from being the fifth to the third largest Group with 64 seats, as a result of the British Conservatives winning 60 of the 81 UK seats on 50 per cent of the vote. The European Conservatives also changed their name to that of the European Democratic Group (EDG). Besides the British Conservatives (and for a while also an Ulster Unionist) they included three members from the Danish Conservatives and one from the Danish Centre Democrats, though the latter subsequently joined the Group of the EPP.

The Communists also did well, advancing from being the sixth largest Group, to being the fourth largest. Their full name was the "Communist and Allies Group". Besides the French, Italian and Greek Communists, they also included the non-Communist Socialist People's Party from Denmark and a number of left-wing independents elected on Communist lists (such as Altiero Spinelli). The Liberals slipped from being the third to become only the fifth largest Group. The European Progressive Democrats obtained only 22 members. They again included the French Gaullists and the *Fianna Fáil* members from Ireland but also recruited a Dane from the anti-tax Progress Party, and Winnie Ewing of the Scottish National Party, who had previously sat as an independent.

Greek accession in 1981 did not lead to major alterations in the political balance, the major beneficiaries being the Socialist Group, who were joined by *PASOK* members, and the EPP Group, who recruited members from New Democracy. The Communists also gained three new members.

The second elections in 1984 led to the creation of an eighth Group, the European Right, with members from Le Pen's *Front National* in France and from the Italian Social Movement (MSI) and one member from the Greek *EPEN*. Another significant change was the transformation of the almost completely heterogeneous Technical Group into a larger and slightly more structured Rainbow Group, consisting of the first set of Greens to be elected to the Parliament (from *Die Grünen* in Germany and *Agalev* and *Ecolo* in Belgium), left alternative parties (such as *Democrazia Proletaria* in Italy and those linked together in the *Groen Progressief Akkoord* in the Netherlands), regionalist parties of the European Free Alliance (such as the Flemish *Volksunie* and the Italian alliance of *Union Valdôtaine-Partito Sardo d'Azione*) and the anti-market Danes in the Danish People's Movement. The Italian Radicals did not participate in the new Rainbow Group, partly because of the Group's suspicion of what they saw as the overpowering personality of Marco Pannella. The other Groups remained unchanged in structure, with the Socialists and European Progressive Democrats gaining seats and the others all losing some.

Spanish and Portuguese accession in 1986 was of greatest advantage to the Socialist Group, which gained 42 new members. The European Democrats (EDG) recruited the main Spanish party of the centre-right *(Alianza Popular)*. Significant gains were also made by the Liberals, in particular through the adhesion of the Portuguese Social Democrats (for whom the Group changed their name yet again to Liberal, Democratic and Reformist Group). The EPP Group, the European Progressive Democrats, the Communists and the Rainbow Group all made lesser gains.

One of the main parties that entered the Parliament was the Social

Democratic Centre (CDS) of former Spanish Prime Minister Adolfo Suarez who remained non-attached. In late 1987 an attempt was made to create a new Technical Group within the Parliament, based on the CDS members, the Italian Radicals and one or two other non-attached members. The Group had only 12 members but quickly lost its Dutch Calvinist member, who decided, in particular, not to be associated with the Radical party of Pannella and "Cicciolina" (the "porno star", Ilona Staller, elected to the Italian parliament on the Radical list). An attempt was made to "lend" two Italians from the Socialist Group to keep the new Group in existence, but this failed, and the new Group collapsed after a few days.

A final development that took place in the second directly elected Parliament was that the Group of the European Progressive Democrats renamed itself the Group of the European Democratic Alliance.

The **third direct elections in June 1989** saw the reinforcement of the two largest Groups, the Socialists and the EPP (which the *Alianza Popular* MEPs now joined), and the fragmentation of the smaller Groups. There were now ten Groups in number instead of eight, as a result of the creation of two completely new Groups. A separate Green Group was formed for the first time, and the divided Communist and Allies Group finally split into two separate Groups, one dominated by the reformist Italians and the other by the orthodox French Communists, but neither calling itself Communist.

Between 1989 and 1994 two of these Groups disappeared. In May 1992, the remaining EDG members (largely UK Conservatives) joined the EPP and in January 1993 the majority of the former Italian Communists (renamed the PDS) joined the Socialist Group. In consequence, the Group of the United European Left, of which the Italians had been the largest component, no longer had enough members to survive as a Group. By the end of the 1989–94 Parliament, the Socialist Group had grown to 198 members and the EPP to 162. The two largest Groups had over 69% of the Parliament's entire membership, compared to a figure of only 54% before the 1989 elections.

After the 1994 elections the Socialists and the EPP were roughly the same size as before, but in an enlarged Parliament their combined membership as a percentage of the total was reduced from over 69% to under 63%. The Liberals, Greens and European Democratic Alliance also continued. A further Group, the "Confederal Group of the European United Left", was not entirely new, in that it was primarily based on former or continuing Communist parties of the "Left Unity Group", but it also absorbed the surviving reformist parties from the former Group of the "United European Left", whose acronym ("GUE") it revived.

On the other hand, three entirely new Groups were founded. One of the main reasons for this was the political fragmentation among the French MEPs, with the list led by Bernard Tapie (*"Energie Radicale"*) taking away votes from the French Socialists, in particular, and the nationalist list of Philippe de Villiers harming the mainstream centre-right list. *Energie Radicale* formed the nucleus of a new Group called the "European Radical Alliance", and the members elected on the de Villiers list helped to establish a Eurosceptic Group called "Europe of Nations". The final new Group, *Forza Europa*, was based on Berlusconi's new *Forza Italia* party in Italy. Of the other Groups that had existed in the 1989–94 Parliament, the former members of the Rainbow Group were either not re-elected or went into the Europe of Nations or European Radical Alliance, and the Group of the Right could not be reconstituted, because it did not have enough members, and because the Italian right-wing *Alleanza Nationale* would not join them. As a result, there was an exceptionally high number of non-attached members (27) at the beginning of the 1994–99 Parliament, 25 of them from the far-right.

Austrian, Finnish and Swedish accession in 1995 saw gains relatively proportional to their size for the Socialist, EPP, Liberal, Green and GUE Groups.

The main change during the 1994–99 Parliament was the substantial increase in the size of the EPP Group. The main reason for this was the controversial adherence to the EPP (after a transit for three years via the EDA Group, which changed its name to "Union for Europe") of most of the members of the *Forza Europa* Group, which was dissolved. Nine Portuguese Social Democrats also left the Liberal Group and joined the EPP Group, whose numbers had thus risen to 201 by the time of the June 1999 elections, only 13 fewer than the Socialist Group. Most of the *Lega Nord* members also left the Liberal Group, and became non-attached.

The 1999 elections saw the EPP overtake the Socialist Group to become by far the biggest Group with 233 members, whereas the latter shrank from 214 to 180 members. The combined numbers of the two big groups, however, was just under 66% of the total number of MEPs, a rise from the 63% figure after the 1994 elections, but almost identical to the figure from just before the 1999 elections.

The Liberal Group, the GUE and the Greens all had significant increases in their membership. The Green Group joined forces with a number of regionalist parties to form the combined Group of the Greens/European Free Alliance. The Union for Europe disappeared as most of its members (French Gaullists) joined the EPP Group. The European Radical Alliance also dissolved (French Radicals not re-elected and the regionalists joining the Greens). The Europe of Nations Group changed into the "Union for a Europe of Nations", recruiting notably the Irish *Fianna Fáil* members of the dissolved Union for Europe Group, but losing its Danish Eurosceptics and Dutch ultra-Calvinists to a new "Europe of Democracies and Diversities Group" set up with the new UK Independence Party and French members elected on a hunting and fishing platform.

A heterogeneous collection of other members, ranging from Emma Bonino's Radicals from Italy to the French *Front National*, tried to create a new Technical Group during the constituent session in July 1999, but its existence was quickly challenged by the other Groups on the grounds of lack of political affinity. The EP decided that the new Group did not, by its own admission, meet the test of Rule 29–1 as regards the need for political affinity. The Technical Group was thus dissolved, although only after fierce protests from Emma Bonino, in particular, and after counterclaims that certain other groups did not have political affinities either.

Table 10: *MEPs and parties in the European Parliament (Oct 1999)*

	B	DK	D	EL	E	F	IRL	I	L	NL	A	P	FIN	S	UK	EP
EPP/ED	6	1	53	9	28	21	5	34	2	9	7	9	5	7	37	233
	CVP 3 PSC 1 CSP 1 MCC 1	KONS 1	CDU 43 CSU 10	ND 9	PP 27 UDC 1	UDF 9 RPR 6 DL 4 SC 1 GE 1	FG 4 Ind 1	FORZA IT 22 PPI 4 UDEUR 1 CCD 2 CDU 2 RI/DINI 1 SVP 1 PENSION 1	CSV 2	CDA 9	ÖVP 7	PPD-PSD 9	KOK 4 SKL 1	M 5 KD 2	Conserv 36 UUP 1	
PES	5	3	33	9	24	22	1	17	2	6	7	12	3	6	30	180
	SP 2 PS 3	SOC 3	SPD 33	PASOK 9	PSOE 22 PDNI 2	PS 18 PRG 2 MDC 2	LAB 1	DS 15 SDI 2	LSAP 2	PvdA 6	SPÖ 7	PS 12	SDP 3	S 6	LAB 29 SDLP 1	
ELDR	5	6	0	0	3	0	1	8	1	8	0	0	5	4	10	51
	VLD 3 PRL+FDF 2	V 5 RV 1			CDC 2 CC 1		Ind 1	PRI/LIB 1 I DEMO 6 Ind 1	DP 1	VVD 6 D66 2			KESK 4 SFP 1	C 1 FP 3	LD 10	
Greens/EFA	7	0	7	0	4	9	2	2	1	4	2	0	2	2	6	48
	AGALEV 2 ECOLO 3 VU-ID21 2		GRÜNEN 7		PA 1 EA 1 BNG 1 PNV 1	Verts 9	GP 2	Fed.Verdi 2	D GRENG 1	GROEN LINKS 4	GRÜNE 2		VIHR 2	MP 2	GREEN P 2 SNP 2 PCYMRU 2	

Table 10 (continued)

	B	DK	D	EL	E	F	IRL	I	L	NL	A	P	FIN	S	UK	EP
EUL/NGL	0	1	6	7	4	11	0	6	0	1	0	2	1	3	0	42
	0	SF 1	PDS 6	KKE 3 SYN 2 DIKKI 2	IU 4	PCF 4 Ind 2 LO/LCR 5		RC 4 CI 2	SP	SP 1		PCP 2	VAS 1	V 3		
UEN	0	1	0	0	0	12	6	9	0	0	0	2	0	0	0	30
		DF 1				RPFIE 12	FF 6	AN/SEGNI 9				CDS-PP 2				
EDD	0	4	0	0	0	6	0	0	0	3	0	0	0	0	3	16
		Juni.B 3				CPNT 6			RPF/SGP/GPV 3						UK Ind. 3	
Non-attached	2	0	0	0	1	6	0	11	0	0	5	0	0	0	1	26
	Vl. Blok 2				EH 1	Ind. 1 FN 5		BONINO 7 LN 3 MSI 1			FPÖ 5				DUP 1	
TOTAL	25	16	99	25	64	87	15	87	6	31	21	25	16	22	87	626

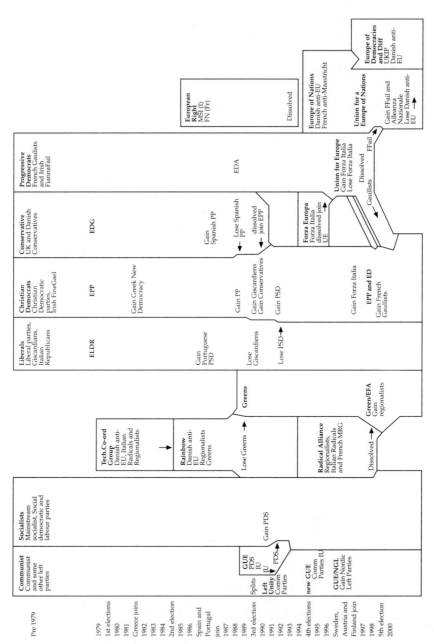

Figure 1 *Evolution of Political Groups*

Composition of the Groups after the 1999 elections

Group of the European People's Party (Christian Democrats) and European Democrats (EPP–ED)

Chairman   Hans-Gert Poettering
Secretary-General   Klaus Welle
Current membership   233
Current Parliament posts   President, 5 Vice-Presidents, 2 Quaestors and
                            8 committee chairs
Group founded   23 June 1953 (Christian Democratic Group
                            until 1979)

Current member parties (1999–2004 Parliament) with number of members

Austria	Österreichische Volkspartei (ÖVP) (7)
Belgium	Christelijke Volkspartij (CVP) (3)
	Parti Social Chrétien (PSC) (1)
	Mouvement des Citoyens pour le Changement (MCC) (1)
	Christliche Soziale Partei (CSP) (1)
Denmark	Det Konservative Folkeparti (1)
Finland	Kansallinen Kokoomus (National Coalition Party) (4)
	Suomen Kristillinen Liitto (SKL) (1)
France	Union pour la Démocratie Française (UDF) (9)
	Rassemblement pour la République (RPR) (6)
	Démocratie Liberale (DL) (4)
	Société Civile (1)
	Génération Ecologie (1)
Germany	Christlich-Demokratische Union (CDU) (43)
	Christlich-Soziale Union (CSU) (10)
Greece	Nea Dimokratia (ND) (9)
Ireland	Fine Gael (4)
	One independent MEP (Dana, Rosemary Scallon)
Italy	Forza Italia (22)
	Partito Popolare Italiano (PPI) (4)
	Centro Cristiano Democratico (CCD) (2)
	Cristiani Democratici Uniti (CDU)(2)
	Unione Democratici Europei (UDEUR) (1)
	Rinnovamento Italiano/Dini (1)
	Partito Pensionati (1)
	Südtiroler Volkspartei (SVP) ()1
Luxembourg	Christlich Soziale Volkspartei (CSV) (2)
Netherlands	Christen Demokratisch Appèl (CDA) (9)
Portugal	Partido Social Democrata (PPD/PSD) (9)
Spain	Partido Popular (27)
	Unió Democràtica de Catalunya (1)
Sweden	Moderata Samlingspartiet (5)
	Kristdemokraterna (2)
United Kingdom	Conservative Party (36)
	Ulster Unionist Party(1)

For the first time since 1975 the Group of the EPP is now the largest Group within the Parliament. It has members from every EU country, and now has 53 more members than the PES. It also contains 33 political parties and movements, far more than in any other Group, and 12 more, for example, than in the PES.

Over recent years the Group has not only grown considerably but also changed its character. Its original nucleus was parties of Christian Democratic inspiration, which generally regarded themselves as centrist, and were keen European federalists. They were represented in all the six original Member States, and were traditionally the largest parties in five of them (the exception being France where they were represented by the relatively small CDS, the *Centre des Démocrates Sociaux*). The largest and most dominant parties within the Group were the CDU/CSU in Germany and the DC in Italy. These parties were all full members of the European People's Party, a federation of Christian Democratic parties in the EC (see below) which saw itself as a European political party, with its own programme and direct membership. It is linked to the European Union of Christian Democrats (which also includes Christian Democratic parties from non-Union countries), with which it has a joint secretariat.

This original Christian Democratic core has now been considerably diluted. An early recruit was the Irish *Fine Gael* party, which joined the Group (and the Federation of the EPP) after Irish accession, and thus pre-empted its larger rival party, *Fianna Fáil*, from joining the same Group.

Since direct elections a large number of other centre-right parties have also joined the Group of the EPP, some of Christian Democratic provenance (the Austrian People's Party, the Finnish and Swedish Christian Democrats), but some from very different backgrounds. Certain of these parties have come directly into the Group (the Greek New Democracy Party, the Finnish and Swedish Conservatives), whereas others have transited through other Groups (the Spanish *Partido Popular* and the British and Danish Conservatives from the former European Democratic Group, the Portuguese Social Democrats and certain French UDF members from the Liberal Group, the French Gaullist party and the Italian *Forza Italia* from the former Union for Europe Group). Some of these new recruits to the Group have become full members of the party, and others have applied (most recently *Forza Italia*), whereas others have remained outside.

There is thus an important distinction between *full* members of the EPP Group (i.e. members from parties which belong to the EPP itself) and *allied* members (i.e. members from parties which do not). One important difference is that full members are bound by the EPP's electoral programme, whereas allied members are not: the latter are bound only by the general principles that underpin the EPP. Both are bound by positions of the EPP Group.

Prominent among the allied members have been the British Conservatives, who, with the Danish Conservatives and (for a while only) the Spanish *Alianza Popular*, had been in their own separate Group from British entry in 1973 until 1992. (Known as the European Conservative Group until 1979, and the European Democratic Group (EDG) from 1979–92, this was the third largest Group in the Parliament from 1979–89, and even provided one EP President, Lord Plumb). After the Spanish members in the re-named

Partido Popular left the EDG to join the EPP Group, the remaining EDG members first sought a close working relationship with the EPP Group and then to join it directly. Although there was majority support for their joining from within the EPP (notably from the German members), there was also opposition from other members who preferred to keep the EDG at arm's length. In April 1992, however, the EPP Group finally voted by 66 to 28 with five abstentions to admit the individual EDG members into the Group of the EPP on the basis of acceptance of the Group's programme. In view of the divisions within the British Conservative Party on European issues, their continued presence in the Group has remained controversial, both within the Conservative Party itself and amongst certain of the EPP member parties. After the 1999 elections, however, the British Conservatives all remained within the Group, but were instrumental in changing its official name to its new and longer form of the "Group of the European People's Party (Christian Democrats) and European Democrats".

The second controversial application to join the Group of the EPP was that of *Forza Italia*. As mentioned above, the former Italian Christian Democratic party the DC had been one of the pillars of the EPP Group and Federation, but its disintegration in the early 1990s left only smaller successor parties within the EP. Silvio Berlusconi's new *Forza Italia* dwarfed them in size but initially formed its own Group, *Forza Europa*. Most of the latter's members later joined the Union for Europe Group (although a handful went to the Liberals). Eventually, however, they broke down the initial resistance to their joining the Group of the EPP, and most of the *Forza Italia* members thus finished up in their third Group within five years.

Since the 1999 elections there are 34 Italian members in the EPP Group. These comprise 22 from *Forza Italia*, a number of members from the fragmented Italian Christian Democratic tradition (four from the PPI, two from the CCD and two from the CDU), and members from other parties, including representatives of a Pensioners' Party, of Lamberto Dini's *Rinnovamento Italiano*, and of the South Tyrol People's Party. In all, there are now eight Italian parties within the EP, the absolute record within the Parliament.

A third complex situation within the Group is that of its French members. The mainstream parties of the French right have tended to be seriously divided within the Parliament, with only the UDF members from the CDS tradition consistently within the EPP, with the other UDF members in the Liberal Group, and with the Gaullists in their own RDE and later UFE Groups. After the 1999 elections they are now finally re-united in the Group of the EPP (even including a member from a Green party, *Génération Écologie*), but the continuing divisions on the French right have eroded the total number of members from these mainstream parties.

A few of the EPP's other components are worth a brief comment. The Belgian delegation includes Gérard Deprez, the former long-serving leader (while he was an MEP) of the *Parti Social Chrétien*: he left it to form a new movement (the MCC) which campaigned along with the Liberals against his old party, but after the elections he was again allowed to join the Group of the EPP. So was the former Eurovision Song Contest winner, Dana (Rosemary Scallon), who was elected as an independent on a Catholic Conservative ticket, and the representative of the Ulster Unionist Party, which has been in several different Groups in the Parliament.

The Group of the European People's Party has provided over half of the Presidents of the Parliament (see table 13), including the two most recent, José Maria Gil-Robles, and the present incumbent, Nicole Fontaine.

Group of the Party of European Socialists (PES/PSE)

Leader	Enrique Baron Crespo
Secretary-General	Christine Verger
Current membership	180
Current Parliament posts	6 Vice-Presidents, 2 Quaestors and committee chairs
Group founded	23 June 1953 (known as Socialist Group until 1993)

Member parties (1999–2004 Parliament) with number of members

Austria	Sozialdemokratische Partei Österreichs (SPÖ) (7)
Belgium	Parti Socialiste (3), Socialistische Partij (2)
Denmark	Socialdemokratiet (3)
Finland	Suomen Sosialidemokraattinen Puolue (3)
France	Parti Socialiste (18)
	Parti Radical de Gauche (PRG) (2)
	Mouvement des Citoyens (MDC) (2)
Germany	Sozialdemokratische Partei Deutschlands (SPD) (33)
Greece	Panellinio Sosialistiko Kinima (PASOK) (9)
Ireland	Labour Party (1)
Italy	Partito Democratico della Sinistra (PDS) (15)
	Socialisti Democratici Italiani (2)
Luxembourg	Letzeburger Sozialistesch Arbechterpartei (LSAP) (2)
Netherlands	Partij van de Arbeid (PvdA) (6)
Portugal	Partido Socialista (12)
Spain	Partido Socialista Obrero Español (PSOE) (22)
	Nueva Izquierda (PDNI) (2)
Sweden	Socialdemokratiska Arbetarepartiet (6)
United Kingdom	Labour Party (29)
	Social Democrat and Labour Party (N. Ireland) (1)

For the first time since direct elections the PES Group was no longer the largest Group within the Parliament after the 1999 elections, and indeed, with 180 members, had 53 fewer members than the EPP. The main reason for this fall in numbers (there had been 198 after the 1994 elections, and 221 after Austrian, Finnish and Swedish accession) was the loss of 33 members from the UK, largely but not exclusively because of the change of electoral system. Compared with 1994 there were also seven fewer members from Germany, although this was offset by an increase in seven members from France. There was also a slight increase in members from Spain (plus three) and Portugal (plus two), and stability or only very small losses elsewhere.

The composition of the Group is straightforward, consisting of the mainstream Socialist and Social Democratic parties in the Member States. The only unusual situation worth pointing out is in Italy where two parties, the Socialist Party (PSI) and the Social Democrats (PSDI), both long-standing members of the Socialist International, had traditionally co-existed within the Group. During the 1989–94 Parliament, the former Italian Communist Party (PCI), the dominant force within what was then the Group of the United European Left, not only changed its name to the *Partito Democratico della Sinistra* (PDS: Democratic Party of the Left), but also transferred allegiance to the Socialist Group. With the collapse of the Italian Socialist and Social Democratic parties, the PDS now provides 15 of the 17 Italian members of the PES.

The Socialist Group is linked with the Party of European Socialists, which has had its headquarters in the Group's offices in Brussels.

European Liberal, Democratic and Reformist Group (ELDR)

Chairman	Pat Cox
Secretary-General	Bo Jensen
Current membership	51
Current Parliament posts	1 Vice-President, 1 Quaestor and 1 committee chair
Group founded	23 June 1953 (as Liberal Group, became Liberal and Democratic Group in November 1976, and Liberal, Democratic, and Reformist Group in 1986)

Member parties (1999–2004 Parliament) with number of members

Belgium	Parti Réformateur Liberale (PRL) (with Front des Francophones) (2)
	Vlaamse Liberalen en Demokraten (VLD) (3)
Denmark	Venstre (Danmarks Liberale Parti) (5)
	Det Radikale Venstre (1)
Finland	Suomen Keskusta (Centre Party) (4)
	Svenska Folkpartiet (Swedish People's Party) (1)
Ireland	1 Independent (Pat Cox)
Italy	Partito Repubblicano Italiano (PRI/LIB) (1)
	I Democratici (6)
	1 Independent (Marco Formentini)
Luxembourg	Demokratesch Partei (DP) (1)
Netherlands	Volkspartij voor Vrijheid en Democratie (VVD) (6)
	D66 (2)
Spain	Convergència Democràtica de Catalunya (CDC) (2)
	Coalición Canaria (CC) (1)
Sweden	Centerpartiet (1)
	Folkpartiet Liberalerna (3)
United Kingdom	Liberal Democrats (10)

The Liberal, Democratic and Reformist Group (LDR) is the third largest Group in the new Parliament. The Group has 51 members from ten countries. As in 1994, it has no members from Greece or Germany, but this time it also has no French, Austrian or Portuguese members. Its membership, but not its composition, has remained relatively stable in recent years in the 40 to 50 range.

After the 1994 elections, there was a considerable shift in the Group's internal balance of power from its southern to its northern members, a shift symbolised by the loss of most of its French and Spanish members, and by the election of a Dutch Liberal to be its new Chair. This was further reinforced during the 1994–99 Parliament by the departure of the Portuguese Social Democrats to the EPP, and by the adhesion of Finnish and Swedish parties from the Liberal and Centre Party traditions. The stronger northern emphasis of the Group has been largely confirmed after the 1999 elections.

The UK Liberal Democrats had finally managed to elect two members of the Parliament in 1994 and, helped by the change to the UK election system, elected ten members in 1999, making them the single largest component in the Group. There are now also 15 members of the Group from the three Nordic countries, with the Danish *Venstre* and Swedish Liberal parties, in particular, substantially increasing their support. Another 14 members of the Group are from the Benelux countries, with the Liberal parties generally doing well in terms of votes (although this was not translated into new seats), apart from the Dutch D 66 party, which lost two of its former four seats.

The main exception to the northern emphasis of the Group is its Italian component. In Italy, the traditional Liberal parties had been the *Partito Liberale* (PLI) and the *Partito Repubblicano* (PRI). In 1994, only the PRI won a seat in the European Parliament, but the Liberal Group's Italian delegation was subsequently greatly increased after it was joined by the six elected members of Umberto Bossi's *Lega Nord*. As a result of the extreme positions later taken up by that party's leadership on the issue of "Padanian" independence, the *Lega* as such was eased out of the Liberal Group, although a couple of its members remained on an individual basis, and were later joined by a couple of dissidents from the *Forza Italia* party. Following the 1999 elections, the Group was joined not only by one member of the Republican Party but also by six members of then Commission President-elect Prodi's "*Asinello*" ("Little Donkey") list. There were also contacts with Emma Bonino and the other members of her list, but these were ultimately unsuccessful. In October 1999 the Group was also joined by independent member Marco Formentini, formerly Mayor of Milan for the *Lega Nord*, but who has now publicly distanced himself from its programme.

The other southern members of the Group are from Spain. There are currently no representatives of Spanish-wide parties (the presence in the Group of several members from Adolfo Suárez's former CDS party did not survive the 1994 elections), but the Catalan regionalist party *Convergència* has long provided one or two members of the Liberal Group. After the 1999 elections their two members were also joined in the Group by a member of the Canarian regionalist party, *Coalición Canaria* (which had been part of a wider electoral coalition of Spanish regionalist parties, *Coalición Europea*, whose other elected member, from the *Partido Andalucista*, has joined the Green/EFA Group).

The final member of the Group is from Ireland. Although the Liberal Group's associated Irish party, the Progressive Democrats, lost their only seat in 1994, their former MEP, Pat Cox, won re-election as an independent and was re-admitted to the Liberal Group. He later became the leader of the Group after Gijs de Vries entered the Dutch government in 1998. He was again chosen to be Group leader in 1999 after his successful re-election as an independent, thus making him the only Political Group leader in the history of the EP not to be a member of a national political party.

The Liberal Group had FDP members from Germany between 1979 and 1984, and again from 1989 to 1994, but the FDP failed to reach the 5 per cent German electoral threshold in 1984, 1994 and 1999. Until recently the Liberal Group also had substantial French membership from UDF members as well as those in the CDS. It had 13 such members at the beginning of the 1989 Parliament, including the Group's then leader, former French President Valéry Giscard D'Estaing. By the 1994–99 Parliament, and after progressive defections to the EPP, there was only one French member of the Group (from the Liberals' one firm French ally, the Radical Party), and after the 1999 elections there are now no French members of the Group. Finally the only Austrian party in the Group, (the Liberales Forum, a breakaway from the right-wing FPÖ) did not win a seat in the 1999 elections.

All the parties within the Group are now also members of the Federation of Liberal, Democratic and Reformist parties of the European Community (ELDR), with the exception of *I Democratici*.

Group of the Greens/European Free Alliance

Co-Presidents	Heidi Hautala and Paul Lannoye
Secretary-General	Hans Nikolaus (Juan) Behrend
Current Membership	48
Current Parliament posts	1 Vice-President and 1 committee chair
Group Founded	July 1989

Member parties (1999–2004 Parliament) with number of members

Austria	Die Grünen (2)
Belgium	Agalev (2)
	Ecolo (3)
	Volksunie-ID 21 (2)
Finland	Vihreät (Greens) (2)
France	Les Verts (9)
Germany	Grünen (7)
Ireland	Green Party (2)
Italy	Federazione dei Verdi (2)
Luxembourg	Dei Greng (1)
Netherlands	Groen-Links (4)
Spain	Coalición Europea: Partido Andalucista (1)
	Coalición Nacionalista Europea de los Pueblos: Eusko Alkartasuna (1)
	Coalición Nacionalista Europea de los Pueblos:Partido Nacionalista Vasco (1)
	Bloque Nacionalista Gallego (1)
Sweden	Miljöpartiet (2)
United Kingdom	Green Party (2)
	Scottish National Party (SNP) (2)
	Plaid Cymru (2)

The Greens/European Free Alliance Group now has 48 members, and is over double the size of the Green Group in 1994.The increase in numbers is partly due to new members from Austria, Finland and Sweden, partly to the considerable success of Green parties in certain countries in the 1999 elections, and partly to the arrival in the Group of regionalist parties which had previously been in other Groups. The Greens had already been allied with regionalist parties in the former Rainbow Group (which also included anti-Market Danes) in the 1984–89 Parliament.

The Greens were first founded as a Group in their own right after the June 1989 elections, with eight Green members from France, eight from Germany and seven from Italy (the latter from four separate lists), as well as members from Belgium, the Netherlands, Portugal and Spain. During the 1989–94 Parliament there was a considerable turnover in the membership of the Group. Seven of the eight French members stood down at the half-way point of the legislature (in line with a campaign promise) and were replaced by the next on the list; two of the German members left to join other Political Groups, as did the Group's only Portuguese representative. One of the Italian members became non-attached. On the other hand, the Danish Socialist People's Party MEP joined the Group in 1992.

After the 1994 elections, the Green Group had fewer members (23 instead of 29). Moreover, the Group now had a much more northern emphasis, with a reinforced German presence, with new Luxembourg and Irish members and with no members from France (the French Greens having fallen victim in the elections to their own internal divisions), Spain or Portugal. The German Greens became the dominant element in the Group with 12 out of 23 members. The second largest number of members was from Italy, with three members from the *Federazione dei Verdi* and the former Christian Democrat Mayor of Palermo, Leoluca Orlando.

For the first time there were two Irish Greens (elected in the Dublin and Leinster constituencies respectively), and one from Luxembourg. Two were elected in Belgium (one *Agalev* and one *Ecolo*, the latter party down from two members in 1989–94) and one in the Netherlands. Finally, the Group again included a Dane from the Socialist People's Party.

After the 1995 enlargement, the Greens gained an additional member from each of the Austrian, Finnish and Swedish Green parties. During the rest of the 1994–99 Parliament there were further modifications in the composition of the Group. The Swedish Greens won three additional seats in the first Swedish direct elections in 1999 (on a platform that was highly critical of the EU). On the other hand the representative of the Danish Socialist People's Party, John Iversen, left the Group (and became a Social Democrat within the Socialist Group) as did the Luxembourg Green, Jup Weber (who joined the ARE Group).

The Greens generally did well in the 1999 elections, and would have been a considerably larger group even without the new EFA component. The French Greens, led by Dany Cohn-Bendit (1968 student leader and a German Green MEP during the 1994–99 Parliament), returned to the Parliament with nine seats, and the two Belgian Green parties, *Ecolo* and *AGALEV*, did very well in the immediate aftermath of the dioxin scandal, and went up from one seat each, to three and two seats respectively. The Dutch *Groen Links*, which went up from one to four seats, also enjoyed considerable success. For the first time two British Greens were also elected, and the Austrian and Finnish Greens both went up from one to two seats. The Irish Greens did well to hold on to their two seats, and a Green from Luxembourg again returned to the Group. On the other hand the German Greens lost five seats compared to 1994, and the Swedes won two fewer seats than in 1995. The Italian Greens also only won two seats.

The Group now also includes members from parties belonging to the European Free Alliance (EFA), and the Group's name has been changed to reflect this. Since its first general assembly in Brussels in 1981, when it adopted its initial declaration of fundamental principles, the EFA has been a framework for cooperation between a number of regionalist parties seeking greater autonomy or independence for their regions. In 1995 they began the process of transforming themselves into a European political party, and took on the new name of "Democratic Party of the Peoples of Europe-European Free Alliance (DPPE-EFA)". 17 parties are currently members of the EFA, whose headquarters are at the EP in Brussels. While its members have been in different Groups within the Parliament their main homes have been the two Rainbow Groups from 1984–94 and the European Radical Alliance from 1994–99. Five of these parties are now in the Green EFA Group.

The Group thus now incorporates two members of the *Volksunie-ID 21* from Belgium, two SNP and two *Plaid Cymru* members (these latter entering the Parliament for the first time) from the UK, as well as four members from three separate Spanish lists. In order to get elected in the single Spanish national constituency, Spanish regional parties have to make coalitions. There are thus two members from the *Coalición Nacionalista Europa de los Pueblos* (one from the largest Basque nationalist party, the PNV, and one from a smaller Basque party, *Eusko Alkartasuna*, itself a breakaway from the PNV); one from the *Coalición Europea* (one member from the *Partido Andalucista*: the coalition's other elected member, from the Canarian regionalists, has joined the Liberal Group); and finally one member from the Galician coalition, the *Bloque Nacionalista Gallego*.

Of those parties who had already been in the EP several had been in the former ARE Group (e.g. the *Volksunie* and the SNP) but the PNV, the main governing party in the Basque country, had been a long-standing member of the EPP. They have now left the EPP, partly in protest at the support that they believe the Group gave to their *Partido Popular* rivals, and have now joined their Basque coalition partners, *Eusko Alkartasuna*, within the Greens/EFA Group.

As in the 1989–94 Parliament, the Group has two co-presidents.

Confederal Group of the European United Left/Nordic Green Left

Chairman	Francis Wurtz
Secretary-General	Maria d'Alimonte
Current membership	41
Current Parliament posts	1 Vice-President and 1 committee chair
Group founded	July 1994

Member parties (1999–2004 Parliament) with number of members

Denmark	Socialistisk Folkeparti (1)
Finland	Vasemmistoliitto (Left Alliance) (1)
France	Parti Communiste Français (4)
	Independents (elected on "Bouge l'Europe" list) (2)
	Lutte Ouvrière/Ligue Communiste Révolutionnaire (5)
Germany	Partei des Demokratischen Sozialismus (PDS) (6)
Greece	Kommounistiko Komma Ellados (2)
	Synaspismos tis Aristeras Kai tis Proodou (2)
	DIKK (Dimokratiko Kininiko Kinima) (2)
Italy	Rifondazione Comunista (4)
	Comunisti Italiani (2)
Netherlands	Socialistische Partij (1)
Portugal	Partido Comunista Portugués (2)
Spain	Izquierda Unida (4)
Sweden	Vänsterpartiet (3)

The GUE Group is now the fifth largest Group in the Parliament, with its membership of 41 drawn from Communist, former Communist and left Socialist parties from ten countries. Its history is a complex one.

From its foundation in October 1973 until 1989, the only Group to the left of the Socialist Group was the Communist and Allies Group. This was soon divided between what, at the risk of oversimplification, could be described as its Eurocommunist and more traditional pro-Moscow wings. The former was dominated by the Italian Communist party, the largest single party within the Group, which always provided the president of the Group. The Italians were supported by the member from the Eurocommunist party in Greece (the smaller of the two Greek Communist parties, and which itself later split in two), by the member from the Danish Socialist People's Party, and later by the members from Spain. The more orthodox faction was dominated by the French Communists, and also included the members from the larger and more orthodox of the two Greek Communist parties and later by the members from the Portuguese Communist party. As a result of these divisions the Group hardly ever held common meetings, and seldom agreed on a common line in committee or plenary meetings.

After the 1989 elections, the two factions formally divided and created two new Groups with confusingly similar names, the Italian Communist-led Group taking on the name "United European Left" (GUE after its French initials) and the more hard-line Group the name "Left Unity".

The Italian Communist Party later changed its name to that of the *Partito Democratico della Sinistra* (PDS: Democratic Party of the Left). A considerable minority of its membership refused to accept the party's change of direction and of name and started a new Communist party under the name *Rifondazione Comunista* along with members from another left-wing Italian party, *Democrazia Proletaria* (Proletarian Democracy). The vast majority of the MEPs remained in the PDS, but two joined *Rifondazione Comunista* at the end of 1991. The PDS members subsequently joined the Socialist Group, leaving the six remaining members of the "United European Left" on their own, and without enough members to keep the Group going. After the 1994 elections, most of them (the Spanish members of *Izquierda Unida*) hesitated whether to join up with the Greens or with the remaining Communist parties of the Left Unity Group. In the end, they opted for the latter but with a new name, and the new GUE Group was born.

All the parties in the Group have a Communist origin but two of them, the Spanish coalition of *Izquierda Unida* and the Greek party *Synaspismou tis Aristeras* no longer called themselves Communist. *Izquierda Unida* included members from the mainstream Spanish and Catalan Communist parties, but also from the left Socialist party *PASOK* and from Green and other backgrounds. With nine members, it was now the largest single force in the new GUE Group and provided its chairman, Alonso Puerta (who was also the leader of *PASOK*). The other parties in the Group still explicitly called themselves Communist, and included 12 members from the French, Greek and Portuguese parties as well as five from the Italian *Rifondazione Comunista* which, in spite of its name, was less hard-line and more pro-European than the others. Divided over internal tactics in Italian politics, *Rifondazione Comunista* later itself split in two, with the veteran Italian Communist, Armando Cossutta, creating yet another party, the *Partito dei Comunisti Italiani*.

After enlargement in 1995, the Group gained Swedish and Finnish members, with the Swedish party being anti-EU, but with the Finnish party being more divided. At the insistence of its new members the Group added a new reference to "Nordic Green Left" at the end of its existing name.

After the 1999 elections the GUE Group enlarged to include members from two additional countries, Germany, with six members from the PDS (the successor to the East German Communist Party), and the Netherlands, with one member from the left-wing *Socialistische Partij*.

In other countries the picture was a mixed one. In France the Communist Party's attempt to broaden its traditional base was unsuccessful, but the Trotskyist alliance of Arlette Laguiller and Alain Krivine managed to elect five members, who were accepted into the Group. In Italy both continuing Communist parties, *Rifondazione* and the *Comunisti Italiani*, obtained seats and entered the Group. The two Greek parties in the former Group (the KKE and *Synaspismos*) were joined by two new members from the breakaway Socialist DIKKI party, and the Group also has five members from the three Nordic countries. The main setback for the Group was the poor performance of *Izquierda Unida*, which went into the 1999 elections internally divided (indeed a couple of its former members are now in the Socialist Group), and went down from nine to only four seats.

The current chairman of the Group is Francis Wurtz (French Communist), who has been an MEP since 1979. In spite of its still varied membership there are signs that the present Group is acting in a more cohesive way than its predecessors, holding, for example, its first ever press briefing session at the first plenary session in October 1999.

Group of Europe of Nations

Chairman	Charles Pasqua
Secretary-General	Frank Barrett
Current membership	30
Group founded	July 1999

Member parties (1999–2004 Parliament) with number of members:

Denmark   Dansk Folkeparti (1)
France   Rassemblement pour la France et l'Indépendence de l'Europe
           (RPFIE) (12)
Ireland   Fianna Fáil (6)
Italy   Alleanza Nazionale/Patto Segni (9)
Portugal   Centro Democrático Social-Partido Popular (CDS-PP) (2)

This is virtually a new Group, whose membership is mainly from the former Europe of Nations Group and partly from the Irish *Fianna Fáil* Members who were in the Union for Europe Group.

The nucleus of the Union for Europe Group (and of its similar predecessors, the European Democratic Union, the European Progressive Democrats and the European Democratic Alliance) had been the long-lasting cooperation between the French Gaullists and the Irish *Fianna Fáil* members. These two parties also had a variety of normally short-lived allies (both parties and dissident individual MEPs) from other countries, including Denmark, Greece, Italy (*Forza Italia*, during their passage from individual Group status towards joining the EPP Group), Netherlands, Portugal, Spain and the UK (the SNP). Meanwhile the largest component of the Eurosceptical Europe of Nations Group, first founded in 1994, had been a number of right-of-centre French members who had been elected on the *Autre Europe* list led by Philippe de Villiers and James Goldsmith. By the 1999 elections Goldsmith had died, but his place as leader of a Eurosceptical French list (RPFIE) had been taken by the prominent anti-Maastricht Gaullist, Charles Pasqua.

There had long been uncertainty whether the mainstream French Gaullists would cut their links with the Irish and other members, and instead join a larger Group. This materialised after the 1999 elections when they finally joined the EPP, leaving their former Union for Europe allies without a Group.

The Irish *Fianna Fáil* and Portuguese CDS members then decided to join up with the 12 elected members of the Pasqua-De Villiers RFPIE list, along with one member from the right-wing Danish People's Party. After some initial uncertainty they were later also joined by the nine members of the *Alleanza Nazionale/Patto Segni*.

Alleanza Nazionale was the successor party to the far-right Italian Social Movement (MSI), which had had MEPs since 1979, and which had been in the Group of the European Right with Le Pen's *Front National* between 1984 and 1989. After 1989 the MSI left this Group, partly over differences of general political emphasis, but more specifically because of differences with the German *Republikaner* over the political situation in the South Tyrol (where the MSI had been the most vocal defenders of the Italian-speaking minority). They thus became non-attached, and retained this status during the 1994–99 Parliament, by which time the MSI's successor, *Alleanza Nazionale*, was seeking new respectability as a mainstream party of government, and did not wish to join up with far-right parties. In the 1999 elections *Alleanza Nazionale* made a common list with Mario Segni, a dissident Christian Democrat who had been in the EPP at the start of the 1994 Parliament.

The Group is likely to have a considerable difference of emphasis among its members as regards attitudes to European integration, with *Fianna Fáil* and *Alleanza Nazionale* being more positive than their French, and to a lesser extent, their Portuguese allies.

Europe of Democracies and Diversities

Co-chairmen   Jens-Peter Bonde, Jean Saint-Josse, Hans Blokland
Secretary-General   Patrick Reynolds
Current membership   16
Group founded   July 1999

Member parties (1999–2004 Parliament), with number of members:

Denmark   Folkebevaegelsen mod EF-Unionen (1)
                       Junibevaegelsen (3)
France   Chasse, Peche, Nature, Traditions (6)
Netherlands   RPF/SGP/GVP (Reformatorische Politieke Federatie/
                       Staatkundig Gereformeerde Partij/Gereformeerde
                       Politiek Verbond) (3)
United Kingdom   UK Independence Party (3)

This is a new Group consisting of parties that are highly critical of the EU and of any further integration, and in some cases, wish their country to leave the EU altogether. The Group's Dutch and Danish parties were in the former Europe of Nations Group, whereas its French and British components are new to the Parliament.

There have long been four Danish members from the anti-EU movement (which only stands in European, not national, elections). In 1994 the movement split, with two competing lists. The "People's Alliance against the European Union" remains opposed to Danish membership in the EU, whereas the two members from the "June Movement" are no longer opposed to Danish EU membership "per se", but to the "Europe of Maastricht".

The Group also contains three MEPs from a coalition of three separate fundamentalist Calvinist parties in the Netherlands, the inspiration of which is primarily religious rather than nationalist.

The French list, "*Chasse, Peche, Nature et Traditions*", represents hunters, fishermen and other rural voters (especially in south-west France) opposed to Brussels directives, notably those on protecting birds. After narrowly falling below the 5 per cent French threshold in 1994 they won six seats in 1999.

Finally the UK Independence Party advocates British withdrawal from the EU, and was able to win three seats after the change in the electoral system in 1999.

The non-attached members

Parties in the 1999–2004 Parliament which are not in any Groups:

Austria   Freiheitliche Partei Österreichs (FPÖ) (5)
Belgium   Vlaams Blok (2)
France   Front National (5)
                       Independent (1) (Marie-France Garaud)

Italy	Lista Emma Bonino (7)
	Lega Nord (3)
	Movimento Sociale Italiano (1)
Spain	Euskal Herritarrok (1)
United Kingdom	Democratic Unionist Party (DUP) (1)
Current total	26

The successful struggle led by Pannella and others at the beginning of the directly elected Parliament in 1979, prevented the numbers required for forming a Political Group from increasing significantly to reflect the much higher membership within the Parliament. As a result, and because of the great advantages accorded to membership of a Political Group, only a small number of members have remained non-attached. These have tended to be members of small political parties or individual personalities sharing little common political ground with any of the existing Groups, or who have positively preferred the complete freedom of movement given them by non-attached status.

After 1994, however, a disproportionate number of the non-attached members came from parties on the right or far right of the political spectrum (the French *Front National*, the Belgian *Vlaams Blok* and *Front National*, the Italian *Alleanza Nazionale* and later the Austrian Freedom Party), which, for a variety of reasons, were unable to form a Group of their own.

After the 1999 elections an attempt was made to form a Technical Group consisting of a variety of non-attached members and parties of very different orientation, ranging from the *Lista* Emma Bonino to the French *Front National*. However, not all the non-attached members (e.g. the representatives of the Austrian Freedom Party, as well as Ian Paisley) wished to join such a Group. As described above, the Technical Group was dissolved in the September 1999 plenary because it was considered not to have the necessary political affinities required in Parliament's Rules. A proposed Rules change was later tabled by Italian non-attached members in order to permit a "Mixed Group" to be formed, that would incorporate all non-attached members, and that would enjoy the normal rights of a Political Group: such Mixed Groups exist, for example, in the Italian and Spanish Parliaments.

In the meantime there are now 26 non-attached members from nine parties from six countries. The largest single delegation is that of the seven Italian Radicals elected on a list headed by former Commissioner (and MEP) Emma Bonino, and also including Marco Pannella, who with only a short break during the last Parliament has been in the Parliament since 1979. There are also three other non-attached Italian members from the *Lega Nord*, and one member from the *Movimento Sociale Italiano*, which consists of those members of the old far-right MSI who refused to accept the party's transformation into the more mainstream *Alleanza Nazionale*.

There are also five members of Jean-Marie Le Pen's *Front National* from France (down from 11 in the last Parliament as a result of the schism in the party between Le Pen and Bruno Megret that had led to an election fight between two separate lists), and five from Jörg Haider's Freedom Party from Austria, as well as two from the Belgian *Vlaams Blok*.

The other non-attached members are Ian Paisley of the Democratic Unionist Party of Northern Ireland (who has been a non-attached member since 1979), a member of the extremist Basque Movement *Euskal Herritarrok*, and an independent French member, Marie France Garaud, who had been elected on Pasqua's RPFIE list, but did not join the others on the list in the UEN Group.

Parliament's Rules lay down certain rights for the non-attached members. The non-attached members are entitled to a Secretariat (Rule 30), and the 27 MEPs have been allocated a staff of 18 by the Bureau, which has also decided to set aside rooms for their disposal on an occasional basis at Parliament's normal working places. The non-attached members are entitled to delegate two of their number to attend meetings of the Conference of Presidents, but without the right to vote (Rule 23.2), and may also nominate members to committees and delegations (Rules 152 and 168) and an equal number of substitutes (Rule 153). Finally, they are allocated an overall speaking time in plenary based on the fractions previously allocated to the different Political Groups (Rule 120–2(c)). The non-attached members are allocated seats at the very back of the hemicycle.

As a general rule non-attached members have been able to make more of an impact in plenary than in committees, through participation in debates, points of order or even demonstrations (such as those made by Mario Capanna in the 1979–84 Parliament when he wore Mohawk head-dresses to protest at the Lake Placid Olympics taking place on Mohawk ancestral ground), including challenges to the authority of the presiding officer (see section on order in the chamber in Chapter 9). Their protests are rarer in committee (though Capanna was once physically removed from the Rules Committee after attempting to interrupt the proceedings), and non-attached members are never allocated the more significant rapporteurships.

Changing Groups

If an MEP changes Group or becomes a non-attached member, he or she retains the seat previously held as a full member of a committee, but not one held as a substitute. Although the Rules have been interpreted to provide that "if a member's change of Political Group has the effect of disturbing the fair representation of political views in a committee, new proposals for the composition of that committee shall be made by the Conference of Presidents", no major problem has yet been caused in this regard. Indeed, members changing Groups can retain Parliament posts such as committee chairmanships, vice-presidencies and quaestorships. One member, Antoni Gutierrez Diaz, even retained his committee chairmanship (Regional Affairs) after his Group no longer existed. This is because such posts are formally elected by members and only informally based on a share-out among Groups at the time of the election.

Support provided by the European Parliament to the Political Groups

Parliament's budget allocates certain appropriations directly to the Political Groups (about €34 million in 2000). The number of members in each Group determines its share of these funds. The non-attached members also receive a proportionate share. The relevant budgetary headings are

Item 3707, which covers the secretariat and administrative expenditure of the Groups and their own political activities, and Item 3708, which finances information activities by the Groups. This latter item was originally used for European election campaigns but this was challenged in the Court of Justice by the French Green Party *Les Verts* in 1983 and the Court ruled that financing of party election campaigns was a national competence until the adoption of a uniform election system (see page 20). The item now funds information activities only and cannot be used for any election campaign or for any information activity in the 30 days prior to European elections.

Besides these items which the Group manage themselves, they also obtain further support from the Parliament in terms of their staff entitlements (see below), office space, meeting rooms and technical facilities. Altogether, the Groups can be said to account for around 15 per cent of Parliament's budget.

Structures of Groups

Each Political Group has its own internal structures, notably a Bureau composed of a Chair, Vice-Chairs, Treasurer and others. Bureaux vary considerably in size and responsibilities, and are obviously more important in the larger Groups where they tend to include one or two members from each national component of the Group, including the leader of each national party delegation. In the Socialist Group, the Bureau must also include at least 40 per cent women, a figure to be reached, if necessary, by electing additional members. Bureaux can play a role in preparing the political discussions and positions of the Group as a whole. They normally also take the decisions regarding the administration and management of the Group and its secretariat.

Group chairs provide political leadership for their Group. They speak on its behalf in major debates and to the outside. They represent the Group in their party, in Parliament's Conference of Presidents, and in negotiations with other Groups, notably in the informal meeting of Group chairs in which many deals are struck

Group chairs are elected by the Group and in most cases remain in office for some years. After the 1999 elections all but the Liberals chose new chairs. The longest-standing chairman was Christian de la Malène of the RDE (Gaullist) Group who was chairman from 1975 to 1994. Some Groups, notably the Greens, have usually had two co-chairs.

Political Group staffing

Precise rules have been established regarding the numbers of staff to which Political Groups are entitled. The most important criterion is the number of members in each Group, but the number of working languages within the Group also plays a role.

Each Group is entitled to a fixed total of two A grade (Administrative) posts, with a further two such posts for every 30 MEPs within the Group, and another A grade post if the Group uses four or five languages, two posts for six or seven languages, three posts for eight or nine languages and four posts for ten or eleven languages. This is topped up by a proportional share, according to the size of the Group, of a pool of 143 posts.

Table 11: *Leaders of the main Political Groups*

Date	No. of years	Name	Country
1. *Socialist Group*			
1953–56	3	Guy MOLLET	F
1956–58	2	Henri FAYAT	B
1958–59	1	Pierre O. LAPIE	F
1959–64	5	Willi BIRKELBACH	D
1964–67	3	Kate STRÖBEL	D
1967–74	7	Francis VALS	F
1974–75	1	Georges SPENALE	F
1975–79	4	Ludwig FELLERMAIER	D
1979–84	5	Ernest GLINNE	B
1984–89	5	Rudi ARNDT	D
1989–94	5	Jean-Pierre COT	F
1994–99	5	Pauline GREEN	UK
1999		Enrique BARON CRESPO	E
2. *Group of the European People's Party* *(until 1979 Christian Democratic Group)*			
1953–58	5	E.M.J.A SASSEN	NL
1958–59	1	Pierre WIGNY	B
1959–66	7	Alain POHER	F
1966–70	4	Joseph ILLERHAUS	D
1970–75	5	Hans A. LÜCKER	D
1975–77	2	Alfred BERTRAND	B
1977–82	5	Egon KLEPSCH	D
1982–84	2	Paolo BARBI	I
1984–92	8	Egon KLEPSCH	D
1992–94	2	Leo TINDEMANS	B
1994–99	5	Wilfried MARTENS	B
1999		Hans Gert PÖTTERING	D
3. *Liberal Group*			
1953–57	4	Yvon DELBOS	F
1957–69	12	Rene PLEVEN	F
1969–73	4	Cornelis BERKHOUWER	NL
1973–78	4	Jean DURIEUX	F
1978–79	1	Jean PINTAT	F
1979–84	5	Martin BANGEMANN	D
1984–89	5	Simone VEIL	F
1989–91	2	Valery GISCARD D'ESTAING	F
1991–94	3	Yves GALLAND	F
1994–98	4	Gijs DE VRIES	NL
1998–		Pat COX	IRL

4. *"Gaullist" Group.*
Union for Europe Group (1995–1999) wound up in 1999
Group of the European Democratic Alliance (1988–95)
Progressive Democrats (1973–1988)
European Democratic Union (1973–1995)

1965	0	Jacques VENDROUX	F
1965–66	1	Andre BORD	F

Table 11: *Continued*

Date	No. of years	Name	Country
1966–67	1	Alain TERRENOIRE	F
1967–68	1	Jean DE LIPKOWSKI	F
1968–72	4	Raymond TRIBOULET	F
1973–75	2	Yvon BOURGES	F
1975–94	19	Christian DE LA MALENE	F
1994–99	5	Jean Claude PASTY	F
1999		Charles PASQUA	F

5. *Green Group*

1989–90	2	Alexander LANGER &	D
		Maria SANTOS	P
1991–93	3	Adelaide AGLIETTA &	I
		Paul LANNOYE	B
1994–95		Alexander LANGER &	D
		Claudia ROTH	D
1995–96		Claudia ROTH	D
1997		Claudia ROTH &	D
		Magda AELVOET	B
1998		Magda AELVOET	B
1999		Heidi HAUTALA &	FIN
		Paul LANNOYE	B

6. *European Democratic Group*
(Founded 1973, until 1979 called European Conservative Group)

1973–77	4	Sir Peter KIRK	UK
1977–78	1	Geoffrey RIPPON	UK
1979–82	3	Sir James SCOTT-HOPKINS	UK
1982–87	5	Sir Henry PLUMB	UK
1987–93	6	Sir Christopher PROUT	UK

(Absorbed into EPP Group in 1993)

7. *Communist Group (founded 1973)*

1973–79	6	Giorgio AMENDOLA	I
1979–84	5	Guido FANTI	I
1984–89	5	Giovanni CERVETTI	I

(Split in 1989 into two groups)

8. *United European Left*
(Founded in 1989 from split in the Communist Group)

1989–93	4	Luigi COLAJANNI	I

(The majority joined the Socialist left in 1994)

9. *European United Left / Nordic Green Left*
(Founded in 1989 from a split in the Communist Group. Called Left Unity Group 1989–94)

1989–94	5	Rene PIQUET	F
1994–99	5	Alonso PUERTA	E
1999		Francis WURTZ	D

The total number of A posts to which a Group is entitled then provides the key to the number of B (Assistant) and C (Secretarial) posts within each Group, with 1.4 B or C posts funded for each A grade post. The total number of posts per Political Group may not exceed the number of members within that Group. There is thus a great difference in the size of Group staffs from only 16 in the smallest Group up to over 150 officials in the EPP-ED Group. The number of staff employed by the Groups has grown in recent years. In the year 2000, 532 posts were budgeted (of which 218 As) – as compared with 285 (of which 123 As) in 1982. This represents an increase of 87% (77% for As), as compared with 38% over the same period for Parliament's own staff (52% for As).

The great majority of these are temporary, not permanent officials, and do not have the same job security enjoyed by permanent officials. They are recruited directly by the Groups (with the national delegations within each Group playing an important role in the recruitment of individual Administrators, in particular), and do not have to pass the open competitions which Parliament's permanent officials have been through. In practice, however, the majority of Group staff do enjoy de facto if not de jure job security, and relatively few of them are made redundant as a result of election defeats, or Group reorganisations, a notable exception being the redundancies of virtually the entire staff of the EDA Group in 1999 when the bulk of its MEPs (French Gaullist) joined the EPP Group. Furthermore there are a number of permanent officials working within the Groups who have passed an open external competition. These may be Group officials who passed an exam but then remained with a Group, or they may be seconded officials at a later stage in their careers.

Recruitment of staff within a Group is sometimes based on political and personal contacts and patronage, but more objective methods are now the norm in the large Groups with both written and oral exams and language tests, though, of course, candidates must normally also have a political affinity with the Group and political experience is taken into account.

Group staff have both general and sectoral responsibilities, examples of the former being administrative or press work, or responsibility for urgency debates in plenary. Some staff work directly to assist the Group leader, whereas others follow particular policy areas. The larger Groups are able to have one or even two officials to follow each committee, whereas an official in a smaller Group may have to follow up to three or four committees at once. They assist their co-ordinators, help to ensure as unified a Group line as possible, and follow votes and new developments. They sometimes have to round up Group members from other committees to help in tight votes in their committee. They must prepare the discussions within their Group meetings, and help their members to formulate a Group position before the plenary session. They may also have to prepare background information for the Group. They help to draw up Group whips both in committee and in plenary. They help maintain contacts with national parties, national governments when their party is in power, Commissioners of their own tendency and other organizations. They must take into account the fact that national, sectoral, or constituency considerations are sometimes of greater importance to an individual member than his or her Group stance.

Group staff sometimes move on to political careers. Among those who have become MEPs are Florus Wijsenbeek and Jessie Larive of the Liberals, Raymonde Dury, Carole Tongue and Richard Corbett of the Socialists, Caroline Jackson and Anne McIntosh of the Conservatives, Bruno Boissière, Alexander De Roo and Monica Frassoni of the Greens and Gianfranco Dell'Alba (non-attached, formerly in the Green Group Secretariat). Others have gone on to national Parliaments.

Working methods within the Groups

Groups generally convene during the "Group week", and during the Strasbourg plenary week. The meetings during Group week are usually held in Brussels (and occasionally other locations, normally at the invitation of one of the member parties of the Group). They last two or three days, and are primarily devoted to examining the next week's plenary agenda. They are also used for discussion of the Group's own activities (campaigns, conferences, publications etc.) and for receiving visiting delegations or leaders of national parties or other personalities (Commissioners, ministers or personalities from third countries). These meetings are both preceded and followed by a variety of Group working parties of both a political and technical nature, as well as meetings of national party delegations.

The meetings in Strasbourg are normally held on four occasions during plenary week: before the beginning of the plenary on Monday, and on Thursday morning (when the plenary only begins at 10:00 am), and also for an hour or so at the close of the plenary on Tuesday and Wednesday evenings. Each Group has its own meeting room and its own rules and practices concerning the confidentiality of its meetings.

The Groups do not normally meet during the committee weeks, except when there is a Brussels plenary sitting the same week, but the Group members within a committee (especially from the two largest Groups, the Socialists and the EPP-ED) get together before the start of the committee meeting to discuss the positions that they will adopt. These meetings are generally led by the Group's co-ordinator on the committee, who is elected by the Group's members on the committee. Large Groups often appoint a shadow rapporteur where another Group has the rapporteurship.

Own activities of the Groups

Apart from work directly related to Parliament, Groups have developed their own political activities. They form an important channel of communication between corresponding parties in different countries and also between the European Union and national politics. In this, they complement Parliament's role as a forum and channel of communication described in Chapter 16.

Groups receive a constant stream of visitors from national parties, including ministers and front-bench spokesmen in national parliaments. They also send delegations to national parties, and Group chairmen or vice-chairmen normally speak at the congress or conference of each national party in the Group. Groups also publish brochures, studies and newsletters aimed in part at national parties. Groups organize seminars and conferences with national parties on European themes.

A particular effort may be made by a Group on behalf of one of its national parties when that Member State holds the Presidency of the Council, especially when that party is in government. Some Groups organise special meetings and briefings for the ministers or shadow ministers concerned and these can provide a valuable alternative to those prepared by national civil servants. As a source of information such briefings are of particular assistance to parties in the smaller Member States.

The Socialists, Christian Democrats and Liberals organise "summits" of their Group chairmen, national party leaders, prime ministers of the countries where they are in government and Commission members, prior to meetings of the European Council. This is done through their party federations (see pages 91–93).

National party delegations

Group members of the same nationality (normally from one political party) form national delegations that serve as an important link to national parties. Most national delegations within the large Groups meet once during "Group week" and again during plenaries. They will sometimes take a collective decision and try to act as a bloc in Group discussions. On important issues, Groups will try to negotiate compromises among their national delegations before taking a decision. When Groups fail to vote cohesively, it is usually because one or more national delegations have decided to opt out of a Group position. Posts within the Group structures (Bureau of Group and Group nominations for posts in Parliament) are often shared among the delegations within a Group using the same proportional method (d'Hondt) as for posts among Groups in Parliament, albeit with greater flexibility.

Most national delegations, especially those from large parties, have their own officers (chairman, treasurer, etc.) and their own staff, partly financed from Group funds, but who can be employed in the national capitals (e.g. press officers, liaison officers with national parties). These staff are relatively few in number (even major parties from large Member States will have scarcely half a dozen).

It is also through national delegations that the bulk of the "information money" (item 3708 mentioned above) is spent. In the Socialist Group, for instance, 82 per cent is allocated to the national delegations (15 per cent of which is shared equally and 85 per cent in proportion to the number of MEPs). Delegations do not have absolute discretion: there are strict Parliament rules preventing the responsibility being delegated any further (e.g. to national parties) and all sums must be spent according to Socialist Group priorities and relate to the activities of the Group and its members. Any printed matter must specify that it is on behalf of the Group and any reference to a national party or an individual member must not be larger in size than the reference to the Group. Information campaign accounts are subject to inspection by the Court of Auditors.

Delegations are normally represented within the structures of their national parties (e.g. national executive committees, back-bench committees in the national parliamentary Groups etc.) where they will be involved notably, but not exclusively, in discussions with a European dimension (often alerting them to that dimension). Some national party leaders have sat in the European Parliament instead of in the national parliament, e.g. Gérard Deprez, leader of the PSC (Walloon Christian Democrats), Karel van Miert, SP (Flemish Socialist) or in both parliaments (many Italian, French, Belgian and Northern Irish party leaders). In other cases, the European Parliamentary leader will be in close contact with the national leader and meet regularly. In the UK, for instance, Conservative, Labour and Liberal MEPs attend their party conferences as of right, and Labour MEPs have the same rights as Westminster MPs in the electoral college for electing the Labour Party leader (Conservative MEPs have only a consultative vote in their leadership elections). In 1990, the Labour delegation gave itself the title "European Parliamentary Labour Party" (EPLP) by analogy with the PLP in Westminster, a term recognised since 1991 by the Labour Party, which at the same time granted the EPLP a number of specific rights within the party structure, including a place for its leader on its National Executive Committee. In 1997, the new Labour Government set up a system of "link members" so that each government ministerial team included an MEP from the appropriate parliamentary committee, ensuring close cooperation at an early stage on policy formulation. One particularly striking example of a national delegation's influence on national policy formation was that of Labour MEPs on the working party that prepared Labour's position on the Amsterdam IGC, described in chapter 16.

Naturally, frequent contacts are not a guarantee of identity of views. MEPs and MPs will inevitably have different perspectives and, on occasion, will accuse each other of, respectively, "having gone native" or being "parochial". However, this does not detract from the utility of such contacts: on the contrary, it makes them more useful for both sides.

Leadership of a national delegation is usually occupied for several years in a row by the same person. As regards the UK, the leaders of the two main parties in the European Parliament have been as follows:

The high turnover of Labour leaders in the 1984–89 Parliament reflects hotly contested elections at a time when pro- and anti-marketeers were evenly divided. Pauline Green's tenure from 1993–94 was brief because she became leader of the whole Socialist Group after the 1994 elections. The

Table 12: *Leaders of the UK Conservative and Labour MEPs*

Conservatives	Labour
Sir Peter Kirk (1973–77)	Sir Michael Stewart (1975–76)
Geoffrey Rippon (1977–79)	John Prescott (1976–79)
Sir James Scott-Hopkins (1979–81)	Barbara Castle (1979–85)
Sir Henry (now Lord) Plumb(1982–86)	Alf Lomas (1985–87)
Sir Christopher Prout (1986–94)	David Martin (1987–88)
Lord Plumb (1994–1995)	Barry Seal (1988–89)
Tom Spencer (1995–1998)	Glyn Ford (1989–93)
Edward McMillan Scott(1998–)	Pauline Green (1993–94)
	Wayne David (1994–1998)
	Alan Donnelly (1998–99)

Liberal Democrat MEPs, first elected in 1994, have had Graham Watson as their leader since then.

Group discipline & whipping

Groups issue voting instructions to their members, both in terms of how to vote on each amendment and text as well as indicating which votes are important (where a number of Groups have taken up the British tradition of issuing one-, two- or three-line whips). Whipping is less tight than in some national parliaments, not least because there is no governing majority to support or to oppose. Some Groups have "whips" ("Le Whip", "Der Whip", etc.) to keep a check on attendance and voting discipline.

Most members follow their Group's voting recommendation most of the time. As the Group's position is defined not by instructions from above but by a process of discussion and negotiation within the Group involving the Group's coordinator in the relevant committees, the leadership and often the leaders of component national party delegations, it is usually acceptable to most members.

Group "whipping" systems are, however, less strict than in most national parliaments, for a number of reasons. First, there is no government emerging from the parliament, requiring systematic support from its majority. Second, the diversity of regional, national party and sectoral interests within a Group make it difficult to agree on a common Group line on some issues. Most Groups accept that, in practice, individual members or whole national party components can opt out of the Group whip on some individual votes and either abstain, or not take part in the vote or even vote the other way. Third, Groups have fewer effective sanctions against dissident members than are usually available in national parliaments. They can give a member a less favourable committee or delegation allocation, but only at the next 2½ year allocation. They can deny new rapporteurships, but not withdraw existing ones. They can decline to offer speaking time in plenary for debates, but not points of order, question time or explanations of votes. The ultimate sanction of not re-nominating a member for election is a prerogative of the national or local party, not the Group.

It is indeed the national party delegation that is in a stronger position to "discipline" individual members, even on matters such as committee allocations when the Group will usually base its nominations on proposals from its national delegations. A national delegation is likely to be able to ask its national party to discipline a member (e.g. to suspend him/her from membership), and in cases of differing views between a national party delegation and the rest of its Group, it is the national party pressure that is usually stronger on a member in those (relatively few) cases where it is crucial. In practice, however, even this discipline is less than in most national parliaments and it is only members who persistently vote against the party line on important issues who are likely to find themselves in trouble.

Despite the above, Group cohesion is strong in most Groups and has got stronger over time (see academic research by Raunio (1996) and Hix (1999)). Most members realise that their main policy and political objectives are more likely to be obtained by coordinated action with those who are close to them politically and with whom they have developed an effective structure.

Group whips also sometimes entrench divisions in that individual members do not have the time or experience to take their own position on every amendment on every issue and usually follow the Group line on the voting list prepared by the Group staff, or the upturned or downturned thumb of their specialist spokesman. Thus, most Groups can count on well over 80 per cent of their members supporting the Group line even in Roll Call votes, and this in turn means that it is the positions taken by Groups that are usually decisive in determining Parliament's position.

Power balances and relationships between the Groups

After each European election much of the attention has focused on whether Parliament has had a left-of-centre or right-of-centre majority. We shall now look at whether this has much validity in predicting how the Parliament operates in practice, or whether other factors are more important. We shall conclude by examining the current relationships between the Groups.

Compared with many national parliaments, the left-right cleavage within the European Parliament is less strong. There are a number of reasons for this. There is no parliamentary divide between government and opposition. The European Parliament, in which over 140 political parties are represented, is heterogeneous with a huge range of different national, regional and sectoral interests, which means that voting patterns are sometimes more related to these factors than to ideological divisions. (Coalitions, for example, of those representing agricultural areas, are often forged across Group boundaries). The division between federalists and Eurosceptics often overrides party differences. At the same time, many members come from countries with more of a consensual political tradition than, say, the UK or France. Certain political situations also reinforce the search for consensus, such as the need for a common front to defend Parliament's institutional prerogatives, or the need for an absolute majority in certain votes in the legislative and budgetary procedures (see Chapters 12 and 13). Much of the EP's work is highly technical, often making left-right arguments irrelevant. The "rapporteurs" system that lies at the heart of the Parliament's work is oriented towards finding a consensus. Last but not least, the range of political beliefs within the individual Groups is often wide.

The Socialist Group, for example, has traditionally covered a wide political spectrum from left to centre, and has frequently acted more as a federation of relatively autonomous national delegations. The British Labour delegation, in particular in the early 1980s when it was controlled by the Eurosceptic "anti-marketeers", frequently voted differently from the mainstream of the Group as a whole. In recent years, however, the Socialist Group has become more cohesive. The Christian Democrats have also been far from ideologically homogeneous, ranging from Social Christian members from the Benelux countries with strong trade union links and who are left-of-centre on certain social questions, to highly conservative CSU members from Bavaria. Furthermore, the traditional Christian Democratic basis of the EPP Group has been diluted, as we saw above, by Spanish, British and Nordic Conservatives as well as, since 1999, French Gaullists. They had a number of serious divisions early in the 1999–2004 Parliament. The

Liberals also cover a wider spectrum than one might imagine, given the size of the Group, with differences between those committed to a more social brand of liberalism and those with strong free market views – and, while generally in favour of European integration, include one or two Nordic Eurosceptics. The Greens sometimes divide between those who see themselves as clearly on the left, and others who claim to be above traditional left-right divisions.

All the above factors tend to undercut the dominance of left-right divisions, or at least make them much more complex. But they are still there. There are important issues that divide the Parliament on traditional left-right lines. Recent research (Raunio (1997), Hix (1999)) on Group voting patterns shows that each Group's votes most frequently coincides with the Groups next to them on the left-right spectrum.

A crucial factor is the nature of the balance of power within the Parliament. The EPP Group is now the largest, but is still over 80 members short of an overall majority. It cannot achieve that majority in combination with the other right-of-centre Groups unless it can unite extreme-right members and Eurosceptics on the one hand and the Liberals on the other, normally not a realistic option. The same was true before the 1999 elections when the Socialist Group was the largest, but could only attempt a left majority if it could rely on solid undivided support from the Greens, Communists, former Communists and regionalists.

The sort of majorities required under certain legislative and budgetary procedures are, to all intents and purposes, impossible to achieve on a narrow left or right basis. Usually, the Socialists and the EPP must negotiate compromises if Parliament is to have an impact. They are the only two Groups that can combine to obtain an overall majority and have been since before direct elections. Their combined forces have always represented over 54% of the members of the Parliament, reaching a peak of 69.5% in 1993 (currently 66%) and any deal struck between them is likely to stick, unlike fragile left or right coalitions. The relationship between the Socialists and the EPP is therefore of central importance. Representatives of the two Groups meet with each other to strike deals over political or patronage issues without smaller Groups to left or right always being consulted. These latter may then be forced to conform on a take-it or leave-it basis.

Certain general rules of operation can be observed. When consensus or special majorities are not of prime importance, the Socialist Group turns initially to the left and the EPP to the right in terms of deal-making. However, in the more usual cases when consensus is important or when special majorities are required, the Socialists and the EPP try to find compromises, often bringing the Liberals and others on board too. The dynamics of inter- group negotiations on plenary resolutions are described in the section "Building majorities: bargaining among Groups" in chapter 9.

European party federations

Besides the Political Groups in the Parliament, the main political families have set up structures outside Parliament bringing together the national parties belonging to them. Three were established before the first direct elections and have now developed a significant infrastructure:

- **The Party of European Socialists** (PES – until 1992 the Confederation of Socialist Parties of the European Community). This brings together the parties affiliated to the Socialist International.
- **The European People's Party** (EPP). This brings together the Christian Democrats or similar parties from the Member States.
- **The European Liberal, Democratic and Reformist Party** (ELDR).

Since then, two more have emerged, namely the **European Federation of Green Parties** and the **Democratic Party of the Peoples of Europe – European Free Alliance** (DPPE-EFA, which brings together regionalist and nationalist parties such as the Scottish National Party, the Flemish *Volksunie*, Basque, Corsican, Sardinian, Catalan and Welsh nationalists). MEPs from both currently sit in the same Group in the Parliament.

The development of the party federations has been gradual and is still rather limited, but through regular working parties they are adopting common policies in a growing number of areas. All organise regular congresses composed of delegates from the respective parties and involving their Group in the European Parliament. All adopt policy, in particular common manifestos for European elections. In practice, their decision-taking tends to be by consensus among the member parties, which means that the content of their policies tends to the lowest common denominator and is, therefore, often less precise than the policies of their corresponding Group in the European Parliament, which can adopt policy by a majority vote. However, the pressure to reach consensus, particularly before elections, is considerable and the effort of convergence does have an impact on the positions of individual parties. The groupings have become more cohesive over the years, in particular the Socialists who, in the 1970s and early 1980s, often had great difficulties in reaching any consensus at all. Most now allow majority voting in their constitutions, though this is not frequently used.

The holding of a "Summit" of heads of government, party leaders, the chair of the Political Group in the European Parliament and members of the Commission of their political family is perhaps one of the most significant activities of the PES and the EPP. This practice has developed in recent years, with most such summits arranged as pre-meetings for European Council meetings. These can be significant as in October 1990 when the EPP leaders agreed to press the case for a strict timetable for monetary union at the subsequent European Council in Rome. This was the so-called "ambush" of Margaret Thatcher, who was left isolated at the Summit with all the other Member States agreeing on a timetable for EMU.

Increasingly, the PES organises meetings of its ministers prior to ordinary Council meetings as well, in which the corresponding Group coordinator and Socialist Commissioner will also participate. This can be an important opportunity for the Group to influence "its" ministers in the Council.

The groupings do occasionally collaborate, and there have been "Summits" of the Presidents of the PES, EPP and ELDR. It was as a result of a joint initiative of the three that the Treaty of Maastricht introduced a new article (then 138(a), now 19, TEC) recognising the importance of European political parties.

The party groupings also have secretariats of up to half-a-dozen administrators. Although the groupings as a whole are co-financed by the participating parties and the corresponding Group in the European Parliament, the staff contingent is largely composed of officials seconded from the Group staff in the corresponding Political Group.

The officers of the five party political federations are as follows:

Party of European Socialists (PES)

President	Rudolf Scharping (Germany)
Secretary-General	Anton Beumer (Netherlands)

The European People's Party

President	Wilfried Martens (Belgium)
Secretary-General	Alejandro Agag (Spain)

The European Liberal and Democratic and Reformist Party

President	Uffe Ellerman Jensen
Secretary-General	vacant

The European Federation of Green Parties

Spokespersons	Niki Korterelgessy (UK) & Franz Floss (Autria)
Secretary-General	Arnold Cassola (Malta)

European Free Alliance

President	Winnie Ewing
Secretary-General	José Luis Linazasoro

6.   Leadership structures

At the beginning of, and halfway through, each term of office (i.e. every two-and-a-half years) the Parliament elects its formal office holders: the President, 14 Vice-Presidents and five Quaestors. At the same time, the opportunity is often taken to renew the leadership of the Political Groups. Although they are only elected from within their Group and not by the Parliament as a whole, the Group leaders play a key role in its leadership structures. Committee chairs are also up for re-election at the beginning and halfway through the legislature.

The two main decision-making bodies within the Parliament (other than the full plenary) are the Conference of Presidents (consisting of the President and the Political Group chairs) and the Bureau (consisting of the President and 14 Vice-Presidents). In addition, the five Quaestors play an important role in managing a number of issues directly concerning members' interests.

The present section looks first at the role of the President, Vice-Presidents and Quaestors, and how they are elected. It then examines the different responsibilities of the Conference of Presidents, the Bureau and the Quaestors, their working methods, and the relationships between them as well as providing some brief background on the Conference of Committee Chairs and the Conference of Delegation Chairs.

The President

There have been 23 different Presidents of the Parliament since the establishment of the Common Assembly in 1952. As Table 13 below indicates, they have come from seven countries and four Political Groups, most regularly the Socialists and Christian Democrats. The President from 1999 to the beginning of 2002 is Nicole Fontaine, a French Christian Democrat.

The President's formal duties, under Rule 19 of the Rules of Procedure, are: "to direct all the activities of Parliament and its bodies"; "to open, suspend and close Parliament's sittings, to ensure observance of (the) Rules, maintain order, call upon speakers, close debates, put matters to the vote and announce the results of votes, and to refer to committees any communications that concern them"; and to represent the Parliament "in international relations, on ceremonial occasions and in administrative, legal or financial matters".

These tasks involve the President in an enormous variety of activities inside and outside the Parliament, some of which can be delegated. In practice, for example, the President does not chair all sittings. He or she chairs the opening sitting of each part-session, formal sittings (when visiting heads of state or political leaders address the Parliament) and important debates

Table 13: *Presidents of the Parliament*

Date	Name	Political Group & Nationality
1952–54	Paul-Henri Spaak	Socialist/B
1954–	Alcide De Gasperi	Christian Democrat/I
1954–56	Giuseppe Pella	Christian Democrat/I
1956–58	Hans Furler	Christian Democrat/D
1958–60	Robert Schuman	Christian Democrat/F
1960–62	Hans Furler	Christian Democrat/D
1962–64	Gaetano Martino	Liberal/I
1964–65	Jean Duvieusart	Christian Democrat/B
1965–66	Victor Leemans	Christian Democrat/B
1966–69	Alain Poher	Christian Democrat/F
1969–71	Mario Scelba	Christian Democrat/I
1971–73	Walter Behrendt	Socialist/D
1973–75	Cornelis Berkhouwer	Liberal/NL
1977–79	Georges Spenale	Socialist/F
1977–79	Emilio Colombo	Christian Democrat/I
1979–82	Simone Veil	Liberal/F
1982–84	Pieter Dankert	Socialist/NL
1984–87	Pierre Pflimlin	Christian Democrat/F
1987–89	Lord Plumb	Conservative/UK
1989–92	Enrique Barón	Socialist/E
1992–94	Egon Klepsch	Christian Democrat/D
1994–97	Klaus Hänsch	Socialist/D
1997–99	José Maria Gil-Robles	Christian Democrat/E
1999–	Nicole Fontaine	Christian Democrat/F

N.B. 1952–58   Common Assembly of the ECSC (nominated)
      1958–79   European Assembly/Parliament (nominated)
      1979–   European Parliament (elected)

or votes. For the remainder of the Parliament's business, the Vice-Presidents are invited to chair. Similarly, the President can invite a Vice-President to represent the institution abroad but all Presidents have a punishing schedule of visits to countries inside and outside the Union, combining a protocol side (audience with the head of state, participation in ceremonies) and a functional side (meetings with the head of government, foreign minister, trade minister etc.) as well as an opportunity to make the European Parliament better known to a wider public through the media.

At the same time, the President's role is wider than Rule 19 suggests. He or she signs into law the Union budget and co-signs with the President-in-Office of Council all legislation adopted under the co-decision procedure. The President chairs the Conference of Presidents and Bureau meetings, unless there are exceptional circumstances, and has a casting vote in the Bureau. The President's role in representing the Parliament *vis-à-vis* the other Union institutions has also developed. He or she enjoys the right to chair the Parliament's delegations in conciliation meetings with the Council, though this task has normally been delegated to one of the Vice-Presidents responsible for conciliation. Furthermore, the President has acquired the right, since the late 1980s and the Presidency of Lord Plumb, to attend and address the opening of all European Council meetings.

In addition, working with Parliament's Secretary-General, the President has an important internal role within the Parliament, in overseeing its day-to-day running and administrative structures. A good example of the effect that this can have was provided by Klaus Hänsch, who in 1996 negotiated an arrangement with the Luxembourg Prime Minister, Jean-Claude Juncker, which guaranteed that the number of Parliament staff working in Luxembourg would in no circumstances fall below 2000 (i.e. about half the Secretariat) up to the end of 2004, thereby providing for an important level of stability in staff planning.

The President (like members of the Commission) is assisted by a personal private office ("*cabinet*"), with a head and deputy head, and with six or seven other administrators, covering a number of nationalities and languages and carrying out a variety of specific functions, such as relations with the press and the preparation of speeches. These *cabinet* members are drawn from the Political Group staff, from Parliament's own civil service or from outside, such as the Commission or a national civil service: most *cabinets* contain a mix of all three. The President may feel, for example, most at home with someone from his or her own political background and nationality, but may also recognise the need to consult someone with a longer experience of Parliament's working methods and traditions, individuals most easily found from within Parliament's own staff. Thus, of the heads of the private offices of the last four Presidents, two had long experience inside the Parliament secretariat and had worked as a secretary-general of a Political Group, while two came from outside, one from the Commission and the other from the diplomatic service of the President's own country.

The way in which each President approaches his or her job varies. Some Presidents adopt a direct style of leadership, others a more consensual one. Presidents also differ in the emphasis they put on the various functions and duties mentioned above. Some have attached a particular importance to their external functions, such as relationships with other Union institutions or their activities in the international sphere. Others have taken a greater interest in Parliament's internal administration. However, the growing volume of responsibilities of the Parliament makes it increasingly important for the President to keep a watchful eye on all areas of his or her responsibility.

The Vice-Presidents

Parliament has 14 Vice-Presidents, whose order of precedence is determined by the number of votes they received at their initial election.

The main formal role of the Vice-Presidents is three-fold: to preside over the plenary sessions when the President is not in the chair, to replace the President in representing the Parliament externally and to take part in the work of the Bureau (the responsibilities agreed for 1999–2002 are shown in Table 14 below).

Although the Vice-Presidents enjoy an order of precedence, determined

Table 14: *The Vice-Presidents: 1999–2002 term of office and responsibilities within the Bureau (in order of precedence)*

David Martin	Socialist/UK	Relations with national parliaments, Information policy
Renzo Imbeni	Socialist/I	Multilateral interparliamentary relations
Gerhard Schmid	Socialist/D	Budget
James Provan	EPP-ED/UK	Internal reform
Ingo Friedrich	EPP-ED/D	Members' statute
Marie-Noelle Lienemann	Socialist/F	Staff policy reforms
Guido Podesta	EPP-ED/I	Relations with national parliaments, enlargement
Alejo Vidal-Quadras Roca	EPP-ED/E	Studies, STOA, information policy
Joan Colom I Naval	Socialist/E	Buildings policy
José Pacheco Pereira	EPP-ED/P	Computing and telecommunications
Luis Marinho	Socialist/P	Members' statute
Jan Wiebenga	Liberal/NL	Members' statute, multilateral inter-parliamentary relations
Alonso Puerta	GUE-NGL/E	Organisation of Question Time
Gérard Onesta	Greens-EFA/F	Members' assistants statute

by the number of votes they receive at their election, this numerical ranking is of limited significance in determining a Vice-President's importance within Parliament's leadership structure. Their role is more likely to depend on other factors, such as whether they have been a former President of the Parliament, whether they are members of a large Political Group, whether they are particularly representative of their own nationality (they may be, for example, the only Dutch MEP in Parliament's leadership structure). But above all, personal factors play a crucial role: a Vice-President, with a strong personality and determination, who is an assiduous attender, can become very influential in shaping the wide range of decisions taken by the Bureau.

There is some specialisation among the Vice-Presidents, with each entrusted with general or specific tasks as indicated in Table 14. In addition, three are appointed by the Groups as permanent members of the Conciliation Committee with Council (see Chapter 12): Renzo Imbeni, James Provan and Ingo Friedrich were given this task in September 1999; two are appointed to lead Parliament's delegation to the COSAC meetings with national parliaments (see Chapter 16) (David Martin and Guido Podesta after the 1999 elections); and one is invited to co-chair, with a member of the European Commission, the European Union Visitors' Programme (EUVP) (see p. 291). Others may have special aptitudes that are put to use. Certain Vice-Presidents, for example, have been well known for their particularly speedy handling of votes in plenary. This was true, for example, of Nicole Fontaine, when she was a Vice-President in the 1994–99 legislature.

The Quaestors

The office of Quaestor was first established by the Parliament in 1977. At first they formed a sub-group of the Bureau, but they have been separately and directly elected by the Parliament since direct elections in 1979. The five Quaestors are responsible for administrative and financial matters concerning members individually, in accordance with guidelines that were laid down by the Bureau in September 1981 and reviewed most recently in June 1996.

At the beginning of their term of office, Quaestors distribute amongst themselves areas of interest covering such diverse issues as security, external information offices, members' assistants, the allocation of offices, visitors' groups, exhibitions and works of art, language courses, official cars, recreational activities and financial questions. Theoretically it is the President of Parliament who presides at meetings of the Quaestors but in practice this only happens at the first meeting of the College. Thereafter they take it in turn (for three months) to chair. The Quaestors also take part in the meetings of the Bureau in an advisory capacity, where they do not have the right to vote but can speak on a wide range of issues, with a strong Quaestor able to have considerable influence.

Table 15: *The Quaestors: 1999–2002 term of office*

Mary Banotti	EPP-ED/IRL
Godelieve Quisthoudt-Rowohl	EPP-ED/D
Daniel Ducarme	Liberals/B
Jacques Poos	Socialist/L
Richard Balfe	Socialist/UK

The election of the President, Vice-Presidents and Quaestors

The choice of its officers has always been determined by the Parliament itself, which resisted any instructions from outside. The precise way in which this choice is organised has evolved over time. Before Parliament became an elected body in 1979, its President was chosen annually. The practice developed of the President being given a second year of office, with election in the second year being by acclamation (only Alain Poher of France was given three years in office). Since 1979 Parliament's officers have been chosen every two-and-a-half years, first in the July session immediately following the June elections and then in mid-term elections which take place in the January session two-and-a-half years later.

The first to be elected is always the President. Until he or she has been elected the chair is taken by the oldest member among the MEPs (not the member with the longest service in the Parliament). Although no other business is transacted while the oldest member is in the chair, a tradition had developed that the oldest member deliver a keynote speech before proceeding with the formal business of supervising the election of the President. The first such speech after direct elections was given by Louise Weiss. The then 86-year-old was a renowned French journalist, a lifetime advocate of women's political rights, and fervent supporter of the European cause.

In 1989, however, the oldest member was a member of the far right French *Front National*, the film director Claude Autant-Lara. His speech was boycotted by a large number of members from the outset, and many others left as a result of his remarks. Parliament's Rules of Procedure were subsequently amended so that the oldest member could no longer deliver an introductory speech, but merely supervise the election of the President. In 1992 and 1994, Otto von Habsburg should have performed this role, but because he was no longer allowed to make a speech, declined to act as oldest member, and had to be replaced by the second oldest member. In 1999 the sitting was due to be chaired by Mário Soares, former President of Portugal, but as he was a candidate for the post of President, he let the next oldest member (Giorgio Napolitano) chair.

Nominations for the office of President are generally put forward by a Political Group or a coalition of Political Groups, but may also be submitted by 32 or more members. The ballot is secret, with members lining up to cast their vote in the centre of the hemicycle, and with the result announced an hour or two later. An absolute majority of the votes cast (not of the total number of MEPs), with abstentions and spoilt ballots not counting, is required for election. If this is not achieved, a second and, if necessary, a third ballot is held, with no obligation on any of the first ballot candidates to stand down, and with the possibility of new candidates (compromise or other) entering the fray. If, however, there is no result in the third ballot, a conclusive fourth ballot is held, in which only the two candidates with the highest votes in the third ballot take part, and in which a simple majority is enough to ensure election.

Nine sets of elections have been held since 1979, and the circumstances and degree of suspense have varied greatly.

In 1979, Simone Veil was the clear front runner on the centre right, with support from the Liberals, Christian Democrats and Conservatives. The left was divided, with Socialist and Communist candidates in the field.

In 1982, the election was much more dramatic. The right was divided, with the European Democratic Group (Conservatives) considering that it was their turn for the Presidency. Not only were they unwilling to give a free run to the EPP, but they were also unenthusiastic about Egon Klepsch, the EPP's candidate. The Socialist candidate, by contrast, Piet Dankert, had made his name as Parliament's Budget rapporteur on the first occasion that the Parliament rejected the budget in 1979 and then as a Vice-President. He enjoyed the sympathy of some members from outside the ranks of the left. In the decisive fourth ballot Dankert won by 16 votes, clearly gaining support (or abstentions) from certain Conservative and other centre-right members.

In 1984, there was again a clear front runner from the centre-right, Pierre Pflimlin of the EPP, a former French Prime Minister and the long standing Mayor of Strasbourg. Dankert was again the Socialist candidate, the only case in the elected Parliament of an outgoing President seeking re-election. Pflimlin easily beat the by then less popular Dankert on the second ballot.

Table 16: *Presidential elections since 1979*

Candidates	1st round	2nd round	3rd round	4th round
1979 *Veil* (Lib/F)	183	192 = absolute majority		
Zagari (SOC)	118	138		
Amendola (Com)	44	47		
De la Malène (EDA)	26	–		
Bonino (Tech. Grp)	9	–		
	380	377		
1982 *Dankert* (SOC)	106	114	162	191
Klepsch (EPP)	140	130	156	175
Scott Hopkins (EDG)	63	67	67	–
Chambeiron (Com)	43	43	–	–
Pannella (Tech. Grp)	16	18	–	–
	368	372	385	366
1984 *Pflimlin* (EPP)	165	221 = absolute majority		
Dankert (SOC)	123	133		
Lady Elles (EDG)	44	–		
Pajetta (Com)	37	–		
Bloch (Rainbow)	17	–		
Le Pen (Right)	16	–		
Spinelli (Com)	11	49		
	413	403		
1986 *Plumb* (EDG)	199	233	241	
Barón (SOC)	206	219	236	
Pannella (Non-Att.)	61	35	–	
Staes (Rainbow)	14	–	–	
	483	487	477	
1989 *Barón* (SOC)	301 = absolute majority			
Von Wechmar (LDR)	93			
Santos (Green)	31			
Ewing (Rainbow)	20			
Le Pen (Right)	18			
Pannella (Non-Att.)	12			
	475			
1992 *Klepsch* (EPP)	253 = absolute majority			
Barzanti (U.Eu.Left)	105			
Defraigne (LDR)	72			
Dillen (Right)	16			
	446			
1994 *Hänsch* (SOC)	365 = absolute majority			
Galland (LDA)	87			
	452			
1997 *Gil-Robles* (EPP)	338 = absolute majority			
Lalumière (ERA)	177			
	515			
1999 *Fontaine* (EPP-ED)	306 = absolute majority			
Soares (SOC)	200			
Hautala (Green-EFA)	49			
	555			

The 1987 elections were the closest yet. Sir Henry Plumb was the candidate of the centre-right and Enrique Barón (Spanish Socialist) of the left. There were two other outsider candidates, Pannella (who won support well beyond his intrinsic strength) and Paul Staes of the Rainbow Group. In the third ballot, with only Plumb and Barón standing, the former won but only by five votes.

In 1989, in contrast, there was a tacit agreement between the two largest Groups, the Socialists and the EPP, to share the two Presidencies of the legislature. The EPP supported Barón in 1989 and in return, the Socialists did not put up a candidate in 1992 against Egon Klepsch, the long-standing Chairman of the EPP Group and the losing candidate in 1982. Both won an absolute majority on the first ballot, although two of the three other candidates in 1992 clearly obtained a considerable number of votes from outside their own Groups.

In the 1994–99 legislature, the agreement between the Socialist and EPP Groups to share out the Presidency continued, despite the complaints of the smaller groups. As a result, Klaus Hänsch and José Maria Gil-Robles were both elected on the first ballot, the first with a record majority.

In 1999, the EPP-ED group succeeded in overtaking the Socialists as the largest Group and both these Groups initially indicated their desire to hold the Presidency of Parliament during the first half of the legislative term. Once it became clear that there was no longer scope to continue the previous 'alternance', both Groups sought to build a majority with other Groups. In the end, the EPP-ED negotiated an agreement with the Liberals, under which the EPP-ED would take the Presidency for the first half of the legislature and the Liberals for the second half.

As a result, for the first time since 1986, the Socialists and the EPP-ED contested the election. The PES candidate, Mário Soares, could not prevent Nicole Fontaine from being elected on the first ballot. It is now expected that following her Presidency, the present leader of the Liberal Group, Pat Cox from Ireland, will be elected President of the Parliament in 2002.

Once the Presidential elections have been settled, they have a bearing on the elections for the Vice-Presidents, and Quaestors (and subsequently on the committee chairmanships, and other posts within the Parliament). These posts are effectively divided between the Political Groups (and within them between their different national delegations) on the basis of their numerical strength (using the d'Hondt system) after taking into account which Political Group has obtained the Presidency.

In order to be elected as Vice-President on the first ballot a candidate has to receive an absolute majority of the votes cast. If 14 candidates are not so elected on the first ballot, there are provisions for a second ballot for the remaining places under the same rules, and finally for a third ballot in which those candidates with the most votes win. The "official" nominees of the Groups are almost always elected, although some of them only on the second or third ballot. Some outsider candidates (such as the popular Green candidates Roelants de Vivier in 1987 and Ripa di Meana in 1994) have come close.

Once the Vice-Presidents have been elected, there is a separate ballot for the Quaestors with similar rules, in which there is usually little suspense. Here, however, the "official" candidates from the Groups have not always been elected. In 1997, the Irish EDA member, Mark Killilea was elected (eliminating Vicenzo Viola from the EPP) and in 1999 Richard Balfe, an outgoing Quaestor seeking re-election, was re-elected (keeping out Nelly Maes from the Green Group). Back-bench MEPs feel less need to support candidates put forward by Groups following the inter-group share-out in the case of the Quaestors, who are elected last and whose job, after all, is precisely to look after the interests of individual members, rather than those of the Groups.

The Conference of Presidents, the Bureau and the College of Quaestors

In 1993, Parliament reorganised its management structures into three separate bodies, each with a specific set of tasks:

* *the Conference of Presidents* composed of the President of Parliament and the chairs of the Political Groups
* *the Bureau* composed of the President and the Vice-Presidents, and
* *the Quaestors*

Prior to 1993, there was an "Enlarged Bureau" instead of the Conference of Presidents. This body brought together the Bureau and the Group chairmen (with Quaestors present as well as non-voting members). It was felt to be an unwieldy body and was replaced by the more compact Conference of Presidents. Normally, the Conference of Presidents works by consensus but, where necessary, it votes in accordance with a weighting based on the number of members in each political group. As a result, the Conference reflects political strengths inside the Parliament more accurately than did the Enlarged Bureau. The closest such vote occurred in November 1995 when the EPP, UPE, ELDR and EDN (with 298 votes) decided against the SOC, GUE, Green and ARE (with 297 votes) to hold over the awarding of the Sakharov prize (see Chapter 16) from December 1995 to January 1996.

The *Conference of Presidents* is responsible for the broad political direction of the Parliament, both internally and externally. Internally, it proposes the membership and competence of parliamentary committees and delegations, adjudicates on disputes of competence between committees, authorises the drafting of reports and draws up the draft agenda of part-sessions. Externally, it decides on inter-institutional relations and relations with Member States and national parliaments, handles matters relating to relations with non-member countries and non-Union institutions and organisations and decides on the sending of delegations to third countries.

The *Bureau* deals with internal financial, organisational and administrative matters as well as staff policy and the management of sittings. Under its financial responsibility, it draws up the preliminary version of the budget of the institution and decides on the size of the establishment plan of the Secretariat, thereby determining how many new staff, if any, can be recruited. In organisational and administrative terms, it takes decisions on the conduct of plenary sittings, authorises committee meetings away from the usual places of work as well as hearings and study and fact-finding journeys by rapporteurs. Last but not least, it appoints the Secretary-General. In addition, the Bureau sometimes uses smaller working parties, to which other members may be co-opted, for example, on the sensitive issues of new buildings and information policy.

The *Quaestors*, as described above, are responsible for administrative and financial matters concerning MEPs individually (e.g. members' office equipment, allowances, use of vehicles, etc.). They also deal with day-to-day matters concerning security, passes, the allocation of offices and the use of buildings, including giving permission for the variety of exhibitions that are organised in the Parliament's buildings in and out of session.

The Conference of Presidents meets at least twice, and normally three or four times, per month. Its meetings are prepared by meetings of the head of the President's *cabinet*, the Secretary-General of Parliament and the Secretaries-General of the Political Groups. The Bureau and the Quaestors normally meet once a month, during part-sessions in Strasbourg, with occasional extra meetings in Brussels.

The meetings of all three bodies are held in camera. Meetings of the Bureau tend to be quite formal affairs, with Vice-Presidents actively participating in the wide range of debates on their agenda. Meetings of the Conference of Presidents, on the other hand, tend to be much more brisk, with interventions limited to what is necessary to formalise agreements and to cut deals between the Groups regarding Parliament's business. Meetings of the Quaestors are particularly robust affairs, often representing a distillation of members' concerns or complaints regarding their working environment.

Attendance at all three is limited to their direct membership, though the non-attached members may also send two non-voting members to the Conference of Presidents. When discussing the draft agenda of Parliament, the Conference of Presidents invites a representative of the Commission and of the Council and the chairman of the Conference of Committee Chairmen within the Parliament (see below).

On the staff side, attendance at the Conference and the Bureau is normally limited to the Secretary-General, the Secretariat of the Conference and Bureau (four or five Parliament offiicals) and that of the Quaestors, the Directors-General of the Parliament and the head of its Legal Service, and one or two members of staff from each Political Group. The minutes of meetings are drawn up by the Secretariat and unlike in committees or the plenary, are reviewed and approved before dissemination, given the sensitivity of some of the decisions that are taken and the need to prevent conflicting interpretations.

The Conference of Committee Chairmen and the Conference of Delegation Chairmen

The chairs of parliamentary committees meet together once a month (usually the Tuesday afternoons of the Strasbourg sessions) to review progress of work in committees and make suggestions to the Conference of Presidents as to forthcoming plenary agendas. For this purpose the chair of the Conference of Committee Chairs attends the Conference of Presidents. The meeting also serves to discuss organisational matters affecting committees, demarcation disputes and common problems that affect more than one committee. The chair of the meeting is elected by the committee chairs themselves.

The Conference began life as an informal gathering until its existence was formally recognised in the Rules of Procedure in 1993. Since 1979 there have been five chairs: Erwin Lange, a German Socialist, had the job from 1979 to 1984; he was succeeded by Michel Poniatowski, a French Liberal, until 1989 when Henri Saby, a French Socialist, took over. He remained in post until 1993 when he was replaced by Ken Collins, the British Chair of the Environment Committee. He held the post for six years until 1999 when he was succeeded by Ana Palacio, the Spanish Chair of the Legal Affairs Committee.

The Conference of Delegation Chairs fulfills a similar function in terms of discussing common organisational and timetable problems. They also elect their own chair: for nearly twenty years from 1981, when the body was established, this was a German Christian Democrat, Günter Rinsche, who was succeeded in July 1999 by Claude Desama, a Belgian Socialist. Like the committee chairs, they meet once a month with the chair representing them in the Bureau and Conference of Presidents when issues pertaining to the functioning of delegations are discussed.

7. The Parliamentary committees

It is in the parliamentary committees that much of the detailed work of the Parliament is carried out and where individual members can play a crucial role. This chapter examines the structure and functioning of the committees. It looks at the division of responsibilities between them, how members are allocated to them, at the way committee office-holders are chosen, at decision-making structures within the committees, and how they are staffed. It considers where and when committees meet, their working methods and workload, notably how committee rapporteurs are chosen, and how reports and opinions progress through committee.

The structure and character of committees

Committees were a central part of the Parliament's work from its inception. The Common Assembly of the Coal and Steel Community had already set up seven committees by 1953. In 1958, with the establishment of the EEC and EURATOM, the number of committees increased to 13 in a structure not very different from that which exists today although over the years there have been occasional changes of committee nomenclature and responsibility.

After direct elections in 1979, 16 standing committees were set up. This gradually increased to 20 by 1999 (see Table 18 with all committee chairs since 1979 at end of this chapter). By then there was a growing feeling that the number of committees and subcommittees should be reviewed with the primary aim of spreading the new legislative responsibilities arising from the Amsterdam Treaty more evenly. As a result the number of committees was reduced from 20 to 17. The Regional and Transport Committees which had been separated in 1979 were combined again; the External Economic Relations and Research Committees were merged into a new Industry, External Trade, Research and Energy Committee, which also took over the industrial policy part of the Economic Committee, and the Rules Committee was merged with the Institutional Committee, which was renamed the Constitutional Affairs Committee. In addition, all sub-committees were abolished and there were some important shifts of responsibility with, notably, the Legal Affairs Committee taking over responsibility for general internal market measures from the Economic and Monetary Affairs Committee.

The 1999 review of the committee structure was the first comprehensive review since direct elections, but the changes eventually made did not go as far as some would have liked. There are a number of reasons for this. First is that radical changes would unravel carefully achieved balances. The normal moment to make changes is at the start of the term of office of a new Parliament, but, in practice, this only leaves a four-week period between direct elections and the first plenary, when there are many new members unfamiliar with the workings of the old Parliament and when there are many other key decisions that need to be taken. The 1999 partial reform was achieved because it was prepared by the Groups in the outgoing Parliament. A second reason is that it is often genuinely difficult to draw up clear demarcation lines between policy areas. Is media policy, for example, a cultural, economic or legal matter? A third is that committees develop an identity and *esprit de corps* of their own with some members serving on them for ten years or more. Members are naturally reluctant to see their committee merged with another or losing some of its responsibilities. Such resistance can be highly successful: in 1999, for example, the Fisheries Committee won a hard-fought battle when threatened with being reunited with the Agriculture Committee.

Individual committees are not necessarily equal in strength and prestige. The Foreign Affairs Committee covers areas where Parliament has few formal powers, yet it has always included a high proportion of the better-known members. The Budgets Committee, too, has traditionally had a high profile in an area where the Parliament has had real powers since the Treaty revisions of 1970 and 1975.

The reinforcement of the Parliament's legislative role and the arrival of the co-decision procedure under Maastricht led to a strengthened role for the Environment and Consumer Protection Committee and the Legal Committee, in particular, and their increased workload is likely to be matched by that of others following the entry into force of the Amsterdam Treaty, notably the Regional Policy, Transport and Tourism Committee, whose transport responsibilities are now all subject to co-decision under Article 251 (see Chapter 12).

A number of committees, however, have a less obviously powerful role, even if they deal with important subjects. These typically have smaller memberships, far fewer legislative proposals to consider, and hold fewer meetings. They tend to concentrate instead on own-initiative reports on issues of their choice (e.g. the Women's Committee) or else have specialised tasks to carry out (e.g. the Committee on Petitions).

Membership of committees

The number, responsibilities and size of committees are initially decided upon during the July session of a newly elected Parliament, and are then re-examined at the half-way point of the Parliament after two-and-a-half years. In 1999 the 17 committees that were established ranged from a high of 65 for the Foreign Affairs Committee and 60 each for the Industry and Environment Committees, down to 21 for the Fisheries and Budgetary Control Committees.

Once the number and size of committees has been determined the appointments of full members and substitutes to committees are then decided upon by the Political Groups in such a way as to ensure that each committee reflects the overall political balance between the Groups in plenary. Only small exceptions – to the tune of one or two extra members perhaps – are normally accepted.

The majority of MEPs serve on one committee as a full member and on another as a substitute. A small number, however, are either full members of two committees and substitutes on another, or else are full members of only one committee but substitutes on two others. This is largely explained by the existence of so-called "neutralised" committees. These are committees on which an MEP can be a full member without prejudicing his or her chances of being a full member of another committee. These "neutralised" committees have included small technical committees such as the Rules and Petitions Committees, and other committees of specialised interest such as Women's Rights and Budgetary Control. If members were restricted to a single committee, there would be too few who would make these committees their only choice.

Some MEPs have been permitted by their groups to be full members of two normal "non-neutralised" committees, and a tiny handful have been full members or substitutes on three or more committees. (In the past these have varied from particularly active to apparently inactive MEPs!) At the other end of the spectrum, a small number of MEPs have not been full members of any committee. These have understandably included the President of the Parliament and others who have preferred not to be active in committees because of their other European parliamentary or domestic political duties. A current example is Pat Cox, the leader of the Liberal Group.

The reasons for members' preferences for individual committees vary greatly. In many cases perceived "constituency" advantage is the decisive factor, in others personal interest or expertise play a greater role. However, while these individual preferences do play an important part in the process of committee allocation, the Political Groups cannot always fulfil these wishes, since some committees are over-subscribed. Less well-known backbenchers in their first term are often at a disadvantage in this distribution.

One safety mechanism for members who are not completely satisfied with their primary committee assignments as full members is their assignment to a second committee as a substitute. In some cases this is the committee on which they would have preferred to have served as a full member, and they may put more effort into this committee than their main one. Substitutes suffer little disadvantage compared to full members. They have full speaking rights, full voting rights (in the place of an absent full member – and there are usually some absences) and can also be rapporteurs and draftsmen, on occasion drawing up some of the major reports within a committee. Substitutes can even become the coordinators of their Political Groups on a particular committee. This was the case with Jean-Louis Bourlanges, EPP coordinator on the Institutional Affairs Committee (and also one of the Committee's two main rapporteurs during the first stages of preparation for the 1996 Inter-Governmental Conference).

Despite the balance generally achieved between Political Groups, committees do tend to develop a corporate identity, and do tend to attract members with a particular sympathy for the sector concerned. Thus, some nationalities and Groups have a strong preference for certain committees: Irish members, for example, have been keen to sit on the Agricultural and Regional Committees.

A further distinctive feature of committee membership within the European Parliament is the relatively high turnover of membership of individual committees. This is particularly true from one Parliament to another. In 1999, for example, only three full members of the Culture Commitee had been members of the same committee in the previous legislature. Only a tiny minority of MEPs stay in one committee for more than ten years. This turnover of membership is in sharp contrast to the much greater continuity in committee membership in the US Congress.

Office-holders and their selection

The formal office-holders ("Bureau") within each committee are its chairman and three vice-chairmen. The chairman presides over the meetings of the committee, speaks for it in the plenary sessions at a time of sensitive votes or decisions and also represents it at the regular meetings of committee chairmen (see Chapter 6). He or she can also have a powerful role in shaping the agenda of the committee, and in acting as its representative outside Parliament.

The chairman and the three vice-chairmen are elected at the committee's constituent meeting, normally during the July plenary of a new Parliament and at the halfway point of the legislature. In practice, all these positions are divided by agreement among the Political Groups on the basis of the number of members within each Group.

The allocation is determined by the d'Hondt system of proportional representation, whereby Groups choose which committees to chair in an order determined by the size of the Group. In 1999, for example, the EPP-ED Group had the right to the first, third, fifth, seventh, tenth, thirteenth, fifteenth and seventeenth choices of committee, the Socialists to the second, fourth, sixth, eleventh, fourteenth and sixteenth choices, the Liberals to the eighth choice, the Greens to the ninth choice and the GUE Group to the twelfth choice among the 17 available committees The same system also covers the allocation of other committee posts, such as chairs of temporary committees and vice-chairmanships of committees, and ensures a distribution of posts roughly proportional to the size of the Groups.

Once a chair has been allocated to a particular Group, the choice depends on a number of factors including the need to take into account the size of the national delegations within a Group, and the experience and expertise of their individual candidates. In contrast with the US Congress, seniority within the Parliament does not play a very great role: four (Gemelli, Gargani, Napolitano and Westendorp) out of the 17 committee chairmanships in 1999 were held by new members of the Parliament. Another key factor is the previous distribution of posts. If a national delegation within a Political Group has already provided a President, Vice-President or Quaestor of Parliament, or the chair of its Political Group, its chances of gaining a major committee chair may diminish since other delegations must also get their turn.

Once chairs have been distributed, a similar process occurs for the first, second and third vice-chairs of the committees, although these are clearly of lesser importance. Preliminary agreement on all these matters is reached by the Groups in the weeks before the first plenary session of a new parliament but it is not until the plenary itself that the final decisions can be taken especially if there is uncertainty as to the size of Groups and as to who will become President.

After the nominations of chairs and vice-chairs have been decided by the Political Groups, the formal decisions are taken by the committees at their constituent meetings. In practice there have rarely been competing candidates, and election of the Political Groups' nominees is normally a formality, by acclamation rather than by vote.

Only occasionally, a candidate has been the subject of controversy. For example, in 1992, the choice of the British Conservative, David Curry, to replace Sir Henry Plumb as Chairman of the Agriculture Committee, was strongly contested by those who perceived him as hostile to the CAP. He failed to get a majority on the first vote, but was eventually elected. In 1993 the EPP candidate to take over as Chairman of the Institutional Affairs Committee, José Maria Gil-Robles, was initially defeated in Committee by another EPP member, Derek Prag. The latter was subsequently persuaded by his Group to resign and Gil-Robles was duly elected.

Even rarer is for a candidate from another Political Group to be elected against the official nominee, as this upsets the carefully constructed political balance between Groups that had been previously agreed upon. The only exception to this so far as regards committee chairmanships came in June 1994. Although the *Forza Europa* Group was entitled to the chair of the Research Committee, the designated nominee, Umberto Scapagnini, lost at the constituent meeting in July on a vote of 12 to 13 to a wildcat candidate proposed from within the Socialist Group, namely the outgoing Committee Chairman, Claude Desama. The latter had been a popular chairman but the main factor in his initial victory was the hostile attitude of many on the left towards *Forza Europa*, its leader, the Italian Prime Minister, Silvio Berlusconi, and his government coalition with the right wing *Alleanza Nazionale*.

The result of the vote was stalemate for several weeks. Not only *Forza Europa* but some other Groups, in particular the EPP, strongly opposed the decision. The re-creation of a monetary sub-committee within the Economic Committee (allocated to a Socialist nominee under D'Hondt criteria) was blocked until the situation in the Research, Technological Development and Energy Committee had been sorted out. In this period, the Research Committee lost its first few planned meetings. The situation was only resolved well into September, when Claude Desama resigned as Chair and Umberto Scapagnini was elected, the whole episode illustrating the strength of political commitment to the d'Hondt system when significant posts are at stake.

The only occasions when the D'Hondt system has not finally prevailed has been over the less important votes for committee vice-chairmen. In 1984 in the Youth Committee, for example, the official Group nominee for one of the vice-chairs was defeated by a candidate from another Group. Another case, also in the Youth Committee, arose half-way through the 1984-89 Parliament, when the third vice-chairmanship was supposed to go to a representative of the Group of the European Right. No nominee was put forward, and there were no representatives of the Group present at the constituent meeting of the Committee, which proceeded to elect an Italian Communist as third vice-chairman. The Group of the European Right protested strongly, but to no avail, a decisive factor being the "outsider" position that the Group had in the political decision-making structure of

Parliament. (In 1987, however, a member of the *Front National*, Devèze, was elected to the Bureau of the Agriculture Committee, despite left opposition.)

After the 1989 elections the whole system was subjected to a more fundamental challenge by the Group of the European Right, which put up candidates against the other Groups' nominees in the vast majority of committees. Not only were all these challenges unsuccessful (although prolonging the duration of the constituent meetings of the committees) but the one "official" nominee from the Group of the European Right (Hans Günter Schodruch for the third vice-chair of the Transport Committee), was challenged and defeated. Hence, the Group remained without a single chairman or vice-chairman.

Once elected, the chairs and vice-chairs have terms of office of two-and-a-half years. Half-way through the five-year term of the Parliament, the whole process is repeated. Fewer changes are made on these occasions to the distribution of committees between Political Groups than at the beginning of each Parliament, especially because there has been far less change in the numerical balance between the Groups. In all four legislatures there was some change to the balance as a result of mid-term enlargements of the Community, and a wish to allocate some committee chairmanships and vice-chairmanships to members from the new countries.

Moreover, certain Groups have felt the need to redistribute posts among their own members for reasons of internal political balance or for other reasons, so even when a committee chairmanship remains with the same Group as before, there is a tendency to change the chairman. In 1992 exactly half the existing committees ended up with new chairmen. A really long-serving chairman is thus the exception rather than the rule. Perhaps the most striking such exception was Ken Collins, Chairman of the Environment Committee for 15 out of his 20 years in the Parliament. Other exceptions have been the German SPD member, Erwin Lange, who was Chair of the Economic and Monetary Committee for four years and then of the Budgets Committee for seven years (1977–84); the Italian Communist, Pancrazio de Pasquale (Chair of the Regional Committee from 1979 to 1989); Heinrich Aigner (Chair of the Budgetary Control Committee from its creation in 1979 to his death in 1988); Michel Poniatowski (Chair of the Development Committee from 1979-84 and of the Energy Committee from 1984-89); Bouke Beumer (Chair of the Culture Committee from 1982-84 and of the Economic Committee from 1987–94), and Willy de Clercq (Chair of the REX Committee from 1989 to 1997 and of the Legal Affairs Committee from 1997 to 1999).

The result of a system of frequent changes of chairman has been that many committees have had a great number of chairs. The Legal Affairs Committee has had 11 chairs since 1979 and the Foreign Affairs Committee and Employment (Social Affairs) Committee have each had ten (see Table 18 at end of chapter). Compared to the US Congress, in particular, the European Parliament continues to be characterised by short-term chairmanships.

Group coordinators

Apart from the official office holders, a very significant part is played within every committee by the Group coordinators. Each Political Group chooses a coordinator as its main spokesman, in most Groups elected by its members of the committee. The coordinators of each Group meet together (normally immediately after the end of a committee meeting) to share out rapporteurships and to discuss the committee's future agenda and outstanding political problems before full discussion in the committee. Coordinators' meetings can also be held during the Strasbourg plenaries to discuss forthcoming votes affecting the committee, possible compromise amendments and so on.

Coordinators allocate tasks among the members of their own Group. Once a report has been allocated to a Group the coordinator often plays the decisive part in the choice of rapporteur from among the members of that Group and of which substitute members may vote in place of an absent full member from the Group. The coordinators often act as "whips", convening meetings of the members of their Group before the start of the full committee meeting, maximizing their Group's presence during key votes, and helping to establish the full Group's voting line and speakers' lists for the plenary sessions.

The balance of decision-making power between the chairman, the bureau and the coordinators differs considerably from committee to committee. The chairman is often in the most powerful position, and can dominate much of the work of a committee. Other chairmen operate through a more collective style of leadership, in conjunction with the Group coordinators.

Staff of committees

Compared to the US Congress (but not to the national parliaments of the Member States) the full-time staff of Parliament's committees is very small. Committees normally have between two and seven administrators under a head of division, most of whom are now in Brussels. There is also a committee assistant to look after the logistics of the meetings, and a number of secretaries. The committee staff have an important role in briefing members of the past activities and positions adopted within the committee, help in background research for rapporteurs, and in the drafting of texts. They frequently tend to be generalists rather than specialists, largely because there are so few of them to cover what is often a wide range of policy areas, but also because of language constraints. A French-speaking expert on a particular subject area may have to hand over to a German-speaking, but non-expert, colleague if the rapporteur he or she is meant to assist speaks only German.

Besides the committee staff, other officials attend committee meetings. Parliament's Directorate-General for Research can help committees with more detailed research and sends one or two of its administrators to keep track of committee developments. Parliament's Directorate-General for Information is also represented and prepares brief records of meetings for information in a daily publication, *News Report*.

A Political Group also has one or sometimes more of its staff whose responsibilities include following an individual committee. The smaller Political Groups are more stretched in this regard, and their staff may have to follow more than one committee (see chapter 5 on Political Groups). Finally, there are members' personal assistants (see Chapter 4). In the early days of the directly elected Parliament their presence at committee meetings was disputed in certain committees, but this is no longer the case. Only a minority of the assistants, however, regularly attend committee meetings, although they are quite often used as the "eyes and ears" of a committee member who is elsewhere engaged. They are not generally called upon for drafting of reports, but do frequently draft amendments.

Place, time and character of meetings

The committees' normal meetings are during the two so-called "committee weeks" which immediately follow the plenary session, and precede the Group week. Regular committee meetings almost invariably begin after lunch (to allow members to travel in the course of that morning if necessary) and end before lunch on a subsequent day. The normal working hours are 3 p.m. to 6:30 p.m.and 9 a.m. to 12:30 p.m. (see Chapter 3). The main exception is the meetings of the Budgets Committee at peak budget time, which often continue until late into the night.

The busier committees now meet at least twice a month for two or four half days on each occasion. Other committees may only meet once a month, although often for four half days. The majority of these meetings take place in Parliament's buildings in Brussels. For many years, there was a general rule that Parliament's committees could meet once a year outside Parliament's "normal working places" (but within the European Community). This was felt to ensure a good balance between showing the flag outside Brussels (and learning about national and regional situations), and not indulging in wasteful extra travel. This practice has now been curtailed. Committees are now no longer allowed to hold external meetings during election years, and have to choose between holding one full external meeting (involving all the committee members) during the rest of the legislature or else sending a number of smaller delegations from the committee to different destinations. In practice the latter solution has become the almost univeral choice.

Committees also meet in the other working places of the Parliament: in Luxembourg or Strasbourg. Such meetings now only rarely take place in Luxembourg, but short extra meetings during Strasbourg plenaries are frequent. They are discouraged in that they compete for scarce room space and interpreters, as well as further undercutting plenary attendance, but Parliament's new legislative responsibilities have made them difficult to avoid.

Prior to direct elections (and for two years after them), Parliament's committees were smaller and used to sit around a long rectangular table, with the chairman at the head. The meetings were very cramped but informal with the Commission representatives also at the same table. Since then meeting rooms have got larger. The chairman sits up on a raised dais, with the vice-chairs on his or her left and the committee secretariat to the right. The members sit in the central bloc of seats, facing the chairman rather than each other, with the Socialists in the front seats on the left, the EPP in the front seats on the right and the smaller Groups behind. The secretariats of the Political Groups, members' assistants and staff sit in the block of seats on one side of the room, with representatives of the Commission or Council in the block of seats on the other side.

As a result there has been a change in atmosphere. The rooms are much more spacious, but the meetings are also more formal, and the distinction between the various Political Groups is sharper. Jacques Delors, Chairman of the Economic Committee from 1979 to 1981, was one who disliked the less intimate atmosphere, which, he said, made him feel more like a teacher in a traditional school. The change was inevitable, however, with the increase in Parliament's membership.

Before direct elections, committee meetings were closed to the public, but they are now practically always open (see Chapter 16). As for the use of languages, there is a greater informality than in plenary sessions, with members more frequently responding to points made by other members in the latter's language rather than their own. For coordinators' meetings, there is sometimes no interpretation, with only English or French being used.

Committee business

Draft reports and opinions

The bulk of committee business is concerned with the consideration and adoption of draft reports and opinions, in fulfilment of Parliament's legislative, budgetary and agenda-setting roles. There are three main bases on which committees draw up such reports or opinions: *first*, to consider draft legislative or other texts from the Council or Commission; *second*, in response to resolutions tabled by individual members, and *third*, as a result of their own initiatives.

When Parliament receives a formal Commission or Council proposal, it is referred to the appropriate committee as "the committee responsible", and to one or more of the other committees for their "opinion". The decision as to where to refer the proposal is prepared by officials in Parliament's legislative coordination unit and is then announced by the President of Parliament in the subsequent plenary session. These decisions may be challenged. During the 1994–99 legislature, there were 79 conflicts of competence which required discussion between committees. Most such conflicts were resolved in the Conference of Committee Chairs (35) but a minority (10) were referred to the Conference of Presidents.

Committees may also request that they be asked to give an opinion on a proposal or suggest that another committee give them such an opinion. Drawing up an opinion for another committee allows for the expression of views, but is less satisfactory than being "the committee responsible". Opinion-giving committees, for example, may table amendments to Commission proposals but are not meant to vote on the Commission proposal as a whole. There is no obligation for the committee responsible to take other committee's amendments on board, though they do have to be voted on. If the amendments are rejected, the opinion-giving committee does not have the right to table amendments in plenary, unless it can obtain the signature of 32 members or the support of a Political Group.

Rule 162 does specify that the main committee must set a fixed deadline for opinion-giving committees, before which date it can not adopt its own report, but the latter are sometimes given very little time to draw up their opinions, which often have to be abandoned, or else take the form of a short letter from the chairman. On other occasions they are adopted so late that they are presented separately from the main reports in the plenary (opinions are otherwise annexed to main committee reports).

General dissatisfaction amongst opinion-giving committees with these arrangements led to the development of two procedures, known as "Gomes" and "Hughes", which remain outside the formal structure of the Rules of Procedure. The Gomes procedure, which requires a decision of the Conference of Presidents, provides for one committee to be responsible, but for (an)other committee(s) to draw up their parts of a report, it being understood that the responsible committee will include in its report without substantial change the entire contribution from the opinion-giving committee(s). This procedure was used, for example, when the structural funds were reformed in 1993, and led to seven committees being given a full role in the development of Parliament's position. The second procedure, known as the Hughes procedure, was introduced in 1995 by the Conference of Commmittee Chairmen and has been much more widely used than Gomes. In this case, the amendments of the opinion-giving committee(s) are not automatically incorporated into the report of the responsible committee but they are treated more carefully, on the basis of more systematic and organised contacts between rapporteurs in the different committees. It has proved a useful way of defusing conflict between committees and ensuring broader and more effective participation in the legislative procedure.

The *second* basis for committee reports and opinions are motions for a resolution tabled by individual members. These are also referred to specific committees which must then decide whether or not and by which procedure such resolutions should be considered. A list of such motions is normally examined by the committee coordinators. The recommendations of the coordinators are then submitted to the full committee. In practice only a few such motions are made the subject of individual committee reports, not least because these now require the approval of the Conference of Presidents (Rule 48). Many raise constituency matters of specific national, regional or sectoral interest only and are not considered to be appropriate for detailed committee consideration. Some committees have informal rules that such resolutions will only be taken further when they raise an issue affecting more than one Member State, though this may be less strictly observed in committees with lesser work loads or when a determined member (especially a Group coordinator) continues to insist on a report. No further action, however, is a very common fate for motions. Alternatively, such a motion can be considered in conjunction with a report being drawn up in another context. In all cases the motions are annexed to the report in question, though the reports themselves may depart quite significantly from the contents of the resolution.

A *third* common basis for committee reports and opinions is when a committee decides that it wishes to draw-up a so-called "own initiative report" on a particular subject on which it has not been consulted. This might, for example, be an entirely new issue on the policy agenda, or a Commission communication on which Parliament has not been formally consulted.

Own initiative reports have always been subject to prior approval, but the rules were significantly tightened in 1994 when the Conference of Presidents took over responsibility from the Bureau for authorising them. Since then there has been a strict quota which allocates two own initiative reports annually to legislative and three to non-legislative committees. However, even within the quota, permission is not automatic. Typical reasons for rejecting requests include that the subject matter is too close to that of another committee's report, or that the issue has been recently handled by Parliament, or simply that the plenary agenda is getting more and more overloaded. The result of these tighter controls was dramatic: between 1990 and 1994, 528 reports based on own initiatives were adopted; in the following five years, the number dropped to 212 or around two per committee per year.

Volume and distribution of reports

To measure the total output of the committees, it is necessary to include a number of other reports, such as those related to the budget or budgetary control, waivers of immunity, changes in the rules of procedure, petitions of particular policy interest, "own initiatives" or any other procedural matters, such as when a proposal's legal base is contested. If these are added together, then between 1994 and 1999, 482 non-legislative reports from the committees were adopted in plenary. To these one can add a further 504 reports on non-legislative consultations, though these often did have some relation to the legislative process.

The balance between the different types of legislative and non-legislative reports has varied greatly from committee to committee (see Table 17). Some committees had a heavy legislative burden involving all three of the consultation, cooperation and co-decision procedures (e.g. the Economic Committee with 143 reports under the three procedures in the 1994–99 Parliament, the Environment Committee with 153 and the Research Committee with 67). Other committees also had a considerable legislative load but primarily restricted to the single reading consultation procedure (e.g. the Agriculture Committee with 85 reports adopted under the consultation procedure in 1994–99 but only three other legislative reports, or the External Economic Relations Committee with 70 reports adopted under the consultation procedure but only one co-decision resolution).

A further set of committees were not involved in legislation at all because they had very specific non-legislative tasks (e.g. the Rules or Petitions Committees) or whose involvement was limited, the main thrust of their work being on own-initiative and other non-legislative reports (e.g. the Foreign Affairs Committee with 23 assents and 12 consultations but 50 consultations on non-legislative issues and 32 own initiatives, the Institutional Affairs Committee with 10 non-legislative consultations and 10 own-initiative but only 3 legislative consultations or the Women's Committee with 7 legislative and 25 non-legislative reports). It was these imbalances between committees which partly explain the revision of the committee structure which took place at the end of the 1994–99 legislature. The revision was designed to balance out legislative and non-legislative work between the committees so that their overall work loads become more evenly spread.

Table 17: *Number of reports adopted in plenary, listed by committee of origin during the 1994–99 legislature*

	A	B	C	D	E	F	G	H	I	J	K	L	M	Total
Foreign Affairs	12					23	50				32	10		127
Agriculture	85	1		2	1		11				7	9		115
Budgets	28		1	1	1		7			58	6	1		104
Budgetary Control	22			2			15			37	8			84
Culture	20	2	2	15	15		8				10	3		75
Development	9	17	17	4		5	11				10			73
Economic	63	4	3	40	33		120				16	8		288
Employment	14	5	8	9	3		40	1			8	11		99
Energy and Research	41	4	5	10	7	1	29	1			8	8		113
Environment	20	23	24	51	35		37				9	8		207
Women's Rights	3	1	1	2			7				10	8		32
Institutional Affairs	3						10				10	1		24
Legal Affairs	12	1	1	27	18	1	30				8	19		117
Civil Liberties	37			3	1		24				17	15		97
Fisheries	86					2	11				8	5		112
Petitions							5				7			12
Regional Policy	6			1	1	4	43				6	9		70
Rules of Procedure									9		5	1	20	35
REX*	70			1		13	15				18	12		129
Transport	7	36	44	22	5	1	31				6	13		165
Temporary or Inquiry											6			6
Grand Total	538	94	106	190	120	50	504	2	9	95	215	141	20	2084

Report Types:
A = Consultation procedure (reports)
B = Cooperation procedure (reports in 1st reading)
C = Cooperation procedure (Recommendation in 2nd reading)
D = Codecision procedure (reports in 1st reading)
E = Codecision procedure (Recommendations in 2nd or 3rd reading)
F = Assent procedure
G = Consultation on non-legislative issues

H = Reports on legal base issues
I = Reports on lifting immunity
J = Budgetary reports
K = Committee "own initiative" reports
L = Reports on motions for a resolution pursuant to Rule 48 (Ex-45)
M = Reports on EP Rules
* = External Economic Relations

Nomination of rapporteurs and draftsmen

Once a committee has decided to draw up a report or opinion its next task is to nominate a rapporteur (when the committee is primarily responsible) or a draftsman (when it has to draw up an opinion for another committee). Only in a few cases are rapporteurs not appointed, namely when a committee decides to apply the procedure without report (Rule 158). Draftsmen of opinions, on the other hand, are quite often not appointed, because the issue is felt to be of little interest to the committee or because the timetable of the committee primarily responsible leaves little time for adequate discussion. On such occasions the committee chairman may send an opinion in the form of a letter approved by the committee.

The system of rapporteurs stems from continental parliamentary practice, and is unfamiliar to those, for example, with British or American parliamentary backgrounds (though the possibility is provided for in the Scottish Parliament). It is the job of the rapporteurs (and of draftsmen) to prepare initial discussion on the subject within the committee, to present a draft text, and to amend it, if necessary, to take account of the committee's observations or of new developments. Once the report is adopted by the committee, the rapporteur presents it in plenary, and is asked to give a view on behalf of the committee on any plenary amendments that have been tabled (normally communicated to the President in advance in writing, although the rapporteur may take the floor on complicated points). The rapporteur must also follow developments after the first Parliament reading, and prepare a recommendation for the second reading. Certain other rapporteurships call for continuing follow-up, especially those of an annual nature, such as those on the budget or competition policy. A rapporteur becomes *ex officio* a member of Parliament's delegation to conciliation with Council (see Chapter 12).

The choice of rapporteurs and draftsmen is normally decided upon within individual committees by a system whose broad lines are common to all committees. Each Political Group receives a quota of points according to its size. Reports and opinions to be distributed are then discussed by the committee coordinators who decide on the number of points each subject is worth, and then make bids on behalf of their Group, the strength of their claim being based in theory (but not always in practice) on the relationship between the number of points already used by the Group and their original quota. A controversial issue may be the subject of competing bids. Groups may then raise the bid up to a maximum level which is normally around five points. If two or more Groups are still in contention, it is normally for the Groups concerned to come to an agreement between themselves, possibly in the form of a package deal whereby one Group receives one report and the other is promised a subsequent one. Occasionally, two co-rapporteurs are appointed, mainly on major reports where the support of the two biggest Groups is more likely to be ensured in this way.

There are certain characteristics of this "auction" system. One is the tendency for Groups not especially interested in a report to try and raise the bids, in order to make other Groups "pay" more for them. A second is that it is often advantageous for a Group to submit the name of a proposed rapporteur as early as possible. If the suggested rapporteur is recognised as a specialist on the issue it is easier to get agreement on his or her nomination. Certain technical issues on which there is little political controversy but on which a committee member is a specialist are again and again referred to that same specialist, often for very few points. A third feature is the general informality of the system. Trade-offs are common between Groups and there are very few formal votes to decide on rapporteurships. If a Group exceeds its total number of points a relaxed attitude is often taken by the other Groups. It is generally only for the most politically important issues that a more rigid and partisan stance is taken.

For certain major and regularly recurring reports a rotation system is sometimes developed between the Political Groups. This is the case for Parliament's most obviously prominent rapporteurship, that on the annual budget, which normally goes to the major Political Groups in turn (see p. 218). Similar rotations are arranged within individual committees for certain annual reports, such as those within the Economic Committee on competition policy.

One innovation that has been attempted has been to name rapporteurs at a much earlier stage on the basis of the annual legislative programme. This is designed to enable rapporteurs to begin their preparatory work in advance of the formal presentation of a legislative proposal by the Commission, thus saving valuable time later on. It provides the possibility for rapporteurs to enter into talks with the Commission, before the latter finalises its proposal, as well as in the case of co-decision, with the Council, should both institutions consider there to be a chance of concluding the legislative procedure at first reading. It also facilitates "trade-offs" and "package deals" between the Political Groups regarding a large number of rapporteurships. So far, however, it has been little used, not least because of the uncertainty about the exact content of the forthcoming proposal.

Choices facing a rapporteur

Once appointed, a rapporteur may proceed in a number of ways. The first element to consider is that of **timing**. Some legislative reports may be presented quickly, especially where the Commission or Council Presidency has indicated that the matter is an immediate priority (or even formally requested urgent treatment by the plenary), or where the Parliament itself has undertaken (e.g. in the context of the annual legislative programme) to give its opinion within a certain time. Other reports, especially those on individual motions, or own-initiative reports, are often less pressing, and sometimes may not be presented for a year or more. A final deadline is the end of the legislature as all rapporteurships lapse when the five year Parliamentary term expires and new rapporteurs have to be appointed (or former rapporteurs reconfirmed).

The rapporteur must also decide what **assistance** to obtain. Some rapporteurs rely heavily on the committee's staff, who are often asked to draft a text on the basis of more or less specific guidelines. Other rapporteurs (a minority) write all their reports themselves. Other possibilities include assistance from a member's research assistant, Group staff, his or her party at home, or from other organisations (such as research institutes). Rapporteurs often seek background information from a wide range of sources, including not only the committee staff but also Parliament's Directorate-General for Research, national governments, employers, trade unions, trade associations, public interest groups and, last but not least, the Commission. They are also likely to make use of information provided by lobbyists. The latter play a valuable role in this respect, although there is always room for debate as to whether a rapporteur is gaining a balanced picture.

In the course of his or her research a rapporteur may decide to consult people outside Brussels, in another country or countries of the Union or even in third countries. As pointed out in Chapter 4, each member has an allowance of €3,000 per annum to be used for travel outside their own country. While this is often used by rapporteurs, they may seek to gain additional financial support from the Parliament, although this is now only rarely granted.

The **structure** of the rapporteur's text usually depends on whether it is legislative or non-legislative. A non-legislative text generally consists of a draft motion for a resolution and an explanatory statement. The motion for a resolution contains first, a number of procedural *citations* ("having regard to", for example, any motions for resolution or Commission memorandum on which the report is based, a list of committees drawing up opinions, etc.), then sometimes a number of factual *recitals* ("whereas . . .") and concludes with the substance of the matter in a number of *paragraphs* ("welcomes", "regrets", "deplores", "calls upon the Commission", etc.) The final paragraph is always procedural in that it calls for the resolution to be transmitted to the Commission, Council, or other bodies including national parliaments.

Accompanying the draft motion for a resolution of a report can be an explanatory statement, which serves to provide background information on the problem, and outlines why certain recommendations were made. Unlike the draft motion this is not put to the vote in the committee, but is drafted by the rapporteur on his or her own responsibility; it is still supposed to reflect the opinion of the committee. Minority statements may be added to an explanatory statement, although this provision is rarely used. In addition, any motion for a resolution serving as a basis for the report, or which was considered in conjunction with it, is annexed at the end.

Until the revision of Parliament's rules following the Single European Act, all Parliament's reports generally followed the above model. Now Parliament's rules provide for a different format for legislative texts. Any suggested amendments to the Commission's proposal or, in second reading, Council's common position, are put forward at the beginning of a report (in the form of a parallel text with the proposal or common position on the left, and the draft Parliament amendments on the right). The amendments should be accompanied by short justifications.

The draft motion for a resolution is now of a procedural nature only, and does not address the substance. It only covers points, such as whether Parliament approves the legal base of a proposal (normally a formality, but of considerable importance if Parliament disagrees, such as when it believes that a proposal should come under the co-decision procedure rather than involve a single reading only), whether Parliament approves the proposal with or without modifications, or whether it rejects it. Other permissible procedural points include a request that Parliament be reconsulted in the event of a substantial change in a proposal or that the 1975 conciliation procedure (see Chapter 12) be opened. Comments of a non-procedural nature are struck out.

Opinions from one committee to another consist of proposed amendments to the draft legislation (for legislative reports) or draft paragraphs (for non-legislative reports). (Until 1999, they were presented in a different form beginning with the draftsman's comments – similar to but not called an explanatory statement – and finishing with a number of "conclusions". Only the conclusions were put to the vote within the committee.) Once adopted, they are transmitted to the main committee, which must put the proposed amendments or paragraphs to the vote.

There are now length limits on parliamentary reports and opinions, which have been imposed because of the proliferation of such texts and consequent difficulties in ensuring translation. As a general rule, motions for a resolution are not meant to exceed two pages, explanatory statements ten pages and opinions five pages. Special derogations are required from the Bureau to exceed these limits, a requirement which has served to discourage over-lengthy texts.

The most obvious constraint on a rapporteur, is that his or her report should be acceptable to a majority of members of the committee. Rapporteurs are the servant of the committee, not their Group. The rapporteur's own personal preferences can more easily be expressed in the explanatory statement, although even here highly partisan statements would be challenged within the committee. On several occasions rapporteurs have lost the confidence of the committee and been replaced by the chairman or another member; on others, rapporteurs have chosen to resign when their basic line was rejected, or their draft text was amended out of all recognition. A more common situation is when a rapporteur expresses a point of view which is controversial, but which still has a chance of winning a narrow majority within the committee, with the risk that this will be subsequently overturned in the plenary. Such a strategy, however, runs counter to the pressure which exists on committees to try and achieve the widest possible consensus whenever there is a need for a special majority in Parliament (above all, for votes on assents, second readings under co-decision and the budget).

The progress of reports through a committee

The process whereby a report goes through committees varies, but there are a number of common stages for most of them. Unless there is particular urgency, in which case these various stages are telescoped into one or two meetings (with a report sometimes being adopted at a special meeting during the plenary), there is normally a period provided for committee discussion before a draft text is produced. Typically the rapporteur will introduce the issue, and give an indication of his or her initial views, and there will then be a possibility for members to give their views. A representative (or representatives) of the Commission will be present to make a statement or answer questions about the Commission's proposals or position. This representative may be the specialist who drafted the proposal, or someone higher up the Commission hierarchy. For more important issues the responsible Director-General or Commissioner will often be present. A Commission representative will normally be present on all occasions when the issue is discussed, although problems are sometimes posed when the committee agenda is changed at short notice. For a committee with a very full agenda there may be ten to 15 Commission officials present at any one moment. In addition, there is likely to be a member of the Council Secretariat and sometimes an official of the Council Presidency present.

At the end of the initial discussion the rapporteur usually undertakes to produce a text by a particular time. It is also often clearer as to whether the issue is controversial within the committee or not. Once ready the text is sent for translation into all working languages (for which at least ten working days is normally required), and then distributed to all members. There follows a fresh discussion, with committee members and the Commission commenting on the rapporteur's text. A deadline for amendments may then be set. The rapporteur can also decide to make modifications to his or her text or even to draft a new text if there are a large number of amendments.

The committee proceeds to vote at a subsequent meeting, first on the amendments, and then on the motion for a resolution as modified. After voting on the amendments but before voting on the proposal as a whole, the Commission is asked to state its position on all the amendments and the Council is invited to comment. If the Commission is not in a position to make such a statement or declares it is not prepared to accept all the amendments, then the committee may postpone the final vote, thereby providing more time for finding a common solution, a particularly important provision in the case of co-decision where the procedure can now be concluded at first reading.

Procedures are generally less formal than in the plenary session. Untranslated amendments and even oral amendments are sometimes allowed, especially when the chairman, rapporteur or co-ordinators put forward compromises. Voting is by show of hands, with the permitted option of standing and sitting being very rarely used. The plenary techniques of requesting roll call votes on sensitive issues or calling for a quorum (in both cases by one quarter of the members of the committee) are available to members, but are seldom used.

Most members consider that committee meetings should retain a greater degree of informality than plenary sessions, and that procedural manoeuvres should be avoided where possible. There have only been occasional exceptions to this (e.g. in the Foreign Affairs Committee, where roll call votes are sometimes requested). A proposal that electronic voting systems be installed in committees as well was rejected by the Bureau of Parliament on the grounds both of cost and lack of necessity. On the rare occasions when it is needed (e.g. to speed up very long votes) committees are allowed to use the plenary chamber in Brussels: the Institutional Affairs Committee did this when it voted on its reports in advance of the Amsterdam IGC.

Once a report has been adopted within a committee it is then collated by the committee secretariat (including any opinions received from other committees) and sent for final translation in all the languages. It is then submitted to plenary as a sessional document (in the A series of documents). Resolutions (and any legislative texts) adopted (for plenary procedures, see

Chapter 9) are forwarded to the Commission and Council (and often to Member States' governments and parliaments as well) and published in the Official Journal of the Communities. The committee report with its explanatory statement is not re-issued.

For non-legislative texts, or for legislative texts involving only one reading, that is generally the end of the procedure as far as a committee is concerned. On the other hand, in reports involving two or more readings by the Parliament, the committee's rapporteur continues to follow developments and may bring the issue up again within the competent committee at any time. Once the Council has adopted a common position, this is announced in the plenary, and is then placed on the next agenda of the competent committee. The Rules were amended in 1999 to encourage the Council to present the common position at that meeting.

The committee adopts a recommendation in second reading, which must go to the plenary within a maximum of three months (four months if extended) of the common position being announced. If conciliation takes place between Parliament and Council, the rapporteur, chair and other members of the committee will participate in Parliament's delegation to the Conciliation Committee. However, the results of conciliation go directly to the plenary for decision without passing through committee though they are also sometimes debated within the committee.

A committee's involvement in a report can be maintained over a longer period as when it is referred back from the plenary to the committee, or when reconsultation of the Parliament is requested. Occasionally committees which wish to have Parliament pronounce on a certain issue, but do not want to produce a final report until a later date, prepare an interim report.

Alternative procedures

Parliament has an increasingly full agenda. Every encouragement has thus been given to committees in recent years to adopt alternative procedures to the classic ones mentioned above, in order to lighten Parliament's agenda, and notably to deal with technical legislation.

Two procedures can be used by a committee provided there is no objection by one-fifth of its members. They are the *procedure without report*, when a legislative procedure can be approved as such without amendment, and the *simplified procedure* where the chair is named as rapporteur and prepares a draft which is sent to members of the committee and deemed to be approved unless there are objections (again by at least one-fifth of the members) within a set time limit of at least 14 days. In both cases, (and also for ordinary reports when there are no amendments to legislative proposals or when requested by the committee), the matter is put to the vote in plenary *without debate*, unless at least 32 members object, in which case the matter will be handled with debate at a subsequent plenary and, in the case of the procedure without report, sent back to committee for reconsideration. These procedures are relatively common – there were 281 procedures without debate in the 1994–99 legislature – and are normally normally used for highly technical consultations where the issues involved are minor.

Another technique is to be found in Rule 62. It provides for a report to be adopted directly by a committee on behalf of the Parliament, without involving a vote in plenary. This rule was originally derived from legislative practice in the Italian Parliament. It works as follows: a request for decision-taking power to be delegated to the appropriate committee is made by the Conference of Presidents (often at the suggestion of the committee concerned) and then applies unless a third of the current members of the committee object. The report then proceeds through the committee in the normal way, except that the committee meeting where the final decision is taken must be open to the public, and the deadline for tabling amendments must be published in the Parliament's own Bulletin. Once adopted in committee, the report is then placed on the next plenary agenda and is considered to be adopted without a vote, unless there is an objection in writing from one tenth of the current members of Parliament belonging to at least three Political Groups.

Until late 1988 Rule 62 (then Rule 52) only applied to legislative reports, and was little used. By the end of the 1984–89 Parliament, however, it was apparent that the plenary workload was becoming increasingly heavy, and it was decided to extend its use to non-legislative reports. As a result, it has come to be a common feature of the work of the committees: during the fourth legislature 207 reports were adopted under this rule.

Treatment of confidential documents in committee

The Parliament is generally a very open institution (see Chapter 16). Most of its committee meetings are open to the public and even draft reports are rather freely available but there is a need for confidentiality in certain cases. The problem became particularly apparent in Parliament's Committee on Budgetary Control, which needed to consult confidential documents in the course of its duties. An agreement on handling these documents was negotiated between the Commission and the Parliament, and adopted by Parliament in February 1989. As a result a new Annex VII was added to Parliament's Rules of Procedure laying down criteria for the consideration of confidential documents communicated to the European Parliament. Individual members may also request application of these procedures to a particular document, but this request must then be accepted by a majority of two-thirds of the members present.

When the confidential procedure is to be applied, attendance at the relevant part of the committee meeting is restricted (to members of the committee, and only those officials and experts who have been designated in advance by the chairman and whose presence is strictly necessary). The relevant documents are numbered and distributed at the meeting, but collected again at the end: no notes of their contents or photocopies may be taken. Procedures are laid down for breach of confidentiality, and the committee chairman can set down any penalties, including reprimand, or a short-term or even permanent exclusion from a committee (with a possibility of appeal to a joint meeting of Parliament's Conference of Presidents, and the bureau of the relevant committee).

Since the introduction of these procedures confidential meetings have been held not only by the Committee on Budgetary Control, but also by the Rules Committee, when dealing with issues of whether to waive a member's immunity.

Subcommittees, working parties and temporary committees

Although the committee structure is flexible, there are times when strong pressure is exerted to create new structures, either within the standing committee framework (such as subcommittees or working parties) or outside it (such as temporary committees).

Subcommittees

The European Parliament has never had the complex system of subcommittees that has been established within the US Congress. It has been reluctant to create too many new permanent bodies, notably in view of constraints of staff numbers and of members' time. A few subcommittees have been established, notably within the Foreign Affairs, Agriculture and Economic Committees. In the 1994–99 legislature, there were three subcommittees, a subcommittee with 26 members on Security and Disarmament and one of 25 members on Human Rights (both of these within the Committee on Foreign Affairs) and a 24 member subcommittee on Monetary Affairs within the Economic Committee. However, at the end of the legislature, all three subcommittees were disbanded and the new Parliament confirmed this decision.

Their degree of autonomy from the main committee varied. Before it was promoted to a full Committee in 1994, the Fisheries Subcommittee, whose area of responsibility was quite distinct from that of the Agriculture Committee as a whole, had a large measure of autonomy, naming its own rapporteurs, voting on reports (though these still had to be ratified formally by the parent committee) and directly receiving the responsible Commissioners and Council President. The subcommittees reporting to the Foreign Affairs Committee, on the other hand, had little autonomy, and acted instead as fora for preparatory discussions before decisions were taken in the main committee. Relations between the Economic Committee and its Monetary Subcommittee were in an intermediate category. Disputes over the Subcommittee's degree of autonomy (including who it could invite to its meetings) and spheres of responsibility helped to delay its creation for a considerable time in early 1992 and occasionally resurfaced. The Subcommittee had a high profile, inviting eminent personalities and holding major hearings, but its rapporteurs were chosen by the main Committee and when it was examining draft reports it could only make recommendations to the main Committee, where the formal votes and decisions were taken.

Working parties

Far more working parties than subcommittees have been set up by Parliament's committees. The former are easier to establish (they generally have no official status and require no prior authorisation from Parliament's leadership) and to discontinue, and they enable committees to respond in a rapid and informal way to shorter-term issues. The vast majority were established in the first two legislatures of the directly-elected Parliament, since when they have become much less common.

While the majority of working parties have been established by individual committees, it is also possible for the Parliament as a whole to authorise the creation of a working party, as happened with the working party within the Agriculture Committee on the monitoring of milk quotas. In such a case a working party can benefit from "official status", with the notable advantage of full interpretation.

There have been around 25 working parties within no fewer than 11 committees of the Parliament. They have differed greatly in duration and public profile. Some have lasted for a long time, e.g. Human Rights 1980–84; Fisheries 1977–85, both of which subsequently became subcommittees; Technical Barriers to Trade 1980–84; Milk Quotas 1984–89; while others have been linked instead to particular events (e.g. those on the Conference on Security and Cooperation in Europe 1979–80, on the Conference of the Regions 1982–84, on the 1986 Year of the Environment, on Lomé III 1982–84). One of them has evolved into a different type of body (the STOA working party). Another was primarily an exercise in raising public consciousness on a policy issue (the 1980 working party on Hunger in the World). Many others have been set up to help tackle a particular problem (e.g. several of the working parties set up within the Budgets Committee, such as those on Own Resources in 1979–80, Financial Regulation in 1980, Budgetary Discipline in 1985-86 and Future Financing 1986–89).

Temporary committees

Temporary committees can take the form of committees of inquiry (discussed in Chapter 15 below), whose work is governed by Treaty provisions and an inter-institutional agreement with the Council and Commission. Here the discussion will be restricted to those temporary committees whose powers, composition, terms of office and mandate are established by the Parliament alone. Such temporary committees have an initial 12-month term of office that can be prolonged. They can also submit interim and final resolutions on which Parliament formally votes.

There have been seven such temporary committees in the four legislatures since 1979:

1983 –   Parliament commissioned two prominent outside experts, Michel Albert and James Ball, to produce a report on ways to stimulate European economic development. Parliament set up a temporary committee on European Economic Recovery to provide the necessary follow-up to the Albert-Ball report. This exercise helped to launch the notion of the "cost of non-Europe" (i.e. the cost to the tax payer, consumer and businessman of the continuing fragmentation of the Community's internal market), which served to stimulate the 1992 internal market programme.

1984 –   Temporary committee on Budgetary Resources.

1987 –   Temporary committee on the Commission's proposals on "Making a success of the Single Act" (the "Delors package"). Lord Plumb, the President of Parliament at the time, chaired the committee which had two co-rapporteurs, Enrique Barón (Socialist) and Karl von Wogau (EPP).

1990 –   Temporary committee on the Impact on the European Community
           of German Unification was set up with 25 members, with
           Fernandez Albor (Spanish, EPP) as chair and with Alan Donnelly
           (UK Socialist Party) as its general rapporteur. Not without some
           opposition from the permanent committees, it also became the first
           temporary committee to be made responsible for the consideration
           of draft legislation (the necessary Community legislation to permit
           German unification) which it completed before the end of 1990.
           The standing committees which would normally have been in
           charge only gave opinions.

1992 –   Temporary committee on the Delors II package on the future
           financing of the European Community. This had 29 full members,
           with Emilio Colombo (EPP) as its chairman. To minimize friction
           with the Budgets Committee the latter's chairman, Thomas Von
           Der Vring (Socialist) was appointed as the temporary committee's
           rapporteur.

1994/5 –   Temporary committee on Employment established with a view to
           making initial recommendations in time for the European Council
           in Essen in December 1994, and completing its work by the
           summer of 1995. It was set-up with 36 members, with Celia
           Villalobos Talero (EPP) as its chair and Ken Coates (Socialist) as its
           general rapporteur.

1997 –   Temporary committee instructed to monitor the action taken on
           the recommendations made concerning BSE (in the report of the
           BSE Committee of Inquiry). It was composed of 20 members with
           Dagmar Roth-Behrendt (SOC) as chair and Reimer Böge (EPP) as
           rapporteur.

Table 18: *Committee chairmanships in the elected Parliament 1979–99*

Date	No. of years	Name	Group & Country
1. Foreign Affairs (formerly Political Affairs)			
July 79–April 80	(1)	Emilio COLOMBO	EPP/I
April 80–July 84	(4)	Mariano RUMOR	EPP/I
July 84–Jan. 87	(2½)	Roberto FORMIGONI	EPP/I
Jan. 87–July 89	(2½)	Sergio ERCINI	EPP/I
July 89–Feb. 91	(1½)	Giovanni GORIA	EPP/I
Feb.91–Jan. 92	(1)	Maria Luisa CASSANMAGNAGO CERRETTI	EPP/I
Jan. 92–July 94	(2½)	Enrique BARON	SOC/E
July 94–Jan. 97	(2½)	Abel MATUTES	EPP/E
Jan. 97–July 99	(2½)	Tom SPENCER	EPP/UK
July 99–		Elmar BROK	EPP/D
2. Agriculture			
July 79–Oct. 82	(3)	Sir Henry PLUMB	ED/UK
Oct. 82–July 84	(2)	David CURRY	ED/UK
July 84–Jan. 87	(2½)	Teun TOLMAN	EPP/NL
Jan. 87–Jan. 92	(5)	Juan Luis COLINO SALAMANCA	SOC/E
Jan. 92–July 94	(2½)	Franco BORGO	EPP/I
July 94–Jan. 97	(2½)	Christian JACOB	RDE/F
Jan. 97–July 99	(2½)	Juan Luis COLINO SALAMANCA	SOC/E

Table 18: *Continued*

Date	No. of years	Name	Group & Country
July 99–		Friedrich-Wilhelm GRAEFE ZU BARINGDORF	GREEN/D

3. Budgets

Date	No. of years	Name	Group & Country
July 79–July 84	(5)	Erwin LANGE	SOC/D
July 84–July 89	(5)	Jean-Pierre COT	SOC/F
July 89–July 94	(5)	Thomas VON DER VRING	SOC/D
July 94–July 99	(5)	Detlev SAMLAND	SOC/D
July 99–		Terry WYNN	SOC/UK

4. Economic & Monetary Affairs

Date	No. of years	Name	Group & Country
July 79–June 81	(2)	Jacques DELORS	SOC/F
June 81–July 84	(3)	Jacques MOREAU	SOC/F
July 84–Jan. 87	(2½)	Barry SEAL	SOC/UK
Jan. 87–July 94	(7½)	Bouke BEUMER	EPP/NL
July 94–July 99	(5)	Karl VON WOGAU	EPP/D
July 99–		Christa RANDZIO-PLATH	SOC/D

5. Research and Energy (and since 1999 Trade and Industry)

Date	No. of years	Name	Group & Country
July 79–July 84	(5)	Hanna WALZ	EPP/D
July 84–July 89	(5)	Michel PONIATOWSKI	LIB/F
July 89–Jan. 92	(2½)	Antonio LA PERGOLA	SOC/I
Jan. 92–Sept.94	(2¾)	Claude DESAMA	SOC/B
Sept.94–July 99	(4¾)	Umberto SCAPAGNINI	FE then EPP/I
July 99–		Carlos WESTENDORP Y CABEZA	SOC/E

6. External Economic Relations

Date	No. of years	Name	Group & Country
July 79–July 84	(5)	Sir Fred CATHERWOOD	ED/UK
July 84–Jan. 87	(2½)	Dame Shelagh ROBERTS	ED/UK
Jan. 87–July 89	(2½)	Jacques MALLET	RDE/F
June 89–Jan. 97	(7½)	Willy DE CLERCQ	LIB/B
Jan.97–Sept. 98	(1¾)	Luciana CASTELLINA	GUE/NGL/I
Sept. 98–July 99	(1)	Philippe A. R. HERZOG	GUE/NGL/F

(merged with Research, Energy and Industry Committee in 1999)

7. Legal Affairs

Date	No. of years	Name	Group & Country
July 79–Jan. 82	(2½)	Mauro FERRI	SOC/I
Jan. 82–July 84	(2½)	Simone VEIL	LIB/F
July 84–Jan. 87	(2½)	Marie-Claude VAYSSADE	SOC/F
Jan. 87–	(0)	Sir Christopher PROUT	ED/UK
Jan. 87–July 89	(2½)	Lady ELLES	ED/UK
July 89–Nov. 92	(3½)	Graf STAUFFENBERG	EPP/D
Feb. 93–June 93	(⅓)	Reinhold BOCKLET	EPP/D
June 93–July 94	(1)	Siegbert ALBER	EPP/D
July 94–Jan. 97	(2½)	Carlo CASINI	PPE/I
Jan. 97–July 99	(2½)	Willy DE CLERQ	LIB/B
July 99–		Ana PALACIO VALLELERSUNDI	EPP/E

8. Employment & Social Affairs

Date	No. of years	Name	Group & Country
July 79–Jan. 82	(2½)	Frans VAN DER GUN	EPP/NL
Jan. 82–July 84	(2½)	Efstratios PAPAEFSTRATIOU	EPP/GR
July 84–Jan. 87	(2½)	Michael WELSH	ED/UK
Jan. 87–July 87	(½)	Rodolfo CRESPO	SOC/P
July 87–Feb. 88	(½)	Jorge CAMPINOS	SOC/P
Feb. 88–July 89	(1½)	Fernando GOMES	SOC/P
July 89–Nov. 89	(½)	Hedy D'ANCONA	SOC/NL
Nov. 89–July 94	(4½)	Wim VAN VELZEN	SOC/NL
July 94–July 99	(5)	Stephen HUGHES	SOC/UK

Table 18: *Continued*

Date	No. of years	Name	Group & Country
July 99–		Michel ROCARD	SOC/F

9. Regional Policy

Date	No. of years	Name	Group & Country
July 79–July 89	(10)	Pancrazio DE PASQUALE	COM/I
July 89–Jan. 92	(2½)	Antoine WAECHTER	GREEN/F
Jan. 92–July 94	(2½)	Antonio GUTIERREZ DIAZ	GUE/E
July 94–Jan. 97	(2½)	Roberto SPECIALE	SOC/I
Jan. 97–July 99	(2½)	Miguel ARIAS CANETE	EPP/E

(Merged with Transport Committee in 1999)

10. Transport & Tourism (merged with Regional policy since 1999)

Date	No. of years	Name	Group & Country
July 79–July 84	(5)	Horst SEEFELD	SOC/D
July 84–July 89	(5)	Giorgios ANASTASSOPOULOS	EPP/GR
July 89–Jan. 92	(2½)	Rui AMARAL	LIB/P
Jan. 92–July 94	(2½)	Nel VAN DIJK	GREEN/NL
July 94–Jan. 97	(2½)	Petrus CORNELISSEN	EPP/NL
Jan. 97–July 99	(2½)	Jean-Pierre BAZIN	UPE/F
July 99–		Konstantinos HATZIDAKIS	EPP/GR

11. Environment & Consumer Protection

Date	No. of years	Name	Group & Country
July 79–July 84	(5)	Ken COLLINS	SOC/UK
July 84–July 89	(5)	Beate WEBER	SOC/D
July 89–July 99	(10)	Ken COLLINS	SOC/UK
July 99–		Caroline F. JACKSON	EPP/UK

12. Culture, Education, Youth and Media

Date	No. of years	Name	Group & Country
July 79–Jan. 82	(2½)	Mario PEDINI	EPP/I
Jan. 82–July 84	(2½)	Bouke BEUMER	EPP/NL
July 84–Jan. 87	(2½)	Winnie EWING	RDE/UK
Jan. 87–July 89	(2½)	Eileen LEMASS	RDE/IRL
July 89–Jan. 92	(2½)	Roberto BARZANTI	GUE/I
Jan. 92–July 94	(2½)	Antonio LA PERGOLA	SOC/I
July 94–Jan. 97	(2½)	Luciana CASTELLINA	GUE/I
Jan. 97–July 99	(2½)	Peter PEX	EPP/NL
July 99–		Giuseppe GARGANI	EPP/I

13. Develpoment Cooperation

Date	No. of years	Name	Group & Country
July 79–Dec. 79	(½)	Colette FLESCH	LIB/LUX
Dec. 79–July 84	(4½)	Michel PONIATOWSKI	LIB/F
July 84–Jan. 87	(2½)	Katherina FOCKE	SOC/D
Jan. 87–July 89	(2½)	Michael McGOWAN	SOC/UK
July 89–July 94	(5)	Henri SABY	SOC/F
July 94–Jan. 97	(2½)	Bernard KOUCHNER	SOC/F
Jan. 97–July 99	(2½)	Michel ROCARD	SOC/F
July 99–		Joaquim MIRANDA	GUE-NGL/P

14. Budgetary Control

Date	No. of years	Name	Group & Country
July 79–March 88	(9)	Heinrich AIGNER	EPP/D
June 88–July 89	(1)	Konrad SCHÖN	EPP/D
July 89–Jan. 92	(2½)	Peter PRICE	ED/UK
Jan. 92–March 93	(1)	Alain LAMASSOURE	PP/F
April 93–July 94	(1)	Jean-Louis BOURLANGES	EPP/F
July 94–		Diemut THEATO	EPP/D

15. Institutional Affairs (created Jan. 82 In 1999 merged with Rules to form Constitutional Committee)

Date	No. of years	Name	Group & Country
Jan. 82–July 84	(2½)	Mauro FERRI	SOC/I
July 84–May 86	(2)	Altiero SPINELLI	COM/I
June 86–July 89	(3)	Sergio SEGRE	COM/I
July 89–June 93	(4)	Marcelino OREJA	EPP/E

Table 18: *Continued*

Date	No. of years	Name	Group & Country
June 93–July 94	(0)	Derek Prag	EPP/UK
June 93–July 94	(1)	José Maria GIL ROBLES	EPP/E
July 94–Jan. 97	(2½)	Fernando MORAN	SOC/E
Jan. 97–July 99	(2½)	Biagio DE GIOVANNI	SOC/I
July 99–		Giorgio NAPOLITANO	SOC/I

16. Women's Rights (created Jan. 1982 as temp. committee, later permanent)

Jan. 82–July 84	(2½)	Maria CINCIARI RODANO	COM/I
July 84–Jan. 87	(2½)	Marlene LENZ	EPP/D
Jan. 87–July 89	(2½)	Hedy D'ANCONA	SOC/NL
July 89–July 94	(5)	Christine CRAWLEY	SOC/UK
July 94–July 98	(4)	Nel VAN DIJK	GREENS/NL
July 98–July 99	(1)	Heidi HAUTALA	V/FIN
July 99–		Maj Britt THEORIN	SOC/S

17. Rules Committee (until 1987 Rules and Petitions, merged with Institutional in 1999)

July 79–July 84	(5)	Kai NYBORG	RDE/DK
July 84–July 89	(5)	Guiseppe AMADEI	SOC/I
July 89–Jan. 92	(2½)	Marc GALLE	SOC/B
Jan. 92–July 94	(2½)	Florus WIJSENBEEK	LIB/NL
July 94–July 99	(5)	Ben FAYOT	SOC/LUX

18. Petitions Committee (created 1987, previously with Rules)

Jan. 87–July 89	(2½)	Raphäel CHANTERIE	EPP/B
July 89–Jan. 92	(2½)	Viviane REDING	EPP/LUX
Jan. 92–July 94	(2½)	Rosi BINDI	EPP/I
July 94–Jan. 97	(2½)	Eddie NEWMAN	SOC/UK
Jan. 97–July 99	(2½)	Allesandro FONTANA	EPP/I
July 99–		Vitalino GEMELLI	EPP/I

19. Civil Liberties and Home Affairs (created 1992)

Jan. 92–July 94	(2½)	Amadée TURNER	ED/UK
July 94–Oct. 95	(1¼)	Antonio VITORINO	SOC/P
Nov 95–Jan. 97	(1¼)	Luis MARINHO	SOC/P
Jan. 97–July 99	(2½)	Hedy D'ANCONA	SOC/NL
July 99–		Graham WATSON	LIB/UK

20. Fisheries (created 1994)

July 94–Jan. 97	(2½)	Miguel ARIAS CANETE	EPP/E
Jan. 97–July 99	(2½)	Carmen FRAGA ESTEVEZ	EPP/S
July 99–		Daniel VARELA SUANZES-CARPEGNA	EPP/E

Note: The credentials of new members were verified in a small separate committee from 1981 to 1987 (previously by Legal Committee). Chairs were FERRI (Legal Committee 1981-82), Tom MEGAHY (SOC/UK 1982-84 and Dieter ROGALLA (SOC/D) 1984-87. The verification of credentials was the responsibility of the Rules Committee from 1987–89 and is now undertaken by the Legal Affairs Committee.

8.   Interparliamentary delegations

Parliament has links with countries outside the European Union and in particular, with its counterparts in the parliamentary bodies of those countries. It has a structure of delegations to maintain these links as well as to respond to specific obligations that arise from international agreements between the European Union and third countries. This structure combines four different kinds of delegations:

- delegations to joint parliamentary committees (JPCs), formally established as part of association agreements signed by the EU with third countries and including a Joint Council at ministerial level: the majority of the JPCs are with countries that have applied to join the EU and that have signed "Europe" agreements;
- delegations to parliamentary cooperation committees, also formally established under partnership and cooperation agreements signed between these countries and the EU;
- delegations designed to foster appropriate contacts at the parliamentary level between the EU and the countries concerned: these have been set up by the Parliament itself or as a result of other kinds of agreement between the country and the EU; and
- the delegation to the ACP-EU Joint Assembly.

The discussion here will concentrate on these four kinds of delegations as well as referring more briefly to links with other interparliamentary assemblies and to less formal *ad hoc* delegations.

Historical development

The first interparliamentary delegation, that for relations with the USA, was established in 1972 but the number increased rapidly, reaching 27 by the end of the second legislature of the elected Parliament in 1989. The origin of the different delegations varied considerably. Some, for example, those for relations with the Maghreb and Mashreq countries and Israel, were set up as a direct result of agreements between the EU and the countries concerned, which called for the "necessary co-operation and contacts" between the Parliament and the parliamentary bodies of the partner countries. Others resulted from initiatives taken by bodies like the Japanese Diet, which itself proposed a regular parliamentary exchange following a visit to Tokyo in 1978 by Parliament's President Emilio Colombo. South Korea mounted a major diplomatic effort in 1985–86 with a view to having its parliament accepted as a "partner", in the Parliament's system of interparliamentary delegations; it succeeded. In 1989 there was also one joint parliamentary committee. This had been established in the 1960s as a result of the Association Agreement signed at that time between the EU and Turkey.

The balance between JPCs and other delegations was to change radically during the 1990s. In January 1992, the number of JPCs was increased to four. Austria was added because the Commission had given a favourable opinion on its application to join the EU, and Cyprus and Malta gained JPC status because, like Turkey, they had association agreements with the Community and had also recently applied for membership. The next step was to create joint parliamentary committees with other countries, which had, or would soon have, special relationships with the Union. JPCs were set up with Finland, Norway and Sweden, once the Commission had delivered favourable opinions on their applications to join the EU. The so-called 'accession JPCs' with the four applicant states met frequently during the period 1992–94, providing an important degree of parliamentary input into the accession negotiations. The JPCs were disbanded following accession but were soon be replaced by others. The association agreements with the Central and East European countries all contained 'parliamentary clauses', which made the setting up of JPCs between the European Parliament and the associated countries mandatory. As a result, JPCs were established between 1995 and 1999 with the Czech and Slovak Republics, Bulgaria, Romania, Slovenia and the Baltic States.

Furthermore, similar clauses in the 'partnership and cooperation agreements' signed by the EU with various countries of the former Soviet Union provides for the setting up of a new type of body, called 'parliamentary cooperation committees'. Such committees exist already for Russia, Ukraine, Moldova and Georgia and are being established progressively for other countries as the agreements enter into force.

To complete the picture, it should be noted that Parliament itself has sometimes proposed the establishment or extension of interparliamentary links. In 1994 it decided in 1994 to create a new delegation for relations with South Africa, reflecting its wish to be closely involved with the new, democratic South African Parliament.

Number and composition of delegations

Following the 1979 direct elections, Parliament began setting up its delegations at the same time as its committees, by way of formal decisions taken after the elections and again at mid-term. These decisions lay down the total number and areas of responsibility of delegations, and reflect the changing political situation as it evolves. As the table below indicates, their size can vary considerably. The current range is from 12 members for all the JPCs to 28 members for the delegation for relations with South East Europe, including Albania, Croatia, Kosovo, Macedonia and the ex-Yugoslavia.

The result of the historical growth in the number of delegations has meant that ever more members of the Parliament have been able to take part in the work of at least one delegation. In 1989 there were 375 places on 27 delegations, including one JPC; in 1999 the figure had increased substantially with 564 places on 34 delegations, including fourteen JPCs. If one includes the places on the ACP-EU Joint Assembly, virtually all MEPs now have a place on an external delegation of some kind.

The number of members on delegations has been a source of controversy for many years. On the one hand, there is a concern to ensure a match between the number of members on delegations and those playing an active part in their work, given the burgeoning cost as well as the sometimes negative impact that large groups of travelling MEPs has had on public opinion; on the other hand, there is a need to avoid offending countries which may see in a reduction in the number of members or of meetings a statement about the attitude of the EU towards them. The Parliament has sought to strike a delicate balance in reforms that were introduced in 1994 whereby the major Political Groups decided to abandon the practice of automatically providing every member with the possibility of travelling with a delegation. The result in budgetary terms was dramatic: the cost of delegations fell from €2 million in 1993 to an average of €800,000 between 1995 and 1998.

At the beginning of the 1999 Parliament it was decided to pursue this objective by inviting the chair of each delegation to take a decision as to how many members should travel with each delegation, on the basis of a pre-established limit, taking account of the areas of activity of each member of the delegation, frequency of participation, interest shown, etc. Such a rule does not necessarily reduce the number of participants: in the case of the ACP-EU Joint Assembly, for example, the number of MEPs has to match the number of ACP delegates. Nevertheless, it does contribute towards a general reduction in costs and tighter and more focused meetings, as well as reducing the cases where members of EP delegations outnumber their partners during interparliamentary meetings.

Table 19: *Interparliamentary delegations and delegations to joint parliamentary committees, with number of members and chairmen (as of October 1999)*

Delegations to Joint Parliamentary Committees (JPCs):

a) *Europe*
- European Economic Area (EEA)   (12 members): McMillan Scott (EPP-ED, UK)
- Switzerland, Iceland and Norway   (15 members): Dimitrakopoulos (EPP-ED, Greece)

b) *Central and Eastern Europe/Baltic States*
- EU – Poland   (12 members): Stenzel (EPP-ED, Austria)
- EU – Hungary   (12 members): Desama (PES, Belgium)
- EU – Czech Republic   (12 members): Olsson (ELDR, Sweden)
- EU – Slovak Republic   (12 members): Martin (PES, Austria)
- EU – Romania   (12 members): Thors (ELDR, Finland)
- EU – Bulgaria   (12 members): Alavanos (EUL-NGL, Greece)
- EU – Estonia   (12 members): Suominen (EPP-ED, Finland)
- EU – Latvia   (12 members): Gomolka (EPP-ED, Germany)
- EU – Lithuania   (12 members): Titley (PES, UK)
- EU – Slovenia   (12 members): Ebner (EPP-ED, Italy)

Delegation for relations with South-East Europe
    (28 members): Pack (EPP-ED, Germany)

Table 19: *Continued*

c) *Newly independent States and Mongolia*

Delegations to parliamentary cooperation committees and delegations for relations with:

– Russia	(25 members) Krehl (PES, Germany)
– Ukraine, Belarus and Moldova	(18 members): Wiersma (PES, Netherlands)
– Transcaucasian republics: Armenia, Azerbaijan, Georgia	(16 members): Schleicher (EPP-ED, Germany)
– Kazakhstan, Kyrgyzstan, Uzbekistan, Tajikistan, Turkmenistan and Mongolia	(17 members): Staes (Greens-EFA, Belgium)

(d) *Mediterranean*

Delegations to the Joint Parliamentary Committees:

– Turkey	(12 members): Cohn-Bendit (Greens-EFA, France)
– Cyprus	(12 members): Rothe (PES, Germany)
– Malta	(12 members): Cocilovo (EPP-ED, Italy)

Delegations for relations with:

– the Maghreb countries and the Arab Maghreb Union	(23 members): Obiols (PES, Spain)
– the Mashreq countries and the Gulf States	(19 members): Dary (PES, France)
– Israel	(17 members): Galeote (EPP-ED, Spain)
– the Palestinian Legislative Council	(17 members): Morgantini (UEL-NGL, Italy)

(e) *The Americas*

– the United States	(25 members): Read (PES, UK)
– Canada	(16 members): Sturdy (EPP-ED, UK)
– the countries of Central America and Mexico	(23 members): Seguro (PES, Portugal)
– the countries of South America and MERCOSUR	(23 members): Di Pietro (ELDR, Italy)

(f) *Asia/Pacific*

Delegations for relations with:

– Japan	(21 members): Schori (PES, Sweden)
– the People's Republic of China	(19 members): Gahrton (UEL-NGL, Sweden)
– the countries of South Asia and the South Asia Association for Regional Cooperation	(18 members): Collins (UEN, Ireland)
– the Member States of ASEAN, South East Asia and the Republic of Korea	(22 members): Nassauer (EPP-ED, Germany)
– Australia and New Zealand	(16 members): Nicholson (EPP-ED, UK)

(g) Delegation for relations with *South Africa*	(17 members): Smet (EPP-ED, Belgium)

Leadership of the delegations

Each delegation is led by a chairman and two vice-chairmen who, like the other members, are elected by the plenary on the basis of nominations submitted to the Conference of Presidents by the Political Groups and the non-attached members. The nominations are designed to ensure as far as possible fair representation of political views and of Member States. This is reflected in the above table whereby the first six Groups in the Parliament by size and all nationalities bar two have delegation chair posts.

In the past, the procedure was somewhat different in that the officers of delegations were appointed by Political Groups on a proportional basis (using the d'Hondt system). In 1989, however, there was intense controversy over this system of appointment, after members of the Technical Group of the Right were chosen as chair of the delegation to Switzerland and vice-chair of the delegation to Israel (with the Technical Group of the Right itself putting forward a German *Republikaner* nominee for the latter post). These nominations were unpopular with the countries concerned, and were also successfully challenged from within the Parliament itself, to the anger of the Technical Group of the Right (see section on Order in the Chamber in Chapter 9).

The change in the system has not eliminated argument. From the end of 1995 to the beginning of 1997, the Canadian parliament refused to cooperate with the Parliament's delegation because it was chaired by a French Europe of Nations member, Georges Berthu, who supported independence for Quebec. The Parliament, for its part, refused to respond to the Canadians' call to find a new chair, taking the view that the choice was a prerogative of the institution and should not be influenced by outsiders. As a result the pattern of annual meetings was broken: there was a break of more than three years between successive meetings of the delegation with its Canadian counterparts.

Role of delegations and joint parliamentary committees

Delegations have a range of tasks. The most obvious of these is to ensure a continuous dialogue and a network of contacts with parliamentary bodies in third countries or in regional organisations such as ASEAN or MERCOSUR, to exchange information on topical issues, to provide parliamentary backing for the Union's external policies, and generally to provide a political counterweight to the work of the Commission and Council in this area.

Another valuable function of delegations is to examine the situation in a third country prior to developments of particular importance to the Union, such as possible accession to the EU, or conclusion of an association agreement, or simply prior to the discussion of the political situation in a country or region within the Parliament.

Delegations, for example, have regularly monitored the situation as regards observance of human rights. An EP delegation was the first ever to be permitted to visit Tibet, in late 1991, where it raised questions of human rights violations with the Tibetan and Chinese authorities. More recently, the Parliament responded to the work of the delegation for relations with the Central Asian Republics by delaying for 18 months its assent to the Partnership and Cooperation Agreement with Uzbekistan. There was a widespread feeling that the human rights clause in the agreement was not being respected and the Parliament insisted on specific improvements before going ahead with its vote in March 1999.

Delegations have also been able to play a role in resolving problems between the Union and third countries. One good example was over the disputes with the United States brought about by the Helms-Burton Act, which seeks to stop third country investment in Cuba, and the Iran-Libya Sanctions Act (ILSA). The delegation has played a significant role in emphasising to Congress that these acts are a breach of international law as well as in brokering a solution. Thus there is at present an understanding in place which has avoided – for the time being – a further escalation of the dispute.

A delegation can help to create new mechanisms for resolving disputes between the EU and third countries. Again, in relation to the United States, there has been a realisation of the importance of early contacts between legislators on both sides of the Atlantic, notably in the wake of the conflict that has arisen over the EU noise pollution directive and the controls that it will impose on aircraft using EU airspace. This conflict arose without either party being fully aware of the likely consequences of the implementation of the directive. As a result, with entry into force of the directive postponed, both sides sought to find a solution, notably through organising meetings of members of the European Parliament and the US Congress. Indeed, there has been a more formal agreement to establish a Transatlantic Legislators' Dialogue, designed to promote early discussions (through a video conference link) on legislative issues likely to generate conflict.

An EP delegation may also use information it acquires to bring influence to bear on other EU institutions rather than on the partner country. This was the case in 1993, when Parliament's CIS delegation received numerous complaints from various former Soviet republics regarding the administration of the TACIS (Technical Assistance to the Commonwealth of Independent States) programme. Too much of the aid money was allegedly being spent on financing studies, often by European consultants, and not enough was actually going in assistance to the beneficiary countries. The delegation, with the help of the Budgets Committee, put in an amendment to the budget effectively freezing part of the 1994 TACIS funds until the Commission, which administered the programme, had made the necessary changes. The Commissioner responsible, Sir Leon Brittan, appeared before the delegation, and promised to set in train appropriate improvements and changes. These were duly implemented, and Parliament was able to release the funds from the budgetary reserve.

A separate word should be added about the role of JPCs since they have recently become of much greater importance in Parliament's work. JPCs operate in the context of association agreements between the EU and countries seeking accession to the Union once the Commission has given a favourable opinion on their accession. In practice many fulfil both functions. In the context of association agreements they examine the workings of the agreement between the Union and the country concerned. In particular, they present a report on the Association Council's annual report and make appropriate recommendations. They may appoint rapporteurs, and their work is thus more formalised than that of traditional interparliamentary delegations. In the context of accession to the Union they monitor the course of the accession negotiations.

Each delegation generally holds an annual interparliamentary meeting, alternately in Strasbourg or Brussels and in the partner country. However, the US delegation traditionally meets twice a year, once in the United States and once in the European Union. The same applies to the Russian delegation and to most of the joint parliamentary committees. Delegations which deal with a geopolitical region rather than with a single country may try to visit two or more of their partners during a single trip abroad, and may likewise host visits in Europe from more than one parliament in a given year.

Besides these regular interparliamentary meetings, preparatory meetings are held in Brussels and Strasbourg, at which members of the delegation discuss the agendas of the visits and the issues to be raised. Ambassadors of the countries accredited to the EU, as well as Commissioners and Commission officials, are often invited to these meetings to brief members.

Relations with the rest of the Parliament

The relationship between delegations and the rest of the Parliament has not always proved easy. The delegations generally operate in an informal way, and are thus not subject to too many political constraints. They must, however, closely reflect the Parliament's resolutions and policy positions if they make any formal declarations during meetings. Working documents drawn up for delegations also follow this same rule, as must those members who are appointed as lead speakers for the delegation on any particular policy issue. Delegations are foreclosed from issuing unilateral statements or bilateral communiqués that contradict Parliament's adopted policy positions. Members expressing a purely personal or Political Group point of view are meant to make this clear.

Despite these rules, there is still a concern to avoid the risk of divergence between the official position of the Parliament and what the members of a delegation say or do. A number of measures have been taken to reduce this risk. Although delegations do not formally adopt reports for the attention of Parliament as a whole, they must all submit a written report on the outcome of each interparliamentary meeting to the Foreign Affairs Committee, which has now placed the work of delegations as a standing item on its agenda. More generally, coordination between delegations and Parliament's standing committees is now a requirement laid down in the Rules of Procedure. When a group of parliamentarians from a third country visits Strasbourg or Brussels, periods of an hour or more are often set aside for joint discussions between them and members of Parliament's relevant committees.

In the same spirit, delegations now regularly invite rapporteurs from the committees to accompany them when their visit relates to the work in committee. In March 1999, for example, Terry Wynn accompanied the relevant delegation on its visit to South Africa, after he had been made rapporteur for the Budgetary Control Committee on a report prepared by the Court of Auditors relating to aid to South Africa. The good management of this aid is of particular importance to the Parliament as the line in the budget was established at its initiative and has now reached a level – €125 million per year – which makes it the largest amount paid from the EU budget to any single country in the world.

As the role and number of delegations increases, their functioning has had to be subject to greater forward planning and to more formalised rules. The activities of the delegations are coordinated by a Conference of Delegation Chairmen (including the Chairmen of JPCs) (see also p. 104). The chair of this meeting is elected by the other chairs and may be invited to attend the relevant meetings of the Conference of Presidents and the Bureau of Parliament. Amongst the duties of the meeting of delegation chairs is the preparation of a calendar of future interparliamentary meetings. The Conference of Presidents then adopts their suggested calendar after consulting the Foreign Affairs Committee. The Conference of Delegation Chairmen also draws up implementing rules for the functioning of delegations, for approval by the Conference of Presidents. These rules codify and formalise the working practices developed within the delegations over the years.

The ACP – EU Joint Assembly

Parliament's day-to-day work on development issues is carried out by its permanent Committee on Development and Cooperation. However, in the specific context of relations with African, Caribbean and Pacific countries, there is a wider body, the ACP-EU Joint Assembly, to which the Parliament nominates a delegation. This Assembly meets twice a year and brings together 142 participants, thereby making it a much larger-scale event than any of the meetings of delegations described in the rest of this chapter. In fact, the Joint Assembly considers itself to be an international parliamentary body in its own right and not simply a forum where delegations from the European Parliament and the ACP countries meet.

The Joint Assembly was established by the Lomé Convention, which links 71 African, Caribbean and Pacific countries. Each ACP country sends one parliamentarian (in almost three-quarters of the cases), or representative (such as their diplomatic representative to the Union) and an equivalent number is sent by the European Parliament, which provides the administrative facilities. The Assembly meets twice a year – once in the EU and once in an ACP country. The meetings in ACP countries rotate around the different ACP Regions, of which there are seven (Pacific, Caribbean and five in Africa), with due consideration, however, being given to reducing costs.

The Lomé Conventions, the fourth of which is at present in force but will expire in February 2000 (after ten years, its three predecessors having been signed for only five years each), have set up a unique instrument of cooperation between a group of developed and a group of developing countries. The main features are: access to the European Union for ACP products, notably free access for manufactured products (other than goods in the agricultural sector); financial co-operation and aid (including STABEX and SYSMIN – which attempt to stabilise export earnings from commodities with fluctuating prices); and on-going dialogue about the ACP countries' economic policies and the EU's support for those policies.

Assembly meetings are attended by the Joint Council and the EU

Commissioner responsible. A Bureau (each side nominating a co-president and twelve vice-presidents) is elected for a term of one year (frequently renewed: on Parliament's side generally for two-and-a-half years as for its own internal bodies, and on the ACP side, for two years) to manage day-to-day affairs. Since direct elections Parliament's co-presidents have all been EPP Group Members:

1979–89   Giovanni Bersani (Italian Christian Democrat)
1989–91   Leo Tindemans (Belgian Christian Democrat)
1991–94   Luisa Cassanmagnago Cerretti (Italian Christian Democrat)
1994–99   Lord Plumb (British Conservative)
1999–   John Corrie (British Conservative)

Ad hoc working parties may be set up (no more than three at any one time) to investigate particular problems in greater depth. Such working parties have ranged very widely dealing with, for example, technology and training, refugees and humanitarian aid, commodities, debt, human rights, industrial development, urbanisation, environmental problems, regional cooperation, fishing, energy, the effects of sanctions and the future of ACP-EU relations.

The main output consists of resolutions. Draft resolutions can be tabled by an ACP representative, a Political Group or ten members of the Joint Assembly, and are then examined by the Bureau before being forwarded to the full Assembly, with recommendations, where appropriate, to negotiate compromises or composites. The Assembly examines a keynote report by a general rapporteur on the whole range of ACP issues. It can appoint rapporteurs on specific issues, and each working group has its rapporteur. A large number of resolutions are examined by the Joint Assembly: 20, for example, were adopted at the meeting in the Bahamas in October 1999.

The Joint Assembly has a question time to the ACP-EU Council of Ministers. Over the last five years the tradition has developed that both ACP and EU Council Presidents-in-Office reply. There is also a question time to the Commission, where the Commissioner for Development replies. Written questions are also possible. Hearings with outside experts are sometimes held.

The Assembly's current priorities include support of democratisation and human rights, conflict prevention, regional cooperation, rural development, the local processing of commodities, better coordination of the Union's development policies with its other policies and the need to promote training in and technology transfer to the developing countries. In the late 1990s it has been particularly involved in the debate on the successor to Lomé IV; indeed it was the central issue at the session in Nassau (Bahamas) in October 1999.

There are several ways in which feedback is provided from the Assembly meetings into Parliament's work as a whole. The main way is through the Parliament's Development and Cooperation Committee, which can draw up reports on specific problems identified at Joint Assembly sessions so that there can be a debate in plenary on what took place, and a resolution adopted on the principal recommendations that have emerged. In addition, the Development Committee draws up an annual report on the work of the Joint Assembly. In view of the weakness of the ACP-EU Council, which is usually attended by very few European ministers (often only by the President-in-Office), the Joint Assembly has acquired an importance that goes far beyond the role that it is allotted formally under the text of the Convention.

Other interparliamentary assemblies

Delegations are involved in the work of other interparliamentary assemblies, which are gradually assuming a greater importance. Thus Parliament's two delegations responsible for Latin America are actively involved in the organisation of the EP-Latin American Parliament Conference. This biennial conference (the fourteenth took place in Brussels in the spring of 1999) is a major event in parliamentary relations, bringing together MEPs with Presidents and high ranking delegations from all over Latin America, together with representatives of other assemblies in the continent including the Andean Parliament and the Central American Parliament (*Parlacen*).

Four delegations (Maghreb, Mashreq, Israel and Palestinian Council) and three JPCs (Turkey, Cyprus and Malta) are active in the development of relations between the EU and the countries of the Mediterranean. The so-called Barcelona process, designed to tighten links between the countries of the Mediterranean, has a parliamentary dimension in the shape of the Euro-Mediterranean Parliamentary Forum. It brings together representatives of the European Parliament, EU Member State parliaments and Mediterranean parliaments.

Parliament also sends members as observers to the WEU Assembly and maintains contacts with the parliamentary assembly of the Council of Europe (which include periodic meetings between delegations of the respective bureaux and cooperation between parliamentary committees). As regards NATO, up to three European Parliament representatives attend the two annual sessions of the North Atlantic Assembly and subsequently report to the Foreign Affairs Committee. The Parliament representatives enjoy informal observer status and may take the floor, both in committee and in plenary.

Ad hoc delegations

Finally, *ad hoc* delegations are sometimes set up by the Conference of Presidents in response to particular political events. Such delegations visited Sarajevo twice during the Bosnian war, and others have undertaken missions to Cyprus (to investigate the question of missing persons), to the Gulf states (following the Iraqi invasion of Kuwait), to the Kurdish regions of Iran and Turkey (to look into alleged human rights abuses), and to Algeria in 1998 at the height of the civil war there.

More often, however, *ad hoc* delegations have been established specifically to observe elections in the numerous countries that have held their first free elections. Since 1989, over 30 such election observation delegations have been dispatched by Parliament to countries around the world. The teams are usually small, consisting of between three and five members assisted by one or two staff. In this way, elections in Kampuchea, Mongolia, various Latin

American and African states and nearly all of the emerging democracies of Central and Eastern Europe have been observed by MEPs, often as part of wider international observation and monitoring efforts.

On three occasions, Parliament has contributed larger election observation teams to European Union 'joint actions'. The first was to observe the Russian general election in December 1993, when 25 MEPs were deployed along with over 100 national MPs from individual Member States. The second was in April 1994, when 14 MEPs joined over 300 EU observers as part of the UN-coordinated observation of the South African parliamentary elections; and the third was to the autonomous Palestinian territories in 1996 on the occasion of the first elections to the Palestinian Legislative Council. More recently, in the summer of 1999, a small group of MEPs observed the independence referendum in East Timor.

Parliament may also send *ad hoc* delegations for its own reasons, to present Parliament's views or to undertake fact-finding activities. Such delegations may well be quite small, consisting of a single member (possibly a rapporteur on the subject) and an official. Parliamentary delegations sometimes participate in international conferences, such as UN, OSCE or G7 Conferences. This is normally done by joining the Union's official delegation, be it the Commission or the Council Presidency.

Overall assessment

The Parliament has established a highly elaborate system of delegations to enable it to develop relations with countries outside the Union. These links have assumed greater importance as the impact of the Union's own internal decisions on the outside world has grown and as the number of agreements requiring the Parliament's assent has increased. The delegations provide one means for the Parliament to acquire the information it needs to make informed judgments on whether or not to give assent as well as to assist the EU as a whole in the pursuit of its objectives.

Delegations have also served to enhance understanding of the EU amongst parliamentarians of third countries and have helped to establish the EU's democratic credentials around the world. The European Parliament uses its delegations to practise a unique form of parliamentary diplomacy. Its delegations, which are often received at the highest levels of state in the countries they visit, act as political ambassadors for Europe in a way that none of the other EU institutions are able or empowered to do.

9.   Plenary

Parliament's plenaries (formally monthly *part-sessions* of an *annual session,* and divided into daily *sittings)* are usually convened for a week each month in Strasbourg with additional days in Brussels (see Chapter 3). The present chapter starts off by examining the setting for each plenary (what it looks like, the seating of members and participation of Commission and Council, staff, press and public) and then outlines the typical timetable of a part-session. It then looks in more detail at the conduct of part-sessions, how the agenda is drawn up, the organisation of debates, voting procedures, order in the chamber, common procedural manoeuvres, and how the session is recorded.

The setting

The Strasbourg sessions took place until May 1999 in the debating chamber or "hemicycle" of the Council of Europe (where the latter's Parliamentary Assembly meets, four times a year). Since the 1999 elections, Parliament uses the debating chamber in the purpose-built building constructed by the French authorities.

The shape of both these chambers is a compromise between differing national parliamentary arrangements. In the UK House of Commons, government and opposition face each other across a central alley; in the German *Bundestag* members face the front in rows and speeches are made from a rostrum; while the French *Assemblée Nationale* sits in a semi-circle in the traditional continental model. The European Parliament is essentially semi-circular, but the opposite ends of the political spectrum do face each other. Every seat in the chamber has a desk, a place to keep documents, and a voting machine.

MEPs sit in the chamber according to their Political Group (before 1958 they sat alphabetically). The Group leaders sit in the front row allocated to the Group. Next to them or immediately behind them are the vice-chairs and other members of the bureau of the Group (normally including leaders of the national delegations within the Group). Behind these are other office holders from the Group (e.g. committee chairs) and then the other members of the Group, seated in alphabetical order. Five of the Groups have their chairmen sitting in the front row of the hemicycle. The other two Groups are situated further back in the chamber, along with the non-attached members.

From the perspective of the President on his dais, the United European Left Group is on the far left of the hemicycle. Next are the Socialists, then the Greens (who previously sat at the back behind the Socialists), then the Liberals. The EPP is now on the right of the chamber with the small

Eurosceptic Groups (Europe of Democracies and Diversities and Europe of Nations) behind them. The non-attached members are in the back mainly on the extreme right, reflecting the political views of the majority of the present non-attached members.

The placing of the Liberals (ELDR) within this seating plan has been the source of some controversy. They used to be on the right of the hemicycle beyond the former European Democratic Group (EDG) which was composed of UK, Danish and Spanish conservatives. The Liberals protested, and some wanted the Group to be located between the EPP and the Socialists. In 1989 the Group was moved over just one place, to sit between the EDG and the EPP. After the members of the EDG joined the EPP in spring 1992, the Liberals again asked to be moved to the centre and were successfully supported in this by the Socialists who wanted to make the point that the EPP, in absorbing the EDG, was becoming more conservative. The EPP were thus shifted further right, but were allowed to stretch across to touch the Socialists (at the back until 1994, subsequently at the front, with the Liberals pushed to the back with other small Groups). In 1999, the Liberals (and the Greens) were given space in the centre all the way from back to front and the EPP, following its absorption of the Gaullists and *Forza Italia*, was moved completely to the right.

Besides the seats allocated to the members, there are a few other seats in the main body of the chamber. A bloc of seats on the left, facing the chamber at an angle, is allocated to the Council, with one seat for a representative from each of the Member States. The seats in the front row are allocated to the relevant minister from the country currently holding the Council Presidency, along with his advisers.

An equivalent bloc of seats on the right, directly opposite the Council, is reserved for the members of the European Commission, with its President occupying one of the seats in the front. While every effort is made to ensure that Commissioners are present to take part in debates affecting their own portfolio, this is not always the case: a rota of Commissioners is established for night sessions and Fridays, when one Commissioner deals with all the business.

At the back, and behind the President's chair, a few seats are reserved for the Political Group staff (one each), and for those Parliament officials whose duties (such as assisting rapporteurs, or following votes on their Committee's reports) require their presence in the chamber. Staff and members can also listen to proceedings on monitors in their offices. There are screens in the chamber and at various locations throughout Parliament's buildings, showing what debate is in progress, and who are the next speakers.

Facing the members are a rostrum and a dais. The rostrum is in practice only used for addresses to the Parliament by distinguished visitors (such as Heads of State), since MEPs and the representatives of the Commission and the Council speak from their seats. On the dais, sits the presiding officer of the Parliament (the President of the Parliament or one of the Vice-Presidents). The presiding officer is flanked by the Secretary-General of the Parliament (on all important occasions) and by other administrators from Parliament's Directorate-General of the Presidency (DGI), who advise the President on difficult procedural points and on matters concerned with the running of the session. Other officials keep tallies on the number of speakers in each debate, and advise members as to how long a debate is scheduled to last, and roughly when they will be called upon to speak.

Two rows of seats behind the dais are used by those officials, including those from Parliament's linguistic services, who keep track of the proceedings for the minutes and daily record of events.

Access to the floor is not open to members of the public and is controlled by parliamentary ushers, who wear a special uniform. They also carry out other tasks in the chamber, such as transmitting messages to or from members, or assisting the President if there is disorder in or immediately outside the chamber.

The public are, however, entitled to follow the sittings from a gallery which is also shared with diplomatic observers and the press. All Parliament's sittings are held in public. In 1999 Parliament deleted a provision in its rules, in practice never used, allowing it to decide by a two-thirds majority, to sit *in camera*.

Behind glass, under the gallery, are interpreters' booths and positions for television crews and technicians, and for those officials from Parliament's information services, whose job it is to follow the sittings.

As in national parliaments, members of the public looking down at the hemicycle may only see a handful of members and wonder where everyone else is. The likelihood is that most of the members are present in the building but are working in their offices (from which they can follow the debates on their television) or taking part in another meeting in one of the many large and small meeting rooms available on the premises. Each Political Group for example has its own meeting room, which can be allocated for other purposes such as for an intergroup (see chapter 10), when it is free. A member may also be addressing a visitors' group, from his or her constituency or elsewhere, or talking to journalists in the press room.

Another frequently used space is the "lobby" immediately outside the hemicycle, which members must cross when leaving the chamber. Seats in this space are often occupied by lobbyists, members of trade associations or the press, and are also used for short meetings between Parliament officials and members. An increasing number of television and radio interviews are conducted outside the hemicycle, and even entire news programmes and chat shows have been made there.

As in all parliaments the bars are also important meeting places, such as the conveniently located Members' Bar near the hemicycle, the Press Bar and the so-called "Swan Bar", which is reached by a passage over the river.

Most of the above-mentioned features apply to the Brussels hemicycle too. The Groups sit in the same pattern and the rostrum and dais are similar.

The typical timetable of a part-session

In a Strasbourg part-session, business begins on **Monday** afternoon, generally with short meetings of the Political Groups, notably to discuss last-minute changes in the agenda, and issues for that day's business.

The sitting in the hemicycle opens at 5:00 p.m., when the President (who presides in person at this stage) makes a number of announcements (such as important procedural statements, announcing the arrival of a new member or the death of another, or that he has sent a message of sympathy to victims of a disaster, or of congratulations, etc.). A number of other procedural declarations (such as which proposals for legislation have been received) are normally not read out in full, but are included instead in that day's minutes.

At the beginning of the sitting there are often a number of more or less bogus points of order from individual members, about constituency or other matters. While these are limited to one minute, they sometimes lead to a mini-debate and can cumulatively take up a considerable amount of time.

The next task is the final fixing of the week's agenda, with Political Groups or numbers of members sometimes trying to make further modifications. Only when this is completed does debate begin on individual items. If there is a report on whether to lift a member's parliamentary immunity (see Chapter 4), this is always taken on Monday. Monday's sitting normally lasts until 7:00 p.m., allowing committees to meet until 9:30 p.m.

The number of **night sittings** lasting until midnight was originally limited to one per week. From 1979–87 these were generally held on Thursdays, but in 1987 they were moved forward to Tuesdays, in order to allow debates on legislation requiring special majorities under the Single European Act to be taken earlier in the week, and thus to permit votes at a time when the maximum of members were present. Since 1992, however, there have been two such sittings at each part-session (usually Monday and Tuesday from 1992–94, now Tuesday and Wednesday).

Tuesday's sitting runs from 9:00 a.m. to 1:00 p.m., 3:00 p.m. to 7:00 p.m., and 9:00 p.m. to midnight. Tuesday's business begins with votes on whether to accept Commission or Council requests for urgent procedure to be applied by Parliament on particular pieces of legislation. There are now usually two or three such requests per session, with Council having agreed in July 1995 to limit such requests. The chairman of the committee responsible is normally called upon to give his or her view, and there can be one speaker in favour, and one against. If urgency is then accepted by Parliament (which happens in about half the cases), the item is usually placed on the Friday's agenda, and if the relevant committee has not already adopted its report on the subject, it will have to hold a special meeting in order to debate and adopt it in the course of the plenary week. (Nevertheless there is nothing to prevent a matter for which urgency has been accepted subsequently being referred back to committee).

The rest of Tuesday's agenda has few particularly distinctive features, although legislative reports are given priority. There is usually a voting time at 12:00 noon, on reports on which the debate has already closed, and which do not require special majorities. Question time to the Commission is usually taken from 5:30 to 7:00 p.m.

Each Council presidency introduces its priorities at the beginning of its term of office, and sums up its achievements at the end. The Commission also presents its annual work programme at the beginning of each year. Debates on Commission and Council programmes of this kind thus occur at least five times a year and usually take place on Tuesdays or Wednesdays. Oral questions with debate, and statements by the Commission or Council (which may be wound up with the adoption of a Parliament resolution) are also usually placed on Tuesday's or Wednesday's agenda. Groups meet again from 7:00 to 9:00 p.m. on Tuesdays and Wednesdays.

Wednesday's sitting lasts from 9:00 a.m. to 1:00 p.m., from 3:00 p.m. to 7:00 p.m., and from 9:00 p.m. to midnight. There is a period of voting time, at 12:00 noon, which can often go on well beyond 1:00 p.m. and includes all votes that may require an absolute majority of Parliament's current members. This is therefore the moment when the highest regular turnout of members must be achieved. A second voting time can be held at 5:00 p.m. Question time to the Council normally takes place from 5.30 to 7.00 p.m.

Thursday's sitting begins at 10:00 a.m.(to allow the Political Groups to meet at 9:00 a.m.), and lasts till 1:00 p.m., and then from 3:00 p.m. to 8:00 p.m. Debates on topical and urgent subjects of major importance are held on Thursday, and take up three hours, with votes thereon grouped together at the end of the debates.

The rest of Thursday's agenda often includes debates carried over from Wednesday's or even Tuesday's agenda. There is one other long voting time on Thursday, beginning at 6:30 p.m., and lasting until 8:00 p.m., or even beyond. Turnout of members is already often lower by this stage, especially if the subject matter is less controversial.

Friday's sitting begins at 9:00 a.m. and goes on as long as is necessary to finish the remaining items unless they are postponed to a subsequent plenary. Friday's sitting may thus last for only a short time, or go on until 1:00 p.m. or even later. Ironically many of the members present on the final morning are those from remote destinations, such as the UK or Ireland, whose most practical way of returning to their country is to take the special plane which leaves at around 2:00 p.m.

Friday begins with votes on those legislative proposals which have been taken without report, and on reports without debate (see Chapter 7), followed by votes on other reports debated the previous day. Once this continuous voting time is over, the agenda continues with the remaining debates. Any resolutions are then put to the vote at the end of the corresponding debate.

The typical week described above refers only to the activities in plenary. Parallel to this are numerous meetings of the Political Groups, intergroups, committees, delegations, etc. Furthermore, the typical schedule can, if necessary, be adjusted (e.g. by starting earlier or curtailing a lunch break). The longest sitting ever was on 13 March 1996 when Parliament sat from 8:00 a.m., and finished at 0:45 a.m. with lunch restricted to 20 minutes.

The timetable of Brussels' plenary sittings is somewhat different. They are now held once between each Strasbourg plenary (except at Christmas and Easter and in October and the summer recess) for just two days, in a week otherwise devoted to committee meetings. They start at 3:00 p.m. on a Wednesday, often with a statement from the Commission, and continue until midnight, resuming the following morning at 10:00 a.m. and finishing with votes at 11:00 or 12:00 p.m., which may go on for an hour or more. Groups meet on the Wednesday morning from 11:00 a.m. to 1:00 p.m. and Thursday from 8:00 or 9:00 a.m. to 10:00 a.m.

How the plenary agenda is drawn up

Unlike many national parliaments, the European Parliament is master of its own agenda. It may discuss (or not) what it likes, when it likes, and according to its own priorities. It cooperates, of course, with the other institutions in dealing with proposals for legislation, and they in turn have a vested interest in cooperating with Parliament in order to ensure smooth passage of proposals. Only as of the second reading of legislative procedures and in the budget procedure is Parliament bound by a formal deadline, laid down in the Treaties.

The drawing up of the plenary agenda is therefore an elaborate process. As regards the legislative and non-legislative reports from committees, informal meetings are held between the officials of Parliament's committees to monitor progress on reports within committees, and to see which items are likely to be ready for forthcoming plenaries. The meeting of committee chairmen, which is held every month, provides a more formal opportunity for stock-taking and to discuss which reports are ready, and which reports could be accelerated or held back. This is then submitted to the Conference of Presidents where each Group chair will also bring the requests of their Group (e.g. for oral questions with debate or for requests for Commission or Council statements) and express a view on the relative priorities of committee reports.

The Conference of Presidents then prepares a preliminary draft agenda, taking account of a number of constraints. Parliament may have undertaken to give a legislative proposal priority, and where possible, to deal with it within a certain time frame within the context of the annual legislative programme (see Chapter 12) established with the Commission and Council. Any Council common positions in the cooperation or co-decision procedures must be considered within three (or a maximum of four) months of their official receipt. Legislative items are thus given priority on Parliament's agenda.

The Commission and the Council try to influence Parliament's agenda and are invited to attend the relevant meeting of the Conference of Presidents. The Political Groups, meeting in the week before the plenary, may push for further changes, and the Conference of Presidents' meeting on the Thursday before the Strasbourg plenary adopts the final draft agenda which is distributed to all MEPs and examined by Parliament at the beginning of the part-session. A Political Group, a committee, or 32 members, may propose changes in writing up to one hour before the opening of the part-session. Each such request is moved by one member and there is one speaker for and one against, followed by a vote on the request.

The agenda is then formally adopted. In practice, however, it is often subsequently modified, either because urgent requests from Commission or Council are accepted by the Parliament on Tuesday morning, or because unexpected events (e.g. emergency debates on Commission declarations) or straightforward delays mean that items are carried over from one day to the next. There can also be, as we shall see, a number of other, procedural manoeuvres to modify the agenda.

Topical and urgent debates

One or two periods, together totalling a maximum of three hours, are set aside each month for debates on topical and urgent subjects of major importance. In practice this now tends to be a single three-hour period on Thursdays of Strasbourg part-sessions.

The Conference of Presidents puts forward up to five subjects in the draft agenda that may be changed when Parliament adopts the agenda. The main criteria for selection of topics are laid down in Annex III of Parliament's Rules of Procedure. These include the need for Parliament to express a view before a particular event has taken place, to react quickly to current events, or to comment on a major issue within the Union's responsibilities. Resolutions can be directed to Council, the Commission, the Member States, third countries or international bodies. The significance of these resolutions is discussed in chapter 16.

Compared to normal plenary debates the debates on topical and urgent issues have several distinctive features. There is much less speaking time. There are no explanations of vote. There can be no requests for inadmissibility of a motion, or for motions to be referred back to a committee. No one can call for a debate to be adjourned, though a quorum call can be made. The votes are taken together at the end.

A compromise motion is put to the vote in place of the first resolution that it is meant to replace. It is now the practice to adopt a single resolution on each issue (except for human rights and disasters). All motions not included in the final list of topics automatically lapse, as do resolutions on which there is no time left to vote.

The allocation of speaking time in debates

Debates in plenary, whatever their origin (legislative or non-legislative reports, oral questions with debate, or debates on statements by the President of the European Council, the Commission or the Council), have many similar features in the way they are structured. A first important decision is on the allocation of speaking time for the debates, on which the President makes proposals after consulting the Political Groups. These proposals are outlined in the draft agenda for the plenary, and are divided into speaking time for debates on Monday, Tuesday, Wednesday and Thursday (with topical and urgent debates subject to a separate procedure and thus excluded). Speaking time is allocated to Commission and Council, rapporteurs and draftsmen of opinions, authors of motions, and finally to Political Groups to allocate to their members. Rule 120 of Parliament's Rules of Procedure lays down the guidelines for distribution of speaking time between members. A first fraction of speaking time is divided equally among all the Political Groups, and a further and more important fraction is divided among the Political Groups and non-attached members in proportion to the total number of their members.

An illustration of what this allocation of speaking time means in practice can be seen in the agenda for the morning of Tuesday 5 October 1999 in which there were 150 minutes of speaking time to be distributed. The Commission was given 40 minutes (including replies); Parliament's rapporteurs ten (five minutes each to two rapporteurs); draftsmen of opinions from other Committees four (two at two minutes each). The remaining 150 minutes were distributed to the Groups as follows: EPP-ED 52, Socialists 41, Liberals 13, Greens 12, European Left 11, Europe of Nations 8, EDD 5 and the non-attached members 8.

Once this allocation of speaking time has been made, the Political Groups then indicate how much of their overall time they wish to use in each individual debate. They also divide up their speaking time among members within their Group.

A typical debate on a committee report begins with a five-minute statement by the rapporteur from the committee responsible presenting its conclusions. If it is a report on a legislative proposal, the Commission will then give its initial response. Draftsmen of opinions from other committees will also often choose to speak, though for a shorter time. The main Group spokespersons for the issue then speak in descending order of the size of Groups. Some Groups may wish to allocate most of their speaking time to their main spokesperson, while others may prefer to give smaller amounts to several members. An electronic board shows how much of a member's speaking time has elapsed, and indicates when it has come to an end by means of flashing asterisks. The presiding officer then requests the speaker to stop, and if he or she fails to do so, can cut off the speaker's microphone.

At the end of a debate the Commission will reply. This is the moment when, for legislative resolutions, the Commission will indicate its position on specific amendments tabled in the report before the Parliament. In some cases the Commission will give a very lengthy reply, which cuts into the time allocated for subsequent debates. The Commission's allocation of speaking time is purely indicative, as the Treaty gives the Commission an unlimited right to intervene.

A debate on a Commission or Council statement will begin with the statement and be followed by Group spokespersons, starting with one from each Group in descending order of their size. The Commission and/or Council will reply at the very end. However, Parliament can decide instead to have thirty minutes of short and concise questions and answers instead of a full debate.

Time for debates is thus strictly limited, with a corresponding lack of scope for spontaneity, or cut and thrust exchanges between individual members. This is reinforced by a tendency for many members to read out their speeches. Nevertheless certain members do try and continue debates through other means, such as attempted points of order, or in their explanations of vote. These are often livelier occasions than the debates themselves, where set positions that have often already been aired in committee, are presented again.

Voting procedures

Members of the public, lobbyists or journalists who attend Parliament's plenary sessions to follow a particular subject are often surprised to find that the vote on a particular report does not usually follow the debate, but comes only at voting time, which may take place a day later (the main exception is Friday morning).

This separation between debate and final vote may seem illogical, but there are several reasons why this is done. One is the unpredictability of the duration of votes: if voting followed each debate, it would be even more difficult to plan the organisation of debates within the small number of days available at each session. The variety of activities that take place during plenary sessions would have to be interrupted every time there was a vote.

Votes are thus grouped at certain fixed moments of the week. The most important such voting time is 12:00 noon on Wednesday when the main legislative votes are taken.

Although members thus have a good indication of when voting time will take place they are also reminded by division bells, which can be heard throughout the buildings, shortly before a vote will take place (as well as ten minutes before a sitting; and when it starts).

Voting is a personal right and no proxy voting is permitted. There are two main ways of voting, by a simple show of hands and by electronic voting. Secret ballots may also be used, but are only required for election of the President, Vice-Presidents and Quaestors. The Rules of Procedure also permit voting by sitting and standing (when a vote by show of hands is unclear) and also by full roll call vote with members replying "yes", "no", or "I abstain" in alphabetical order, but electronic voting has now replaced both methods in practically all instances. Electronic voting is used when the result of a vote is unclear, or if a formal roll call vote has been requested in writing by at least 32 members or a Political Group before voting has begun, or to check that a particular majority of members has been obtained when required by the Treaties.

The electronic voting system was first installed in May 1980. Members must insert their voting card in the voting machine on their desk, (or, indeed, any desk as the machine will recognise their card) and press the appropriate button: a green light comes on for a "yes" vote, red for a "no" vote, and yellow for an abstention (and blue for a secret ballot). When the President announces an electronic vote, a reference to the text being voted (a paragraph, amendment or final text) is displayed on a small screen built in to the voting machine as well as on the electronic scoreboard. Members out of their places must then rush back to them in time, creating a scramble at moments of close and tense voting. Sometimes before the result is finally announced, certain members will catch the attention of the President to say that their voting machine was not working, and telling him or her how they voted. These are then added to the tally.

The final results (which appear after about five seconds) are displayed on the screens and on the electronic scoreboard. If a roll call vote (RCV) has been requested, the result of each member's vote is formally recorded, first in a special annex to the minutes which appears the next day, and later in the translated minutes which come out in the Official Journal of the European Communities about three months later (although unofficially a print-out is available in the press room within half an hour of the vote).

Roll call votes tend to be called by Political Groups for three main reasons. First, to put a Group's position on an issue firmly on record; second to embarrass another Group by forcing the latter to take a publicly recorded stance on an issue; and third, to keep a check on their own members' participation in a vote, and the position they take.

Whatever the reason for a recorded roll call vote, it provides a very valuable but currently relatively under-utilised source for assessing the political positions taken by a Political Group and by individual members. It could, for instance, be used by European interest groups the way American congressmen's voting records are assessed by the Washington-based lobbies. However, it is a tool that must be used with caution. It is easiest, for example, to assess a roll call vote on the finally adopted text, whereas the most significant vote may have been on a specific amendment. Deciding which vote was significant requires considerable knowledge of the issue at stake.

The electronic voting system has also had the great advantage of ensuring that Parliament's votes are now comparatively rarely contested, except when only one or two votes separate the two sides, and members complain that their voting machines did not work, and that they did not catch the eye of the President beforehand. There have been accusations that certain members have double voted by voting for absent colleagues but these have been extremely rare. The system works remarkably well.

Voting order

Parliament has laid down standard procedures for the order in which votes are taken, that differ as between non-legislative and legislative texts.

When a **non-legislative** text is put to the vote, Parliament first votes on amendments to specific parts of a resolution. When there are several amendments it normally begins by voting on that furthest removed from the original text, although the President has discretion to do otherwise. He may also put complementary or similar amendments to the vote en bloc. If an amendment is adopted, then subsequent contradictory amendments or text fall. Requests may also be made for separate votes on an amendment or the original paragraph so that votes can be taken on its component parts. Such a request for a split vote may be made by a Group or 32 members the evening before the vote (so that Group whips have advance notice).

Once the voting on the separate amendments is concluded, Parliament then votes on the motion for a resolution as a whole, as amended. An opportunity is given for explanations of vote by individual members (orally or in writing, see Chapter 4), normally after this final vote. Oral explanations are limited to one minute for individual members and two minutes for an explanation of vote on behalf of a Group. Written explanations of vote are limited to 200 words, and are included in the verbatim record of proceedings. Explanations are not allowed on procedural matters.

Most votes on non-legislative resolutions require simple majorities only. Unless a quorum call is made (see below) or an electronic vote taken there is no check on how many members are actually voting.

Certain non-legislative votes of a procedural or decision-making nature, however, do require special majorities. These include amendments to Parliament's Rules of Procedure, which require a majority of the total number of members, and censure votes on the Commission which require a two-thirds majority of the votes cast, representing a majority of the current members of Parliament.

Voting on **legislative texts** is similar in terms of the order of voting on amendments, and the possibility of explanations of vote. The main difference is that a distinction is made between voting on the Commission or Council text (including amendments to it, specific paragraphs or articles of the text, and the proposal as a whole) and voting on the accompanying draft legislative resolution. After voting on the former is completed but before Parliament completes its procedure by voting on the draft legislative resolution, the Commission is asked to react to (and the Council to comment on) Parliament's amendments or in extreme cases, its rejection of the proposal. If the Commission gives an unsatisfactory response, or is not in a position to react immediately, the vote on the draft legislative resolution may then be postponed for a period sufficient to allow the responsible committee time to examine the situation. This period may not exceed two months unless the Parliament decides to extend it. Until Parliament finally votes on the draft legislative resolution, it has not officially spoken.

This possibility for separating votes on a Commission proposal and the accompanying draft legislative resolution is an important procedural device developed by the Parliament to reinforce its role in the legislative process. Its significance is described in greater detail in Chapter 12.

The above procedure applies to legislative resolutions in first reading or if there is a single reading by the Parliament. In second or third readings special procedures apply. Whereas single readings or first readings require simple majorities, in second reading, if Parliament wishes to amend or reject Council's position, an absolute majority is required. Furthermore, Parliament cannot delay, as it must act within three months, with the possibility of a further extension of one month. Parliament has developed rules for determining the moment from which the three-month period is to run, namely when it has received, in all the official languages, the common position, the Council's explanation of how it was reached, and the Commission's reaction. Only then does the President of Parliament announce receipt of the common position during the relevant plenary session.

In second reading Parliament may adopt the Council's common position as such, reject it outright or adopt amendments. In the first case there need be no plenary vote at all (with the President of Parliament simply declaring it to be adopted in the absence of any other proposal). In the second and third cases, however, an absolute majority of the current members is required to reject a text or to amend it. The consequences of these procedures are again described in more detail in Chapter 12.

In third reading, Parliament votes on a proposal from its delegation to the conciliation committee with Council. If agreement has been reached in the committee, a simply majority is enough to approve or reject it.

A final word should be added as regards the **amendments** that are voted upon in plenary. These are subject to certain rules. First, they must be tabled by a deadline set down for each report or resolution. For most reports this is mid-day on the Thursday of the week preceding the plenary session, but for more urgent topics the deadline is set for a moment during the plenary itself, and is announced by the President of Parliament. Second, amendments are generally put to the vote only when they have been printed and distributed in all the official languages. Parliament may decide otherwise, but not if 12 members or more object. Inevitably the practice in plenaries is more formal in this respect than in committee meetings. Third, plenary amendments may only be tabled by a Political Group, the committee responsible for the report, or at least 32 members. Committees asked for an opinion, for example, may not table amendments in plenary.

Building majorities: bargaining among Groups

The only major exception to the deadline for tabling amendments is where compromise amendments are put forward by Political Groups, or committee chairmen or rapporteurs. The President of Parliament must examine their admissibility, and must then obtain the agreement of Parliament before they are put to the vote. Such compromise amendments would typically entail the withdrawal of texts tabled by different Groups in favour of one composite text. It is relatively difficult to reach last-minute agreement on a compromise amendment that will satisfy all Political Groups, and agreement is often reached between two or three Groups only, notably when these Groups together constitute a majority. It is also common for two or more Groups to agree to support some of each other's amendments without any being formally withdrawn.

In the case of resolutions winding up debates on statements by the Commission, Council or European Council, or on oral questions, or on topical or urgent debates where most Political Groups will have tabled their own motion for resolution, the "compromise amendment" may take the form of a compromise resolution tabled by some (or possibly all) Groups. If adopted, the other motions fall.

The technical aspects of the compromise negotiations are taken care of by the secretariat of the Political Group chairing the meetings of the Group chairs for a six month period, which is responsible for issuing invitations, booking rooms, providing secretarial assistance, etc.). Normally, all Groups that have introduced a resolution are invited to participate in the negotiations on the compromise text. There are no fixed rules as to who represents a Political Group at the meeting (a Group member, a Group member accompanied by a staff member, a staff member) or about the number of representatives.

Compromise resolutions are often elaborated under considerable time pressure, which does not facilitate the preparation of quality texts. A commitment to sign a compromise text is normally taken at the end of the negotiations. It may happen that concessions are made to a particular Group during the negotiation process on a specific point, without any guarantee that this Group will sign the compromise.

There is no distinct pattern as to the coalitions that are formed during negotiations, but the fact that the EPP and the PES can together reach a majority means that there is a premium on compromises between them. The smaller Groups often intervene mainly on those points where they have a particular interest.

A particular problem arises from the fact that the EPP has a working method that differs substantially from that of the PES. On key issues (summits etc.) the EPP elaborates a lengthy resolution, with a number of chapters, each being drafted under the authority of a particular member. Furthermore, all the specialists involved participate in the negotiations, with the result that other Groups' single representatives can be confronted with four or five EPP members during negotiations – though this is not necessarily to the EPP's advantage.

Despite efforts to draft concise texts with clear priorities, texts tend to be made longer during the negotiations, as a compromise can be more easily obtained by including more issues.

Common procedural manoeuvres

Parliament's Rules provide considerable scope for procedural man-oeuvres by individual members or by Groups. The most important of these are the right to make points of order, request whether there is a quorum and to request referral back to committee. Other possibilities are to move the inadmissibility of a matter, the closure or adjournment of a debate or the suspension or closure of the sitting.

By far the most frequently used of these devices are points of order (Rule 142). They last for one minute and take precedence over other business. They are meant to refer to abuse of a specific rule, or to request clarification from the President of Parliament (e.g., pointing out that a text has not been translated into the speaker's language). However, bogus points of order are used to bring totally different subjects onto the agenda, to respond to an event that has just taken place, to make a constituency point, to criticise another member, to criticise a ruling by the President, to participate in a debate when not due to do so, or to continue a concluded debate by other means. On certain occasions, such as the opening of the sitting on Monday afternoon, or after a controversial ruling by the presiding officer of the Parliament, they can lead to mini-debates.

The other procedural devices cited above are mainly used for one reason, to get a controversial item off the plenary agenda, and thus to postpone or block Parliament's decision on the matter. The most commonly used rule to achieve this is Rule 144, providing for referral of a matter back to commit-tee. This is often done by the responsible committee itself, if difficulties have emerged during a debate, or if new developments or an unsatisfactory response by the Commission require reconsideration of the matter within the committee.

A request for referral back, however, may only be made when the agenda is adopted, or at the start of the debate, or at the vote. As on other pro-cedural matters, the President, after having heard the mover of the motion, will then call for one speaker in favour and one against. If it is a committee report, the committee chairman, or rapporteur, may also speak. Parliament then proceeds to a vote on the request, and if it is adopted, the debate (if applicable) and the final vote are postponed to a future plenary. Requests for referral back are sometimes accompanied by requests that the matter be placed on the next plenary agenda, but this is not automatic.

Another, and more controversial, device to postpone a vote is through a request to ascertain the quorum. Most plenary decisions can be taken by simple majority, without any particular number of members being present (unlike committee decisions, where a quarter of the membership must be present), unless there is an objection that the quorum of one-third of Parliament's members is not present. At least 32 members (but not a Political Group) may request that the quroum be checked. The President asks these members to stand up so that they can be counted. The President will then put a particular amendment or point to the vote, and announce whether or not the quorum (209 members) has been attained. If it has not been, the vote is then placed on the agenda of the next sitting.

The 32 or more members who request a quorum count are automatically included in the number of members counted as being present in the chamber for the purpose of establishing the quorum. This interpretation of the Rule was made after an incident when one particular group of members made a quorum call, and subsequently walked out of the chamber to ensure that a quorum was indeed not present.

Quorum calls are most likely on a Friday morning, when attendance is at its lowest. Fridays therefore tend to be reserved for less controversial items. Quorum calls may not be used for preventing debate or for preventing the adoption of the agenda or the minutes. In other words, they cannot bring Parliament itself to a halt.

Other procedural devices are less frequently used. To find that a matter is inadmissible, for example, is relatively rare, since the range of issues debated by the Parliament is so vast. Motions to move closure or adjournment of a debate tend to be used only for genuine timetabling reasons. One other reason used to be to challenge the legal base of a proposal and insist that a report not be voted upon in plenary until the Legal Affairs Committee had given its view as to whether the proposed treaty article for the proposal was the correct one. However, the rules were changed in 1999 to require any such challenges to have been raised already at committee stage.

An extreme case of procedural moves being used to try to block a report was during Parliament's consideration of the Prag report on the working place of the Parliament in January 1989 (see Chapter 3), which was strongly opposed by members supporting Strasbourg and Luxembourg in particular. A number of procedural devices were used to try and get the issue off the agenda. First, when the agenda was set, an unsuccessful attempt was made to remove the report from the agenda. When the debate started, a further unsuccessful attempt was made to refer it back to committee. A request for the debate to be adjourned until Friday was adopted, but the sitting was then suspended, and the President used his discretion to propose to reinstate the item at its original place on the Wednesday agenda, to which Parliament agreed. Finally, when the text was put to the vote (after a successful motion to close the debate prematurely) roll call votes were requested on each amendment, and a further unsuccessful attempt made to suspend the sitting.

Order in the chamber

Lack of order is only rarely a problem within the European Parliament, whose proceedings are usually rather calm, especially in comparison with certain national parliaments like the UK House of Commons. The variety of languages used, and of also of national parliamentary traditions, means that there tends to be less spontaneous repartee between individual members, and fewer interruptions of members while they are speaking. Furthermore, many debates are rather technical. Nevertheless the European Parliament is livelier than some of the national parliaments in the Member States. When Hanja Maij-Weggen, a long-serving MEP, was appointed as Minister in the Dutch government, and her aggressive debating style was commented upon in the Dutch Parliament, she claimed to have learnt the technique from British members of the European Parliament. Although there are relatively few moments of high drama within the European Parliament, this does not mean that there are not occasionally very lively debates, or periods of unrest in the chamber when a presiding officer's decision is contested.

There have also been a number of individual demonstrations within the chamber, many by the Parliament's "outsider" members, though it is fair to say that in recent years such incidents have been rare, perhaps reflecting Parliaments' transition from being just a forum to being a partner in the EU's decision- taking procedures. In February 1981 Mario Capanna (of the Italian Proletarian Democracy Party) held up a Palestinian flag in the Chamber during an address to Parliament by President Sadat of Egypt. Ian Paisley disrupted the visit of the Pope and had to be removed from the chamber after having been warned by the President. In July 1989, Green MEPs came into the Chamber wearing UK Green T-shirts to protest against the absence of UK Greens due to the British electoral system. In October 1989, members of the then Group of the Right protested at their exclusion from leadership posts within Parliament's interparliamentary delegations, eventually causing a scuffle, with the suspension of the sitting and with the lights being switched off in the chamber.

As a result of this incident, Parliament revised its Rules of Procedure to provide for members to be called twice to order by the President if they create a disturbance in the chamber. On the second occasion their offence is recorded in the minutes. If there is a further repetition, the President may exclude the offender from the chamber for the rest of the sitting (Parliament's ushers are given the delicate task of actually removing the member from the chamber if he or she refuses to leave). Parliament may pass a vote of censure in serious cases of disorder, automatically involving immediate exclusion from the chamber, and suspension for two to five days, including loss of attendance allowance. (This power was used against a Portuguese member, Rosado, who hit a Danish member, Blak, in December 1997 after a vigorous exchange in a debate on tobacco subsidies.)

A final such rule provides for closure or suspension of the sitting by the President when disturbances in Parliament threaten to obstruct the business of the house or if an unexpected political situation arises. This rule has only been used sparingly, and more for political deadlocks needing compromise during votes than for disturbances.

Record of plenary sittings

Two sets of documents are prepared on a daily basis. First, there are the daily *minutes* of each session, which are divided into two parts. Part I records the business that took place, who spoke, the procedural decisions, the overall results of voting on amendments and texts and the complete register of members present for the day's business (prepared on the basis of lists signed by members at one of two locations within the chamber). Part II contains the texts finally adopted by the Parliament. The minutes are translated into all the official languages for distribution at least half an hour before the opening of the next sitting (i.e. usually the following morning). They are approved on that occasion, unless objections are raised. The minutes are subsequently published in the Official Journal of the European Communities.

Second, there is the *verbatim report* of the proceedings of each sitting. The initial version, available the following day at around noon, is familiarly known as the "Rainbow" because it contains the members' speeches in the languages in which they were given. Members wishing to make technical corrections to the transcripts of their speeches are required to do so not later than the day following that on which they received them. The "Rainbow" is eventually translated into all the official languages, and published as an annex to the Official Journal of the European Communities, which thus serves as a full record of what was said on which subject at each plenary session. This is important not just in terms of recording for posterity the views of MEPs, but also as an official record of positions taken by the Commission and Council on subjects not always of their own choosing. Attempts to cut down on the translation of debates on the grounds of cost have so far all failed.

Besides these official records, Parliament's press and information service publishes a daily summary of debates and events.

"Open" Bureau and Conference of Presidents

In 1991–92, before an equipped hemicycle was available in Brussels, a number of meetings held in similar conditions to plenary sittings took place in Brussels, although they were expressly not described as such. They were referred to instead as meetings of the Enlarged Bureau open to all members. The origins of this innovation are described on page 30. They were used mainly for topical statements by the Commission and, on occasion, for contacts with visiting statesmen. They have now been superseded by Brussels part-sessions. However the practice was revived in 1999 as open meetings of the Conference of Presidents in order to hear statements from the Commission on the decisions taken at its weekly meetings on Wednesdays, and to answer questions. It has been suggested that these meetings might become short weekly plenary sittings.

Formal sittings

Parliament accepts requests by Heads of State of the Member States or of third countries to address the Parliament in so-called "formal sittings". These are often held on the Wednesday of the Strasbourg plenary week, and are not treated as a normal sitting in that there can be no points of order, procedural motions, etc.

10. Intergroups

A striking development in the Parliament since direct elections has been the creation of a large number of informal "intergroups", consisting of members from different Political Groups with a common interest in a particular political theme (similar to "all party groups" in the UK House of Commons). This chapter briefly traces the evolution of intergroups, gives an indication of their scale and diversity and examines their advantages and disadvantages, including the rules to which they are subject. It concludes by looking in more detail at three specific intergroups as case studies, dealing variously with a European Constitution, Welfare and Conservation of Animals, and Sport.

The evolution of intergroups since 1979

A number of intergroups were established shortly after the first direct elections in 1979 and requested official recognition (i.e. that Parliament provide and finance the necessary logistics, such as a meeting room and interpretation). It was very quickly realised, however, that Parliament would not be able to provide facilities for all intergroups. The Parliament's Bureau took a restrictive position, deciding only to give official recognition to the Intergroup of Elected Local and Regional Representatives, founded in 1980. No other intergroups have been granted formal status since, despite many requests. Intergroups, therefore, have to meet with only restricted facilities, or with facilities provided by sympathetic Political Groups.

This has not, however, prevented a dramatic growth in the number of intergroups. The precise number is hard to gauge but towards the end of the 1994-99 Parliament, 58 intergroups were registered with the EP Secretary-General, of which 12 claimed to have funding, and over 30 a special logo. At the beginning of the 1999–2004 legislature the total figure was still higher at around 80 as indicated in Table 20 at the end of this chapter. The list can only be indicative: it does not necessarily include all intergroups and may include some whose level of activity is very low or sporadic. Nevertheless, it gives a good sense of the diversity of intergroups.

The importance of the groups in the list is far from uniform. Some hold regular meetings, have prominent visiting speakers, large attendances and their own secretariat, sometimes on a practically full-time basis. Others represent the hobby-horses of a small group of members and have few resources and infrequent meetings. Their sources of support are also extremely varied: some are assisted by the Political Groups, others get backing from the Commission's budget and others again obtain help in terms of staffing and finance from industry. Groups in the last category include the

Kangaroo Group, a group which is committed to the elimination of all barriers to the free movement of goods, services and people across the internal frontiers of the European Union: it is funded by a corporate membership scheme. Rules on membership also vary widely: in some cases, it is limited to MEPs, in others, members can also include trade association or other external members. An intergroup has even been founded (Global Legislators for a Balanced Environment, GLOBE for short) with members from the US Congress, Japanese Diet, Russian Parliament and others.

A few intergroups have broad-focus political goals, such as the European Constitution Intergroup and the Animal Welfare and Conservation Group (both discussed below), or the Consumer Affairs and Minority Languages intergroups. Others have less explicit political goals, but provide a focus for those interested in sharing their experiences (such as the Intergroup of Elected Local and Regional Representatives) or discussing issues within a particular field (such as the Audiovisual Intergroup).

Others have a narrower focus, and concentrate more on promoting specific interests, be they industrial (in the past, for example, there was Wings of Europe, concerned with the aeronautical industry, and a TGV or High Speed Train Intergroup), regional (mining regions, Atlantic regions, islands and maritime regions in the EU), or particular national or political causes (Tibet, East Timor, Euro-Arab, Friends of Israel, Friends of Hong Kong, etc.).

The scale of intergroup activity is significant, especially during the plenary sessions in Strasbourg where their meetings are normally held and feature prominently on the list of scheduled meetings on Parliament's notice boards, in meeting rooms often put at their disposal by individual Political Groups. There are fewer such meetings in Brussels. Members tend to be in Brussels more frequently but for shorter lengths of time. Strasbourg, which is more difficult to reach and leave, and where members come for longer, and where there is much more overlapping of attendance, is thus more suitable for intergroup activities.

Advantages and disadvantages

Intergroups have developed because they have a number of major advantages. They permit members to focus on a particular set of issues of specific national, constituency or personal concern. They enable them to specialise, make contacts with outside interest groups on a more informal basis than in committee meetings, and make political contacts outside their own Political Groups. A member may sometimes find that he or she has more in common on some issues with certain members in other Groups. Intergroups thus not only help to form cross-Group coalitions on specific issues, but to forge wider political friendships which can be useful in other circumstances, and can help to build that wider consensus which is often essential in the European Parliament. Finally, intergroups can also provide new roles and responsibilities for members and their assistants.

The very success of intergroups, however, has meant that they can constitute a rival centre of attention to official parliamentary activities, and in certain circumstances may undercut the latter. They may lead to lower attendances at committee and plenary. There have even been occasions when prominent outside speakers have been reluctant to address a committee meeting because they have already appeared before an intergroup.

There have also been concerns that a few intergroups are too closely linked with, or are even being manipulated by certain lobbies. For all these reasons attempts have been made to limit their proliferation. The Political Group chairmen in June 1995 reached an agreement, subsequently ratified by the Conference of Presidents in December 1995, in which they reaffirmed that intergroups had no official status, were not organs of the Parliament, could not express the Parliament's point of view, and could not use its name or logo, or any other denominations which could lead to confusion with other official organs of the Parliament. At the same time they established specific rules governing the provision of technical facilities by Political Groups, including:

- the obligation never to meet during a scheduled voting session of the Parliament;
- the communication to the chairmen of the Political Groups concerned of the list of persons responsible, from at least three Political Groups, the denomination of the intergroup and its logo, if any, and funding sources; and
- the obligation to comply with the rules concerning the declaration of financial interests of MEPs and assistants and the rules on lobbyists.

The responsible committee of Parliament later examined (in 1998–99) a draft report on the financing and operation of groups of members. This pointed out that it was still not possible to make an adequate assessment of the influence of outside interests on intergroups (for example, several groups were registered as having no external source of finance although they received secretarial aid from outside bodies). It also noted that there was no one consolidated and easily accessible register of groupings receiving outside support (the register at the Secretary-General's office only gave an intergroup's leadership, and did not indicate which MEPs are members or regular participants of which grouping).

As a result of the report, the provisions of Annex 1 of the EP Rules on transparency and members' financial interests were tightened up. Chairmen of intergroups and other unofficial groupings of members were required to declare any support, whether in cash or kind (e.g. secretarial assistance) which would have to be declared if offered to members as individuals. The Quaestors were also made responsible for keeping a register and drawing up detailed rules for the declaration of outside support by such groupings.

In November 1999 a new draft set of rules was being examined by Parliament's governing bodies as regards the constitution of intergroups. This would further reinforce existing rules. The declaration of financial interests would have to be made on an annual basis, the Quaestors' register would have to be made public, the precise objectives of each intergroup would have to be clarified, and there would be strict regulation of when they could meet. The establishment of an intergroup would require the agreement of three Group chairs, each of whom could support only a limited number.

Specific intergroups

To provide something of the flavour of the way in which intergroups operate, a brief description is given below of the objectives and working methods of three intergroups. The first is committed to establishing a European Constitution, the second is concerned with issues linked to the welfare and conservation of animals and the third was set up to promote sport at the European level.

European Constitution Intergroup

Set up in 1999, this is the latest in a series of intergroups that have followed on from the original Crocodile Club established after the first direct elections. The Crocodile Club was an informal discussion group, named after the Strasbourg restaurant where it first met, and created by Altiero Spinelli, with the aim of getting Parliament to take the initiative in constitutional change in the Community. The Crocodile Club was the initiator of the decision to create a special Committee on Institutional Affairs within Parliament, and it was this committee which prepared Parliament's proposal for a "Treaty on European Union" in 1984, which in turn led to the negotiation of the Single European Act (see Chapter 17).

The Federalist Intergroup was set up in 1986, soon after the death of Altiero Spinelli, by those who considered the Single Act to be an insufficient step towards European Union, and who sought to continue Spinelli's work for "achieving European Union through the effort of the European Parliament, the only democratically representative institution at Community level". It immediately attracted about 150 members, despite a hefty membership fee. These members covered all Political Groups (except the European Right) and all nationalities. It held monthly meetings during sessions in Strasbourg (and extra ones in Brussels), adopted a Political Declaration and detailed rules of procedure and set up a Bureau whose dozen members rotated monthly in the chairmanship. It appointed a Secretary-General, Virgilio Dastoli, the former personal assistant of Spinelli, who was assisted by a volunteer Federalist Intergroup Support Group (FIGS) composed of students in Brussels in the Federalist Youth Movement.

The intergroup's activities were mainly directed outside Parliament, but it also co-ordinated the position of the more "maximalist" members of the Committee on Institutional Affairs. It set up federalist intergroups in a number of national parliaments, which held joint meetings. It sponsored several opinion polls in all the Member States (financed by selling exclusive rights to newspapers). These showed clear majorities in all except two Member States (UK and Denmark) for such things as a European government accountable to the European Parliament, legislative powers for the European Parliament, and giving Parliament the task of drafting a constitution for European Union. The referendum held in Italy at the same time as the 1989 European elections on this last point was a direct result of the intergroup pressing for this, together with its counterpart in the Italian Parliament and the Federalist Movement in Italy.

After the negotiations for the Maastricht Treaty it became less active but was later revived as "SOS-Europe" by members disillusioned by the lack of progress on institutional matters in the Treaty of Amsterdam. Its initial leadership consisted of Jean-Louis Bourlanges (EPP,France), Dany Cohn-Bendit (Greens, then Germany), Olivier Duhamel (PES, France), Gianfranco dell'Alba (ERA, Italy) and Antoinette Spaak (ELDR, Belgium), and 55 other members associated themselves with the initiative. In particular, it saw itself as a lobby for making more sweeping institutional reforms to better prepare the EU for its future enlargement.

After the 1999 elections a new European Constitution Intergroup was established. Its main objectives are the "constitutionalisation " of the current Treaty texts, a new and more democratic method of Treaty revision (with more use of "community" methods, and application of the "constitutional co-decision procedure between the elected representatives of the European citizens in the European Parliament and the representatives of the Member States of the European Union"), strengthening of the major EU policies, and major reform of the EU institutions.

Its initial steering committee consisted of Jo Leinen (PES, Germany), Alain Lamassoure (EPP-ED, France), Andrew Duff (ELDR, UK), Monica Frassoni (Greens, Belgium), Mihail Papayannakis (GUE, Greece), Carlos Carnero Gonzalez (PES, Spain) and Cecilia Malmstrom (ELDR, Sweden). 125 members expressed initial interest in its work.

The intergroup meets on the Wednesday afternoon of each Strasbourg plenary, and has continued to attract a large number of members to its meetings. It plans to work closely with national parliaments, and to encourage the establishment of parallel intergroups within them: one such intergroup was set up within the Italian Parliament in October 1999, and was almost immediately joined by 113 members of the Italian Chamber of Deputies.

Intergroup on the Welfare and Conservation of Animals

This intergroup is aimed at mobilising cross-party support for animal welfare and conservation, which overlap the remit of several of Parliament's standing committees, especially those on agriculture, the environment and legal affairs. It exists to exchange information on topical issues, to put pressure on the Commission to come up with new legislative initiatives, and then to follow these through. It also takes an interest in related conservation and environmental issues.

The Eurogroup for Animal Welfare was set up in 1980 to coordinate the various national societies for the protection of animals and is now represented in all 15 Member States. Its first director was Edward Seymour-Rouse. It then had no special links with MEPs. In 1983, however, a British Conservative member, Stanley Johnson, along with five other like-minded members, established an Animal Welfare Intergroup. Members from all Political Groups took part in its work, and its secretariat was provided by the Eurogroup. Stanley Johnson was chairman for the first few months, and was later succeeded by Lieselotte Seibel-Emmerling (German SPD) for around two-and-a-half years and then by Madron Seligman (British Conservative). After the 1989 elections a hotly contested election for the chairmanship between Hanja Maij-Weggen (Dutch Christian Democrat) and Hemmo Muntingh (Dutch Socialist) was won by the former, with around 90 MEPs taking part in the meeting, and even with party whips being applied. Shortly afterwards, however, Maij-Weggen was appointed as a member of the Dutch government, and was replaced as chair by Mary Banotti (Irish *Fine Gael*). Its next president was Anita Pollack (British Labour). After the 1994 election, Hanja Maij-Weggen was again elected to chair the intergroup, and was later succeeded by Michael Elliot (Labour). After the 1999 elections former EP President, José Maria Gil-Robles, was elected as chairman. Hanja Maij-Weggen is the honorary secretary, and there are also nine vice-presidents.

David Wilkins has been the director of the intergroup since 1992. He spends half his time with the intergroup, giving scientific and political advice to MEPs and the rest lobbying the Commission and other European institutions. A second member of staff is in charge of the lobby activities in the European Parliament and part of her job is dedicated to the intergroup. Coordinating campaigns on enlargement and communications with member organisations are the tasks of the deputy director and her assistant. An administrative officer runs the office, and a communications officer is in charge of the minutes of the intergroup and the *Eurobulletin* (a monthly publication concerning all EU developments on animal protection).

The intergroup does not have card-carrying members, and its meetings are open to all MEPs. Turnout at its meetings has ranged between a tiny handful and 90, but the average attendance tends to be around 25–35. Some members attend practically all of its meetings, others come occasionally, or when a specific item of interest to them is on the agenda. Sometimes opponents (e.g. supporters of the fur trade, hunting or farming interests, etc.) turn up at meetings, which are thus considerably enlivened.

The most regular attenders tend to be British and Dutch MEPs, who often receive the most constituency mail on animal welfare issues, followed by German, Swedish and Irish members, whereas Spanish, French and Greek members have tended to be less involved. In terms of political allegiance the intergroup has tried to achieve the widest possible spread. Six Political Groups are thus represented among the chairman and vice-chairmen.

The main working session of the intergroup is its monthly meeting in Strasbourg. Invitations to this meeting are issued to all members of the Parliament at the beginning of the week. Press conferences are also often held in Strasbourg. Meetings are not held in Brussels. The intergroup's executive meets every three months.

As a general rule, only MEPs can speak at the meetings of the intergroup, although experts can be called upon to speak on the invitation of the chair. The agenda for the meetings is drawn up jointly by the leadership of the intergroup and the secretariat. It would typically begin with a discussion of legislative strategy on current Commission initiatives having a bearing on animal welfare. There are then discussions of items of general interest, such as issues that the intergroup would like the EU to tackle. On all these items an individual member will introduce the discussion. Other issues are put on the agenda as a result of concern expressed by an individual member, or by a national animal welfare association, or simply as a matter of topical interest.

The intergroup's meetings are held in rooms provided by individual Political Groups. Interpretation is provided in English, French and German, and in other languages where possible. The minutes, however, are drawn up in English and French alone. Wherever possible, the intergroup tries to work on a consensus basis.

The intergroup drafts motions for resolution and seeks to have reports drawn up on them by the committees to which they are referred. It also seeks the direct adoption of written declarations under Rule 51. If and when the Commission responds to Parliament's pressure, the intergroup then tries to mobilise support within the Parliament, and to fend off counter-lobbies.

Another feature of the intergroup's working methods is that its secretariat will also help individual members in their correspondence on animal welfare issues. The Eurogroup has a permanent office in Brussels, but its secretariat comes every session to Strasbourg.

The intergroup has played a prominent role in a number of major animal welfare initiatives, and has been unusually successful in getting the Commission to take up legislative initiatives. Its best-publicised initial success was in obtaining the ban on imports of baby seal products into the European Community. Other successes have been achieved on the issues of animal experimentation, phasing out the battery-cage system for laying hens, a ban on the import of certain furs from animals caught in leghold traps and a Zoos Directive. A particular success has been that of an 8-hour limitation for the transport of farm animals to slaughter. The Council had been deadlocked, but following intergroup action a compromise was achieved. The intergroup also initiated Parliament's successful request to have animals classed as "sentient beings", rather than mere products, in the Amsterdam Treaty. The intergroup has been less successful on certain other issues where a consensus approach has proved hard to achieve, such as on some hunting issues.

The Sports Intergroup

The Sports Intergroup was established in 1991 in order to promote sport at a European level and in response to the growing impact of EU legislation on the world of sport. The intergroup also recognised the potential of sport in shaping a European identity through international sporting events. Much of its activity was directed towards securing European funding for such projects but equally there was a concern to improve the dialogue between sport at all levels and the EU.

A consistent guiding principle for the intergroup was that it should always be a forum for informal discussion on sport but should never to seek to reach policy conclusions. Policy conclusions were seen as the prerogative of Parliament – the intergroup was composed of parliamentarian lovers of sport, motivated by a common view that for many European citizens sport was at least as important a factor in European integration as either the single market or the single currency.

From its creation in 1991 until the 1999 elections, the Sports Intergroup was chaired by the Socialist MEP John Tomlinson. Other active members included the Dutch Liberal Jessica Larive, the Irish Christian Democrat Mary Banotti and the British Socialist Angela Billingham.

Membership of the Sports Intergroup was entirely open, with all MEPs invited in writing to attend the bi-monthly meetings and to propose items for discussion. MEPs were joined by representatives from other EU institutions and from governmental and non-governmental sports organisations in the EU and its Member States. With the meeting agendas and related documents made available on the Internet from 1995 onwards, the attendance at Intergroup meetings became ever more diverse, with interested members of the public, such as European Studies students, welcomed to the meetings. The Sports Intergroup operated without any financial assistance from inside or outside the Parliament. It was run through the Brussels office of John Tomlinson, with meeting rooms and interpretation provided by the Socialist Group. Assistance in the planning of meetings and the production of minutes was provided on a voluntary basis by the UK's Central Council for Physical Recreation.

One of the main achievements of the intergroup was its role in helping to secure and then to develop budget lines for sport within the European Commission budget, in particular, the 'Eurathlon' programme, which promotes amateur sporting competition between citizens from different EU Member States, and the Sport for the Disabled programme. The collaboration between the intergroup and the European Commission was therefore a close one, with DGX of the Commission being present at all intergroup meetings, often represented by its Director-General. Similarly, the Sports Intergroup was represented at all meetings of the then DGX's Sports Steering Committee, which brought together representatives of ministries of sport from the EU Member States as well as representatives of the non-governmental sports organisations in Europe. The Steering Committee itself was created in response to pressure from the intergroup.

During the 1994–99 Parliament, the intergroup discussed a wide variety of issues including EU funding for sport in developing countries, tobacco advertising in sport, the need for a specific mention of sport in the Treaty of Amsterdam, arbitration in sports disputes, virtual advertising at sporting fixtures, hooliganism at European football tournaments and racism in sport. Intergroup members were instrumental in arranging a 'Kick Racism out of Sport' event in Parliament in Brussels in February 1998, which consisted of an exhibition by all the EU Football Associations and a meeting addressed by, amongst others, former Tottenham and England player Garth Crooks.

The intergroup is best known however for its role in raising the profile of European Court of Justice cases affecting the world of sport. In November 1995, between the publication of the Advocate-General's opinion in the Bosman case and the final Court Decision in December, members of the intergroup arranged a conference in Brussels to highlight the implications of the case for professional football in Europe. Organised with only ten days' notice, the conference succeeded in bringing together over 300 representatives from the worlds of sport, law and politics. The discussions centred around presentations by the lawyers of both Bosman and of UEFA, with club and association directors from various professional and amateur sports in the EU Member States describing the possible impacts for their sports of the likely judgment. As in subsequent intergroup meetings in which Court of Justice cases were presented, the French Socialist MEP Jean-Pierre Cot provided the intergroup with an expert legal analysis of the issues involved.

The possibility of organising such an important meeting with so little notice as an issue arises, is one that intergroups are often better able to realise than the formal committees of the Parliament. The Bosman conference also demonstrated the way that intergroups can be used to address issues that European citizens care passionately about.

In January 1998, in what was undoubtedly one of its most entertaining meetings, the Sports Intergroup was addressed by the then UK Sports Minister Tony Banks MP. It was events such as this that ensured that the Sports Intergroup was one of the best attended throughout the 1994-99 Parliament.

Table 20: *Indicative list of intergroups at beginning of 1999–2004 legislature (chair/ president/convenor in brackets)*

Ageing (Guido Podestá)
All Parties Friends of Cycling
Amici Curiae
Animal Welfare (José Maria Gil Robles Gil-Delgado)
Anti-personnel landmines (Geoffrey van Orden)
Anti-Racism (Fodé Sylla)
Atlantic Regions
Automobile users
Beer Club (Robert Sturdy)
Bioethics (Evelyne Gebhardt)
Biotech (Peter Liese)
Books & Reading
Camino de Santiago (Jaime Valdivielso De Cué)
Ceramics Intergroup (Malcolm Harbour)
Ciel et Espace Européen (Claude Desama
Cinema & Audio-visual (Walter Veltroni & Ruth Hieronymi)
Comité Quart Monde au PE
Commerce and Distribution (Christos Folias)
Complementary medicines (Nuala Ahern)
Conservation & Durable Development
Consumer Forum (Astrid Thors)
Crane Group
Disability (Richard Howitt)
Duty Free
East Timor (Heidi Hautala & Carlos Costa Neves)
Ecumenical Prayer Group
Elimination of the Embargo against Cuba
Equal rights for Gays and Lesbians
Euro-Arab Intergroup
European Constitution Intergroup (Joe Leinen et al.)
European Defence Industries
Eurosun
Family, children and solidarity (Marie Thérèse Hermange)
Fieldsports, Fishing and Conservation (Michel Ebner)
Financial Services (José Garcia-Margallo)
Food & Health (Marianne Thyssen)
Forests
Fourth World European Committee
Friends of Hong Kong (Richard Balfe & Willy De Clercq)
Friends of Israel (Willy De Clercq)

Friends of Music
Friendship with Morocco
Friends with Tunisia
GLOBE
Groupe d'amitié PE- Taiwan
Health Forum (Mel Read)
Horse (Francis Decourrière)
Indigenous Peoples
Intellectual Property Rights (Geneviève Fraisse)
Intergroupe Francophone
Internet Intergroup (Diana Wallis)
Islands (Fernando Fernandez)
Kangaroo group (Karl von Wogau)
Land Use & Food Policy (Jan Mulder)
L'Europe contre la Douleur (Françoise Grossetête)
Local and Regional Representatives (Maria Berger)
Maritime (Brigitte Langenhagen)
Mediterranean
Mining regions (Bernard Rapkay)
Minority Languages (Eluned Morgan)
Non Food Uses of Agricultural Products
North Sea
Paneuropean Parliamentarians
Peace for the Saharaui People (Margot Kessler)
Peace & Disarmament (Luisa Morgantini)
Pharmaceutical Products
Population, sustainable development and reproductive health
Reform the WTO
Social exclusion (Stephen Hughes)
Solidarity with the people of East Timor
SOS Democracy Group (Jens Peter Bonde)
Sports (Glyn Ford)
Sustainable Development (Karl-Erik Olsson)
Taxation of capital, tax policy and globalisation (Harlem Désir)
Textile, Clothing and Leather (Concepió Ferrer)
Third Sector – Social Economy (Fiorella Ghilardotti)
Tibet
Tourism
Trade Unions
Viticulture, tradition and quality (Astrid Lulling)

11. The Parliament secretariat

Who are the staff of the Parliament?

"Cut it out, whose stooge are you?" said the sceptical Canadian political staffer to one of the co-authors of this book when the latter tried to explain that he had been recruited through an open examination, and was not beholden to any one Political Group or national administration.

Parliament's permanent officials are European civil servants, subject to the same terms and conditions as those working in the other institutions. They are recruited directly by the European Parliament by means of open external competitions, which are normally held every two or three years for each category of staff. The competitions are organised by language groups rather than by nationality: Irish and British candidates compete for posts as English-language administrators, along with any other candidates from a country of the Union with a sufficient knowledge of English. Language competence is one of the factors in candidate recruitment but is not necessarily decisive. The minimum requirement is "satisfactory" knowledge of one official language in addition to the mother tongue but extra points are awarded for other languages.

The Staff Regulations lay down that "an official shall carry out his duties and conduct himself solely with the interests of the Communities in mind", and "shall neither seek nor take instructions from any government, authority, organisation or person outside his institution". They go on to specify that "no posts shall be reserved for nationals of any specific Member State". In practice a strong attempt is made to ensure rough balance between the nationalities, especially for senior posts: hence in 1999 the eight Director-General posts were filled by officials from six different nationalities.

The European Parliament now has an establishment plan that provides for 4,118 posts (figures for the year 2000). Of these, slightly more than half are in Luxembourg, something under half in Brussels, a small antenna of 28 people in Strasbourg and 153 spread over the information offices in the Member States (see Appendix 3). Out of this grand total 532 are temporary agents in the Political Groups, nearly all in Brussels, who are recruited directly by the Groups (and whose separate role and status have been discussed in Chapter 5), along with a small number of other temporary posts elsewhere in the Parliament, designed to cover special needs, such as assistance to the Vice-Presidents. In addition, the Parliament recruits free-lance interpreters to complement the full-time interpreters, short-term auxiliaries (to replace, for example, staff on maternity leave and in Strasbourg, and to cope with the extra demands of plenary sessions, such as the printing and distribution of documents), and some staff linked to external contract (to ensure, for example, the security of the buildings).

There are four categories of officials: A, administrators; B, executive assistants; C, clerical staff (mainly secretaries), and D, manual or service staff. Language staff – translators and interpreters – are classed as LA. The largest of these categories – over 1500 – are C officials; the smallest category – under 250 – are D staff. Permanent administrative posts totalled 420 or just over 10 per cent of the total; LA posts amounted to 841 (583 translators and 258 interpreters), underlining the effort required to translate documents and interpret speeches into all the languages of the Union. (2000 Budget).

Within each category there are a number of grades. Newly recruited administrators, for example, tend to come in at A8 or A7 level; a Director-General is at A1 level. It is possible to move from one category to another and this is done through internal examinations. When the Parliament was smaller and more informal some officials succeeded in rising rapidly from one category to another through the system, but this has become much more difficult. There are now a substantial number of officials who find themselves at the top of their grade, say C1, without necessarily having the chance to become a B official. This poses a challenge of motivation of staff and has contributed to a number of reforms of staff policy that will be discussed below.

Certain countries are better represented among the staff than are others. The nationals of countries that joined the Union earlier tend to be more numerous proportionately than those from countries that joined later. This is particularly evident in the case of the latest entrants, Austria, Finland and Sweden, the nationals of each of which form a smaller percentage of the total staff than nationals of any of the other 12 countries. It is a situation that

Table 21: *Breakdown of permanent officials (excluding LA) by category and nationality (as at May 1998)*

Nationality	A Grade	B Grade	C Grade	D Grade	Total
German	54 (13.9%)	44 (9.9%)	116 (7.9%)	14 (5.1%)	228 (8.9%)
French	58 (14.9%)	79 (17.7%)	222 (15.2%)	22 (7.9%)	381 (14.8%)
Italian	45 (11.6%)	56 (12.6%)	195 (13.3%)	88 (31.8%)	384 (14.9%)
British	47 (12.1%)	34 (7.6%)	75 (5.1%)	17 (6.1%)	173 (6.7%)
Spanish	37 (9.5%)	16 (3.6%)	89 (6.1%)	18 (6.5%)	160 (6.2%)
Dutch	16 (4.1%)	20 (4.5%)	67 (4.6%)	18 (6.5%)	121 (4.7%)
Belgian	27 (6.9%)	96 (21.5%)	193 (13.2%)	27 (9.8%)	343 (13.3%)
Greek	19 (4.9%)	21 (4.7%)	78 (5.3%)	13 (4.7%)	131 (5.1%)
Portuguese	15 (3.9%)	13 (2.9%)	80 (5.5%)	12 (4.3%)	120 (4.7%)
Swedish	17 (4.4%)	5 (1.1%)	35 (2.4%)	3 (1.1%)	60 (2.3%)
Austrian	11 (2.8%)	5 (1.1%)	9 (0.6%)	3 (1.1%)	28 (1.1%)
Danish	18 (4.6%)	22 (4.9%)	79 (5.4%)	5 (1.8%)	124 (4.8%)
Finnish	9 (2.3%)	8 (1.8%)	37 (2.5%)	2 (0.7%)	56 (2.2%)
Irish	12 (3.1%)	7 (1.6%)	43 (2.9%)	1 (0.4%)	63 (2.5%)
Luxembourgish	4 (1%)	20 (4.5%)	144 (9.8%)	34 (12.3%)	202 (7.8%)
TOTAL	389	446	1463	277	2575

can only change gradually given the restrictions on the growth of the size of the establishment plan but naturally the figures are closely watched by parliamentarians from the countries concerned. The best-represented nationality are the Italians, by virtue, in particular, of their large number among the manual or service staff (they make up just under one-third of all D grade staff). They are followed by the French, who provide the largest number of administrators and clerical staff, around 15 per cent in each case. Largely because of the location of the Parliament's offices, Belgians and Luxembourgers are also proportionately over-represented. In contrast, the Germans and British are slightly under-represented amongst A grades but conspicuously so in the B, C and D categories.

The structure of the Secretariat

The Secretary-General is the highest official within the Parliament and is formally appointed by the Bureau. Since 1958, there have only been five Secretaries-General, Julian Priestley being the latest and youngest.

Table 22: *Secretaries-General of the European Parliament*

1958–1960	M.F.F.A. de Nerée tot Babberich
1961–1979	Hans Nord
1979–1986	Hans Joachim Opitz
1986–1997	Enrico Vinci
1997–	Julian Priestley

The central unit of organisation of the Parliament is the Directorate-General or DG. Before 1973 there were four DGs but British, Irish and Danish accession was followed by the creation of a Directorate-General for Research. Two further DGs were added after the accession of Spain and Portugal and in 1998 staff and finance matters were separated to give us the present number of eight Directorates-General along with the Legal Service (see Figure 2).

DG I, the *Directorate General for the Presidency* has three main roles:

- providing assistance and the secretariat for the leadership bodies discussed in Chapter 6 (Conference of Presidents, Bureau, Quaestors);
- assuring the smooth running of the plenary sessions (e.g. planning and preparation of the agenda, the tabling of amendments for the plenary, assisting the President or Vice-Presidents in the chair, preparing the daily plenary minutes, summary of debates, etc.); and
- managing specific activities of individual members including written and oral questions and the members' register of financial interests.

It is also responsible for the Protocol, Security, IT and Mail Services.

DG II for *Parliamentary Committees and Delegations* organises the work of the 17 standing parliamentary committees (along with any temporary committees of inquiry that are established), 14 joint parliamentary committees and 20 interparliamentary delegations as well as of the ACP-EU Assembly and the EU-Latin America Conference. Its five directorates include a Human

Figure 2: *European Parliament Secretariat*

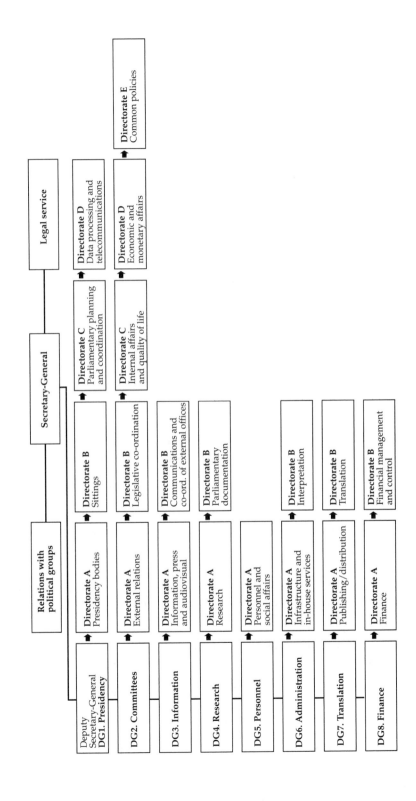

Rights Unit, a division to coordinate relations with national Parliaments, a unit for legislative planning and coordination and the secretariat for the Parliament's delegations to the conciliation committee. It has over 150 administrators, nearly 40 per cent of the A grades of the Secretariat, the majority servicing the committees described in Chapter 7. As compared with national parliaments in Europe (though not the US Congress), the secretariats of European Parliament committees have a larger staff to cover the range of languages of members and to provide detailed help in the preparation of reports.

DG III for *Information and Public Relations* has as its main role to liaise with and brief the press on the activities of the European Parliament. It also provides information for the general public, responding to general enquiries, and looks after visitors' groups. It publishes regular briefings on what is taking place within Parliament's committees and also prepares previews of the plenary session and reports on what takes place there. Monthly newspapers are produced in each of the Community languages: the English language version is called *EP News* (see Chapter 16 and Appendix 4).

DG III has information offices in the capital cities of all Union countries as well as a regional office in Strasbourg. In the run-up to the 1999 European elections it was also decided to set up on a pilot basis small regional offices alongside the Commission in Barcelona, Edinburgh, Marseilles and Milan. After the elections these offices were made permanent along with a further regional office in Munich. The offices in the capitals usually have two or three administrators and act as national contact points for the European Parliament. In all but two cities (Athens and London), the offices are now in close proximity to the information offices of the European Commission. Facilities are often also provided at these offices for the respective national delegations of MEPs. Finally, DG III also has its own television crew, which films Parliament's plenaries as well as important events in the committees and then makes the end product available to national television channels.

The Directorate-General for *Research*, DG IV, includes 30 researchers who produce background studies, briefings and notes in response to requests notably from the President, committees and delegations. Since 1990, a programme of studies requested by the committee chairmen is agreed annually including items to be sub-contracted to external organisations such as universities, research institutes, etc.

DG IV also has a number of "documentalists", and runs Parliament's European Documentation Service in Brussels. The main Library used to be in Luxembourg but under pressure from many MEPs, who rarely, if ever, go to Luxembourg as part of their work, the facilities provided in Brussels have been developed substantially in recent years with a large selection of journals, books and newspapers as well as a growing number of staff able to respond to requests for information.

Parliament's various administrative tasks are now divided between three of its Directorate-Generals, DG V (Personnel), DG VI (Buildings and Administration) and DG VIII (Budget and Finance). Translation and publishing, which used to be carried out within the DG of the Presidency, now has its own Directorate-General, DG VII. These Directorates-General play a major role in ensuring the smooth running of the Parliament. The Buildings Directorate-General, for example, managed in Brussels one of the largest building projects in Western Europe, and in Strasbourg and Brussels is coping with the complexity of owning rather than renting, following the Parliament's decision not to continue with the expensive practice of renting all its premises. The Directorate-General for Translation and Publishing, based almost entirely in Luxembourg, is the largest Directorate-General of all, with some 1200 staff, obliged to find ways of responding to clients for its services who are nearly all in Brussels, 200 kilometres away. Despite technological progress, this is not always easy!

A further service, created in 1985 but growing in importance, is the *Legal Service*. It handles legal cases taken on behalf of or against the Parliament, cases that are increasing in number and complexity. It is also often asked for its view by the committees, and by other Parliament services, especially in disputes over the legal base of Community legislation. The most significant developments in its work result from the co-decision procedure. Under this procedure, as the next chapter explains, the Parliament is jointly responsible with Council for adopting, signing and publishing the final text of European legislation. As a result, not only does the Legal Service have to scrutinise more carefully the quality of the texts of the Parliament, it also checks the first reading of the Council (known as the "common position") and is invited by the Council to give its comments before the text is transmitted to the Parliament. To do this work Parliament established a service of "jurist linguists," translators with specialist legal knowledge, analogous to those used by the European Court of Justice, the Commission and the Council of Ministers.

In addition, the joint adoption and signing of legislative texts under co-decision has meant that the Legal Services of the Parliament and the Council can be obliged to act together in defending the outcome of the co-decision procedure in the event of a case being brought before the European Court of Justice (see Chapter 12).

Issues affecting the Secretariat

Three issues deserve further discussion: the question of the overall size of the Secretariat, its relationship with the Political Groups, and new developments in staff policy, notably mobility and staff reports.

Since the Assembly's beginning in 1952, there has been an enormous rise in the number of Parliament's staff. A figure of 37 posts in 1952–53 rose to 1,995 by 1979, 2,966 by 1984 and is now over 4,000. The rate of increase can be compared with that of the Council, which had almost the same number of officials in the early 1950s but now is considerably smaller with something over 2,500 staff. The rise in the number of Parliament staff has resulted from a number of factors: the increase in Parliament's membership from 78 to over 600; the increase in the number of working languages from four to eleven (between a quarter and a third of Parliament's officials are in its linguistic services); the rise in the number of nationalities from six to 15; and, last but not least, the increased range of Parliament's tasks and responsibilities.

Over the last 15 years, there has been a determined attempt to keep the overall numbers of permanent staff in check. Already in June 1983 Parliament voted for a freeze on the size of its establishment plan over the following four years. This was not achieved, mainly because of the increase in staff numbers after Spanish and Portuguese accession, but the rate of increase in the number of Parliament staff did slow down. The Committee on Budgets, in particular, has been consistently reluctant to provide the appropriations necessary to finance extra posts. It insisted in 1993 and 1994 on a detailed screening exercise to establish priorities and to identify areas where there could be staff cutbacks. Despite the inevitable demands posed by enlargement in 1995, there is no question that the days of rapid growth in the number of permanent officials are over: new tasks will have to be met through re-deployment of existing staff rather than new recruitment.

What has grown more rapidly, however, is the number of staff of the Political Groups and of members' personal assistants. This changed balance between permanent officials recruited through open examinations and temporary staff owing their allegiance to a particular Political Group or parliamentarian has considerable implications for the future. Some argue that it will result in a lesser role for the permanent officials, but up to now there is little evidence of this. The growth in the powers of the Parliament has meant that both sets of staff have found themselves confronted with new challenges, with the Secretariat having to master, for example, the intricacies of new procedures, such as co-decision and the hearings for prospective Commissioners, and the Groups being obliged to pay growing attention to the relationship between their activities and the activities of their parties at the national level.

The permanent staff of the Parliament secretariat are civil servants carrying out their duties in a politically neutral way. None the less, they are not prevented from being active members of political parties in their spare time, or from standing as candidates in local, national or European elections. To do this they must take leave during the election campaign. If elected to any office, they must take indefinite leave but if subsequently they leave that office or are defeated, they may return to Parliament's staff.

In practice, few permanent Parliament officials have stood for national or European elections. One who became a senior government minister was Hans Apel, elected to the German *Bundestag* in the 1970s. He always retained the right to return to Parliament's staff but never exercised it. A more recent case is Ben Patterson, who worked in the London office of the Parliament before 1979, was elected as an MEP that year and remained a member until 1994. He then lost his seat and returned to the Secretariat. Richard Corbett, one of the co-authors of this book, is the only case of someone who has been a *stagiaire*, a civil servant, a senior Group official and an MEP.

There is also some movement between the staff of the Political Groups and that of the Parliament as a whole. Some of the staff of the Groups have passed Parliament's open competitions and can thus be re-deployed as permanent staff without difficulties. A number of long-serving permanent officials have moved the other way and gone to work in the Political Groups, on a temporary or longer-term basis. The present Secretary-General of Parliament, Julian Priestley, who had previously stood on two occasions in Westminster elections as a Labour candidate, was from 1989 to 1994 Secretary-General of the Socialist Group, then head of the Private Office of the President of Parliament. Another example is Sergio Guccione who left the Secretariat to work as Secretary-General of the EPP Group and then returned to become the Director-General of DG III (Information).

There is little direct Political Group influence on appointments at lower levels within the Parliament (and where attempted, it is usually successfully resisted). At the higher levels (A3 and above), political factors do play a role alongside nationality, seniority and ability. This has not led to the domination of one political or national interest. Parliament's staff are protected not only by those who defend the concept of a neutral European civil service, but also by the sheer variety and number of political forces and nationalities represented within the Parliament, which act as counterweights to each other.

Finally, there are a number of new developments in staff policy which are starting to have a significant effect on the running of the Secretariat. The system of promotions is being overhauled with annual staff reports assuming a greater weight than they had in the past. All officials are to be interviewed annually to review their progress and to see how they wish their careers to develop. Everyone is gaining a clear idea of how long they are likely to stay in their present grade in the light of the staff appraisals they receive. A new administrator, for example, can expect to wait five years before moving from A7 to A6 unless she or he shows exceptional ability. In addition, much more stress is being laid on mobility as a desirable aim and one that will be taken account of in promotion decisions, in particular in the administrative grades. All A grade officials below A3 can only stay in their present post for five years (for A3s the period is seven years) at which point the post is advertised for anyone to apply for. This is a remarkable change in an institution where in the past officials could often spend ten or 15 years in the same job.

As indicated earlier, Parliament's employees are subject to the same terms and conditions as those that apply to officials in the other institutions. Hence some aspects of staff policy are subject to inter-institutional bargaining and discussion. A good example is staff salaries, which are fixed by the Council on a proposal of the Commission and after consulting Parliament and negotiating with the inter-institutional trade unions. At the end of 1991, there was considerable friction and even limited strike action, but an agreement was reached for a ten-year "method" for adapting staff salaries, linked to an index which takes account of price movements and of the average change in the salary level of national civil servants. This agreement is up for review in 2001 and will be part of the package of general staff reform to be undertaken by the Prodi Commission and in particular, the Vice-President, Neil Kinnock.

III: THE POWERS OF THE PARLIAMENT

12. The Parliament and legislation

The Treaties initially gave Parliament only a consultative role in the adoption of Community legislation. The legislative power handed over by national parliaments to the Community was placed in the hands of the Council (composed of ministers from the national governments). The first President of the Council, Konrad Adenauer, in his first speech to the Parliament in 1952, asserted that Parliament was a sovereign assembly, and compared Council and Parliament to two chambers in a national parliament. It was not until the 1990s, however, with the arrival of the co-decision procedure, that it became realistic to talk of a bicameral system, with the Parliament acting as a co-legislator alongside the Council. This chapter will describe how this change came about.

The consultation procedure

Under the ECSC Treaty, Parliament exercised a power of control over the High Authority (Commission) but did not participate in the adoption of legislation. The EEC and Euratom Treaties, which entered into force in 1958, gave the Community wider-ranging power to adopt legislation and provided for the Parliament's participation in legislative procedures. This was done by laying down in 22 articles in the EEC Treaty and 11 articles in the Euratom Treaty provisions obliging Council to consult the European Parliament on Commission proposals before their adoption (for an illustration of the process, see Figure 3).

The Treaties provided for Council to consult the Economic and Social Committee as well in certain cases, but the Council could lay down a deadline within which the Committee must adopt its opinion. No such deadline was provided for in the case of the Parliament and this difference was to prove very important.

Over the years, through agreements with the other institutions and through interpretation of the Treaties, Parliament sought to maximise the significance of this consultation procedure. Even before direct elections a number of important steps forward were achieved.

Extension of the scope of the procedure

In response to parliamentary pressure, Council undertook in March 1960 to extend the consultation procedure to all important problems, even where the Treaties did not specifically require the consultation of Parliament. These are known as "voluntary consultations". In February 1964 the Council went further by agreeing to extend such consultation beyond "important

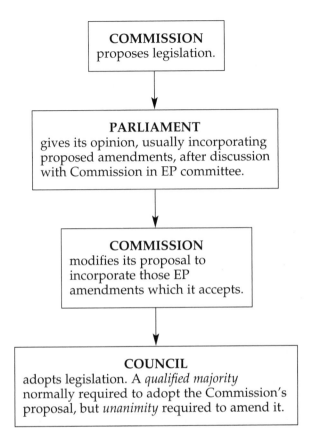

Figure 3: *The consultation procedure*

problems", though without defining the new limits. In practice, by the mid-1970s, Council consulted Parliament on virtually all legislative proposals referred to it except those of a purely technical or temporary nature. This continues to be important as there are still today many articles of the Treaties that do not specifically provide for consultation of the Parliament (see Table 23 at end of this chapter).

In November 1968, Council also undertook to consult Parliament on non-legislative texts. These include Commission memoranda and Council resolutions which, whilst not legally binding, nevertheless lay down guidelines, timetables and commitments which provide the framework for forthcoming legislative measures. At the same time, the Commission undertook to send to Parliament all memoranda and communications that it sends to Council. Parliament does not normally go so far as to draft its own report on these or adopt a resolution on them, but that option is available and the documents can, in any case, provide useful additional information.

Improving the quality of the procedure

In successive letters in November 1969, March 1970 and July 1970, Council committed itself to informing Parliament of the reasons for departing from Parliament's opinion when it adopts Community legislation, initially for legislation with financial consequences and subsequently for all important questions. This information would be provided upon request either orally or in writing.

The Paris Summit of Heads of Government, following the first enlargement of the Community in 1973, invited the Council and the Commission "to put into effect without delay practical measures designed to achieve the reinforcement of the powers of control of the European Parliament and to improve the relations both of Council and of the Commission with the Assembly". As a result of this Declaration, Council agreed in October 1973:

- that it would consult the European Parliament on Commission proposals, in principle, within one week of receiving the proposal;
- that it would not "except in cases of urgency when it will enter into contact with the Parliament, and subject to the fulfilment of its obligations . . . examine a proposal of the Commission on which the Parliament has been consulted until the opinion of the Parliament has been received, provided that such opinions are given by an appropriate date which may, in certain cases, be fixed by common agreement";
- that it would provide better information to Parliament as to the action taken by Council on its opinions and to this end, in addition to existing procedures, would have quarterly meetings of the Presidents of Parliament and Council.

Also pursuant to the 1973 Summit, the Commission agreed on 30 May 1973:

- to propose consulting Parliament on all proposals of any kind other than those of minor importance or confidential matters;
- to express its opinion in Parliament's plenary on all amendments and to justify its opposition to any amendments, either in writing or orally in plenary;
- to amend its proposals to Council in order to incorporate Parliament's amendments, even when these were only technical. (It should be recalled that Council can only amend the Commission's text unanimously whereas a qualified majority is often sufficient to adopt it.)
- to send directly to Parliament the proposals it sends to Council.

In the same year, Commission and Council also agreed that Parliament should be reconsulted whenever significant changes were envisaged to the text on which Parliament initially delivered its opinion.

These developments gave MEPs the opportunity of being involved in all discussions on Community legislation and policy-making. However, until direct elections and the arrival of full-time MEPs in 1979, the practical use made of them was limited. In any case, no matter how extensive the possibilities for parliamentary involvement, the bottom line of being able to block proposals or oblige the other institutions to accept changes to them was lacking. The European Parliament could make its opinion known at all stages, but it had no bargaining power if the other institutions failed to respond to its views. This situation first began to change following a major ruling of the European Court of Justice in 1980.

Giving teeth to the procedure: the Court ruling of 1980 and its repercussions

The *Isoglucose* ruling of the Court of Justice in 1980 in Cases 138 and 139/79 annulled a piece of Community legislation adopted by Council on the grounds that Parliament had not yet given its opinion. The Court made it clear that Council cannot adopt Community legislation before receiving Parliament's opinion, where this is required under the Treaties. In this ruling, the Court made a link between consultation of the Parliament and the democratic character of the Community. It stated that the provisions in the Treaty requiring the consultation of Parliament are:

> "the means which allows the Parliament to play an actual part in the legislative process of the Community. Such a power represents an essential factor in the institutional balance intended by the Treaty. Although limited, it reflects at Community level the fundamental democratic principle that the people should take part in the exercise of power through the intermediary of a representative assembly. Due consultation of the Parliament in the cases provided for by the Treaty therefore constitutes an essential formality, disregard of which means that the measure concerned is void".

The Court ruled in favour of the Parliament despite the fact that:

– Parliament had had a debate in plenary on the basis of a committee report and had finished its examination of the proposal. However, it had not taken a final vote on the resolution as a whole but instead referred the text back to the relevant parliamentary committee.
– There were objective reasons for taking a quick decision in order to avoid a legal lacuna when previous legislation lapsed.
– Council maintained that, in the circumstances, it did try to get Parliament's opinion but that "Parliament, by its own conduct, made the observance of that requirement impossible".
– The Commission intervened on the side of Council.

Parliament included in the arguments on its side of the case the fact that Council had not exhausted all the possibilities of obtaining the opinion of Parliament, in that it had not requested the application of the urgency procedure provided for by the internal rules of Parliament. Likewise it had not taken the opportunity it had under Article 196 of the Treaty to ask for an extraordinary session of Parliament. In its judgment, the Court expressly avoided taking a position on what the situation would have been had Council availed itself of these procedures and had Parliament still not delivered its opinion. Some observers doubted whether, if Council were to exhaust its procedural possibilities to obtain Parliament's opinion, or if Parliament were to state openly that it was withholding its opinion in order deliberately to block decision-taking in the Community, the Court would rule the same way. These doubts were to re-emerge in the mid-1990s after a new Court ruling, as we shall see below.

Taking advantage of the Isoglucose ruling

The *Isoglucose* ruling coincided with a major overhaul of Parliament's internal Rules of Procedure following the first direct elections. Parliament sought to take advantage of the Court's ruling that its opinion was an indispensable part of the legislative procedure that Council must obtain. Notably, Parliament adopted new Rules, still applicable today in Article 69 of the Rules of Procedure, whereby it could decide, on a proposal from the Chairman or rapporteur of the committee responsible, to postpone the vote on the Commission's proposal until the Commission had taken a position on Parliament's amendments. Where the Commission refused to accept these, Parliament could refer the matter back to committee for reconsideration, thereby delaying its "opinion" and holding up the procedure. When it gained a sufficient assurance from the Commission or when a compromise was reached, it could move to a final vote in plenary. The significance of the Commission's acceptance of Parliament's amendments lay in the fact that they would then be incorporated into a revised proposal that Council could only change by unanimity.

Parliament was careful to avoid *explicitly* blocking decisions by withholding its opinion indefinitely, instead pleading a need to get further information, to investigate the social consequences, to pursue discussions with other institutions or interested parties, to hold public hearings, or to wait for related events.

These procedures were initially used rather infrequently, and a number of weaknesses became apparent. Referral back was not automatic (the chair or rapporteur was until 1987 not obliged to make a recommendation) and was sometimes not requested when it should have been. The most serious difficulty for Parliament, however, arose where Council took a decision "in principle" or "subject to Parliament's opinion" before this opinion had been delivered. This broke Council's 1973 undertaking, and broached the spirit of the *Isoglucose* principle in that it was unrealistic to think that in such circumstances Parliament's opinion would be taken into account in any serious way by the Council. (It is also an issue that has continued to affect relations with the Council to the present day: in the 1994–99 legislature, "political agreements" were reached in Council in advance of Parliament's first reading on 49 occasions).

Notwithstanding these difficulties, the *Isoglucose* ruling gave Parliament an important mechanism where it is not satisfied with the response from the other institutions. It is a mechanism that is more significant for urgent matters, where delay can cause problems, than for items that have been in the pipeline for ten years and could equally well remain there for another ten. Urgency strengthens the bargaining position of the Parliament, even if a Court ruling of 1995, to which we shall now turn, does impose on the Parliament a special duty of loyal cooperation.

The limits of the Isoglucose ruling

The Parliament has been obliged to recognise the limits of the 1980 *Isoglucose* ruling following a further judgement in 1995 when the Court rejected the Parliament's application for the annulment of a regulation adopted by the Council without Parliament's opinion (Case C-65/93). On 22 October 1993 the Council had requested an opinion on a regulation for a proposal for the extension of the system of generalised tariff preferences for 1993, stressing the urgency of the matter as the existing regulation expired at the end of the year. Whilst acknowledging the urgency, Parliament postponed consideration of the proposal twice, the second time at the last session of the year in December, after which Council adopted the regulation, stressing the exceptional circumstances.

The Court argued that the consultation procedure required sincere cooperation between the institutions and that the Parliament had failed in this regard because its second decision to postpone consideration, due to an adjournment motion, was for reasons unconnected with the contents of the regulation. This decision would appear to restrict the right of the Parliament to delay giving its opinion by imposing an implicit obligation to have good reasons for such a delay. However, the issue has not been subject to further test in the Court since 1995.

The 1975 conciliation procedure

This procedure resulted from a realisation that the European Parliament might be in a position to use its new budgetary powers (see Chapter 13) to prevent the implementation of legislation with budgetary consequences. Council was therefore willing to negotiate and agree on a mechanism aimed at reducing the risk of such conflicts by first seeking agreement with Parliament on the legislation.

The procedure was established by the following Joint Declaration of Parliament, Council and Commission (our emphasis):

Joint Declaration of 4 March 1975

(i)   A conciliation procedure between the European Parliament and the Council with the active assistance of the Commission is hereby instituted.

(ii) This procedure may be followed for Community acts of general application which have *appreciable financial implications,* and of which the adoption is not required by virtue of acts already in existence.

(iii) When submitting its proposal the Commission shall indicate whether the act in question is, in its opinion, capable of being the subject of the conciliation procedure. The European Parliament, when giving its opinion, and the Council may request that this procedure be initiated.

(iv) The procedure shall be initiated if the criteria laid down in paragraph (ii) are met and if the Council intends to depart from the opinion adopted by the European Parliament.

(v)   The conciliation procedure shall take place in a "Conciliation

Committee" consisting of the Council and representatives of the European Parliament. The Commission shall participate in the work of the Conciliation Committee.

(vi) *The aim of the procedure shall be to seek an agreement between the European Parliament and the Council.* The procedure should normally take place during a period not exceeding three months, unless the act in question has to be adopted before a specific date or if the matter is urgent, in which case the Council may fix an appropriate time limit.

(vii) *When the positions of the two institutions are sufficiently close,* the European Parliament may give a new opinion, after which the Council shall take definitive action.

Such a Joint Declaration can be considered to be a sort of constitutional convention between Council and Parliament, laying down procedures that they both undertake to follow. Whether such provisions are legally binding has not yet been tested, though the Court of Justice has referred to their existence. It needs therefore to be distinguished from the conciliation procedure that applies in the co-decision procedure, which is specified in the Treaties and which we will examine later. (In French it is called *concertation*, which usefully distinguishes it from "conciliation", as applicable under co-decision). The Declaration uses terms that imply a certain number of obligations for Council, and its formal aim is to "seek agreement between the European Parliament and the Council". However, as the ultimate power to legislate remained with the Council, the procedure was little more than an opportunity to ask it to think again. The parliamentary delegation had no bargaining position *vis-à-vis* Council other than, possibly, threatening not to vote the necessary credits when it came to the following year's budget. Unless Parliament was totally opposed to the proposal, such a stance lacked credibility. Council had, therefore, little incentive to make major concessions to Parliament in the conciliation negotiations, especially when this would re-open negotiations within Council itself and quite possibly endanger a compromise which Council may have reached only with the greatest difficulty.

During the 1980s, attempts were made to extend the procedure to all "important" Community acts, as indeed Parliament provided for unilaterally in its Rules of Procedure. The initial scope was found to be small (only seven procedures from 1975 to 1982). In 1981, the Commission submitted a draft for a second Joint Declaration, the main points of which Parliament accepted (De Pasquale Report, 1983). Council, however, was unable to reach agreement on the principle because of a reservation on the part of the Danish Government. In the Stuttgart "Solemn Declaration", the European Council undertook to "enter into talks with the European Parliament and the Commission with the aim, within the framework of a new agreement, of improving and extending the scope of the conciliation procedure". Despite this, Denmark, alone, continued to block the matter within Council and the other Member States were unwilling to proceed on this constitutional issue without consensus.

Instead, Council sometimes agreed to interpret the concept of legislation with "appreciable financial implications" flexibly, allowing conciliation, in some cases, on proposals that do not obviously fall in this category, such as the Social Charter. In addition, some "informal conciliations" were held (such as on the proposals for the first stage of monetary union) by means of a meeting between the Council President, his successor, two Commissioners, and Parliament's rapporteurs and relevant committee chairmen. Council also agreed in 1989 to authorise its Presidents to hold preparatory meetings with the other institutions, prior to conciliation meetings. This enables detailed discussion to solve issues before the meeting.

Such flexibility contributed to a wide range of reasonably successful conciliations during the 1980s. These included: the Food Aid Regulation (1986); the New Community Instrument Regulation (NIC IV) (1987), extending the Community's borrowing and lending capacity to assist small- and medium-sized undertakings; the new regulation on agricultural structures (1987); the budgetary discipline provisions of 1988; and the regulation on the collection of own resources (1989) which strengthened the Commission's rights of inspection in Member States.

Since then this kind of conciliation has been much less common. There were meetings on the reform of the structural funds in 1994 and 1999 but the Council has shown a decreasing level of interest, refusing, for example, a conciliation on the Cohesion Fund in 1994 on the grounds that Parliament now had a power of assent and that conciliation only applied where Parliament is consulted. Only in one area has the procedure continued to be important and that is in revisions to the Financial Regulation, which lays down the details governing the establishment and implementation of the budget. The Financial Regulation specifically refers to the 1975 Declaration and as a result the Parliament can always insist on using the procedure. This occurred, for example, towards the end of 1999 when it was agreed to create a specific section for the Ombudsman in the general budget of the EC and to abolish the common organisational structure of the Economic and Social Committee and the Committee of the Regions.

The importance of the 1975 conciliation procedure resides above all in the principle that it embodied. It made possible a direct negotiation between Parliament and Council. Ministers could meet MEPs face-to-face and the Parliament could make a direct input to Council that had not been filtered by national officials or by the Commission. In this sense it acted as a precursor of the much more developed system of conciliation that exists under co-decision which will be discussed below.

Consultation after Amsterdam

As we shall see, most attention after the entry into force of the Amsterdam Treaty is on the co-decision procedure and the increased role that it gives the Parliament. However, the following list shows just how wide are the areas still subject to the more limited consultation procedure, covering many important Community policies, institutional and budgetary matters, issues of citizens' rights and third pillar questions (new areas under Amsterdam are marked with an asterisk):

Legal bases covered by consultation under the Amsterdam Treaty

− Common Community policies (TEC Treaty):

Agriculture (Article 37.2)
Abolition of restrictions on the freedom of establishment and on the provision of
    services (Article 52)
Asylum, immigration and visa issues (Articles 62, 63, 65 and 66)*
Private sector competition (Article 83)
Regulations for state aids (Article 89)
Harmonisation of indirect taxation (Article 93)
Harmonisation of national provisions which affect the common market (Article 94)
Certain aspects of EMU (Articles 104(14), 107(6), 111(1), 112, 117(1) and (7), 121)
Certain social policy and employment matters (Articles 128(2)*, 130*, 137(3))
Extension of the scope of the common commercial policy (Article 133(5)*
Specific industrial policy measures (Article 157)
Specific actions outside the structural funds (Article 159)
Specific research programmes and the setting up of joint undertakings for research
    Articles 166(4) and 172
Fiscal aspects of environmental policy (Article 175(2))
Application of the Treaty to remote regions (Article 299)
International agreements other than those requiring EP assent, except Article 133
    agreements (Article 300)
Further measures to attain one of the Community's objectives (Article 308)
Nuclear energy and radiation (11 articles in Euratom treaty)

− Institutional matters (TEC Treaty):

Authorisation re flexible integration (Article 11)*
Appointment of President and members of the Board of the Central Bank (Article
    112)
Framework decision on implementing powers for the Commission (Article 202)
Determining classes of action covered by the Court of First Instance (Article 225)
Amendments to Title III of the Statute of the Court of Justice (Article 245)
Appointment of the members of the Court of Auditors (Article 247(3))
Adoption of the Staff Regulations (Article 283)
Calling an intergovernmental conference to modify the Treaty (Article 48)

− Budgetary matters (TEC Treaty):

Decision on the Community's own resources (Article 269)
Rules of budget implementation (Article 279).

− Citizens' rights (TEC Treaty):

Anti-discrimination measures (Article 13)*
Voting in European and local elections (Article 19)
Application and extension of citizens' rights (Article 22)

− Police and judicial cooperation (TEU − Treaty on European Union):

Adoption and implementation of measures (Article 34)
Transfers to the EC pillar (Article 42)

Amsterdam thus not only incorporated eight new Treaty articles under consultation, it also introduced a new form of consultation in relation to third pillar questions dealing with police and judicial cooperation. For decisions under Article 34 (TEU) the Council is required to request the Parliament's opinion but it can also fix a deadline for that opinion which cannot be less than three months. If the Parliament fails to give its opinion within the deadline laid down, the Council can go ahead and adopt the measure. This is an important restriction on the Parliament's rights that enables the Council to escape the requirements of the *Isoglucose* judgement. The Parliament will certainly be eager to ensure that the precedent is not applied in other areas.

The cooperation procedure

This procedure (see Figure 4) was introduced by the Single European Act in 1987 and played an important part in the development of the powers of the Parliament between then and the entry into force of the Amsterdam Treaty in 1999. Under the Amsterdam provisions all legal bases subject to cooperation were transferred to co-decision with the exception of the following, all in the area of Economic and Monetary Union:

Article 99(5)   – Rules for the multilateral surveillance procedure
Article 102(2) – Definitions for the application of the prohibition of
                       privileged access
Article 103(2) – Definitions for guarantees against Community liability
Article 106(2) – Measures to harmonise the denominations and technical
                       specifications of Euro coins

Despite the limited scope of the procedure in the future, it remains useful to present it and the way in which it helped the Parliament to improve its position, applying as it did to about one third of the legislation that Parliament considered, notably the bulk of legislative harmonisations necessary for the single market.

The central new feature of the cooperation procedure, as compared with consultation, was that it provided for two readings of legislation rather than one, the first of which is equivalent to the simple consultation procedure: Commission proposal, Parliament opinion (possibly delayed to obtain concessions) and Council decision. However, the Council decision is not final. It is called a "common position" (even if it is adopted by qualified majority) and returns to Parliament for a second reading in which Parliament may do one of three things within a three-month deadline:

- *Explicitly approve* the text (or, by remaining silent, approve it tacitly) in which case Council "shall definitively adopt the act in question in accordance with the common position";
- *Reject* the text, in which case it will fall unless Council unanimously agrees within three months and with the agreement of the Commission (which can always withdraw the proposal) to overrule Parliament;
- *Propose amendments* which, if supported by the Commission, are incorporated into a revised proposal which Council can only modify by unanimity whereas a qualified majority will suffice to adopt it. Council

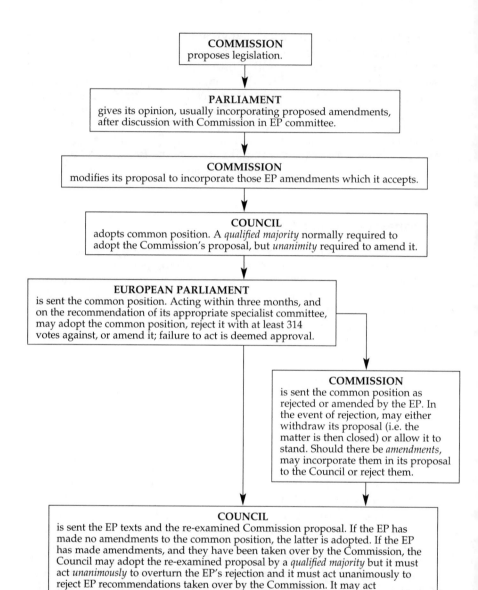

Notes

1. The *Commission* and *Council* do not meet in public. The *EP* and its committees meet in *public*.

2. The *Commission* attends *all* meetings/sittings of the Council, the EP, and their committees.

3. The three-month deadlines may be extended to four by joint agreement between Parliament and Council.

Figure 4: *The cooperation procedure*

has three months to choose one of these options, failing which the proposal falls. Any amendments not supported by the Commission require unanimity to be adopted by Council.

In these last two cases, Parliament can only act by a majority of its members and not a simple majority of those voting. The three-month deadline may be extended to four by joint agreement between Council and Parliament.

Was this a significant increase in Parliament's powers? After all, parliamentary amendments not accepted by Council in first reading seem unlikely to fare better in second reading, when Council positions have been fixed and where Parliament cannot act so easily (needing an absolute majority of members and unable to threaten to delay). Similarly, rejection is an unattractive option as Parliament is usually in the position of persuading a reluctant Council to act. On the other hand, as only legislation that Council *wants* will reach the stage of second reading, a Commission-Parliament alliance puts a lot of pressure on Council, as it must choose within a short deadline whether to accept an amended proposal or lose it entirely. Unanimity would be required to change it back again. A single ally within Council can thus strengthen Parliament's position, and the threat of rejection if Parliament's views are not taken into account can strengthen the bargaining position within Council (already in first reading) of any state agreeing with Parliament. The threat of rejection can also be used by Parliament against the Commission, to put pressure on it to accept amendments instead.

In any case, the second reading gave Parliament a chance to react to Council's position and to respond to the opinions expressed outside the institutions to that position. As a result, the habit of two readings gave the impression of a classic bicameral legislative procedure at European level, and helped pave the way towards full co-decision. Moreover, it opened an additional area in which to test the consultative powers of the Parliament before the Court of Justice on the grounds of the choice of legal base.

A good example of how Parliament can use these powers was when, in 1989, it considered exhaust emission standards for small cars. Here, it was faced with a Council common position that fell below the standards it supported in its first reading. Parliament was keen on raising these standards to levels equivalent to those required in, for instance, the USA and Sweden, and it was known that some Member States shared Parliament's concern, but had been in a minority in Council. Parliament's Committee on the Environment therefore prepared second reading amendments that would restore the higher standards. In the debate, pressure was put on the Commission to accept these amendments before Parliament took its final vote. It was made clear that if the Commission did not do so, Parliament would instead reject the common position, and the legislation would fall as there was no clear unanimity within Council to overrule Parliament. The Commission therefore accepted Parliament's amendments, which were duly incorporated into a reviewed proposal. Council then had three months in which to approve it by a qualified majority, amend it by unanimity (which it could not do as at least three Member States agreed with Parliament) or see it fall (which it could not countenance, as this would have

created havoc in the car industry with a divided internal market and uncertainty as to what standards to adapt to while the whole procedure started
again). A reluctant majority in Council therefore adopted the reviewed text.

Rejection of proposals by Parliament is infrequent, but it is significant that
on most occasions when it was used, the rejection has been sustained, either
because Council was unable to find the necessary unanimity to overrule
Parliament (e.g. Benzene directive, 1988), or because the Commission with-
drew the proposal (e.g. directive on use of sweeteners in foodstuffs, May
1992).

The co-decision procedure

One of the most significant constitutional changes contained in the Treaty
of Maastricht, and subsequently extended and improved by the Treaty of
Amsterdam, was the introduction of a new legislative procedure known as
the "co-decision procedure" (although the name was not retained in the
Treaty, owing to the objections of the UK government!). This procedure
effectively sets up a bicameral legislative authority in the EU where
Parliament and Council jointly adopt legislation, the approval of both being
necessary.

The nature of the procedure

The essence of the procedure can be summed up in a single sentence. If,
after two readings each, Council and Parliament have not agreed the same
text (which, in practice, they usually have), the matter is referred to a conciliation committee (composed of equal numbers from each side) which has
the job of negotiating a compromise text to be submitted for final approval
to Parliament and Council. The details, however, need more space to
explain.

Up until the second reading in Parliament the procedure is identical to the
cooperation procedure, i.e., a Commission proposal, Parliament's first reading "opinion" (possibly delayed while haggling for acceptance of amendments), Council "common position" and Parliament's second reading,
approving, amending or rejecting the common position.

If Parliament *rejects* the common position, by a majority of its members,
the legislation falls, unlike the cooperation procedure where Council could
still adopt the text if it were unanimous. (The Maastricht Treaty also contained a complex provision deleted by the Amsterdam Treaty in 1999,
whereby Parliament had first to announce its "intention to reject" and then
confirm this in a new vote following an optional conciliation meeting with
Council).

If Parliament *approves* the common position, it is adopted (without
needing any further confirmation by Council as is required under the
cooperation procedure and was required under the Maastricht version of
the co-decision procedure, a provision deleted by Amsterdam).

If Parliament *amends* the common position, it returns to Council. If
Council accepts each and every Parliament amendment, the text is deemed
to have been adopted. Failing that, the matter is referred automatically to
the conciliation committee. The committee is composed of the members of

the Council or their representatives and an equal number of members of the European Parliament (at present 15 on each side). This committee, also attended by the Commission, has six to eight weeks during which it is required to negotiate a compromise text based on the common position of the Council and the amendments voted by the Parliament at second reading. If they succeed in reaching an agreement, then within a further six to eight weeks the text has to be submitted for approval by the committee to the plenary of the Parliament and to the Council. If they both support the text (the Parliament voting by simple majority, the Council normally by qualified majority), it is signed into law by the Presidents of the two institutions; if either institution fails to support the text, it falls. The whole procedure can be presented visually as in Figure 5 below.

If the conciliation committee fails to reach agreement within the prescribed time, the text automatically falls and cannot become law, without the whole legislative procedure being restarted from the beginning. This is a significant improvement as compared with the Maastricht provisions, from the Parliament's point of view. Under Maastricht, if the conciliation committee could not reach an agreement, Council could adopt a text unilaterally which would become law unless Parliament rejected it by a majority of its members. In fact Council only tried this once in 1994 on a complex proposal relating to voice telephony. For its part, Parliament found the necessary majority (with 377 votes in favour of rejection) and Council never tried this again! Indeed, in 1998, when the conciliation committee failed to reach an agreement on a directive on a Securities Committee, Council decided to anticipate the provisions of Amsterdam and not to take advantage of its right to challenge the Parliament to overrule its position.

This right to say "no", whether at second reading or during conciliation, gives Parliament a bargaining position which it has hitherto lacked regarding Community legislation, and is of fundamental importance to public perceptions of its role – it can no longer be accused of lacking teeth. It is not that the Parliament will necessarily say no (in fact, it only did so on two occasions between 1994 and 1999) but rather that the Council recognises that this is a possibility if it does not negotiate seriously. The very fact that there have only been two rejections is testimony to the fact that the Council has been willing to look for common ground with the Parliament and to modify its common position in the process.

Another change with respect to the cooperation procedure concerns the role of the Commission and its view on the second reading amendments of the Parliament. In the cooperation procedure, it is critical for the Parliament to win the support of the Commission for its amendments. If these are accepted by the Commission, they are incorporated into the Commission's proposal and can only be taken out or modified by Council, if it is unanimous, whereas a qualified majority will suffice to approve the text as a whole. (Amendments not accepted by the Commission need unanimity, which, against the will of the Commission, is unlikely and they are therefore effectively dead.) Under the co-decision procedure, the Commission does express its views on the Parliament's second reading amendments, but whether or not the Commission is favourable to them, as soon as it emerges that the Council cannot accept all of the Parliament's amendments, attention turns to the conciliation committee negotiations where Council (normally by

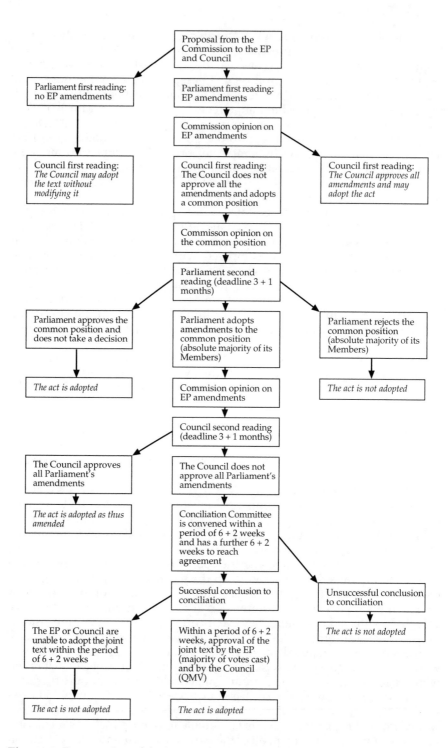

Figure 5: *Presentation of the new co-decision procedure*

qualified majority voting) and Parliament are free to reach an agreement on individual amendments independently of the opinion of the Commission.

A new development introduced by Amsterdam (and not present under Maastricht), is that agreement can be reached at first reading without the Council having to adopt a common position. In other words, if the Council can accept the amendments voted by Parliament at first reading or concurs with the Parliament's approval of the Commission proposal as it stands then the text as voted by Parliament becomes law. Similarly, if Parliament can approve Council's common position, it can vote the text into law there and then. This change underlines the role of Parliament as a legislator. Although it is uncertain how often it will in practice be possible to reach agreements at such an early stage of the legislative procedure, except for the least controversial of issues, the sheer volume of co-decision procedures after Amsterdam means that both institutions have an important interest in not allowing all disagreements to spill over into the conciliation process. As a result, there will be much more intense contact between the institutions earlier in the procedure.

Scope of the procedure

The field of application of the co-decision procedure has been extended under the Amsterdam Treaty. When first introduced under Maastricht, co-decision applied to 15 areas or types of Community action, amounting to about one quarter of the legislative texts that pass through Parliament. The areas covered included most internal market legislation, public health, consumer protection, educational and cultural measures, equivalence of diplomas and qualifications, the free movement of workers, the framework programme for research, and the guidelines for trans-European networks. The Amsterdam Treaty extended this list substantially, so that now 38 areas or types of Community action, spread over 31 Treaty articles, are covered (see list below). These include a number of new areas such as transport (previously almost exclusively governed by cooperation), the fight against fraud, development cooperation, environment policy, customs cooperation, non-discrimination and some social policy and employment measures. As a result co-decision is now the normal legislative procedure for the Parliament, covering more than half of Community legislation, with the possibility of adding two further areas relating to the format and issuing of visas (Article 62 (TEC)) within five years if the Council so decides.

The extension of the scope of the procedure at Amsterdam was impressive and prompted some to call Parliament the big winner of the negotiations. Nevertheless, there are still important exceptions as indicated earlier: co-decision does not apply to economic and monetary union, agriculture, fisheries and fiscal harmonisation. In addition, there are still four co-decision areas (citizenship, freedom of movement for workers, measures concerning the self-employed and cultural actions) where *unanimity* is required in Council. Since the essence of co-decision is the negotiation of compromises between Parliament and Council, and it is more difficult for Council to modify its position where unanimity is required (it may well have only reached its position with great internal difficulties), this particular requirement does weakens the procedure.

It has also been argued that the granting of co-decision rights regarding the internal market was of limited significance, given that almost all the legislation necessary to complete the single market was adopted by the time the Maastricht Treaty came into force. This view, however, proved entirely inaccurate: the bulk of the legislation (60 per cent) adopted under co-decision between 1994 and 1999 was covered by the single market provisions (Article 100A at the time, now Article 95). There is no reason to imagine that this will change, even if there is less new legislation. Once in place, the Community's internal market legislation can only be modified pursuant to the same Treaty articles as those under which it was adopted. Any text which proves unsatisfactory or which, over time, becomes out of date or is no longer politically acceptable will require modification using the relevant procedure – henceforth co-decision. There are already approaching 1,000 items of European legislation adopted pursuant to Article 95, amounting to a huge volume of legislation enacted at Union rather than national level. The areas concerned are thus governed at European level and, as regards any changes to legislation, will come under the co-decision procedure.

Legal bases covered by co-decision under the Amsterdam Treaty

Article 12		prohibition of any discrimination on grounds of nationality
Article 18	**	citizenship: right of citizens to move and reside freely within the territory of the Member States
Article 40		freedom of movement for workers
Article 42	**	freedom of movement for workers: social security of migrant workers in the Community
Article 44		right of establishment
Article 46		right of establishment: special treatment for foreign nationals
Article 47(1)		taking up and pursuing activities as self-employed persons, training and conditions of access to professions: mutual recognition of diplomas
Article 47(2)	**	measures concerning the self-employed: amendment of national legislation
Article 55		right of establishment: services
Article 71(1)		transport: common rules applicable to international transport, conditions under which non-resident carriers may operate transport services within a Member State, measures to improve transport safety
Article 80(2)		sea and air transport
Article 95(1)		harmonisation of the internal market
Article 129		employment: incentive measures
Article 135		customs cooperation
Article 137 (1–2)		social policy: workers' health and safety, working conditions, information and consultation of workers, equality between men and women, measures to encourage cooperation in fight against social exclusion

Article 141		social policy: equal opportunities and pay
Article 148		Social Fund: implementing decisions
Article 149(4)		education: incentive measures
Article 150		vocational training: measures to contribute to the achievement of objectives
Article 151(5)	**	incentive measures in respect of culture
Article 152(4)		public health: minimum standards of quality and safety of organs and substances of human origin, blood and blood derivatives, measures in the veterinary and phytosanitary fields designed to protect public health, action to improve public health
Article 153(4)		consumer protection
Article 156		trans-European networks: establishment, funding
Article 162		European Regional Development Fund (implementing decisions)
Article 166		framework programme for research and technological development
Article 172		research: adoption of programmes
Article 175(1), (3)		environment: measures, adoption and implementation of programmes
Article 179		development cooperation
Article 255		transparency: general principles and limits on access to documents
Article 280		measures to counter fraud
Article 285		statistics
Article 286		protection of data: establishment of an independent supervisory body

**In the case of articles marked with two asterisks the Council votes by unanimity

The impact of the procedure

Has the co-decision procedure made any difference? At the outset in 1993 one could have been tempted to make the assumption that the behaviour of the Council of Ministers would not change fundamentally. The Council had enjoyed a legislative monopoly for forty years and would be eager to find ways of maintaining its position or at least not conceding more that it had been obliged to under the cooperation procedure, as provided for under the Single Act.

The results of the procedure over the last five years contradict such a view. As we have seen, only once (in 1994 on Voice Telephony (ONP)) did the Council reintroduce its common position after a failed conciliation and thereby challenge the Parliament to find an absolute majority to vote it down. Over the next four-and-a-half years only two procedures failed: the directive on the patenting of biotechnological inventions in 1995, where the plenary of the Parliament declined to ratify the results of the conciliation negotiation, and the Securities Committee directive in 1998 where the Council took a decision not to reintroduce the common position in anticipation of the Amsterdam provisions.

However, the impact of the Parliament is not just a question of whether or not procedures are completed. Both in quantitative and in qualitative terms, there is strong evidence that Parliament has made a significant difference to the shape of Community legislation, a difference that goes well beyond what could have been achieved under either the consultation or cooperation procedures. Co-decision has created a new dynamic within the legislative arena of the European Union.

Up until the entry into force of the Amsterdam Treaty, 165 co-decision procedures were completed. In 99 cases (60 per cent) agreement was reached without convening the conciliation committee (63 cases where the common position was accepted by the Parliament without amendment plus a further 36 where it did amend Council's common position but Council accepted all Parliament's amendments). This leaves 66 cases where the conciliation committee was convened, of which 63 were completed successfully.

Consider the amendments discussed in the course of the successful conciliation procedures that took place under the Maastricht provisions. As the list below indicates, Parliament has been remarkably successful not just in persuading the Council to accept, in full or in part, amendments voted in second reading but also in developing with the Council strategies designed to find mutually acceptable outcomes, which were not part of the starting point of either party.

Amendments adopted by the European Parliament in second reading   913
– amendments accepted without modification   244
– amendments accepted in compromise form   328
– amendments accepted in compromise form with a commitment for the future 59
– amendments accepted in compromise form along with a declaration   45
– amendments already covered by another part of the common position   35
– amendments not accepted, including those replaced by a declaration   202

These figures can be variously interpreted. If one groups together the first four categories, one can say that 74 per cent of the amendments of the Parliament were accepted as they stood or in the form of a compromise more or less favourable to the Parliament's position. However, even if one prefers to restrict the analysis to the first category, the figure of amendments adopted as they stand at 27 per cent of the total is still surprising. Since the introduction of cooperation in 1987, the Parliament has imposed upon itself the constraint of normally not considering at second reading amendments that were not passed at first reading. Hence the Council has had an opportunity, under co-decision as much as under cooperation, to consider the contents of what become Parliament's second reading amendments when establishing its common position. In other words, all these amendments are based on ones originally rejected by Council.

The percentage can also be looked at in a comparative perspective. Under the cooperation procedure in the five years preceding the entry into force of the Maastricht Treaty, 24 per cent of the Parliament's second reading amendments were adopted by the Council, including those in modified form. Hence Parliament persuaded the Council to adopt a greater percentage of its amendments under the co-decision procedure than under cooperation.

The figures need also to be disaggregated over the period from 1993 to

1999. At the beginning of the co-decision procedure the Council was tempted to modify its style of behaviour as little as possible. It would divide the Parliament's amendments into two groups, one that it could accept and the other that it rejected. The Parliament was encouraged to agree to the offer as a reasonable division of the cake but it declined to accept such logic, thereby provoking a period of considerable conflict. Over time, attitudes changed and there was a greater willingness on both sides to look for a third way that did not correspond to the starting position of either side, with the Parliament acquiring a highly-developed capacity for negotiating compromises and the Council coming to recognise and value this parliamentary role.

This change is reflected in the decline in the percentage of amendments adopted as they stood and the increase in the importance of compromises based on the amendments of the Parliament. In 1994, amendments adopted as they stood constituted 44 per cent of the total, but they declined to 14 per cent in 1998 and 8 per cent in 1999; as for compromises based on Parliament amendments, the average between 1994 and 1999 was 36 per cent, but the figure rose as high as 57 per cent in 1998 and 59 per cent in 1999. At the same time, the percentage of amendments not accepted consistently remained below one quarter, except in 1996 when it rose to 42 per cent.

The figures also suggest that strategies were developed to improve the chances of a successful outcome. As the period progressed, the Parliament, for its part, took greater care to avoid repeating amendments from first reading which were effectively incorporated into the common position: there were only four such amendments in 1998 and 1999 combined, as compared with 35 in 1994. Both parties likewise came to accept that certain issues could more easily be resolved by a declaration printed with the legislative text in the Official Journal, offering an opportunity for the institutions to present a joint interpretation of the text, or allowing the Commission or Council to make a commitment for the future. In neither case was there a significant trend visible over the period: compromises involving a commitment for the future, for example, varied between 2 per cent and 13 per cent of the total. Nevertheless, they were a useful device, notably for inciting the Commission to contemplate legislative initiatives in the future. This was particularly important for Parliament, which as a result did not need to have recourse to the much heavier "initiative" procedure provided for under Article 192 (former Article 138B).

Numbers alone do not offer an adequate view of the impact of the Parliament. It is almost as tempting to take the percentages of amendments adopted as a sign of the influence of the institution as it is to assume that the only amendments that the Council would be willing to accept are ones that are of marginal importance. Some Parliament amendments adopted by Council are of minor significance but equally the adoption of one amendment out of many can have a major impact on the direction of Community legislation.

What follows are some illustrations of the kinds of difference that the new procedure enabled the Parliament to make to the content of legislation. These differences can be broadly identified by looking at the period in advance of conciliation and the period of conciliation itself.

The prospect of conciliation

Conciliation casts a backward shadow over the whole co-decision procedure. The prospect of this final phase of negotiations, as much as the negotiations themselves, has substantially altered the behaviour of both the
Council and the Parliament. In particular, there has been a realisation on
both sides that conciliation should not be seen as the automatic and sole
mechanism for resolving conflicts of opinion. Some highly sensitive issues
have not reached conciliation but the Parliament has still been able to have
an impact. This can be illustrated by two cases from the first half of 1998,
where Parliament accepted the common position without amendment: the
directive on the banning of tobacco advertising and the directive on the
patenting of biotechnological inventions.

In the first case, the majority view in the Parliament that emerged after
long argument was that the exemptions agreed by the Council in its
common position, notably for sporting events such as Formula One racing,
were unpalatable but, on balance, did not justify amendment. Rather it was
felt that it would be wiser to avoid conciliation, given the fragility of the
coalition of states that had agreed the common position. The country that
was going to head Council's conciliation delegation in the second half of
1998 was Austria which, with Germany, had voted against the common position. All efforts to have amendments carried at second reading were
rejected. Hence the Parliament's action served to protect and maintain a
common position which could only have been weakened rather than
strengthened by conciliation negotiations. The result was that a ban on
tobacco advertising, a proposal initially made by Parliament in 1990, did
come into force.

The second case of biotechnological inventions was a directive with a very
special history. In 1995 this same issue had provided the first and so far only
case where an agreement made by the Parliament's delegation in conciliation was rejected by the plenary. When a revised version of the same directive came back for consideration in 1997, there was a strong desire on both
sides to avoid a similar outcome. The rapporteur, Willy Rothley, made contact with the Council even before first reading, to see how the concerns of
the Parliament could be accommodated by the Council. The relative success
of this strategy was seen in the willingness of the Council in its common
position to accept, in one form or another, almost all the Parliament's 40 or
so amendments. As a result, when the Parliament came to vote its second
reading, a majority felt there was no need for any further amendments. As
with tobacco advertising, the sensitivity of an issue served to shorten rather
than lengthen the co-decision procedure but this time the shape of the outcome could be more easily identified in amendments incorporated into
legislation.

The process of conciliation

Inside the conciliation procedure, a process of exchange has developed
with both sides ready to make concessions but at a price that only becomes
clear in the course of the negotiations. This exchange provides an opportunity for the Parliament to press its point in a much more intensive way

than it ever could under the consultation or cooperation procedures. And the evidence shows that it can get through conciliation changes to the common position which do make a substantial difference to the content of legislation. Two examples from 1998: the Auto-Oil package and the 5th Framework Programme for Research and Technology, show this clearly.

The Auto-Oil package concerned measures to be taken against air pollution resulting from emissions from cars and light commercial vehicles, as well as the quality of petrol and diesel fuels sold in the European Union. The Parliament adopted more than 100 amendments at second reading that contributed to the complexity of the negotiations but also provided the material for trade-offs between the two parties.

The Parliament found itself facing a British Presidency, which had a strong domestic interest in finding a solution. The Deputy Prime Minister, John Prescott, had returned from the Kyoto Summit at the end of 1997, committed to reducing the level of CO_2 emissions in Europe. He was, therefore, eager to ensure that a deal was reached on the Auto-Oil package as a way of showing to the outside world that the EU was respecting the Kyoto deal. The British Presidency made it clear that it wanted to find a compromise with the Parliament. The central element of that compromise was an acceptance by the Parliament of the limit values laid down in the common position but on the basis that those standards should be compulsory by the year 2005 rather than optional as proposed in the common position. Thus the bargaining process led to an outcome which resulted in an EU-wide obligation for improved standards (which would have a marked effect for the general public as well as for the car and oil industries).

A second example of the changes that can be secured by the Parliament is the 5th Framework Programme for Research and Technology, which was adopted in December 1998. This was a particularly unpromising case for influence by the Parliament as it was an area where agreement in the Council had to be by unanimity. The Austrian Presidency did not have the option of working towards a qualified majority. This was particularly important as the Spanish government had insisted on including in the common position what became known as the "guillotine clause", under which any budgetary allocation agreed for the new programme would be subject to review pending the outcome of the negotiations on the Agenda 2000 revision of EU funding. These negotiations also made other delegations, notably the Netherlands and the UK, very reluctant to contemplate any significant increase beyond the common position which had set aside €14bn for the four year period of the programme, and able to veto it.

The Parliament insisted that the current level of Community research could not be maintained under the terms of the common position. It voted at second reading a figure of €16.3bn, and thus the two institutions entered the negotiations more than €2bn apart. Remarkably, an agreement was finally agreed on a figure just short of €15bn, thereby effectively providing for a sharing of the spoils.

Again there was a degree of dissatisfaction in the Parliament with the outcome but there is little question that without co-decision it would have been impossible to reach such an agreement. The cooperation procedure, for example, would have allowed the Commission to propose the Parliament's starting figure after second reading but there would have been unanimity in

Council to re-establish the common position at a far lower level than that finally agreed. Furthermore, the process of negotiation allowed the two parties to revise the "guillotine clause": it was accepted that the EP would be involved through co-decision in any revision of the figures arising from the new agreement on future financing under Agenda 2000. So despite the undoubted difficulties posed by unanimity in Council, it does not make it impossible for the Parliament to influence the outcome.

Composition of the conciliation committee

In deciding how to compose its delegation to the conciliation committee, Parliament examined two models. One was the USA where, for conciliations (conference) between the Senate and the House of Representatives each side composes its delegation on an *ad hoc* basis for each item of legislation, drawing heavily from members of the responsible committee. The other was the German model for conciliations between the *Bundesrat* and the *Bundestag* where the conciliation committee is set up with permanent members who handle each and every item coming to it. Parliament chose a compromise, providing for three permanent members to be drawn from among the Vice-Presidents of the European Parliament and for the remaining members to be drawn predominantly from the committees responsible and including automatically the chairman and rapporteur of the responsible committee.

In addition, the delegation as a whole is meant to reflect the political balance in the Parliament. For most of the period covered by the Parliament elected in 1994, each delegation comprised six Socialists, five EPP, one Liberal, and one Union for Europe, with the two remaining places rotating among the smaller groups. This changed after the 1999 elections, with the Conference of Presidents agreeing to a delegation composed of six EPP-ED and five Socialist members plus one Liberal, one Green/European Free Alliance and one United European Left/Nordic Green Left member, with the final place revolving between the Union for a Europe of Nations and the Europe of Democracies and Diversities Groups. Each Group nominates members to the delegation within this quota, but they must include those members whose presence is required ex-officio (e.g., if the EPP-ED Group provides the chairman and rapporteur of the responsible committee as well as two of the three permanent vice-presidents, they have only two more places to fill).

The permanent members (from 1999, James Provan and Ingo Friedrich from the EPP-ED Group and Renzo Imbeni from the PES Group) are able to become experts in the procedures, practices and precedents of conciliation and to keep an eye on horizontal issues that arise (e.g., comitology). One of the permanent members also chairs Parliament's delegation unless the President of Parliament himself is present (which is rarely the case). The remaining members of the Parliament delegation are meant to bring expertise on the subject matter of the item concerned.

On Council's side the delegation is always chaired by a minister from the country holding the Council Presidency, but the rest of the delegation is usually composed of deputy permanent representatives (COREPER I). Only for particularly important conciliations are there more than a handful of ministers. The Commission's delegation is usually led by the relevant Commissioner.

The conciliation meetings are formally co-chaired and in practice chaired alternately by the leaders of the Parliament and the Council delegations. If a conciliation on one subject is first chaired by the Council (in a Council meeting room) the next conciliation on another subject will normally be chaired by the Parliament on Parliament premises. A second meeting on the same subject will also be chaired by the institution that did not chair the first meeting.

At the very first conciliation meeting, the Parliament and Council delegations initially sat opposite each other. In subsequent meetings the two chairs have sat next to each other with their delegations to their left and right respectively and the Commission sitting opposite them. The new arrangement has been chosen to emphasise the fact that the conciliation committee is indeed a single committee with equal responsibilities among all its members.

Negotiations with 15 on each side of the table are of course impractical. Indeed, as each participant on Council's side is normally accompanied by one or two civil servants and Parliament's own delegation is accompanied by advisors, there can be over a hundred people in the room when the full conciliation committee meets. A trend has therefore emerged of preliminary contacts being taken between the Parliament representatives (usually the chair and/or rapporteur of the responsible committee) and the Council Presidency with the Commission also present. These meetings, known as *trialogues*, have become an essential part of the conciliation process, with each side able to negotiate more freely in the search for compromise than is possible in the full conciliation meeting.

The full conciliation meetings tend to be lengthy, especially since they are frequently interrupted to give time for the Parliament and the Council delegations to meet on their own to decide whether they can accept compromises that have been put forward in the meeting. Each side will also hold preparatory meetings. Parliament's preparatory meeting usually involves the committee chair and/or rapporteur reporting back on the contacts taken with the Council Presidency, and discussion of the strategy to follow in the committee. A typical sequence of events emerging from the initial meetings is as follows:

– Council informs Parliament that it cannot accept all of its second reading amendments, hence triggering the conciliation procedure,
– The Parliament's delegation is chosen and holds a first preparatory meeting to decide on its strategy and to give a negotiating mandate to the chair and/or the rapporteur of the responsible committee for their informal contacts with the Council Presidency,
– An informal meeting is held between Parliament's chairman and/or rapporteur and the Council Presidency at Permanent Representative level. At this meeting the differences between the two delegations' positions are explored and "non-papers" containing possible compromises are exchanged,
– A full conciliation committee meeting is held, typically with the following timetable:

2pm –   meeting of Parliament's delegation
3pm –   *trialogue* between the leaders of the three delegations

3.30pm – full conciliation meeting
4.30pm – separate meetings of each delegation to consider new offers
5.30pm – resumption of the full conciliation meeting to approve an agree-
           ment or to note that no agreement has been reached and to agree
           on a date for a new meeting within the 6–8 week deadline.

Each conciliation must reach an agreement within this deadline of six weeks, which may be extended at the initiative of either institution to eight weeks. In order to maximise the time effectively available, the meetings have formally been convened on the same day as their first meeting (although advance notice is of course sent out beforehand).

Once agreement has been reached in the conciliation committee, the texts are examined by "jurists-linguists" (translators with special legal qualifi-cations). When finalised, they are submitted to the Parliament and the Council for approval by a simple majority in the former and normally a qualified majority in the latter. If approval is forthcoming, the text is signed by the Presidents of the Parliament and of the Council, published in the Official Journal and thereby becomes a piece of Community legislation which both sides have from then on to defend, notably if there is a legal challenge in the Court of Justice.

Developments resulting from the cooperation and co-decision procedures

The increase in Parliament's legislative work, arising both from the intro-duction of two readings and from the growing volume of Community legis-lation generally, has led to a shift of emphasis in Parliament's work. The number of legislative reports adopted (covering consultation, cooperation, co-decision and assent) has increased substantially: in 1986, 135 legislative resolutions were considered in plenary, whereas between 1990 and 1999, the figure ran at between 200 and 250 per year. Consultation remained the most important procedure in numerical terms but co-decision rose to represent about a third of the total. As for the number of non-legislative reports, it remained reasonably constant during the 1990s at around 170 per year. However, within the category there were many fewer own initiative reports and more non-legislative consultations, responding notably to White or Green Papers, which were likely to be the basis of subsequent legislation.

At the same time, Parliament tightened up its Rules to lay down that leg-islative resolutions deal only with procedural points and state whether Parliament approves, rejects or amends the text in front of it. They no longer contain lengthy comments on the proposal: any substantive points must be made by amending the Commission proposal or Council's common position directly. Thus Parliament now focuses on the details of the legislation itself rather than giving general comments on it as it did when it was only a con-sultative body.

Determination of the legal base of proposals

With different procedures applicable to different sectors of legislation, it became important for Parliament to ascertain that Commission proposals are put forward under the correct article of the Treaty. This "legal base" for proposals determines which procedure applies and hence Parliament has been vigilant to ensure that Treaty articles requiring the most favourable procedure are used in preference to those that do not, wherever there is scope for interpretation. A procedure for challenging the legal base has been provided for in Parliament's Rules (Rule 63), allowing the committee responsible, after consulting the Committee on Legal Affairs, to report straight back to the plenary on this point alone.

Reconsultation of Parliament

Where, in its common position, Council departs markedly from the text on which Parliament deliberated in its first reading, and especially where new elements are incorporated into that text by the Commission or Council, Parliament must be reconsulted (i.e. have a "second first-reading") in the same way as it is reconsulted in similar circumstances under the traditional consultation procedure. A second reading under the cooperation or co-decision procedure is not sufficient if the changes made to the Commission's proposal are major ones (unless obviously, they are the changes proposed by Parliament).

Council accepts this in principle, but difficulties sometimes arise, such as in the case of the second directive on insurance other than life insurance, where the Council forwarded to Parliament a text that it regarded as its common position but which Parliament insisted on treating as a basic text on which it was being reconsulted on first reading. Clearly, however, Parliament is often reluctant to demand reconsultation when this would hold up a matter that it is keen to see dealt with urgently.

One special example of reconsultation is where Council amends the legal base from an article requiring two readings to one requiring only a single reading. Council should then reconsult Parliament, which gives a second opinion under the ordinary consultation procedure (first-reading pro-cedure) on Council's "common orientation" (rather than "common pos-ition"). However, Council sometimes reconsults Parliament not on the text as a whole but only on the change of legal base.

Negotiations and dialogue with the Council and Commission

The increase of its formal powers strengthens Parliament's position in the contacts and discussions with other institutions that inevitably accompany the consideration of legislative proposals. The extent of those contacts has increased in line with the development of the Parliament's legislative powers.

A good example of this developing contact is the way in which the Council has come to fulfil its obligation to inform the Parliament fully of the reasons that led it to adopt its common position. Such an obligation is, of course, open to very wide interpretation. Council quickly agreed to present its justification to Parliament in writing. However, the first such justification received by Parliament (after the cooperation procedure got underway in 1987) merely referred in the covering letter to the preambles of the draft directives in question as constituting Council's justification. Parliament objected strongly to this. Informal contacts were taken with Council, but Parliament's President (then Lord Plumb) had to return to this subject again and make a formal statement to plenary on 28 October 1987 on the unacceptability of Council's position. He stated that "as a minimum, the Council should provide a specific and explained reaction to each of Parliament's amendments". The explanations provided by Council have now improved to the extent that they provide an account of Council's viewpoint on the substantive issues raised in the consideration of draft legislation and show where the Council is acting against the wishes of the Commission. The absence of detailed justifications on individual amendments has proved less of a handicap than one might have considered as a result of the improving informal contacts between the two institutions. There is now a much better awareness in the Parliament as to why particular Parliament amendments are rejected in Council and which countries opposed them, even if this information is obtained informally.

At the same time, there is a clear trend towards providing the Parliament and the public with more information about what is decided in the Council. In October 1993, following an inter-institutional agreement between Parliament, Council and the Commission on democracy and transparency in the European institutions, the Council agreed to publish the results of votes taken on legislation and on common positions. This not only improves transparency, but also enables Parliament to know what support might be forthcoming for possible second-reading amendments. Such information is likely to be extended when the institutions agree on new rules for transparency as required by the Treaty of Amsterdam (Article 255 (TEC)).

The written material provided by the Council can acquire much greater relevance if it is accompanied by direct contacts. Here too there have been significant developments over recent years. Dialogue with Council now takes place through the regular appearances of the Presidents-in-Office of the various specialised Councils before the responsible parliamentary committees. Most appear twice during their six-month term. Since the entry into force of the cooperation procedure and even more so, with the arrival of co-decision, these appearances have become an opportunity to discuss – formally in the meeting or informally in the corridor – the take-up of parliamentary amendments to legislative proposals still being considered by Council.

Meetings and correspondence between committee chairmen/rapporteurs and presidents-in-office have also increased. On rare occasions, committee chairmen have been invited to speak at the relevant Council meetings. Contacts between officials in the committee secretariats and their counterparts in the Commission and Council are also being developed. This has been facilitated by the transfer of most of the officials working in the committees of the Parliament's secretariat from the relative isolation of Luxembourg to Brussels, where virtually all committee meetings now take place.

Parliament is also exploring reinforced forms of dialogue with Council following the entry into force of the Amsterdam Treaty and the increased importance of co-decision. It modified its Rules of Procedure to make it possible for the Council:

- to come before its committees in person and to comment on draft amendments on a proposal at first reading before the committee proceeds to its
  final vote (Rule 66);
- to present its common position to committee responsible, so that the written communication can be complemented by additional oral explanations
  (Rule 76.2);
- to enter into dialogue with the committee chair or rapporteur to look for
  possible compromise amendments at second reading (Article 76.5).

Such rules do not bind the Council – no doubt they will present the Council
with certain difficulties of organisation – but they do point to a very clear
trend. Both institutions recognise that they need to work together and
cannot afford to stay isolated, one from the other, if the legislative procedures are to operate successfully.

Assent procedure

The Single European Act introduced, and the Treaties of Maastricht and
Amsterdam extended, a procedure (see Figure 6) whereby the approval of
Parliament is required in a single reading before Council can enact a
measure. Under the Single European Act, this applied only to association
agreements with third countries and the accession of new Member States
(see next section). As a result of the Maastricht and Amsterdam Treaties, a
further six categories of decision are now covered by assent:

- sanctions in the event of serious and persistent breach of fundamental
  rights by a Member State (Article 7 of EU Treaty);

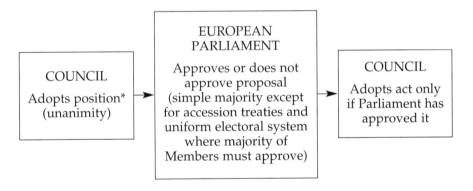

* Council acts on a proposal of
  - the Commission (Articles 105(6), 161, 300 (3) TEC)
  - the Parliament (Article 190 (4) TEC)
  - the Central Bank[1] or the Commission (Article 107 (5) TEC)
  - applicant states, after consulting the Commission (Article 49 TEU)

[1] in which case Council may act by a qualified majority

Figure 6: *Assent procedure*

- special tasks to be entrusted to the European Central Bank (Article 105 (6))
- amendments to the protocol of the European System of Central Banks (Article 107 (5))
- the definition of the tasks, objectives, methods of organisation and co-ordination of the structural funds and the creation of the cohesion fund (Article 161);
- the uniform procedure for European elections (Article 190.4); and
- international agreements establishing a specific institutional framework, agreements having important budgetary implications for the Community and agreements entailing amendment of an act adopted under co-decision (Article 300.3).

The explicit approval by Parliament by a simple majority of those voting is the normal requirement, but in three areas the approval of the majority of members of Parliament (i.e. abstentions or absences counting against) is required. These are the accession of new Member States, the uniform electoral system for European elections and sanctions in the event of a breach of human rights. This absolute majority was also required under the terms of the Single Act for association agreements with third countries, but the Treaty of Maastricht modified the requirement to a simple majority.

The assent procedure is a cruder form of co-decision in that there is no scope for Parliament to put forward amendments to the measure in question. This is normal when it comes to international agreements negotiated by the Commission which, as in national parliaments, have to be dealt with on a take it or leave it basis (see below). It is also understandable for "constitutional" type measures. However, its continuing application to measures that are typically legislative in character, such as the operational rules for the structural funds, is curious.

In two further cases, the assent procedure is reversed in that it is the Council that must give its assent to an act of the Parliament. These two cases are the "statute" of the Ombudsman laying down the general conditions governing his duties (see Chapter 14) and that of the members of the Parliament (see Chapter 4). Whichever way round assent is given, it amounts to a crude form of co-decision in that the agreement of both Council and Parliament are necessary.

Parliament and the approval of international agreements

The Treaties allow the Community to be party to various sorts of international agreements. Agreements are negotiated by the Commission (except accession agreements whereby new states join the Community, where the Member States negotiate after a decision in principle by Council). However, a variety of provisions were laid down in the Treaties for authorising the Commission to open negotiations and for concluding (ratifying) the resulting agreement:

- under the ECSC Treaty, no provisions were laid down for international agreements, but in practice the Commission, within the limits of its fields of responsibility, may negotiate and conclude agreements;
- under the EEC Treaty, Art. 228 originally provided for the Commission

to negotiate agreements which "shall be concluded by the Council after consulting the Parliament, where required by this Treaty". Only Article 238 (association agreements) provided, in fact, for such consultation of Parliament. The main instrument for international agreements, articles 113-114, (trade, commerce and tariffs) provided for no such consultation. This, as we shall see, has now been modified considerably;

- under the EURATOM Treaty, it is again only for association agreements that Parliament is consulted (Art. 206). Ordinary agreements (Art. 101) are concluded by the Commission with the approval of Council (or even without Council's approval if no implementing provisions by Council are required and if the budget is not overstepped).

The European Parliament was thus in a weak position under the initial provisions of the Treaties. It was only consulted in the case of association agreements, and had no say at all concerning the bulk of agreements entered into by the Community. This weakness was all the greater as the Commission negotiated under Art. 133 (ex-113) TEC and 101 EURATOM on the basis of negotiating mandates decided on by Council, and Parliament had no say in drawing up such mandates.

From the outset, Parliament sought to modify this situation and improve its position, both by agreement with the other institutions and by obtaining important changes to the Treaties.

The Luns procedure

A first step forward for Parliament came as early as 1964 when Council, through a letter of its President Luns, undertook to involve Parliament in the discussion preceding the opening of negotiations for an association agreement and to keep it informed during the negotiations. According to this procedure, Parliament may hold a debate before negotiations open, the Commission briefs Parliament's responsible committees during the negotiations, and when they have finished, Council's President or his representative appear before the same committees to brief them confidentially and informally, of the contents of the agreement.

The AETR ruling of the Court

In an important judgement in 1971 (Case C-22/70) the Court ruled that the Community as such is also responsible for the external aspects of its internal policies. This implies that the same Treaty provisions would apply in approving external agreements as apply to the policy area in question. Where this provided for consultation of Parliament, Parliament would therefore also be consulted on the external agreements. This has been important notably in the areas of agriculture, transport and for general economic cooperation agreements.

The Luns-Westerterp procedure

Until the 1970s, Council had refused to give any rights such as those incorporated in the Luns procedure to Parliament for trade and commercial agreements, although these were more numerous and frequently more important (e.g. GATT) than association agreements. The climate in Council changed somewhat in the early 1970s, partly as a result of the AETR ruling, partly because of the Paris Summit of 1973 agreeing to reinforce Parliament's powers and especially because of a realisation that Parliament's new budgetary powers might enable it to cause problems for the implementation of agreements that have budgetary implications. First, the Commission agreed in its Memorandum to Parliament of 30 May 1973, to participate in any debate that Parliament decided to organise in plenary or in committee on the negotiation of commercial agreements, and to brief parliamentary committees during the negotiations (as in the Luns procedure). Then, in October 1973, Council President Westerterp undertook in a letter to Parliament on behalf of Council, to apply a modified version of the Luns procedure to commercial agreements. The text of Council's letter was virtually the same as that of 1964, except that it made no reference to the Commission briefing committees (covered already by the Commission's Memorandum) and it undertook to supplement the informal confidential briefing of Parliament's committees before signature of an agreement with a formal and public information to plenary after signature but before conclusion.

Improvement of the Luns-Westerterp procedures

The growing number of agreements entered into by the Community and the constant need to update and revise them led to further developments in 1977 when Council, through a letter of its President, Tony Crosland, agreed to distinguish between two types of agreement:

- Important agreements, where the Council President's briefing of Parliament's committees would take place at a special meeting (normally in Brussels) instead of at the fringe of a plenary session, and where the President would submit a written aide-memoire in advance.
- Other agreements, where Council would simply inform Parliament in writing of the opening and the conclusion of negotiations, but where Parliament could, if it expressed the wish within two weeks, follow the procedure for important agreements instead.

At the same time, the Community was entering into more and more "cooperation agreements", a sort of half-way house between commercial agreements and association agreements, involving such things as trade, technical co-operation, aid, loans, etc. These, not being specifically provided for under the treaty, required the use of Article 235 (now 308) as a legal base and this in turn required consulting Parliament.

The Stuttgart "Solemn Declaration on European Union"

In this Declaration the European Council agreed that Parliament should be formally consulted on all "significant" international agreements before their conclusion, as well as on accession treaties. The Luns-Westerterp procedures were also extended to cover all important agreements (i.e. even those outside the scope of the then Articles 113 and 238 EEC).

The assent procedure introduced by the Single European Act

The Single European Act modified two articles of the EEC treaty in order to require the assent of the European Parliament for the conclusion of association agreements (Art. 310) and for the accession of new Member States (Art. 49).

Accession of new Member States is not something that arises every month, but the growing list of applicants is a reminder that Parliament could block accession if certain conditions that it feels are important are not met and, in particular, if it considers that the right balance between widening and deepening is not achieved. This possibility means that the other institutions as well as the applicant states are more inclined to take the Parliament seriously during the negotiations and not to assume that it will vote in favour.

The importance of this power was evident in the final stages of the negotiations for the accession of Austria, Sweden, Finland and (it was then thought) Norway. A new threshold for obtaining a qualified majority (previously 54 votes out of 76) had to be defined for a Council with 90 votes. Most Member States wanted the new threshold to be 64, which represented the same proportion (71 per cent) as the previous level. A minority, including the UK, wanted the threshold to be 68, representing the same "blocking minority" of 23 votes. This, however, would have made decision-taking more difficult and MEPs made it clear that Parliament would not give its assent to accession if it contained such a weakening of the Union. This helped to persuade the Member States to agree, in the so-called Ioannina Declaration, on a threshold of 64, with a blocking minority of 27 votes, subject to a provision that "if members of the Council representing a total of 23 to 26 votes indicate their intention to oppose the adoption by the Council of a decision by a qualified majority", then " a reasonable time" would be allowed to elapse to see if an agreement could be found before the new blocking minority figure of 27 was used. Parliament was not entirely happy with this compromise but its pressure had helped to reduce the damage. Hence it felt able to approve the four accessions in May 1994 by overwhelming majorities.

The assent procedure also applies to the substantial number of association agreements with third countries or groups of countries. Indeed, this power has been far more significant than had been supposed by some of those involved in negotiating the Single European Act. The then UK Permanent Representative, for instance, thought that there would be no such procedures "coming forward in the life of this Parliament". In fact, there were over 30 cases between the entry into force of the Single Act and the end of the 1984-89 Parliament. The large number arose because of the need for parliamentary assent not just for the original agreement, but also for revisions or additions to agreements, such as financial protocols, which may be adopted only for limited periods and require renewal.

Three examples show how Parliament can make use of this power. First, in 1988, Parliament initially refused to give its assent to three agreements with Israel. Parliament was unhappy with the conditions for exports to the Community for Palestinian producers in the occupied territories. The dispute occurred at the time of the beginning of the *Intifada* in the West Bank and Gaza. Parliament therefore rejected three protocols to the EEC/Israel Association Agreement. The agreements were referred back to Council. Council in turn referred them back to Parliament, which agreed to put the proposals back on its agenda, but postponed consideration of them for several months. During this period the Commission, as well as MEPs from various Political Groups and Parliament's Committee on External Economic Relations, had discussions with Israeli representatives which produced some concessions on West Bank exports. Parliament then approved the protocols.

Second, Parliament refused its assent to financial protocols with Syria and Morocco in 1992 to protest at the human rights situation in these countries. This caused a serious diplomatic rift with Morocco in particular, which refused, in retaliation, to renew a fishing agreement with the Community for several months.

Finally, there was a long-running argument in the Parliament about whether or not to give its assent to the EU-Turkey customs union agreement. The human rights situation in Turkey was a source of major concern inside the Parliament and there was a strong sense in the summer of 1995 that there would not be a majority for the agreement. In the end, and after Turkey agreed to change its Constitution, a sufficient number of members were persuaded that the deal should go ahead, with 343 votes in favour, 149 against and 36 abstentions at the December 1995 plenary.

The extension of the assent procedure by the Treaty of Maastricht

The Single Act led to a discrepancy in Parliament's powers. Whereas its *assent* was necessary for what could often be relatively minor adjustments or additional protocols to an association agreement, it was, according to the Treaties, only *consulted* for some major agreements such as the first trade and economic co-operation agreements with Eastern European countries. Indeed, for purely trade agreements based on Art. 133, such as GATT, it was not formally consulted at all.

Parliament sought to overcome this anomaly in two ways. First, it pressed the Commission and Council to make greater use of the then Article 238 (Association Agreements) wherever there was scope for interpretation as to the nature of the agreement. As a result of this, the "Europe" agreements with Central and Eastern European countries and the European Economic Area agreement with the EFTA countries were classified as association agreements. Second, Parliament provided in its own Rules of Procedure that it would treat any "significant international agreement" (i.e. the category which the Stuttgart Solemn Declaration provided for Parliament to be consulted on) according to the same procedures as it applied to association agreements. This meant that Parliament would give or refuse its assent to the conclusion, renewal or modification of such agreements in the same way as it did for association agreements, and that it would expect Council not to conclude an agreement that did not receive the assent of Parliament.

This approach gained acceptance to the extent that the Member States agreed in the Treaty of Maastricht to change the provisions of the EC treaty in order to require Parliament's assent for all important agreements. These were defined as any agreement establishing a specific institutional framework, or having important implications for the Community budget, or requiring the amendment of Community legislation pursuant to the co-decision procedure. For all other agreements (except Article 133 (3) agree-ments) Parliament is now consulted, but with the derogation from normal practice that Council may lay down a deadline for Parliament's opinion.

These changes considerably strengthen Parliament's role in the approval of international agreements (if not in determining the negotiating man-dates). They take place at a time when the external relations of the Community are of growing importance, notably with the development of a common foreign and security policy. The Treaty of Maastricht provided for Parliament to be consulted by Council on the main aspects and basic choices of the common foreign policy, but Parliament's main legal power over Council in external relations will be its right to give or refuse assent for important international agreements. Greater use of this power is to be expected in the coming years.

The Commission also undertook, following a statement made by Jacques Delors to Parliament in February 1990, to include MEPs as observers in its delegations to important multilateral conferences (such as WTO ministeri-als). In 1998 the Council formally agreed to the principle of MEPs being able to join delegations of the Union at international conferences, subject to a request being submitted at least four weeks in advance by the President of the Parliament.

Parliament has thus come a long way from its initial position regarding international agreements, where it was merely consulted on a limited cat-egory of such agreements and received no information on their negotiations. Its powers, under the assent procedure, are comparable to the right to authorise ratification that most national parliaments enjoy, and its access to information on the conduct of such negotiations is actually better than that of many national parliaments.

Right to initiate legislation

The right to initiate legislative proposals is one that is traditionally associ-ated with parliaments. But in practice, in most countries, this role has been taken over completely, or almost completely, by governments. In the UK, for example, MPs have to rely on a lottery system (the ballot for "private members' bills") to introduce a limited category of legislative proposals themselves. In France, the government is given a virtual monopoly in this respect by the Constitution. Even in countries where there are no consti-tutional or regulatory limitations on Parliament, the detailed and technical nature of much modern legislation means that, in practice, most legislation is initiated by the executive.

So it is in the European Union, where the Commission has a near mon-opoly of legislative initiative. The European Parliament itself has no formal right under the Treaty to initiate legislation, except for the purpose of adopt-ing a uniform electoral procedure for European elections and the statute for its members. Indeed it has not sought such a right, underlining the com-parability between its position and that of the Council, which also cannot normally initiate Community legislation. Nevertheless, as in national situ-ations, the formal provisions do not grant the executive a monopoly on ideas or the right to exercise these powers without due regard to the wishes of Council and Parliament. Council, indeed, was given the right under the original Treaties (now Article 208) to request the Commission to undertake studies and to submit to it any appropriate proposals.

Under the Maastricht Treaty the Parliament was awarded a right that can be compared with the existing right of the Council. Under Article 192, it can request, by an absolute majority of its members, that the Commission "submit any appropriate proposal on matters on which it considers that a Community act is required for the purpose of implementing this Treaty". Before the Amsterdam Treaty came into force, this right was only used very sparingly. There were six such resolutions adopted in the 1994–99 legislature as follows:

- *Hotel fire safety* (20 April 1994)
- *Environmental damage* (4 May 1994)
- *Settlement of claims arising from traffic accidents occurring outside the claimant's country of origin* (26 October 1995)
- *Health cards* (17 April 1996)
- *Forest strategy* (30 January 1997)
- *Network access for renewable energies* (17 June 1998)

Up to now only one of these resolutions has been followed up by a specific legislative proposal. The Rothley report on the settlement of claims arising from traffic accidents gave rise to the proposal for a Fourth Motor Insurance Directive, which was examined in second reading by the Parliament in the autumn of 1999. This provision should not, however, be seen in isolation: the Parliament has developed various other techniques that continue to be relevant despite the existence of Article 192.

Resolutions seeking to initiate legislation

Reference has already been made to Parliament's procedures governing the adoption of reports at its own initiative (either "own initiative" reports of parliamentary committees, or reports drawn up in response to Rule 48 motions for resolution tabled by MEPs, or indeed resolutions adopted through the urgency procedure or to wind up a debate). Being an independent institution, whose majority is not beholden to the Commission, Parliament frequently uses these opportunities to call on the Commission to take action of one sort of another, and this frequently includes calls for new legislative proposals. Naturally, individual MEPs or Political Groups or indeed parliamentary committees frequently make such proposals in their own right, but those carrying the most weight are own initiative reports drawn up after due consideration (possibly including public hearings) by the responsible parliamentary committee and adopted after due debate in plenary.

The Commission first responds to such initiatives in the debate in plenary. The Commission agreed in 1982 (in its "report on inter-institutional relations", the so-called Andriessen report, Bulletin EEC supplement 3/82) in principle to take up any parliamentary proposals to which it did not have any major objection. Where it had an objection, it undertook to explain its attitude in detail to Parliament. Since March 1983, when it made a commitment to do so through an exchange of letters with Parliament's President

(Piet Dankert), the Commission has submitted written reports every six months explaining how it has responded to Parliament's initiatives and what action it has taken. In November 1994, it was agreed to replace this with a more regular report to be examined within the relevant committees.

The most famous historical example of how Parliament has used this power was the 1982 initiative to press for a ban on the import of baby seal skins into the Community. It was supported by a large amount of public campaigning including a petition with over a million signatures. These efforts resulted in Commission proposals, then backed by Parliament in the legislative procedure, and the adoption of a Council regulation, despite initial reluctance by both the Commission and Council. Another example, this time without much support from public opinion, was the Community's directive on trans-frontier television broadcasts, laying down rules for such broadcasts, which was adopted under co-decision in 1997. This can also be traced back to an own initiative report of Parliament's. Similarly, the proposal to ban tobacco advertising, discussed earlier in this chapter, which passed in 1998 under the co-decision procedure, could be traced back to a Parliament initiative of 1990.

In the field of external relations too, parliamentary initiatives can lead to results. The STABEX fund in the Lomé Convention, which helps stabilise the exports earnings for certain products of the ACP countries, as well as the human rights clauses in that same Convention, owe their origin to parliamentary initiatives.

Finally, it is important to recall that the Parliament has consistently used its budgetary powers to initiate new Community policies. How it has done so is discussed in Chapter 13.

Annual legislative programme

In the revision of its Rules of Procedure following the Single European Act, Parliament provided for it and the Commission to agree on an annual legislative programme and timetable. Parliament's need to manage its workload and the fact that (unlike some national parliaments) it is master of its own agenda, persuaded the Commission of the advantages of negotiating an agreed programme. It therefore accepted the procedure, and the first such programme was agreed in March 1988. It was largely an exercise in determining a timetable for Commission proposals and parliamentary consideration thereof on a quarter-by-quarter basis but it did open the door for Parliament to influence the priorities in the Commission's programme and to press for the inclusion of new items (e.g. following up parliamentary "initiative" reports) or even the exclusion of items.

The 1989 programme included a preamble in which the two institutions agreed to give priority to certain sectors (completion of the internal market, social policy, environment policy and monetary integration) and to improve procedures by providing for trilateral meetings (Commissioner responsible, Council President and Parliament committee chairman and rapporteur). The following year difficult discussions were held on re-scheduling various legislative proposals but agreement was finally reached both on this and on a "code of conduct" in which the Commission undertook to improve its cooperation with Parliament.

In the years that followed, various measures were to taken to improve the operation of the system. To address complaints about the relative slowness with which the programme was adopted, the Commission agreed in the inter-institutional Declaration of October 1993 to finalise its work programme (upon which its version of the legislative programme is based), by October of the previous year. For its part, Parliament indicated in its Rules of Procedure (Rule 57) its determination to complete the process of dealing with the legislative programme before the end of the preceding year.

In principle, these commitments opened the way to the programme becoming a more effective device for planning and monitoring the legislative activity of the Union but in practice, it did not live up to expectations, with discussions on the programme assuming a somewhat mechanical flavour. Its contents tended to combine a list of all the proposals that were in the pipeline in the Commission services with a general introduction which, far from being the equivalent of the "Queen's Speech", was designed to cause minimum offence. It was very hard to assess how important the individual items all were or indeed when precisely they could be expected to arrive in the Parliament. There was little sense of difficult choices having been made inside the Commission between competing priorities. The prospect of a new dynamic being introduced into the process appeared with the promise of the Prodi Commission to put a political programme in front of the Parliament at the beginning of 2000.

Such a programme will offer an interesting contrast with the documents that are now produced in the Council. Originally the Council was unwilling to become involved in the preparation of the Commission legislative programme but the situation changed, following the adoption of the Inter-institutional Declaration on democracy, transparency and subsidiarity on 25 October 1993. The Council agreed to "state its position on the programme in a declaration and undertake to implement as soon as possible the provisions to which it attaches priority". Thus in its declaration on the Commission's programme for 1999, for example, the Council presented a range of areas, internally and externally, where it intended to lay emphasis. These included very specific measures such as the Statute for a European Company, abolition of the tax exemption for kerosene, revision of the regulation on dual-use goods in relation to arms exports and the negotiation of Euro-Mediterannean agreements with Egypt, Lebanon, Syria and Algeria. Priorities of this kind combined with the often very detailed programmes of each Presidency do now start to provide an important benchmark against which the progress of the Council can be judged by the European Parliament and indeed by national parliaments.

Overall assessment

The European Parliament's role in the Community's legislative procedure has increased from having, initially, no role whatsoever, to having a consultative role, to exercising formal powers that as Table 23 below, which gives an overview of the Parliament's role after Amsterdam, shows, justify the description of the Parliament as a co-legislator with the Council. The European Parliament has demonstrated its ability to initiate new legislation in areas of concern to the public, to force substantial amendments to major legislative proposals, to prevent legislative provision where this is not clearly justified and to secure changes of detail which, when cumulated, have led to a generally higher standard of protection for consumers, workers and other participants in the Single European Market.

More specifically, Parliament has used its powers to strengthen consumer protection in package holidays, to tighten rules on insider trading, to provide for greater transparency in the pricing of pharmaceuticals, to limit advertising on trans-frontier broadcasts to 15 per cent of transmission time, to raise minimum standards for safety and health at work (and to provide for information and consultation procedures for workers in this context), to modify the content of Community research programmes (notably to boost research on cancer and AIDS), to ensure transparency in methods of calculating and advertising consumer credit, to make car insurance regulations when travelling abroad more favourable to victims and to ban certain hormones in meat.

The European Parliament is not a sovereign Parliament in the sense of its word being final when it comes to the adoption of legislation in all areas for which it is competent. On the other hand, it is not a rubber-stamp Parliament whose real powers are in practice exercised merely to legitimise a government's legislative wishes. It is an independent institution whose members are not bound to support a particular governing majority, which does not have a permanent majority coalition and whose party structures are not all-pervasive. In this sense it can be compared with the US Congress, with its own identity, independent legitimacy and separation from the executive, whilst seeking to interact intensely with that executive.

The European Parliament is now a clearly identifiable part of an institutional triangle. This fact in itself is remarkable in historical terms. The term "institutional triangle" was virtually unused two decades ago when most commentators referred to a bicephalous Community made up of the Commission and the Council. Now the argument is rather one about preserving and developing the equal status that the Parliament has won with regard to the other two institutions and of making European electorates aware of the contribution that the Parliament is increasingly making to the content of European laws affecting us all.

Table 23: Distribution of legislative procedures and voting methods in Council under Amsterdam Treaty provisions

Treaty articles & descriptions	Legislative procedure:				Council voting:	
	co-decision	consultation	assent/cooperation*	no consultation	unanimity	qualified majority
principles (1–16)	12	13 11(2)	–	–	13	12 11(2)
citizenship 17–22	18(2)	19(1), 22	–	–	19(1), 22 18(2)	–
goods (23–31)	–	–	–	26	–	26
agriculture (32–38)	–	37(3)	–	–	–	37(3)
people, services & capital (39–69)	40, 44, 55 42, 46(2) 47(2)	47, 52(1) 67(1&3)	–	45, 49 57(2) 59, 60(1&2) 64(2)	57(2) 42, 47 67(1)	40, 44, 45, 49, 55 57(2), 59, 60(1&2) 42, 46(2), 47(2) 52(1), 64(2), 67(3)
transport (70–90)	71(1) 80(2)	71(2)	–	75(3), 80(2)	71(2)	75(3), 80(2) 71(1), 80(2)
competition, tax & laws (81–97)	95(1)	83, 89 93, 94	–	88(2), 92, 96	88(2), 93, 94	83, 89, 92, 95(1) 96
economic & monetary policy (98–124)	–	104(4) 107(6) 110(3) 111(1&4) 121(3&4) 122(2)	99(5)* 102(2)* 103(2)* 105(6) 106(2)* 107(5)	99(2), 100(1) 100(2), 104(6) 111(1–4), 114(3) 119(2&3) 120(3), 122(1) 123(4&5)	100(1&2) 105(6), 107(5) 111(1&4) 123(4&5)	99(2&5), 100(2) 102(2), 103(2) 104(4&6), 106(2) 107(5&6), 110(3) 111(1–4), 114(3) 119(2&3), 120(3) 121(3&4), 122(1&2)
employment (125–130)	129	128(2)	–	128(4)	–	128(2&4), 129
commercial & customs (131–135)	135	133(5)	–	132(1), 133(4)	133(5)	132(1), 133(4) 135

Table 23: *Continued*

Treaty articles & descriptions	Legislative procedure:				Council voting:	
	co-decision	consultation	assent/ cooperation*	no consultation	unanimity	qualified majority
social, culture, health & consumer protection (136–153)	149(4), 151, 152(4c), 153(4), **137(1&2)**, **148, 150(4)**, **141**, **152(4a&b)**	**137(3)**	–	139(2), 144, 149(4), 151(5), 152(4), **139(2)**	144, 151, 151(5), **137(3), 139(2)**	139(2), 149(4), 152(4&4c), 153(4), **137(1&2), 148**, **150(4)**, **141, 152(4a&b)**
industry, TENs cohesion and R&D (154–173)	156(i), **156, 162**, **166, 172**	157(3), 159, 166(4), **172(1)**	161	–	157(3), 159, 161	156(i), 166(4), **156, 162, 166, 172**, **172(1)**
environment (174–176)	175(3), **175(1)**	175(2)	–	–	175(2)	175(3), **175(1)**
development & OCTs (177–188)	**179**	–	–	187	187	179
institutional & financial provisions (189–280)	255(2), **280(4)**	225(2), 245(ii), 247(3), 269, 270, 279	190(4)	210, 213(1), 215, 221, 222, 225(4), 245(iii), 247(8), 258(ii& iv), 263, 272(3), 273(ii), **207(2)**	190(4), 213(1), 215, 221, 222, 225(2&4), 245(ii &iii), 247(3), 258(ii), 263, 269, 270, 279, **207(2)**	210, 247(8), 272(3), 273(ii), **258(iv)**, 255(2), **280(4)**
general & final provisions (281–314)	285(1), **286(2)**	283, 300(2 &2ii), 308, **299(2)**	300(3)	290, 296(2), 301, **309(2&3)**	296(2), 290, 300(2ii&3), 308	283, 300(2&2ii), 301, **299(2), 309(2&3)**, 285(1), **286(2)**

Source: European Commission

13. The budgetary role

Just as Parliament has come to acquire a position of greater equality in relation to legislation, so it also enjoys a substantial degree of equality with Council in relation to the budget. However, this has come about in a very different way. Whereas for legislation Parliament made progress by successive changes to the Treaty in the late 1980s and 1990s, in budgetary affairs, the formal Treaty provisions governing the establishment of the budget have remained unchanged for nearly thirty years. The powers that the Parliament now has emerged from the decision in 1970 to replace national contributions as a means of financing Community policies with a system of "own resources". This change was not only important in making the resources collective Community property which Member States were legally obliged to make available, it also generated a debate about who should exercise control over the revenue collected and who should decide how it be allocated and used. It was agreed that the limit on the revenue available to the Community be fixed by the Member States with any change requiring ratification by national parliaments, but that within this overall limit, expenditure be determined jointly by Parliament and Council. In this context the two institutions came to be known as the twin arms of the "budgetary authority."

These changes, as consolidated by a further Treaty revision in 1975, established four major powers for the Parliament. The first three relate to the procedure for establishing the budget, the fourth concerns scrutiny of the implementation of the budget, which will be discussed in Chapter 14. The Parliament:

- First, acquired **the right to increase or to reduce Community expenditure**, within certain defined limits, without having to obtain the approval of the Council.
- Second, gained the opportunity **to redistribute spending**, without an increase or reduction, from one sector of the budget to another.
- Third, was granted **the power to reject** the whole annual budget or any supplementary budget.
- Fourth, was given **the exclusive right to grant a discharge to the Commission** in respect of the implementation of the budget, i.e. to approve or not the way in which the Commission spends the money voted in the budget.

The formal mechanisms that give effect to the three powers relating to the establishment of the budget are included in Article 272 TEC (ex-203). They can be summarised as follows:

Article 272 – the formal rules for establishing the budget

Before July the Commission presents its estimates of its own spending (along with that of each of the other institutions) in the form of a *preliminary draft budget* which it must forward to Council. Council, acting by a qualified majority, adopts a *draft budget*, which it must forward to Parliament by October 5 at the latest.

Parliament has 45 days in which to act. If it fails to do so or if it approves the Council draft, the draft stands as finally adopted. Otherwise, the Parliament has the right to:

– Adopt "modifications" to "compulsory expenditure" (CE) by a simple majority of those voting;
– Adopt "amendments" to "non-compulsory expenditure" (NCE) by a majority of its members.

The budget is then referred back to Council, which has 15 days in which to complete a second reading. If it does not do so, the Parliament version is deemed adopted. To amend Parliament's "modifications" to compulsory expenditure, the Council needs:

– A qualified majority to *approve* any modification that increases expenditure;
– A qualified majority to *overrule* any modification that does not increase expenditure (reductions or transfers from one area to another).

Council may also modify Parliament's "amendments" to non-compulsory expenditure, but only by a qualified majority. Such modifications are referred back to Parliament, which has 15 days to amend them at its second reading. To do so, it requires three-fifths of the vote cast and at least a majority of members.

For NCE, the institutions are obliged to respect a maximum rate of increase fixed annually in the light of the growth of the Member States' GNPs, the variation in national budgets and the trend in the cost of living. Regardless of the level of NCE in the draft budget of the Council, Parliament retains the right to increase NCE beyond the figure in the Council's draft budget by half the maximum rate. The level of the maximum rate itself can be increased if there is agreement between Council, acting by qualified majority, and Parliament, acting by a majority of its members and three fifths of the votes cast.

Parliament may also by a two thirds majority reject the draft budget as a whole, in which case the whole procedure must start again, Community expenditure in the meantime being frozen at the previous year's level on a month-by-month basis.

Finally, it is up to the President of Parliament to sign the budget into law when all the procedures have been completed.

However, Article 272 only gives a very incomplete picture of the role of Parliament in contributing to budgetary policy. Most importantly, since 1988

Parliament, Council and Commission have signed three inter-institutional agreements on budgetary discipline and the improvement of the budgetary procedure. Each of these agreements has included a multi-annual financial perspective, which lays down expenditure ceilings for a range of policy areas, which all three institutions agree to respect in the course of the annual budgetary procedure. The 1999 agreement (Official Journal, C 172 of 18 June 1999) provides alternative frameworks for the period up to 2006, based either on a Union of 15 or on a Union of 21, the latter assuming the first enlargement will take place in 2002. In both cases, the budgetary authority is called upon to respect the ceilings laid down, though there are provisions for modifications to the ceilings in the event of changed circumstances.

In addition, the 1999 agreement has codified in one document a range of procedures and rules, relating notably to inter-institutional cooperation, the classification of expenditure, the incorporation of financial provisions in legislative acts, and the requirement of a legal base and expenditure on Common Foreign and Security Policy (CFSP). These have transformed the character of the budgetary procedure as laid down in the Treaty. Article 272 has remained fixed but the Parliament's role has evolved and in a way that has reinforced the degree of co-decision with the Council. The two institutions increasingly seek mutually acceptable outcomes based on a shared perception of each other's role, rather than Parliament attempting to use the Treaty articles to impose its will on the Council. The combined effect of the financial perspective and the new rules and procedures has been to reinforce substantially the smooth running and predictability of the budgetary procedure.

The annual budgetary procedure

To see how Parliament behaves to take advantage of its budgetary powers, it is useful to follow the progress of budget discussions through the year.

Preparing for the preliminary draft budget

The first step is taken by the Committee on Budgets, which nominates two rapporteurs. One has responsibility for the Commission's administrative and operational budgets, which include all spending on EU policies and amount to over 98 per cent of the total Union budget; the second examines the administrative budgets of the other institutions, including that of the Parliament itself. Normally these appointments are made in January of the year preceding the financial year under discussion. (In the Union, the financial year runs from January to December.) These posts are much sought after and subject to long negotiation within and between the Groups. As the following lists show, the EPP-ED and PES Groups provided most, but not all, of the rapporteurs, in the decade from 1990 to 2000:

Commission budget	Other institutions
1990 John TOMLINSON (PES)	Diemut THEATO (EPP)
1991 Alain LAMASSOURE (ELDR)	Diemut THEATO (EPP)
1992 Pam CORNELISSEN (EPP)	John TOMLINSON (PES)
1993 Detlev SAMLAND (PES)	Jean Claude PASTY (RDE)
1994 Terry WYNN (PES)	Pasqualina NAPOLETANO (PES)

1995	Terry WYNN (PES)	Piet DANKERT (PES)
1996	James ELLES (EPP)	Joaquim MIRANDA (EUL-NGL)
1997	Laurens BRINKHORST (ELDR)	Juan Manuel FABRA VALLES (EPP)
1998	Stanislaw TILLICH (EPP)	John TOMLINSON (PES)
1999	Barbara DÜHRKOP DÜHRKOP (PES)	Vincenzo VIOLA (EPP)
2000	Jean-Louis BOURLANGES (EPP-ED)	Kyösti VIRRANKOSKI (ELDR)

The rapporteur for the administrative budgets of the institutions other than the Commission has responsibility in the first half of the year for guiding the estimates of the Parliament itself through the plenary, usually at its May session. This involves discussions extending beyond the Budgets Committee: the Bureau and the Group chairs also play a major role. The Bureau draws up the first version of the Parliament's spending plans for the following year, known as the preliminary draft estimates. It also decides upon the number of new posts to be created in the establishment plan, with the Budgets Committee able to determine when the related appropriations should be granted. The Group chairs have a specific responsibility in relation to budgetary matters affecting the Political Groups.

During the same period before the summer the rapporteur for the Commission budget has the specific task of steering through committee and plenary a set of guidelines laying down the Parliament's priorities with the aim of influencing the content of the Commission's preliminary draft. To give greater weight to this report, a *trialogue* meeting is organised between delegations of the three institutions, the Parliament's led by the Chair of the Budgets Committee, the Council's by the President of the Budgets Council and the Commission's by the Commissioner responsible for the budget. This meeting discusses possible priorities for the budget in advance of the Commission publishing its plans with a view to enabling the Commission to take account of the positions of the two branches of the budgetary authority.

The Commission usually presents the preliminary draft to Parliament in April, though Article 272, as we have seen, does not oblige it to do so until July. The draft is made up of the consolidated estimates of revenue and expenditure of all institutions and is at present divided into six sections. The preliminary draft distinguishes between "payment appropriations", relating to expenditure restricted to the year in question, and "commitment appropriations", which authorise expenditure over a number of years for multi-annual programmes. The payment appropriations proposed for 2000 were as follows:

Section I	Parliament with an annex for the Ombudsman	€923m
Section II	Council	€324m
Section III	Commission	€83,500m
Section IV	Court of Justice, including the Court of First Instance	€122m
Section V	Court of Auditors	€60m
Section VI	Economic and Social Committee and Committee of the Regions	€101m

These figures underline the importance of the role of the Commission in preparing its section in the preliminary draft. Although the draft does in part reflect the spending priorities of the Union established over previous years, the Commission still has a significant power of initiative, comparable to that which it enjoys in the realm of legislation. Its proposals serve as an important reference point for Parliament and Council throughout the procedure. Any comparison of the preliminary draft with the budget finally voted reveals that a large part of the initial proposal made by the Commission survives.

Responding to the draft budget as adopted by the Council

After the presentation of the preliminary draft, the Council normally adopts the draft budget in July, well in advance of the date of 5 October laid down in Article 272. On one occasion, however, the Council failed to respect the date laid down in the Treaty. In 1987, due to the severity of the revenue crisis faced by the Community, it did not adopt a draft until February of the following year. Both Parliament and Commission took Council to the Court of Justice for failure to respect the Treaty but by the time the Court ruled, the procedure had been resumed. The one sanction applied to the Council was to oblige it to pay the costs of the case!

A second *trialogue* takes place in advance of the Council's adoption of the draft budget with a view to seeking agreement on the shape and content of the budget. This meeting enables the institutions to fulfil their commitment under the 1999 Inter-institutional Agreement to seek an agreement on the overall level and breakdown of CFSP expenditure on the basis of the Commission preliminary draft. If there is no agreement, the amount in the previous year's budget or that in the preliminary budget, whichever is the lower, is entered in the draft. Parliament is, at the same time, committed not to enter any of the CFSP appropriations in the reserve (see below under "Implementation of the budget") in the course of the rest of the procedure, even though they are considered non-compulsory. In addition, the meeting has come to provide a specific opportunity to discuss agricultural guarantee spending as well as expenditure on fisheries agreements. On the basis of the discussion in the *trialogue*, the Budgets Committee presents to the plenary in July its opinion on the preliminary draft budget and invites the whole Parliament to support its strategy in advance of the conciliation meeting with the Council.

The *conciliation* meeting brings together a delegation of the Parliament and the budget ministers in the Council, on the date set by the Council for establishing the draft budget. The conciliation meeting (and the lunch that follows!) provide an important opportunity for the two sides to explain their respective priorities and to narrow the range of differences in advance of the Council's own deliberations.

Once the conciliation meeting is at an end, Council continues its work in closed session, adopts the draft budget and forwards it to Parliament. Traditionally, Council saw its role as reducing the preliminary budget presented by the Commission to what it considered more reasonable proportions. However, such an approach is less relevant in the context of a multi-annual financial perspective, which lays down annual ceilings for the various categories of expenditure. The Council is now committed to accept the maximum rates of increase for NCE arising from a budget established within these ceilings and is aware that the Parliament can reintroduce non-compulsory appropriations that are cut by the Council. In addition, the

Council is itself bound by formal and informal commitments to leave some appropriations intact: the successive agreements on the size of the structural funds have meant that it has normally had to leave this part of the preliminary draft untouched; in areas where a legislative act adopted under co-decision has included a figure for the level of funding, there is only limited scope to modify the figures proposed; and in relation to the Parliament's administrative budget, there is a gentlemen's agreement that the Council will not alter the figures and that Parliament in turn will not amend the budget of the Council.

First reading of the draft budget in Parliament

Following adoption of the Council's draft at the end of July, it is forwarded to the Parliament. By informal agreement between the two institutions, this does not take place formally until the beginning of September. From that moment Parliament has 45 days in accordance with Article 272 to respond to Council's first reading. This is a period of intense activity, particularly within the Budgets Committee, the committee which co-ordinates Parliament's response and mediates between the different interests within Parliament.

It is the task of the rapporteurs to propose the main lines of response to be given to the Council and to suggest how the Budgets Committee should choose between the competing demands presented by the committees of the Parliament that deal with policy areas involving EU expenditure. Both are the subject of considerable lobbying, particularly from within Community institutions. The Commissioner responsible for the budget will be in close contact with the rapporteur for the Commission's budget, although this will not stop approaches from other parts of the Commission, including those who may have been disappointed by the decisions incorporated in the preliminary draft. And, although the budgets of the other institutions are very much smaller than that of the Commission, contacts with the rapporteur responsible can be very intense.

Parliament also remains in close touch with the Council during this period. A third *trialogue* meeting, which can be followed by a conciliation, takes place before the first reading in Parliament. The meeting provides for an exchange of views on the state of implementation of the current budget and in particular, on a Commission proposal, known as the "omnibus transfer", for the redistribution of appropriations between budgetary lines that are underspent and those that risk being overspent. It can also serve as an occasion to discuss any supplementary and amending budget for the year in progress that may have proved necessary due to unexpected circumstances.

The ideas of the rapporteurs, based on these various consultations, are presented to the committee in a series of detailed working documents designed to justify their proposed treatment of the individual lines in the budget. At the same time, the Political Group co-ordinators discuss the general guidelines presented by the rapporteurs, and in particular the one dealing with the Commission budget, and seek to develop an agreed strategy in advance of the vote in committee. This is particularly important when it comes to the amendments that are tabled by the other committees, individual members of the Parliament (draft amendments require the signature of at least nine members) or Political Groups. As we have seen, the Treaty lays down that at first reading (unlike the first reading of legislative texts), amendments to non-compulsory expenditure require the support of at least a majority of the members of the Parliament (at present 314). There is therefore a high premium on gaining a broad consensus within the committee and thereafter in the Parliament as a whole. Failure to reach such a consensus seriously endangers the chance of amendments being adopted.

Although absolute majorities in the Parliament can be obtained by various political combinations, the budgetary procedure is comparable to the legislative co-decision procedure in that it places particularly strong pressure on the EPP-ED and PES groups to reach agreement. If they can, then it is most probable that the majorities needed will be gained. However, if either one of them is unwilling to go along with a particular amendment, then it is highly unlikely that it will be adopted in plenary. The success of this process of mediation and consensus-seeking in the Budgets Committee can be measured by the fact that the proposals of the committee are defeated on only a handful of occasions in the plenary. All recognise the vital role of the committee in establishing an overall coherence in the position of Parliament, even if its individual decisions may be less well received.

From first to second reading

The second October session in Strasbourg is devoted in large part to the debate and vote on the first reading of the budget, with the vote taking place on the Thursday morning. It is a highly complex affair not least because the number of amendments (to NCE) and proposed modifications (to CE) can total more than 1000. Great care is taken to ensure that the vote proceeds smoothly. In view of the absolute majority required for amendments to NCE, the Groups usually issue "three line whips" to their members in advance of the plenary. Before any amendment is voted, there is often an electronic check to verify attendance. Thereafter the vote proceeds at a considerable pace, with members frequently agreeing to vote en bloc on series of amendments proposed by the Committee on Budgets. If the work of the Budgets Committee has been successful, the votes are usually clear and are carried by a show of hands. However, where there is uncertainty, there will be an electronic check. And if a Group wishes to see how its members or those of another Group have voted on a particular amendment, then there can be a Roll Call Vote (RCV) which subsequently is recorded in the minutes.

The amendments and proposed modifications voted by Parliament are collated and sent as Parliament's first reading to Council for its discussion at second reading. Council, for its part, has 15 days in which to respond. During this period a fourth *trialogue* is organised with the Council. This meeting is designed to discuss in particular a letter of amendment that the Commission has to draw up before the end of October. This letter updates *inter alia* the figures underlying the estimate of agricultural guarantee expenditure (45 per cent of the total budget in commitment appropriations) contained in the preliminary draft budget. The aim is to make it possible for the two institutions to adopt this letter of amendment in one reading and thereby provides an opportunity for Parliament to influence the level of compulsory expenditure in accordance with its vote at first reading. Article 272 lays down that proposed increases in CE require a qualified majority in Council in order to be accepted, whereas if a proposed modification involves a decrease in expenditure or an increase is compensated for by a reduction in another area, the Council requires a qualified majority to *over-rule* the proposed modification. However, the purpose of this *trialogue* is to enable Parliament and Council to negotiate an agreed position on this compulsory part of the budget rather than rely on the formal provisions of the Treaty.

At the end of the fifteen days, the results of this *trialogue* are discussed at a further conciliation meeting in advance of – normally the day before – the meeting of Budgets Ministers to adopt the Council's second reading. At this stage the positions of the two parties are much better known but Parliament has an opportunity to make it clear what it expects from the Council in the light of its own first reading.

In the 2000 procedure, for example, this November conciliation meeting was dominated by the issue of how to finance aid for the reconstruction of Kosovo. Council considered that this should be done by top-slicing other external policy lines, thereby avoiding a revision of the financial perspective. For its part, Parliament at first reading had voted for an upward revision of the ceiling of this category of the financial perspective, arguing that there was a substantial volume of revenue available within the overall resource ceiling and that it was important for the Union to show its willingness not to finance Eastern Europe at the expense of other external priorities, including the developing world. No agreement was reached and it took further discussions with the Council to reach a compromise making adoption of the budget in December possible.

Once Council has concluded its second reading, the draft budget returns to Parliament. It can no longer modify the compulsory expenditure in the budget but it does have fifteen days in which to amend the modifications to non-compulsory expenditure made by the Council. These final modifications require a higher majority than that provided for at first reading: not only must a majority of members vote in favour but the majority must represent at least three fifths of the votes cast. Normally these votes, which take place at the December session, are the subject of much less drama than the vote at first reading. Nevertheless, the result is immediately the subject of comment from the Council (normally the President in Office of the Budgets Council). He or she indicates whether the Council considers the outcome to be in conformity with the Treaty and the provisions of the financial perspective. In recent years, with the exception of the 1995 budget to be discussed below, the Council has accepted the result and thereby paved the way for the President of the Parliament to sign the budget into law.

The option of rejection

An agreed result is not inevitable. The Treaty also provides for the option of Parliament rejecting the budget by a two-thirds majority. It has exercised this option on three occasions: in December 1979 during the budgetary procedure that followed the first direct elections to the Parliament; in 1982, in relation to a supplementary budget, designed to finance the British rebate;

and in December 1984 following the second direct elections. On all three occasions, Parliament was dissatisfied with the budget that Council was prepared to accept and called for a new draft to be submitted to it.

Such a decision does not bring the whole Union to a standstill. A complex arrangement comes into force on 1 January if no budget is voted by that time, whereby the Commission is only allowed to spend each month the equivalent of one twelfth of the expenditure included in the previous year's budget or in the draft budget under preparation before it was rejected, whichever is the lower. This allows the Union to function but it does not allow it to start any new activity.

Implementation of the budget

Once the budget is voted, it is then the duty of the Commission, under the Treaty, to implement it. This does not mean that Parliament's involvement ceases. Rather the nature of its role changes to one of scrutiny and control.

In the course of the financial year the Commission (and the other institutions) regularly present to the budgetary authority requests for transfers of appropriations between the various chapters of the budget or from the reserve. In the first case, Parliament and Council are invited to agree to changes brought about by changes of priority or circumstances in the course of the year. In the case of items entered in the reserve, a majority are included during the budgetary procedure without controversy. Where, in particular, the legislative base for expenditure has not yet been agreed, it is accepted practice that the related appropriations be entered in the reserve, only to be released when the legislation is passed.

However, entry in the reserve is also used as a discreet form of bargaining, whereby Parliament and Council can get assurances on the use of particular budget lines and the implementation of programmes. Once appropriations are placed in the reserve (Chapter B0–40 for the Commission's operational expenditure on policies; Chapter 100 for the administrative expenditure of all the institutions), the institution concerned is obliged to come to the budgetary authority during the financial year to justify in writing and orally a request for release of the appropriations. If they are compulsory, Council has the last word but if they are non-compulsory, Parliament decides. In the latter case, the decision is taken by the Committee on Budgets which can reject or approve (wholly or partially) the institution's request or else invite it to provide further information before taking a decision.

Parliament does not only wait for transfer requests but also scrutinises the implementation of the budget with great care to see whether its wishes are being adhered to, and if not, why not. A particular procedure (known originally as the "Notenboom Procedure" after the Dutch MEP who first proposed it) exists for the Commission to comment on the level of implementation of appropriations voted in the budget in the autumn of the financial year. As we have seen, this leads to the preparation of an omnibus transfer request which is discussed between Council and Parliament before Parliament's first reading and contributes to the debate on the appropriate level of appropriations for the following year. More generally, the Commission provides monthly data on the use of appropriations as well as reports on agricultural spending, known as early warning reports, designed to indicate whether agricultural spending is likely to exceed the financial envelope provided for it.

Finally, Parliament has the right to grant discharge to the Commission and the other institutions for their implementation of their budgets. This task is at the centre of the work of the Budgetary Control Committee and starts at the beginning of the second year after the financial year in question. It is discussed in more detail in Chapter 14.

Parliament's budgetary objectives

To complete the above description of the annual budgetary procedure, it is useful to consider the nature of Parliament's budgetary objectives. These objectives have often been linked to the development of the powers of Parliament. The budget has been consistently used by Parliament as a lever to influence the shape of policies and thereby to increase democratic control over the political decisions taken in the Union. However, over time the methods used by Parliament have been adapted to take account of the changing relationship with Council. The conflict that characterised relations in the 1980s has been replaced by a closer degree of cooperation, illustrated by the range of *trialogues* and conciliation meetings described above and explicitly recognised by all the institutions in the 1999 Inter-institutional Agreement. The way in which these changes have come about can be examined by looking at a number of strategies used by Parliament to improve its democratic competencies in the budgetary arena.

Developing Non-Compulsory Expenditure

As Article 272 indicates, the Union budget incorporates a distinction between compulsory and non-compulsory expenditure and Parliament has different rights depending on whether expenditure is defined as compulsory or not. It has the autonomous right to allocate and increase non-compulsory expenditure, within certain defined limits, but it does not enjoy this right in relation to compulsory expenditure. Once the Council has voted at its second reading on the modifications to compulsory expenditure proposed by Parliament, the level of that expenditure is fixed and cannot be altered at Parliament's second reading.

The difference in powers prompts the question of the nature of the distinction between the two types of expenditure. The Treaty suggests that compulsory expenditure is "expenditure necessarily resulting from this Treaty or from acts adopted in accordance therewith". This definition has been used to justify the argument that compulsory expenditure is unavoidable expenditure to which third parties have a legal claim, whether they be farmers benefiting from guaranteed prices or non-EU countries linked to the Union by international agreements, which have a financial component. Non-compulsory expenditure should thus be defined as avoidable expenditure where the Union enjoys broad discretion as to the level of expenditure that it incurs.

Such a definition is less helpful than it appears at first sight. Over the years agricultural policy has been modified to include such measures as set-aside, but even though the policy did not involve unavoidable expenditure, Council insisted it be classified as compulsory. At the same time, the salaries of officials have always been classified as non-compulsory expenditure, even though there is a legal obligation to pay salaries.

These examples illustrate that the distinction is much more a political than a technical one. It serves to cordon off a large part of the budget (most notably, the Common Agricultural Policy) and to reduce the Parliament's power to shape that part. This is not a situation that the Parliament has accepted willingly. Over many years it has fought to change the frontiers between the two kinds of expenditure and has enjoyed considerable success. Twenty years ago less than 20 per cent of the budget was non-compulsory, whereas the figure is now more than 50 per cent, a change due in large part to the major growth of the structural funds which reached 35 per cent of the total budget in 2000. The section of the budget where Parliament makes the final allocation has thus become a bigger proportion of a bigger budget.

However, the Parliament has also consistently sought to persuade the Council to review what it considers to be an artificial boundary between the two categories and to contemplate eliminating the distinction altogether. The Council agreed to consider the issue in the context of the 1996 IGC negotiations but the Treaty of Amsterdam did not bring about any change. In the meantime, Parliament had clashed openly with the Council. In the 1995 budgetary procedure, the Parliament adopted 131 amendments to what the Council and the Commission adjudged to be compulsory expenditure. The Council considered the vote to be in breach of the Treaty and took the Parliament to the Court of Justice to have the budget annulled (Case C-41/95). In its judgment of December 1995, the Court ruled that when the President of the Parliament declared the budget adopted, the budgetary procedure was not completed since there was still disagreement between the two arms of the budgetary authority. It therefore declared the act illegal and the budget invalid. The Court did not, however, express a view on whether the expenditure was compulsory or non-compulsory but left it to the institutions concerned to reach an agreement.

As a result there were negotiations between the two institutions that culminated in Annex IV in the 1999 Inter-institutional Agreement. This lays down the classification of expenditure for all categories of the financial perspective. Although the agreement maintains the existence of the distinction for the foreseeable future, it does embody one very important change, namely that the Council has accepted that some agricultural expenditure, representing over 10 per cent of the total, should be considered non-compulsory. This was an important success for Parliament.

Using the Maximum Rate of Increase

Although the Parliament enjoys some scope for influencing compulsory expenditure, the bulk of its activity is geared to discussing non-compulsory expenditure where it enjoys "the last word". This last phrase should not be misunderstood. It does not mean that Parliament is free to enter in the budget any increase it wishes. At first reading it can theoretically adopt amendments up to any level of expenditure but at second reading the increases have to be reduced to the level permissible under the Treaties. The

Treaties specify that non-compulsory expenditure can increase from one year to the next by no more than what is called "the maximum rate of increase". As indicated earlier, this is a statistical measure calculated by the Commission, which takes account of economic growth, government expenditure and the rates of inflation in the Member States. For the 2000 budgetary year, for example, it amounted to 3 per cent.

According to Article 272 (TEC), the Parliament can always enter amounts totalling at least half the maximum rate (i.e. if Council enters increases that account for all or most of the maximum rate, Parliament still retains the right to enter an amount equal to half the rate). Until the late 1980s, this meant that Council, at its first reading, entered half the maximum rate, leaving it to Parliament to enter the other half. The amount involved inevitably varied depending on the maximum rate: it was regularly of the order of 600–700 million ECUs. In other words, the Parliament had the opportunity to add and distribute expenditure of between 300–400 million ECUs (now EUROs).

However, the Treaty also allows Parliament and Council to jointly agree to increase the maximum rate set by the Commission. Parliament often sought in that period to persuade the Council to agree to a new maximum rate. It regularly argued that Council was not making adequate provision for what was required in areas other than agriculture. Parliament even unilaterally exceeded the maximum rate, most famously in 1985. It maintained that in the draft budget for 1986 Council had failed to provide adequate finance for 12 Member States on the eve of Spanish and Portuguese accession and had ignored the problem of the "weight of the past", i.e. accumulated commitments from previous years which were liable for payment. At the end of the procedure, the Parliament's President signed a budget that went more than 600 million ECUs beyond the maximum rate figure to which the Council could agree. The result was that the Council took the Parliament to court in Case C-34/86, and won in the sense that the Court ruled that any new maximum rate had to be *explicitly* agreed between the Council and the Parliament. However, the new budget that was agreed in July 1986 included virtually identical increases in the structural funds to those voted by the Parliament in December 1985 as well as important increases in agricultural spending in the EAGGF Guarantee Section.

The 1986 case showed that the Parliament was not able to act unilaterally and the following year the impact of the case was again underlined. In December 1986 Parliament voted amendments in non-compulsory expenditure which went beyond the maximum rate of 8.1 per cent. However, the President of the Parliament, whose job it is to sign the budget into law, recognised the force of the Court ruling and did not sign the budget on the grounds that there had not been an agreement between the Council and Parliament on the new maximum rate. The following February, agreement was reached following some movement on the vexed question of agriculture expenditure and using a face-saving formula on non-compulsory expenditure whereby Council agreed to an increase of 8.149 per cent, arguing that the maximum rate only applied to the first decimal point. Parliament, for its part, was able to claim that the maximum rate had been exceeded and honour was saved on both sides.

This debate about increases in the maximum rate took on a radically different form after February 1988. At the Brussels European Council meeting a new framework for Community financing was agreed which allowed for a major expansion in the revenue available to the Community, as well as stricter controls on the development of expenditure, with particular reference to agriculture. In relation to expenditure there was agreement to set down in advance what the budget of the Community should look like in 1992, not just in overall terms but by category of expenditure. Subsequently, in negotiations between Council, Parliament and the Commission, it proved possible to fill out the figures agreed by the Heads of State and Government and to establish a financial framework for each year leading up to 1992. The three institutions signed what was the first "inter-institutional agreement on budgetary discipline and the improvement of the budgetary procedure".

This agreement transformed the argument about the maximum rate of increase. In particular, it provided for major increases in the structural funds to enable those funds to be doubled by 1993. Such doubling could not take place without the normal maximum rates being substantially exceeded. Hence, the inter-institutional agreement contained within it the effective agreement of the institutions to go beyond the maximum rate **in advance of** the relevant budgetary procedures. Parliament interpreted this agreement as allowing it to go up to the ceilings of expenditure in each area and to assume that the resultant maximum rate was acceptable to the Council. The Council did not accept this interpretation but declined to challenge it in the Court of Justice. In the 1992 budgetary procedure it threatened to do so when the Parliament entered the maximum available below the ceiling for research expenditure. The Council argued that the legislative provisions for research laid down the amount that could be entered in the budget and that this amount was lower than the figure voted by the Parliament. The conflict was only resolved in February 1992 when Parliament accepted to reduce research expenditure in exchange for increases elsewhere.

After the 1988 Inter-institutional Agreement expired at the end of 1992 there was a period of uncertainty as to whether a new agreement could be negotiated or not. At the Edinburgh European Council meeting in December 1992 a wide-ranging deal was reached by the Member States on the development of the financing of the Union up to 1999. New revenue ceilings were established allowing spending to rise to 1.27 per cent of the GNP of the Union by 1999 and annual expenditure ceilings were established covering six categories. The extreme detail of the agreement reached at Edinburgh left the Parliament with little room to discuss figures. Hence negotiations with the Council concentrated on the powers of Parliament and the agreement reached in October 1993 gave Parliament reason to be satisfied. In particular, it persuaded the Council to drop its earlier objections and to accept in advance the maximum rates of increase for non-compulsory expenditure deriving from the budgets established within the ceilings set by the financial perspective. In return, it accepted the principle that space should be left below the annual ceilings to make room for additional spending that might prove necessary in the course of the year.

In 1999 Parliament voted at its May session to accept a third Inter-institutional Agreement with a financial perspective based on the conclusions reached at the Berlin European Council meeting. It was the subject of considerable controversy with some arguing that, like the previous two agreements, it should be approved by a majority of MEPs. In fact, it won a substantial but not absolute majority, reflecting a degree of dissatisfaction with the very tight budgetary constraints imposed by the agreement. Some members argued that Parliament would have a greater margin for manoeuvre if it applied the provisions of Article 272 relating to the maximum rate, thereby reviving the strategies of the 1980s. A majority felt that this was too drastic a step, pointing out that the new agreement contained a number of elements favourable to Parliament. These included an increase in the amount provided for internal policies beyond the Berlin agreement and a Council undertaking that it would agree any revision of the financial perspective up to 0.03 per cent of GNP (about €2.2bn) by qualified majority, rather than unanimity.

Promoting policies through the budget

Parliament has always been eager to use the budget to promote new policies, a role that has traditionally provoked major conflict with Council. After the Treaties were revised in 1975 to extend Parliament's budgetary powers, Parliament found itself with an important budgetary role but, at the same time, saw that this increased role had to be exercised in an environment where Council was effectively the sole legislator. To compensate for this weakness, Parliament made maximum use of its budgetary powers to influence the development of legislation.

Initially Parliament argued that if money were entered in the budget, then it had to be implemented by the Commission in accordance with the wishes of the budgetary authority. This point of view was strongly resisted by Council, which argued that the budget was not a sufficient legal base. It claimed that the Commission could only act if there was an agreed legislative framework, a framework within which, of course, Council itself had the final word at that time.

A temporary truce was declared in 1982 when Council, Commission and Parliament signed a Joint Declaration specifying that a legislative base was required for "significant new Community actions". For such actions it was agreed that the three institutions would use their best endeavours to ensure that a decision on a new legislative framework was provided by May of the financial year concerned. This did not stop the argument. It left unclear what was to be considered a "significant" new Community action, with Parliament arguing that much activity lay outside this definition. Such a tendency was only encouraged by the fact that the "best endeavours" of the institutions rarely did prove sufficient to agree basic legislation by the May deadline.

In the course of the 1980s the nature of the argument changed because of the major difficulties encountered in controlling expenditure, notably in the agricultural sector. The Parliament now found that not only was the budget not sufficient to *authorise* significant new Community actions but also that it could not prevent the amounts provided in the budget from being *exceeded*, if the legislation adopted by the Council made extra budgetary provision necessary.

Once again, Parliament went on the offensive and succeeded in the 1988 Inter-institutional Agreement in persuading the Council that where the financial provision for a legislative act was not available, then the implementation of the policy could not take place until the budget was suitably amended, a process in which of course Parliament itself has a direct part to play. This change was given further backing at Maastricht. A specific article (now Article 270(TEC)) was written into the Treaties obliging the Commission not to make any proposal with appreciable budgetary implications unless it could guarantee that the proposal could be financed within the limits of revenue available.

1988 improved the position of the Parliament in its strategy to use the budget to develop policy in a further way. Before 1988, it had devoted a large part of its margin for manoeuvre (i.e. at least half of the maximum rate allowed under the Treaties) to increase spending on the structural funds. The agreement reached at the Brussels European Council in February 1988 to double the funds in real terms by 1993, and the subsequent Edinburgh decision at the end of 1992 to ensure a further significant increase up to 1999, meant that the Parliament was no longer obliged to do this, and it has since concentrated on other areas.

However, these "successes" displaced the argument with the Council elsewhere. In relation to multi-annual expenditure programmes, the Council started to specify the volume of permissible expenditure for each year of the programme within the relevant legislation. The inclusion of such "amounts deemed necessary" (often referred to as "MENs", from the French *montants estimés nécessaires*) effectively served as a limitation on the budgetary power of Parliament and its right to have the last word over non-compulsory expenditure. This was made still clearer by the Commission's readiness to treat the MENs as ceilings which could not be exceeded even where Parliament adopted amendments, incorporated in the budget, which took expenditure on specific programmes beyond that laid down in the accompanying legislation.

The issue assumed greater salience with the introduction of the co-decision procedure in the Maastricht Treaty (see Chapter 12). Parliament now had a more equal say with the Council on the content of legislation and hence came to view the entry of a specific level of finance in acts adopted under co-decision in a different light. In an agreement first entered into in 1995 and then confirmed in the Inter-institutional Agreement in 1999, the institutions agreed that multi-annual programmes adopted under the co-decision procedure should include a provision in which the legislative authority (i.e., Council and Parliament) lays down the financial framework for the programme for its entire duration. This amount constitutes what is called "the prime reference" for the budgetary authority during the annual budgetary procedure and can only exceeded if "new, objective, long-term circumstances arise for which explicit and precise reasons are given". At the same time, where co-decision does not apply, it was agreed that there would not be any reference to an "amount deemed necessary" but an optional figure which in no way binds the budgetary authority.

These provisions have meant that a whole range of co-decision procedures have included arguments about the level of financing of multi-annual programmes. The most significant was that concerning the Fifth Research Framework Agreement which was finally agreed at the December plenary in 1998. After the Council adopted a common position envisaging expenditure of €14bn over five years and Parliament voted for €16.3bn at its second reading, four meetings of the conciliation committee enabled the two sides to come to a deal at €14.96bn, an amount corresponding to around 60 per cent of all expenditure under category three (internal policies) of the financial perspective. In this way, legislative committees have been able to use the co-decision and conciliation procedures to acquire a degree of budgetary security for the programmes they support.

Such agreements on funding reached outside the budgetary procedure have provoked concern amongst budget experts. They are sceptical about the ability of Parliament to do better in the legislative than in the budgetary procedure and fear a lack of prioritisation of the various interests of the institution. And yet such concerns have to be put in context. First, in the conciliation procedure the two institutions do not now fix figures for individual years of a programme, something which remains the preserve of the budgetary authority. Second, even a prime reference figure does not necessarily have to be met if the budgetary authority considers that other priorities warrant putting money elsewhere. Third, the budgetary authority continues to play the main role in fixing the overall level of expenditure through the financial perspective and can thereby strongly influence the content of all legislative discussions. Co-decision has changed much but it has not reduced the role of the budgetary authority and the Committee on Budgets as significantly as is sometimes claimed.

Even with co-decision there is still plenty of scope for the Parliament to develop policy through the budget and it remains an important feature of every budgetary procedure. In some cases, Parliament acts to defend policies that Council has under-funded. Parliament has, for example, consistently entered substantial funds to induce Council to develop transport policy, notably to finance the Trans-European Networks that Council had itself approved; in others, it has acted together with Council to promote a shared concern. The classic example of this came in the 1998 budgetary procedure where the two institutions agreed to launch an employment initiative and to provide funding totalling 150 million ECUs, a sum which was found by redeploying appropriations within the "Internal Policies" category of the financial perspective.

Parliament also continues to use the budget to develop new policies and policies which may not be of specific concern to Council. Examples from the last decade include the KONVER programme for the conversion of the arms industry and military sites and the URBAN programme as new initiatives within the structural funds, and the environmental programme LIFE. Yet the status of such initiatives continued to provoke conflict with the Council as long as there was no legal base. Here too, though, an agreement was reached which is incorporated in the 1999 Inter-institutional Agreement. Parliament accepted that implementation of appropriations in the budget for any Community action requires the prior adoption of a basic legislative act. However, Council agreed that no basic act is needed for the implementation of four specific kinds of appropriations:

– those designed to finance pilot schemes aimed at testing the feasibility of an action, the total amount being restricted to €32m over two years;
– those relating to preparatory actions intended to pave the way for specific

legislative proposals, the total being restricted to €30m per year and no more than €75m over three years;
- those linked to actions carried out by the Commission by virtue of prerogatives specifically conferred on it; and
- those intended for the administrative operation of each institution.

This very detailed agreement will certainly reduce the scope for the kinds of argument that have divided Council and Parliament over the development of policy through the budget since 1975.

Influencing the level of revenue

Finally, a brief word about revenue. It is often commented that the present arrangements give Parliament the right to increase expenditure within certain limits, but without being responsible for determining the type of revenue needed to cover that expenditure. Any increase is automatically financed by a rise in the take-up by the Union of the "own resources" allocated to it but these resources are laid down in a decision taken by the Council and ratified by the Member States. Parliament is only consulted, something it has always wanted to remedy and thereby meet the complaint that it enjoys the "luxury of revenue irresponsibility".

For many years Parliament has also argued that a direct link should be created between the European citizen and the European budget, by, for example, identifying the part of the national VAT take going to fund European-level policies or introducing an additional resource, without increasing the total burden on taxpayers. Such suggestions have made no progress. The Union is increasingly financing its activities by the so-called "fourth resource", which is calculated on the basis of the relative wealth of the Member States. The revenue components originally provided for in 1970 – customs duties, agricultural levies and a proportion of the VAT tax base – are declining in importance (in 2000, they accounted for only just over half of total revenue). As a result, the Union's revenue structure is becoming more like that of traditional international organisations.

There is little enthusiasm at present for any kind of new form of resource for the Union, in part as a result of the efforts that Member States have already made to reform their finances to be eligible for Economic and Monetary Union and the single currency. Despite the demands of enlargement, it is therefore extremely likely that the upper limit of Union expenditure will remain fixed at 1.27 per cent of Union GNP for the foreseeable future. Indeed no budget up to 2006 is anticipated, under the terms of the financial perspective, to exceed 1.19 per cent. By the same token, we can expect that there will be no change in either the components of revenue or the limited consultative role that Parliament has in influencing their shape. There remains a large gap between the major strides Parliament has made in developing its right to co-decide the shape of Union expenditure with the Council and its very limited impact on the structure of the revenue used to finance that expenditure.

14. Appointment and dismissal

Introduction

The Parliament was originally given no formal role in the EU appointments process, which was essentially an inter-governmental one, with each country putting forward its own nominees on the basis of domestic rather than European considerations, and with the other Member States accepting each other's nominees on a consensus basis. Individual appointments, such as to the Presidency of the Commission, were usually made on a rough-and-ready rotation basis. The Parliament was not consulted, nor did it even have any informal say.

On the other hand, the Parliament has long had a Treaty right to dismiss the Commission as a whole. The very powerful nature of this weapon has meant that the Parliament was, until 1999, very reluctant to attempt to use it, and it has thus proved ineffective as a tool of parliamentary accountability. The absence of any right to dismiss individual Commissioners reduced its utility still further as regards individual problem areas within the Commission. Nevertheless, this power has always been there in reserve.

Events in 1998–99 have shown how much the situation has now changed. The Parliament's public hearings on the nominations to the Executive Board of the European Central Bank in 1998 and to the Prodi Commission in 1999 have been considerable media events, and have demonstrated how much the Parliament's powers have grown as regards the EU appointment process. The Parliament's formal powers have not developed as regards censure, but in January 1999 Parliament showed that it was really prepared for the first time to contemplate dismissal of the entire Commission. While the Commission did survive the January vote, a chain of events was unleashed that led to the collective resignation of the Commission in March 1999. Moreover, a serious debate has opened up as to how to increase the accountability of individual Commissioners to Parliament. The rest of this section looks at all these issues in more detail, as well as the rights of the Parliament as regards other EU institutions and bodies.

The development of the Parliament's formal powers as regards EU appointments

The initial step in relation to the power of appointment was taken after the creation of the European Court of Auditors in 1975, when the Parliament was given the right to be consulted in the appointment of the Court's members (Article 247 EC).

The major breakthrough, however, came with the Maastricht Treaty. First, the Parliament was given an important role as regards appointment of the Commission, with it first being consulted on the nominee for President, and later being asked to give its approval on the entire College of Commissioners (Article 214 TEC). Second, the Maastricht Treaty provided for the Parliament to be consulted on the nominee for President of the European Monetary Institute (Article 117 TEC), and on the nominees for President, Vice-President and other members of the Executive Board of the European Central Bank (Article 114 TEC). Finally, the Treaty gave Parliament the direct power to appoint the EU Ombudsman (Article 195 TEC).

The Amsterdam Treaty only introduced one further change, albeit an important one in formal terms, in that it gave the Parliament the power not just to be consulted but to approve the nominee for Commission President.

Besides these formal Treaty changes to the Parliament's role in appointments, Parliament is now also involved in appointing some members of the executive boards of certain EU agencies, and also plays a key part in the appointment of the Director of the new European anti-fraud office (OLAF).

Parliament and the appointment of the Commission

Prior to the Treaty of Maastricht, the Commission was appointed collectively by the governments of the Member States for a four-year term of office. The President of the Commission was, according to the Treaty, nominated for a two-year period from among the members of the Commission. In practice, the President was invariably agreed on first by the Member States and was automatically re-appointed mid-way through the Commission's term of office. Most Commission presidents thus stayed for the full four-year term.

Once the Parliament became directly elected, it introduced into its own procedures provisions for a debate and a *vote of confidence* on an incoming Commission when it presented itself to Parliament for the first time with its programme. This became an established practice and was recognized by national governments in the 1983 Stuttgart Solemn Declaration on European Union. Parliament followed this procedure for the appointment of the Thorn Commission in 1981 and three Delors Commissions in 1985, 1989 and 1993 (see Table 24). On these last three occasions, the Commission waited until it had received the vote of confidence from Parliament before taking the oath of office at the Court of Justice. This was an important gesture and precedent, showing that the Commission accepted that without the confidence of Parliament it should not take office.

Also in the Stuttgart Declaration of 1983, the Member States agreed that the Enlarged Bureau of the Parliament should be consulted on the choice of President of the Commission. In 1984 and 1992, the Presidents-in-office of the European Council (respectively the Irish and Portuguese Prime Ministers) carried out this consultation by attending a meeting of the Enlarged Bureau to discuss the issue. In 1988, this consultation was done through the President of the Parliament, who attended the relevant part of the European Council meeting and acted in consultation with the Enlarged Bureau.

The Treaty of Maastricht built on these existing practices. First, it reinforced the consultation of Parliament concerning the choice of the

President by providing for consultation of Parliament as a whole rather than just its Enlarged Bureau. This meant that there was now a public vote by the whole Parliament on the President-designate – politically much more significant, although still short of a power of formal approval.

In July 1993 when the nomination of Jacques Santer, the Luxembourg Prime Minister, was under discussion (and looked under threat, partly owing to resentment at the UK's veto of the candidacy of Jean-Luc Dehaene), he made it clear that he would withdraw if the vote in Parliament went against him. This view was also expressed by the President of the European Council, Chancellor Kohl, when he met the Conference of Presidents of the Parliament to consult them on the nomination, prior to the meeting of the European Council at which the candidacy of Santer was agreed.

The nature of the debate on Santer in July 1994, following his statement to the House, and the meetings he held with the three largest Political Groups, illustrated the character of the procedure as one of building up a parliamentary majority for the confirmation vote. The Amsterdam Treaty later recognised this by turning the vote on the President into a legally binding one and giving the President thus approved the right to choose the remaining Commissioners jointly with the Member State governments.

Second, the Maastricht Treaty formalised the vote of confidence but reinforced it by providing explicitly for it to take place prior to the Commission taking office. The Parliament then sought to expand on this. In Rule 33 of its Rules of Procedure it provided for the vote to be taken only after the proposed Commissioners had appeared in confirmation hearings before the appropriate parliamentary committees, according to their prospective fields of responsibility. In the autumn of 1994, this Rule was duly invoked for the first time. Despite initial reluctance (the outgoing President Delors was opposed, for example), the proposed Commissioners agreed to participate in the exercise, not least because President-elect Santer wanted to show goodwill to the Parliament after the close vote in Parliament on his nomination in July 1994, and because Parliament would otherwise not have taken the vote of confidence. The procedure also required Member States to complete their selection of nominees for Commissioner much more swiftly than in the past, enabling the Commission President to allocate portfolios before the end of October.

In the event, Parliament decided to hold over its hearings and vote on the new Commissioners until the New Year so as to allow parliamentarians from the new Member States to be involved in the process. It also decided that the hearings should be held in public, thus giving maximum exposure to the process and ensuring that any commitments entered into by the candidates were well-known before they entered into the Commission. It was a dramatic move in strengthening the accountability of the Commission to the Parliament.

Third, the Maastricht Treaty now provided for the Commission to have a five-year term of office instead of four, linked to that of the Parliament. The procedures for appointing the President and the rest of the Commission were designed to begin after each European election and the new Commission, if approved, would take office the following January. The coincidence of term of office facilitated parliamentary scrutiny and control

Table 24: *Votes of confidence on incoming Commisions and incoming Commission Presidents (formalised in Treaty since 1993)*

Incoming Commissions		
February 1981	Thorn Commission	155 votes for, 31 against
January 1985	Delors I Commission	209 votes for, 34 against
January 1989	Delors II Commission	Votes not recorded, overwhelming majority in favour
January 1993	Delors III Commission	256 votes for, 84 against
January 1995	Santer Commission	417 votes for, 104 against
September 1999	Prodi Commission (for unfilled portion of Santer term)	427 votes for, 138 against (29 abstentions)
September 1999	Prodi Commission (for full 2000–5 term of office)	404 votes for, 153 against (37 abstentions)
Incoming Commission Presidents		
July 1992	Jacques Delors (third term)	278 votes for, 9 against
July 1994	Jacques Santer	260 votes for, 238 against (23 abstentions)
May 1999	Romano Prodi (vote by out-going European Parliament on Prodi for unfilled portion of Santer term)	392 in favour, 72 against (41 abstentions)
September 1999	Romano Prodi (vote by incoming European Parliament on Prodi for unfilled portion of Santer term)	446 in favour to 123 against (23 abstentions)
September 1999	Romano Prodi (vote by incoming European Parliament on Prodi for full 2000–05 term of office)	426 in favour to 134 against (32 abstentions)

as well as the feeling of Commissioners that they were accountable to Parliament.

The Parliament's approval of the Prodi Commission in 1999 came in dramatic circumstances after the collective resignation of the Santer Commission in March 1999, with the public spotlight being more on the Parliament than during the previous exercise, and with Parliament being able to use its new post-Amsterdam power of being able to approve formally (and thus also to reject) the proposed Commission.

In other respects, however, the timing of the process was not ideal, in that it overlapped with the elections for a new Parliament, and gave little time for the newly elected Parliament to prepare for the hearings.

The hearings themselves were held under similar rules to those in 1995, but there were a number of significant practical changes. All the nominees were now asked to reply in advance to a prior written questionnaire, with the (often lengthy!) replies being put on both the Commission and Parliament websites. Each of the hearings lasted for three hours, and there were no overlaps between them. Full verbatim transcripts were prepared, translated into different languages, and placed on the Internet.

Further improvements are likely in future, but these changes already represent significant progress in strengthening the accountability of the Commission to the Parliament. They make the relationship between the Community's executive and its elected parliamentary body rather more like that which exists between the government and the lower chamber of a parliament in many countries, thus reinforcing democratic legitimacy within the Union.

The process has also had a number of other advantages. The nominees' suitability for the post of Commissioner is being better and more publicly scrutinised than before, and their personalities and views are becoming clearer at an earlier stage. Wider issues related to the organisational structure and policy priorities of the Commission are also being more thoroughly explored, and benchmarks are being established to judge subsequent Commission performance. Finally, while domestic political considerations still loom large as regards the choice of Member States' candidates, the whole appointments process has also raised wider European considerations, such as the need for better overall political and gender balance. For example, the Prodi Commission, like the previous Santer Commission, contains more women than there almost certainly would have been without pressure from the Parliament. There had been no women at all in any Commission until 1989, and the need for adequate representation of women was a central feature of a European Parliament resolution of 21 April 1994 (based on a report by Froment-Meurice) setting out some criteria for implementation of the Parliament's new post-Maastricht powers on Commission investiture.The new Amsterdam Treaty right of the President of the Commission to choose the Commissioners jointly has reinforced this trend.

On the other hand, there are still unresolved questions as regards the involvement of the Parliament in the appointment of the Commission. One such problem is how best to judge individual nominees for Commissioner when the Parliament has no formal power to weed out individuals but only to approve or reject the Commission as a whole. In both 1995 and 1999 the main result of hearings was letters from the relevant committee (or committees) to the President of the Parliament, which were then published. On both occasions some of these letters contained sharply critical comments (for example, on Bjerregaard and Flynn in 1995 and on Busquin in 1999), but many members were frustrated that they had no real means of forcing individual candidates to withdraw, or be redeployed, without voting against the Commission as a whole. For this reason some would like the Treaty to give them the possibility of voting on individuals, though others point out that few national parliaments can vote to confirm individual members of governments.

A second issue is the Parliament's role in choosing the President of the Commission. While the Parliament can now say yes or no to the proposed candidate, he or she is still designated by the Member States. The idea has been put forward that the Political Groups could, before the Parliament elections, each propose the candidate that they would like to see appointed as President of the Commission, and the European election campaign would then focus on those candidates. The elections would gain in visibility and relevance, and the candidates in legitimacy. There are, however, many practical problems with the proposal, which was mooted within the Parliament but not ultimately supported before the 1999 Parliament elections. In particular, it would constitute a major challenge to national political and party structures, which, at least for the time being, seem unlikely to permit such an initiative. The idea may, however, again be put forward in the future.

Appointments to the Central Bank and European Monetary Institute

The Treaty since Maastricht provides for Parliament to be consulted on the appointment of the President, Vice-President and the members of the Board of the European Central Bank. Given the significant powers of the Board of the Central Bank, these appointments are of great importance.

Although Parliament's role is only consultative, it is potentially crucial. Like for other appointments where Parliament is consulted, when it comes to a public vote in an elected parliament on an individual, it would be surprising if that individual wished to take office should Parliament reject his or her candidacy. If he or she wished to proceed, it is also doubtful that the Member States would retain the necessary unanimity to proceed with the appointment.

In exercising its new rights, Parliament again decided to organise public confirmation hearings at which candidates were invited to defend their suitability for office. This first occurred in November 1993, when Lamfalussy, the nominee for President of the European Monetary Institute (EMI), appeared before the Economic Committee. He had replied in writing beforehand to a series of specific questions and answered detailed oral questions for three hours at a public meeting. Subsequently, Parliament gave its approval for his nomination. A similar hearing was later held when Wim Duisenberg replaced Lamfalussy as President of the EMI.

In May 1998 the Parliament's new responsibilities as regards nominations were again illustrated when it came to consultation of the Parliament on the appointment of the first President, Vice-President and other members of the Executive Board of the newly established European Central Bank (ECB).

The Maastricht Treaty gave the ECB a very large degree of independence from political control by national governments and parliaments and also by the European Parliament. The nomination process for the first Executive Board of the ECB was thus a very important opportunity for the Parliament, not least because the staggered terms of office established for individual members of the initial Board meant that this would be the only occasion when all the members of the Board would be up for appointment at the same time. The nomination process could thus be helpful in scrutinising the different candidates, and in establishing the terms of the future dialogue between the Parliament and the ECB.

To meet these objectives it was again indispensable that there be European Parliament hearings on the individual candidates. There was little doubt that the nominee for President (Duisenberg) would agree to such a hearing. In the event, not only Duisenberg but also all the other candidates agreed to attend such hearings, and to reply in advance to written questionnaires, and the precedent was set.

The preparations made for the hearings were more systematic than for previous Parliament hearings, not only within the competent Parliament committee (Economic and Monetary Affairs), but also within the individual Political Groups: the Socialist Group, for instance, went so far as to organize a video-conference between certain of its members in Strasbourg and Alan Blinder, former Vice-President of the US Federal Reserve in Washington, at which he was asked for his views on possible lines of questioning of the ECB nominees. For their part, the ECB nominees also met up in Frankfurt to discuss their handling of the written questionnaires and of the hearings.

The hearings of 7–8 May 1998 were held in public and lasted for three hours in the case of Duisenberg, 1hr 45mins in the case of Noyer (the candidate for Vice-President) and 1hr 30mins for the other nominees. The entire transcript of the hearings was placed in the original languages on the Internet. All the nominees were later approved by the plenary on 12 May 1998 by substantial majorities.

There were a number of positive results to this process. Duisenberg, who had appeared to have agreed to stand down before the end of his official term of office in favour of a French nominee, succeeded in getting across the message that there was nothing automatic about this promise and that he retained a personal margin of manoeuvre. He also committed himself to a regular dialogue with the Parliament, and to appear before its Economic Committee on at least a quarterly basis. Perhaps most importantly of all, MEPs (and journalists and any others attending the hearings) were able to get a much clearer idea of the personalities and views of the different candidates, including those who would not normally be appearing in the future in front of a parliamentary committee. Without the Parliament's involvement in the process, such knowledge would have been limited to a much more restricted group of insiders. Another – limited but still significant – breach in the traditional EU appointments model had been made.

Appointments to the Court of Auditors

As pointed out above, consultation in respect of appointments to the Court of Auditors became, in 1975, the first example of the Parliament being given such a role as regards EU appointments. A first significant step was taken in 1981 when the Parliament's Budgetary Control Committee began the practice of inviting the nominees to a hearing where they were cross-examined on their expertise and views. The advantages and limitations of such a consultative role in appointments can be seen by observing how the provisions laid down for the Court of Auditors have been applied.

The bottom line of such a consultative procedure is what happens when Parliament gives a negative opinion on a proposed candidate. Such a case first occurred in November 1989, when Parliament was consulted on the appointment or reappointment of six candidates. Parliament approved four of them but felt "unable to give a favourable opinion" in respect of two of them, the French and Greek candidates. The French government immediately responded by withdrawing the nominated candidate and putting forward a new candidate who, after he appeared before Parliament's Budgetary Control Committee, was approved by Parliament at its next part-session and duly appointed. The Greek government, which was in the middle of a government crisis and between two general elections in succession, claimed to be unable to find a more suitable candidate. Parliament chose not to fight, being pleased enough with the French reaction, and merely regretted the Greek government's position. In contrast, in 1993 the Council ignored the reservation of the Parliament on two candidates, one an incumbent member of the Court.

Appointments to the Office of Ombudsman

The most far-reaching change of all to the traditional EU appointments model was that introduced by the Maastricht Treaty as regards the new post of EU Ombudsman. Article 195 TEC provides for appointment by the Parliament after each parliamentary election for the duration of its term of office. The Member States are given no say at all in the nominations process, which is left entirely to the Parliament.

Parliament has provided in its Rules for a call for nominations to be published in the Official Journal of the European Communities and for nominations to have the support of a minimum of 32 members who are nationals of at least two Member States. The competent committee (the Petitions Committee) then holds public hearings on the candidates and, in the current version of the rule, submits a list of admissible nominations in alphabetical order to the full Parliament, which takes the final decision by secret ballot on the basis of a majority of the votes cast. To prevent this being taken on too low a vote, a quorum of at least half of Parliament's component members have to be present. If no candidate has been elected after the first two ballots, only the two candidates obtaining the largest number of votes in the second ballot may continue to stand.

On the first occasion when the Parliament exercised its new powers there was initially a stalemate when there was a tied vote in the relevant committee between two candidates, (Siegbert Alber, a former Vice- President of Parliament, and Gil-Robles, Ombudsman of Spain).The Rules of Procedure provided in their initial version for only one name to be submitted to the plenary, and without a means of breaking any such tie. The Rules were then modified to provide for the committee to submit a list of names in alphabetical order to the plenary, and for the eldest candidate to prevail in the event of any tie there. A Finnish candidate, Jacob Söderman, was subsequently elected by Parliament after nominations had been reopened to allow candidates from the three countries that had joined the EU in the meantime.

The Parliament again had to consider appointment of a new Ombudsman in the autumn of 1999. Söderman was again a candidate, as was former MEP (and long-serving Parliament Vice-President) Giorgios Anastasopoulos. Hearings on the two candidates were held in October 1999, and Söderman was narrowly re-elected by the Parliament on 27 October 1999. (See chapter 16 below for further discussion of the relationship between the Parliament and the Ombudsman).

European Parliament role in other appointments

Besides the main cases mentioned above, the Parliament has a role as regards certain other appointments as well, for example holding hearings on the nomination of the Director of the new anti-fraud office (OLAF) in the autumn of 1999.

A different case is that of certain decentralised EU agencies and bodies for which the Parliament has been given the right to choose two members of their management boards. This is the case, for example, with the European Environment Agency, the European Agency for the Evaluation of Medicinal Products, the European Monitoring Centre for Drugs and Drug Addiction, and the European Monitoring Centre on Racism and Xenophobia.

Procedures have been developed to choose the Parliament nominees and were codified by the Conference of Presidents on 5 March 1998 in the form of new "rules on the designation by the European Parliament of members of the management boards of the specialized agencies and bodies".

Candidates are to be initially designated by a Political Group or 32 members and are sifted by the committee responsible. Candidates are also asked to disclose to the committee any relevant financial interests or incompatibilities. The committee then adopts a list, in the order of votes obtained, of persons eligible to be appointed as full members and as alternates. The final decision is then taken by the Conference of Presidents. The rules also contain provisions for scrutiny of the appointments and for withdrawal, after a prior hearing of the appointee, of the mandate from any appointee who fails to fulfil his or her obligations, or else violates the principles of impartiality or independence.

Possible future changes in appointments to other European Union posts

Besides its changes as regards the President of the Commission, the Amsterdam Treaty did not otherwise modify the EU's appointment procedures as regards other institutions and bodies, in spite of a number of specific (and repeated!) proposals to this effect being put forward within the Parliament.

The Parliament's initial requests had dated from the early 1980s. The Spinelli Draft Treaty establishing European Union had called for judges at the European Court of Justice to be chosen half by the Parliament and half by the Council, and for the Parliament to choose the extra judge if there were to be an uneven number of judges. It also called for members of the Court of Auditors to be appointed on a similar 50–50 basis.

In the run-up to the Maastricht and Amsterdam IGCs, the Parliament asked instead for the right to give its assent to all nominations to the Court of Justice, the Court of First Instance, the Court of Auditors and the members of the Executive Board of the European Central Bank.

There was no response to these requests by the IGC negotiators, although both the Court of Justice and the Court of First Instance reacted to the Parliament's proposals in their respective IGC contributions of May 1995, in which there was an interesting difference of emphasis between the two. The Court of Justice considered "that a reform involving a hearing of each nominee by a parliamentary committee would be unacceptable". The argument used was that "prospective appointees would be unable adequately to answer the questions put to them without betraying the discretion incumbent upon persons whose independence must, in the words of the Treaties, be beyond doubt and without prejudging positions they might have to adopt with regard to contentious issues which they would have to decide in the exercise of their judicial function".

The Court of First Instance adopted a less dismissive stance, drawing "the attention of the Conference to the fact that any projected intervention by the Parliament in the procedure for appointing judges should be confined to the initial appointment, for the obvious reason that it cannot extend to a review of the manner in which judicial functions have actually been carried out". Moreover, "any such intervention by the Parliament should be solely for the purpose of ascertaining whether the prospective nominees possess the qualifications required by the Treaty in order to exercise their functions". A footnote cited with approval a working document on behalf of the Parliament's Institutional Affairs Committee which had called for the Parliament approval process to avoid political considerations and to concentrate on verifying the qualifications required in Articles 223 and 225 (former 167 and 168(a) of the Treaty), namely "that a nominee can demonstrate his or her independence and that they have held high judicial office or can otherwise show outstanding legal abilities".

The above considerations have been cited at some length since they illustrate some of the questions that will have to be tackled as regards the scope of the Parliament's role in the appointment process if it is to be further extended. The Parliament is likely to repeat its requests in any forthcoming IGC, and there may be new requests as regards such bodies as the European Investment Bank or the EBRD. The case for a formal extension of democratic accountability of these institutions and bodies is a powerful one but the nature of the Parliament's role will then have to be carefully defined.

In the meantime, and even in the absence of such formal Treaty changes, the European Parliament's 1999 revision of its Rules of Procedure (Corbett/Palacio/Gutierrez report) has sought to extend Parliament's informal role within the context of the existing Treaty as regards certain appointments in the field of foreign policy. Parliament recognises that it can have no direct say, for example, in the appointment of the High Representative for the Common Foreign and Security Policy pursuant to Article 207(2) TEC or of any special representatives pursuant to Article 18(5) TEU, but in its new Rules 99 and 100, Parliament lays down procedures for the Council to be invited to make statements prior to the appointments being made. Moreover, both the High Representative and any special representative may be invited to appear before the responsible parliamentary committee to make a statement and to answer questions once they have been appointed, but before they have taken up their duties. Following this the Parliament may adopt recommendations. In addition, Parliament's new Rule 102 provides that a nominee to be the head of a Commission external delegation may be invited to appear before the relevant body of Parliament to make a statement and answer questions.

All the above proposals fall far short of a change in the EU appointment model but are aimed at ensuring wider democratic accountability of such nominees and of newly appointed office-holders.

The Parliament is increasingly reluctant to accept a passive role, and its experience of "confirmation hearings" where it does have a formal role in appointments, has been leading it to call for an extension of possibilities for dialogue where this does not exist.

The right of censure

One of the Parliament's most dramatic powers is being able to dismiss the Commission. Indeed, only Parliament, and not the Council or the national governments, can force a Commission to resign before the end of its term of office.

The ECSC Treaty only allowed Parliament to censure the Commission ("High Authority" as it was then) when the latter presented its annual report. This limitation was not included in the EEC and Euratom Treaties. When a single Commission for these Communities was set up in 1965, the Treaty provided for a general right of censure, which, if carried by a two-thirds majority comprising half the Members of Parliament, would force the Commission to resign. This is now incorporated in Article 201 EC.

Parliament has to date never adopted a censure motion, but in March 1999 the Commission resigned when faced with the near certainty of the adoption of a censure motion. Prior to this a number were threatened and nine actually tabled in Parliament (see Table 25 below) but all were rejected or withdrawn. Four of these pre-dated direct elections in 1979. Four motions were tabled by smaller Political Groups, and were all decisively defeated (Conservative Group in 1976 on milk powder, Gaullists in 1977 on butter sales, European Right in 1990 on the Commission's agricultural policy and 1991 on the Commission's conduct in external relations).

A higher level of support for a censure motion was obtained in December 1992 for a motion tabled by various members, including the Greens and the extreme Right, on the issue of the GATT talks on the grounds that the Commission's negotiating tactics had given too much away in the agricultural sector. It obtained 96 votes in favour but 246 members opposed it. There was even more support for a motion tabled by José Happart (Belgian Socialist) on the Commission's handling of the BSE crisis, with 118 members supporting censure.

The most serious crisis to date, however, arose in 1998-99 after the Parliament declined to give the 1996 discharge at its December 1998 plenary. A censure motion was then tabled by Pauline Green and other members of the Socialist Group, which was initially intended as a confidence vote in the Commission, and which was ultimately withdrawn. By this time support elsewhere within the Parliament for censure of the Commission had grown considerably, accentuated by the Commission's awkward " back us or sack us" handling of the crisis. A second censure motion was thus tabled by 70 members from a variety of Groups, and was put to the vote during the January 1999 plenary. A compromise had already been supported by the Parliament whereby, rather than move to an immediate censure, a Committee of Independent Experts would be set up to investigate the actions of the Commission, and the censure motion was rejected.

Nevertheless, it was still supported by 232 members, including a majority of German (by 83 votes to 7), French, Dutch, Belgian, Danish and Swedish members. The Commission had only been given a temporary reprieve and the subsequent critical report of the Independent Experts in March 1999 later led to the collective resignation of the Santer Commission, within hours of the reaction of Political Groups making it clear that there was a majority for censure.

Dismissal of the Commission is, of course, only a last resort, and can only be threatened sparingly. The Parliament has in practice forged a close working relationship with the Commission, and has had growing influence on its proposals. When conflicts have broken out between the two institutions they have been resolved in other ways than by censure. It remains a reserve power, but just as national parliaments only rarely make use of their power to dismiss governments, the fact that they *can* do so is enough to encourage the executive to pay some attention to their viewpoint.

This was illustrated in December 1989 and January 1990 when the Socialist Group considered a proposal from one of its members to table a censure motion in Parliament. Although this found little support, and was decisively turned down in the Group, it did provoke a flurry of extra meetings between Commissioners and Socialist Group leaders, and led to greater attention being paid to the "social dimension" of the Commission's 1990 work programme then being prepared. An earlier example was in 1976 when a censure motion was tabled over the issue of Parliament's access to Commission documents, and then withdrawn when the Commission backed down. Similarly, in 1972, a motion was withdrawn when the Commission undertook to submit a proposal to increase Parliament's budgetary powers, which ultimately led to the 1975 revision of the Treaties and the increase of Parliament's budgetary powers, as described in the previous chapter.

A motion of censure can only be addressed to the Commission as a whole, reflecting the doctrine of collective accountability. Although a vote of censure cannot be passed on an individual Commissioner, there is nothing to prevent Parliament adopting a resolution criticising an individual Commissioner or, indeed, calling upon him or her to resign. Such a resolution would carry even more weight if it were implied that Parliament might move to censure the Commission as a whole if he/she did not resign. Such a cause of action was proposed in January 1999 by the Liberal and EPP Groups at one stage in the events which led to the resignation of the Santer Commission. The idea has since been included in the EP's resolution of 15 September 1999 investing the Prodi Commission, and is likely to figure in the new framework agreement between the EP and the Commission.A formal Treaty change to permit individual dismissal of a Commissioner is also supported by some members, but is unlikely to win majority support because of the potentially adverse implications for the collegial nature of the Commission.

The Parliament does not have any other formal powers of direct censure other than that concerning the Commission.The one limited exception is provided by Article 195–2 of the TEC , which allows for the Ombudsman to be dismissed by the Court of Justice at the request of the European Parliament. This power has not been used.

Table 25: *Motions of censure tabled within the European Parliament*

December 1972	Spénale (French S)	EP power of control over the EC budget	Withdrawn (in favour of compromise resolution)	
June 1976	Kirk (British Conservative)	Incorporation of skimmed milk powder in animal feed	Votes cast: 131 For: 18 Against: 109 Abstentions: 4	
December 1976	Aigner (German EPP)	Parliament's right of control-access to documents	Withdrawn (Commission agreed to provide documentation)	
March 1977	Cointat (French RDE)	Butter sales to Eastern Europe	Votes cast: 111 For: 15 Against: 95 Abstentions: 1	
15 February 1990	Group of the European Right	The CAP and the Commission's competences	Members Votes cast For Against Abstentions	567 264 16 243 5
11 July 1991	Group of the European Right	Commission and Council policy on Yugoslavia	Members Votes cast For Against Abstentions	567 219 8 206 5
17 December 1992	Paul Lannoye (Green Group, B) and 71 other Members	Position adopted by the Commission during the GATT negotiations	Members Votes cast For Against Abstentions	567 357 96 246 15
20 February 1997	José Happart	BSE	Members Votes cast For Against Abstentions	626 459 118 326 15
14 January 1999	Fabre-Aubrespy and 69 other Members	The 1996 discharge	Members Votes cast For Against Abstentions	626 552 232 293 27

15. Scrutiny and control of the executive

Scrutiny and control of the executive has always been one of the main functions of parliaments. As the sheer size of administration has grown, and governments have assumed ever greater powers to influence people's lives, so the importance of parliamentary oversight has grown as a means to ensuring democratic accountability.

In the European Union, similar trends can be observed. The powers exercised at European level, although limited, have expanded dramatically since the founding of the European Coal and Steel Community in 1950. What was once an organisation with powers concentrated in specific sectors of the economy has now become a system of governance covering important aspects of our lives. The decision to move towards a single currency managed by a European Central Bank and the agreement to extend the activities of the Union more deeply into foreign and security policy are two telling examples of where the Union has moved into areas which have been traditionally seen as at the centre of the prerogatives of national governments, and where there is a compelling case for ensuring that the decisions taken are subject to proper democratic scrutiny at European level.

The issue of democratic control at European level is made particularly difficult by the complex nature of the governmental structure. Executive responsibilities are distributed between a number of institutions, in particular the Commission, the Council and the European Central Bank, all of which can take decisions affecting European citizens directly.

The Commission has major powers accorded it under the Treaties. It has a virtual monopoly on drafting and proposing new legislation. It can adopt implementing measures independently (it adopted 1,354 such instruments in 1998, more than double the number of proposals for legislation (576) forwarded for adoption by Council or by Parliament and Council). It can take Member States to the European Court of Justice for failing to apply European law; and it is the competition authority empowered to ensure fair play in the single market. Moreover, although the number of civil servants working for the Commission is often exaggerated (fewer than a major UK city council or the BBC, for example), it has grown considerably: in 1980, the number of permanent posts was 8,435, but by 1999 this had gone up to 20,810.

The Council is often mistakenly perceived as the "government" of the Community, a misperception reinforced by the usage of the term "Council of Ministers" which (like the "Cabinet" in the UK) is the term used for the government in some countries such as Italy and France. In fact, unlike the

Commission, it has no right of legislative initiative and no power to implement the budget and its permanent staff is relatively small (2,584 in 1999).

Nevertheless, it does exercise some important executive responsibilities: it may, in specific cases, reserve implementing powers to itself (Article 202) and outside the Community framework, it has powers to conduct Common Foreign and Security Policy and police and judicial cooperation, under the so-called second and third pillars. The exercise of these latter powers is particularly problematical as they are for the time being outside the reach of review by the European Court of Justice.

The European Central Bank was established under the terms of the Maastricht Treaty to manage the Euro, the single European currency, with a view to maintain price stability. It sets the interest rate of the Euro, has the exclusive right to issue Euro banknotes, conducts foreign exchange operations and manages the foreign reserves of the participating states. The extent of these powers and the fact that they are exercised independently of national governments necessarily raises the question of how they can be subject to democratic oversight at European level.

The growth of executive power in the European Union has prompted a vigorous response from the European Parliament. Initially it was granted limited supervisory powers by the Treaties: the right to receive and debate an annual report of activities, the right to receive oral and written replies to parliamentary questions and, as we have seen, the right to dismiss the Commission by a vote of censure. Over time it has worked to extend these powers and in this chapter we will complement the discussion in the previous chapter on appointment and dismissal by looking at its general power of scrutiny through debates, questions and reports, alongside the more particular instruments of control over expenditure and secondary legislation, committees of inquiry and judicial review.

Scrutiny through debates, questions and reports

The European Parliament has followed national parliaments in seeking to exert greater control over executive decisions by obliging those responsible for such decisions to come and take part in debates in the Parliament, answer questions from members, either in oral or written form, and submit reports on their activities. Some of these mechanisms are laid down in the Treaties but others have been established by practice over time and accepted as part of the parliamentary system at European level.

Debates on statements

The Commission is expected to come before Parliament and explain its actions on a very regular basis. During the hearings on the Prodi Commission at the end of August 1999, prospective Commissioners were specifically asked to ensure that any initiatives be announced in Parliament before they were made known to the press. With this in mind the Parliament has started to organise its work to enable the Commission President to present the outcome of the weekly meetings of the Commissioners, normally held on Wednesdays, to Parliament the same day. This will make it possible to discuss directly decisions taken by the Commission.

More generally, Parliament regularly asks the Commission (or Council) to make a statement in plenary on important issues of current interest. A good example was when, in October 1999, the Agriculture Commissioner presented to the plenary the Commission's point of view on the refusal of France to admit British beef, an issue which was being discussed at the same moment by a scientific committee in Brussels. The procedure is not unlike the requests in national parliaments for statements by departmental ministers, followed by a short debate. Such statements feature in most part-sessions, and Parliament frequently uses the possibility to wind up the debate with a resolution.

Debate is not restricted to plenary. There is an increasing range of activity in parliamentary committees to which the other institutions are invited to contribute. The presence of individual members of the Commission at committee meetings is a routine event. A major committee will often have one or even two Commissioners speaking and answering questions for periods of up to two hours at each of its bi-monthly meetings.

The presence of ministers from the country holding the Council Presidency has also become a normal part of the work of the Parliament. During a six-month Council Presidency, there are normally some 20–30 ministerial appearances in front of parliamentary committees, and an important committee may be visited by two or three ministers, who will speak and answer questions on developments within their sphere of competence. On Common Foreign and Security Policy, the Foreign Affairs Committee holds a special "colloquy" four times a year with the President-in-Office and its bureau meets in between with the chairman of the "political directors" of national foreign ministries.

An important new development is the appearance of the President of the European Central Bank (ECB) before Parliament in plenary and also the Economic and Monetary Affairs Committee. During the hearings that preceded his appointment Wim Duisenberg agreed to appear at least four times a year in front of this committee to keep it informed on the work of the ECB and to answer questions. This forum has become an important mechanism for shedding light on the activities of the Bank within Economic and Monetary Union.

The Director of the European Investment Bank and the heads of various Community auxiliary organs (such as the Environment Agency) also appear on occasion before the relevant committees.

Parliamentary questions

Written and oral questions are an opportunity to obtain precise information on particular points or to force a policy statement to be made. The Treaty itself provided for written and oral questions to the Commission. Council accepted to answer questions as well, an arrangement formalised in 1973. In 1976, at the Paris summit, the Heads of Government agreed to extend this to the Foreign Ministers meeting in political co-operation (now also a Council responsibility). The Solemn Declaration on European Union of 1983 further entrenched these practices.

Parliament for its part has developed three different procedures to take advantage of its right to put questions:

Written questions may be tabled by any member. The question and the replies are published in the Official Journal. Questions requiring an immediate answer are to be answered within three weeks with each member entitled to put one such priority question per month. Non-priority questions are to be answered within six weeks. If the question is not answered within the time limit, the issue can be placed on the agenda of the next meeting of the committee responsible, at the request of the member. Unanswered questions are also listed in the Official Journal as well, a technique likely to embarrass the institution concerned.

Questions for oral answer (with debate) may be tabled only by a committee, a Political Group or at least 32 members. These are filtered by the Conference of Presidents, which decides whether and in what order they should be taken. Questions to the Commission must be referred to it at least one week before the sitting on whose agenda they are to appear and questions to the Council at least three weeks before that date. The reply of Commission or Council is followed by a debate and Parliament may decide to follow this by the adoption of a resolution. If so, a Political Group, a committee, or 32 members may propose such a resolution, which is put to the vote on the same day.

Questions at question time is a procedure introduced in 1973, following British parliamentary practice. Any member may table questions, and the President of Parliament decides on their admissibility and on the order in which they are to be taken. Answers are given during 90 minute periods set aside for this purpose known as "question time". One such period at each part-session is for the Commission, and one for the Council. Each member may only table one question to each institution per month. The author may ask a supplementary question following the reply, and extra supplementaries may be taken from other members. Questions not reached are answered in writing.

Questions at question time rarely have the cut and thrust of the Westminster highlights of the Leader of the Opposition questioning the Prime Minister. It is more like Westminster question time for departmental ministers – not so exciting in media terms but a useful vehicle none the less.

In 1994, Parliament and the Commission experimented with a new format of one hour's worth of impromptu one-minute questions and answers on a major topic to a single member of the Commission, with no predetermined list. This is known as the "Delors format", as it was first used with President Delors himself. In addition, apart from regular questioning of Commissioners and their civil servants, some committees have introduced a more formalised question time to the Commission.

Generally, questions (of all categories) put to the Commission are more rewarding than those to the Council. Commission answers are given by the responsible Commissioner, who has his departmental services to help him prepare. Council answers are given by the President-in-Office, who is not a specialist, and anyway cannot easily take positions on behalf of a body that represents the Member States. The initial draft replies are, indeed, prepared by the Council Secretariat and circulated to all the Permanent Representatives of the Member States and to the Commission for comments or objections (hence the longer deadlines for Council replies). If there are any such comments, the draft reply is discussed in COREPER, otherwise it is approved without discussion. The Commission, too, sends copies of its draft replies to the Permanent Representations when they may be sensitive for national governments, allowing them 48 hours to comment (and a further 48 hours if a national government requests a translation of this draft reply), but the Commission has the final say over its own answers. The Council President does not.

Table 26: *Parliamentary questions tabled during the fourth legislature 1994–99*

Destination	Oral questions	Question Time	Written questions	Overall total
Commission	731	3,430	16,935	21,096
Council	393	1,733	1,832	3,958
Total:	1,124	5,163	18,767	25,054

As the above table indicates, easily the largest category of questions is written questions to the Commission: these far exceed the number of written questions to the Council. Oral questions and questions raised at question time that are addressed to the Commission also outnumber the same categories addressed to the Council but by a much lower percentage (twice as many rather than eight times as many).

If one considers the figures on an annual basis, then over the last decade there has been an increase in the number of written questions (over 4,000 per year from 1996–98, compared with an average of about 3,300 in 1990–93), a decline in the number of questions for oral answer with debate (from 411 in 1990 to 203 in 1998), and a stable level of questions at question time (at around 1,300). All types dip in election years reflecting the smaller number of sittings. Although far more questions are tabled to the Commission than to Council, there has been a slight but constant growth in the latter, reflecting interest in the activities under the second and third pillars where the Presidency plays a role in carrying out policies and the Commission role is smaller.

Besides questions, members may, of course, enter into correspondence with the Commission. There is an ever-growing volume of such correspondence, which can sometimes elicit a quicker reply than a written question. The Commission's internal rules provide for MEPs' letters to receive an acknowledgement immediately. A detailed reply should follow within no more than one month. MEPs also have access to some of the Commission's databases (e.g. on Regional Fund spending).

Reports

The Treaties originally provided for an annual report of activities to be submitted by the Commission to Parliament for debate. This has now been complemented by further reporting mechanisms for the Commission, as well as for the Council, the Court of Auditors and the European Council. These reports provide formal, public, quotable information, the essential raw material for adequate control and scrutiny.

In addition to its annual general report, the Commission now submits to Parliament two three-yearly reports, nine yearly reports and four more regular reports as follows:

- monthly reports (printed as an annex to the "Debates of the EP") on how the Commission has responded to Parliament's amendments to legislative proposals;
- periodic reports (approximately every six weeks) on how the Commission has responded to Parliament's "own-initiative" resolutions and requests for action under Article 192: these are destined for the responsible committee and may be updated if anything further develops;
- monthly reports on the implementation of the budget (introduced in 1988 as a result of Parliament's pressure to limit agricultural spending, but of more general use in the control of expenditure);
- monthly reports, known as "early warning" reports, on agricultural spending, designed to indicate whether such spending is likely to remain within the budgetary limits laid down;
- an annual report on the application of Community law;
- an annual report on competition policy;
- an annual report on the agricultural situation in the Community;
- an annual report on social developments within the Community;
- an annual report on the functioning of the internal market;
- an annual report on the application of the principle of subsidiarity;
- an annual report on regional policy within the Community;
- an annual report on research and technological development activities;
- an annual report on American trade barriers;
- a three-yearly report on the application of the citizenship provisions of the treaty;
- a three-yearly report on progress towards economic and social cohesion.

The other institutions also present a wide variety of reports to Parliament, some of which are provided for in the Treaties and others that have developed as a practice over time:

- the European Council of Heads of State and Government presents an annual written report on "progress towards European Union";
- the Council submits an annual communication on foreign policy and an annual report on human rights;
- the Court of Auditors draws up an annual report after the close of each financial year as well as special reports on specific questions, both designed under Article 248 of the Treaties to assist the Parliament and the Council to exercise their powers of control over the implementation of the budget. The annual report constitutes the first stage in the discussion in the Parliament on whether or not to grant discharge to the Commission and other Community institutions;
- the President of the European Central Bank is required under the Treaties (Article 113) to present an annual report to Parliament meeting in plenary.

In addition to this wide range of reports from outside the institution, Parliament has also sought to generate reports internally, designed to reduce its dependence for information on the very executive it is supposed to control. Its Directorate-General for Research (DG IV) produces background briefings and notes on a broad range of issues, gathering information from a network of researchers in parliaments in Europe, known as the European Centre for Parliamentary Research and Documentation. It also often commissions studies from external organisations such as universities, research institutes, etc. However, it cannot easily match the Commission and national governments in terms of providing an alternative, but equally detailed, viewpoint on controversial complex subjects.

In the scientific field, Parliament decided to address this weakness by establishing in 1987 a small unit within DG IV known as the office for "Scientific and Technical Options Assessment" (STOA). This office, supervised by a panel of MEPs, is designed to help committees and MEPs who increasingly find themselves having to take positions on matters with a scientific or technological component. It is an attempt to respond to the rise in public interest in the social, cultural and political consequences of the growth of scientific knowledge and the application of new technologies. Its goal is to create and maintain the widest possible network of contacts with university departments, research institutes, industrial laboratories and others with a contribution to make. Consultation takes the form of commissions for studies, which are remunerated, and invitations to submit evidence, which are not.

It has, therefore, a vocation similar to that of the POST (Parliamentary Office of Science and Technology) in the UK Parliament and the *Office Parlémentaire des Choix Scientifiques et Techniques* (OPECST) in the French National Assembly. Both of these were established after STOA but like it, took their inspiration from the now defunct Office of Technical Assessment (OTA) attached to the US Congress.

The staff remains small – two A grades plus a number of trainees (known as Ramon y Cajal scholarships) who come for a number of months. Hence the work consists essentially of managing an external research budget, in contrast, for example, with POST which generally produces studies in-house using its own small but expert staff. Nevertheless, STOA has produced a number of reports, for example, on thermonuclear fusion, BSE and ECHELON, which have attracted widespread attention and shown that the Parliament can at least in part make up for its limited technical knowledge.

Control of expenditure

As we saw in chapter 13, Parliament can put pressure on the Commission (and sometimes the other institutions), by freezing items in the budget and only releasing them when certain conditions have been met. However, budgetary control is a much broader concept linked to the power that Parliament has to grant annual discharge to the Commission (and other institutions) for their execution of the budget. It is a power that has come to assume much greater importance in the context of the crisis that led to the downfall of the Santer Commission on the Ides of March of 1999.

At the end of each financial year, all the institutions must draw up their audited accounts for submission to the Court of Auditors. The Court, set up by the 1975 Treaty and made a full institution of the Union in the Maastricht Treaty, is responsible for examining the legality, regularity and sound financial management of all revenue and expenditure of the Community. On the basis of its findings and in accordance with Article 248 of the TEC Treaty, the Court draws up:

(i)   an Annual Report on the activities of each of the institutions over the financial year (incorporating its own observations and the replies of the Institutions),

(ii)   a series of discretionary *ad hoc* special reports, dealing with specific areas of budgetary management, and,

(iii)   since the Maastricht Treaty, a "statement of assurance as to the reliability of the accounts and the legality and regularity of the underlying transactions" (universally known by its French acronym 'DAS').

These documents are submitted – the Annual Report and the DAS each November, special reports as they are published – to the European Parliament and the Council for consideration under the annual discharge procedure (Article 276).

Responsibility for developing Parliament's approach to discharge, including its response to the Court's reports, rests with the Committee on Budgetary Control. Its most fundamental task is to discuss whether the Commission should be granted discharge at all, i.e. whether Parliament should give its approval for the way in which the budget was implemented in the financial year under consideration. More broadly, Parliament looks in some detail at all issues of financial management and difficulties of budgetary implementation and makes recommendations for improvement.

Granting discharge is a formal statement that Parliament is satisfied with the implementation of the budget by the Commission. It is the political endorsement of the Commission's stewardship of the Union's budget. The right to give such an endorsement can be traced back to the Treaty of 22 July 1975, which gave the European Parliament on its own the right of discharge. Between 1970 and 1975, Parliament had shared the power of discharge with the Council, whilst before 1970, the decision lay exclusively with the Council, Parliament only making a recommendation. Nowadays the Council discusses the Court of Auditors' reports and gives its opinion to Parliament but that opinion is usually couched in general terms and leaves Parliament with considerable scope for defining its response.

The right to grant discharge is the basis of Parliament's powers of budgetary control. Discharge is the necessary final act in adopting the Communities' accounts. The act of granting discharge is more than a mere endorsement. Article 89 of the Financial Regulation, which lays down the detailed rules for preparing and executing the budget, requires all institutions to "take all appropriate steps to act on the comments appearing in the decisions giving discharge". The same Article also requires them to report on the measures taken in the light of these comments, if requested by Parliament. These requirements were given treaty status by the Treaty of Maastricht as regards the Commission, which is also required under the provisions of Article 276 para 2 to "submit any necessary information to the European Parliament at [its] request."

This final provision makes it clear that discharge is much more than an annual ritual: it is as much a *power* as a procedure. Increasingly in recent years, Parliament's Committee on Budgetary Control has pressed its right to be fully informed as to all matters affecting expenditure from the Union's budget. In practice, this has entailed probing with ever-greater insistence into allegations of specific occurrences of financial mismanagement, irregularity, fraud and corruption both in the Member States and in the Commission itself. The ultimate outcome of this insistence was the institutional crisis of 1999 – a crisis with its roots not only in the specific cases and dysfunctions which came to light, but also in the very processes of democratic accountability by which they did so, with a central dispute being over the reluctance of the Commission to provide certain kinds of information requested for the purposes of discharge.

The political and legal ramifications of a refusal to grant discharge on the part of Parliament have never been clear. The events of 1999, during which the Parliament rejected a motion to grant discharge to the Commission for the implementation of the 1996 financial year, though underlining and reinforcing the political status of the discharge decision, in fact did little to clarify the legal situation. What is, and was, obvious is that a refusal to grant discharge represents a major political reprimand for the Commission. It is a public statement by Parliament that the Commission has failed in one of its central tasks: its management of the budget has either been irregular and/or uneconomic or has failed to respect the political objectives set when the budget was adopted. Notwithstanding the significance of such a statement, neither the Treaties nor the Communities' Financial Regulation deal with the consequences of a refusal to grant discharge. Prior to 1999, the only formal statement by the Commission on the matter dated from 7 July 1977, when Budget Commissioner Tugendhat stated to Parliament that "refusal to grant discharge is a political sanction which would be extremely serious; the Commission thus censured would, I think, have to be replaced".

It was generally believed that Parliament would feel bound to follow a refusal of discharge with a motion of censure should the Commission fail to resign. In November 1984, Parliament did refuse discharge for the 1982 financial year, but the Commission was at the end of its term and due to leave office a few weeks later. In 1999, no such coincidence allowed the consequences for the Commission to be obscured in this fashion. At the same time, however, the politics of the Parliament combined with procedural ambiguities to muddy the waters somewhat.

In its vote of December 1998 on the 1996 discharge, Parliament rejected a report proposing the granting of discharge. For this, only a simple majority was required. However, for Parliament explicitly to *refuse* discharge, its own rules of procedure require the support of a majority of its membership, i.e. 314 votes. Given the official pro-discharge position of the largest group at the time, the Socialists, this majority was unattainable. In effect, Parliament risked falling into a procedural limbo between the two options of granting and refusing discharge. In an attempt to clarify the situation, the Socialist Group tabled a motion of censure with the paradoxical intention of using it as a confidence motion by voting against it (as a confidence mechanism is not foreseen in Parliament's procedures).

Pressure of events to some extent overtook this plan. When a motion of censure (not that of the Socialist Group but another one introduced by Hervé Fabre-Aubrespy of the Europe of Nations Group) came before the house, 232 voted in favour, with 293 votes against and 27 abstentions. It was by far the closest that Parliament has come to adopting a motion of censure (93 votes being the previous record), and this despite the adoption of a compromise resolution immediately beforehand appointing a "Committee of Independent Experts" to examine the allegations against the Commission and to report its findings six weeks later. Crucially, the Commission undertook to accept the findings of the Committee and to act accordingly. The Committee report absolved the Commission of fraud but its criticisms were much more sweeping than had been expected. The Commission decided to tender its resignation, though only after an announcement by the then leader of the Socialist Group, Pauline Green, that her Group would now vote in favour of a motion of censure, thereby making it clear that there was now a majority in Parliament for censure.

The events described above, which are widely seen as having marked a turning point in the institutional "balance of power" and to have brought to an end an era of complicit co-existence between Commission and Parliament, though doing little to resolve the legal ambiguities surrounding a refusal of discharge, nevertheless significantly boosted the perceived significance of the discharge procedure. Above all, they demonstrated beyond question the importance of the *power* of discharge to the European Parliament. The power of censure too, though not exercised in a legal sense, was an essential component in the process and demonstrated its close connection with the power of discharge.

The combination of circumstances that occurred in 1999 was, of course, atypical. In the normal run of events, the discharge procedure is less dramatic. It remains true, for example, that the effectiveness of parliamentary control is limited by the time gaps involved, and by the fact that many discharge decisions concern preceding Commissions. Parliament has, therefore, generally concentrated on extracting concessions and undertakings from the Commission through its "comments" on which the Commission is obliged to act, and, if necessary, by delaying discharge in order to extract extra information. The Budgetary Control Committee attempts to enhance the continuity and consistency of its monitoring by allocating specific sectors to each of its members for them to specialise in for a number of years. It also works with the parliamentary committees responsible for the policy areas covered by Community spending policies. Some of these committees have themselves introduced systems whereby every few months they are briefed by the Commission officials responsible on the implementation of their areas of the budget.

Scrutiny of executive decisions and implementing measures: the issue of "comitology"

What is comitology?

Just as national legislation often empowers the government to adopt secondary legislation in the form of "statutory instruments" or "orders in Council" (UK) or "decrees" (several continental countries), so European legislation frequently gives the Commission the right to adopt implementing measures or to adapt legislation to technical progress through Commission regulations, directives or decisions.

Such decisions can be controversial and major commercial interests are often at stake. For example, when the Union adopts a directive on common rules for the single market, for, say, authorising food additives or labelling dangerous chemicals, it is often up to the Commission (subject to the rules and procedures described below) to decide subsequently which new additives can be approved or which new chemicals fall under a particular category for labelling purposes.

The legislation that delegates such powers to the Commission obliges it to work with national civil servants in different kinds of committee. Such is the variety of committees and procedures provided for that the term "comitology" was coined to describe it.

For Parliament this system has consistently raised questions of democratic accountability. Behind the apparently technical decisions taken by these committees there are frequently issues of considerable political and commercial sensitivity. As the legislative rights of Parliament have grown, so it has felt increasingly that it should be accorded the right to be informed and to comment on comitology decisions on a comparable basis to the other branch of the legislative authority, the Council.

The 1987 comitology decision

The system of comitology committees was first developed in the 1960s in the agricultural area, and was subsequently extended to other policy areas in an *ad hoc* manner, with different procedures for different committees. The various sorts of committee were standardised in 1987, following the entry into force of the Single European Act, which was supposed to strengthen the Commission's executive powers. On the basis of the then Article 145 (now 202) of the EEC Treaty, Council adopted a decision (87/373/EEC) on 13 July 1987 which established three main types of procedure, type 1(Advisory Committees), type II (Management Committees) and type III (Regulatory Committees), the last two types with two variants. Type I only required the Commission to ask the representatives of the Member States for their opinion, type II allowed a qualified majority to refer a decision to Council, and type III specified that a matter be referred to Council unless supported by a qualified majority. When a measure was referred to Council, Council had a three-month deadline to take a decision, failing which the Commission could proceed with its decision, except under variant B of type III where the Council could, by a simple majority, continue to block the Commission even when it could not agree on an alternative measure.

Parliament objected to these arrangements for three main reasons:

- they were very bureaucratic, retaining too many types of committee and weakening the Commission's ability to implement agreed legislation (especially in the case of Regulatory Committees, where a small minority could block the Commission);
- only Council (or Member State) appointed committees could block a Commission decision and refer it back to the legislative authority; Parliament was given no such role although the Commission was, under the Treaty, responsible to Parliament (indeed, the 1987 Council decision did not even provide for Parliament to be informed about the Commission's proposals); and

– decisions that were blocked were referred only to part of the legislative authority, namely to Council alone and not to Parliament.

Parliament decided to take Council to the Court of Justice on the grounds that the decision did not conform to the intention of the Single Act of strengthening the Commission's executive powers. However, the Court ruled that Parliament did not have the right to bring this type of case. The substance was thus never examined (see section on judicial review, p. 267).

Following the entry into force of the 1987 decision, Parliament sought to remedy the above problems in two main ways. First, it pushed for those committee procedures to be used which gave more discretion to the Commission, because it believed that the Commission must be allowed to act effectively, and because the Commission, unlike the Council, is accountable to Parliament for its actions. It thus frequently attempted to amend legislative proposals to avoid the types of comitology that most restricted the Commission (notably type III (b) Regulatory Committees). (A minority, notably in the Environment Committee, was more wary of the Commission, considering, for instance, that it tended to take too liberal a line on allowing dangerous chemicals on to the Community market and that national civil servants might at least act as a brake on this tendency).

Second, Parliament sought more information on what was being sent to comitology committees (was their content merely technical, or did they contain sensitive matters?) and about the committees themselves (what was their composition, how often did they meet?).

The Plumb-Delors procedure

The Commission agreed in 1988 to transmit draft implementing measures to Parliament (with the exception of routine management documents with a limited period of validity and documents whose adoption was complicated by considerations of secrecy or urgency) at the same time as they were forwarded to the relevant committee of Member State experts, and in the same working languages. This was known as the Plumb-Delors procedure after the then Presidents of the Parliament and Commission who signed the agreement, and it gave the Parliament the chance to respond to matters coming up for decision in the committees.

An example of this procedure was when Parliament challenged a Commission proposal concerning infant formula milk. This was one of several Commission measures to implement a previous directive on foods for particular nutritional uses. Parliament was keen to apply World Health Organisation principles that manufacturers of infant formula milk should not be able to distribute free samples to young mothers without any independent medical advice, and that advertising of such products should be limited to medical journals. The draft was forwarded to Parliament and examined by the Environment Committee, which challenged the Commission on the grounds that its draft implementing measure did not include sufficiently strict provisions. Commission officials appeared before the committee, the committee chairman (Ken Collins) held talks with the Commissioner concerned, and the matter was eventually raised in plenary.

As a result, the Commission modified its proposal to incorporate restrictions on the free distribution of samples and advertising as sought by the Parliament.

This was, however, an unusual case. In general, the system did not work well. Whether because of the exceptions in the Plumb-Delors procedure (which had not been precisely defined), or because of ignorance of the procedure in some of the Commission services concerned, many draft implementing measures were not forwarded to the Parliament. Moreover, the lack of any obligation on the Commission to indicate a timetable for adoption of the measure often made it difficult for Parliament's committees to know how much time they had to react.

The "Modus Vivendi" of December 1994

With the entry into force of Maastricht, a new situation was created, at least with regard to those policy areas subject to the co-decision procedure. Parliament was in a stronger position politically to argue its case with Council as the two institutions now *jointly* adopted legislation containing provisions for implementing powers. It also argued that the legal situation had changed: existing comitology procedures could not be applied in the case of acts adopted by co-decision because Article 145 of the EC Treaty, on which the procedures were based, referred to rules for the implementation of acts of the Council. In the view of the Parliament, co-decision acts were not "acts of the Council", but "acts of the Parliament and the Council", a view that was subsequently rejected by the Court (see section on judicial review).

Parliament maintained that a new system must be agreed such that Council and Parliament not only jointly delegated but also jointly scrutinised and, if necessary, jointly retrieved, implementing powers. It put forward a proposal to this effect in December 1993 (De Giovanni Report Doc. A3–417/93). The Commission responded with a proposal for an Inter-institutional Agreement along similar lines. The Council, however, was extremely reticent and indeed continued to claim that co-decision acts were still acts of the Council, and that the 1987 decision was, therefore, fully applicable.

Disputes between Parliament and Council over comitology became a feature of most of the first conciliations under Article 251, with the Parliament frequently refusing to accept Regulatory Committees unless the Parliament was also given equivalent rights. Attempts to find *ad hoc* solutions (for instance, by deleting all comitology provisions) were not always successful and in one case (ONP voice telephony) the newly elected Parliament in July 1994 rejected the measure primarily over the issue of comitology.

Fears of legislative gridlock meant that serious inter-institutional talks over comitology finally took place in the autumn of 1994. The positions of the Parliament and the Council remained far apart, however. The Commission, which had always disliked the restrictions that comitology placed on its own autonomy, was none the less cautious about a reform that would enhance Parliament's powers.

In the end, it was agreed by all concerned that, pending IGC examination of the matter, a temporary truce would have to be called. The consequent

"*Modus Vivendi*" gave Parliament enhanced rights of scrutiny, but falling short of equality with Council. It provided that Parliament would receive *all* draft implementing measures for general application and the timetables relating to their adoption. The Commission would be obliged to "take account to the greatest extent possible" of the views of the Parliament and to inform Parliament of how it had done so. Where a matter was referred to Council as a result of the deliberations of a comitology-type committee, the Commission would brief Parliament's committee. Council could only adopt a measure after having informed Parliament and giving it a reasonable deadline to give its opinion. If Parliament's opinion was negative, an attempt would be made "within the appropriate framework" to find "a solution". What that framework might be was not defined.

Although it was a step forward, the *Modus Vivendi* did not fully meet Parliament's concerns, and did not prevent further disputes over comitology in co-decision legislation. In 1998, for example, negotiations with the Council on a proposed directive establishing a Securities Committee broke down over the Council's insistence on having a type III(b) committee.

Related developments

Besides these agreements of general application there have been a number of other *ad hoc* agreements, including ones between the Parliament and Commission Presidents, between the Parliament President and an individual Commissioner, and even one between a parliamentary committee chairman and the Commission Secretary-General! In July 1993 a code of conduct was negotiated on the implementation of structural policies by the Commission (the so-called Klepsch-Millan agreement), and this was replaced by a new agreement (the Gil Robles-Santer agreement) in May 1999. These codes have contained far-reaching provisions for informing and involving the Parliament on the structural and cohesion fund decisions in particular.

A further Samland-Williamson agreement was reached in 1996 between the then chairman of the Parliament's Budgets Committee, and the then Secretary-General of the Commission. The Parliament had been using its budgetary arm to obtain concessions in the field of comitology (including temporary blocking of the funds for comitology committee meetings). The new agreement went further than the others in certain important aspects. In particular, its last indent stated that "if the Parliament, or a parliamentary committee, wishes to attend the discussion on certain items on the agenda of a committee, the chairman will put the request to the committee. If the committee does not accept the request, the chairman must duly justify the decision..." In practice this latter procedure never succeeded in its intention of opening up comitology committee meetings, because of systematic objections from the representatives of certain Member States.

The Council Decision of 28 June 1999

The 1994 *Modus Vivendi* referred comitology to the Amsterdam IGC. In fact the IGC hardly discussed the matter, simply inviting the Commission to put forward a new proposal to replace the still contentious 1987 Decision.

Parliament was not satisfied with the ensuing Commission text, and called for major amendments. After lengthy discussions, a new Council Decision (1999/468/EC) was adopted in June 1999. This is now the main reference text for comitology procedures.

The new decision goes further than its predecessors. It simplifies procedures (though not as far as Parliament would have liked) by providing for only one variant of management and regulatory committees, and also establishes criteria for the choice of a particular type of committee procedure. It also removed the provision allowing the Council to block measures by a simple majority even if it could not agree an alternative. This will now only be possible by qualified majority. Although it did not give Parliament the equality with Council that it had sought as regards scrutiny of implementing measures stemming from co-decision, it did reinforce the Parliament's right to receive information and give its views. Two articles of the decision are of particular interest:

– *Article 7.3* states that "the European Parliament shall be informed by the Commission of committee proceedings on a regular basis. To that end, it shall receive agendas for committee meetings, draft measures submitted to the committees for the implementation of instruments adopted by co-decision, and the results of voting and summary records of the meetings and lists of the authorities and organisations to which the persons designated by the Member States to represent them belong. The EP shall also be kept informed whenever the Commission transmits to the Council measures or proposals for measures to be taken". The right of Parliament to receive information on committee meetings thus applies in all circumstances, but the right to receive the draft implementing measures themselves is specified only as regards measures implementing co-decision legislation. For other measures, Parliament will have to specifically request the relevant documents.
– *Article 8* lays down the procedures for permitting Parliament to request re-examination of a draft implementing measure, but only where it is implementing co-decision legislation, and only when it considers that such a measure "would exceed the implementing powers provided for in the basic instrument." In other words, it does not provide for Parliament to contest the content of a decision if it is not *ultra vires*.

Full application of the decision required resolution of a number of practical problems (by means of an agreement between the Parliament and the Commission). It will also put a heavy burden on the Parliament's staff resources: the amount of information to be sifted is impressive, and difficult for those who are not directly affected by the measures to assess properly. Appropriate internal procedures will have to be developed within Parliament.

Concluding remarks on comitology

"Comitology" is both extraordinarily confusing for the outsider and easily subject to misinterpretation. Even within Parliament, reservations have been expressed, both by members from countries whose parliamentary tradition does not include detailed scrutiny of such implementing measures, and by those who fear that such disputes are difficult to explain to public opinion, especially if they lead to the blocking of important legislation.

The counter-argument has been that, stripped of the jargon, the issues at stake are openness and accountability of the decision-making system. No one is claiming that Parliament should be involved in all the details of technical implementation measures, merely that it should have the opportunity to step in when these measures raise significant or politically sensitive policy issues. The Council has always insisted on this right, and Parliament, as the other branch of the legislature, is also entitled to do so. The issue will not go away.

Committees of Inquiry

Committees of inquiry enable in-depth investigation of a particular issue. They also put the public spotlight on the issue concerned and in that sense are useful not only for placing issues on the political agenda but also for enhancing Parliament's scrutiny and control.

Parliament first started to make systematic use of this parliamentary instrument soon after the first direct elections in 1979. It established a committee of inquiry into the situation of women in Europe. This committee led to the establishment of a permanent committee on women's affairs. This is the only instance of an inquiry committee being converted into a permanent committee.

Apart from this case, the following committees were set up in the ten-year period before the entry into force of the Maastricht Treaty:

- Committee of inquiry into the treatment of toxic and dangerous substances by the European Community and its Member States (1983–84): this committee examined the procedures applicable for handling these substances, in particular where trans-frontier shipment of dangerous waste was concerned, in the light notably of the scandal surrounding the waste from the Seveso accident. Its report stimulated new legislation in this field. This committee also set the precedent of all national governments except one agreeing to send officials to testify before the committee, despite the lack of any legal requirement to do so.
- Committee of inquiry into the rise of fascism and racism in Europe: this was set up following the 1984 European elections and the entry into the Parliament of sufficient members to form the "European Right" Group led by Jean-Marie Le Pen. The other Political Groups wished to make a political point in reaction to this. The report drawn up represented a systematic study of these phenomena in the different Member States, examining the links between extreme right groups across Europe. It is thus a useful reference tool for people working against racism in the Member States. Its work led to the adoption by Council, Commission, Parliament and the representatives of the Member States of the Joint Declaration against racism and xenophobia on 11 June 1986. This Declaration, known as the Evrigenis Declaration after the rapporteur of Parliament's committee of inquiry who died just before its adoption, was a solemn affirmation of the determination of the signatories to work against racism and all forms of intolerance.

- Committee of inquiry into the drugs problem (1985–86): this compared the methods used by the different Member States to deal with this problem and examined the problem of extradition of drug traffickers. It also looked at the problems facing developing countries where drugs are produced. It stimulated the interest of Member States to co-operate in this field, an interest which culminated in the third "Pillar" of the Maastricht Treaty dealing with Home and Judicial Affairs. The combating of drug addiction is a specific aim identified within that Pillar.
- Committee of inquiry on agricultural stocks (1986–87): this committee investigated the causes and ramifications of agricultural stocks at a time when debate on the reform of the CAP was at a crucial juncture. Its conclusions contributed to shaping the reformed CAP and the de-stocking policy.
- Committee of inquiry on the handling of nuclear materials (1988): this committee investigated the Mol/Transnuclear scandal. Its investigations concluded that Community officials were not involved in the scandal, but that there were lacunae in Community regulations pertaining to the trans-frontier shipment of nuclear waste. The Commission undertook to bring forward new legislative proposals as a result. This committee of inquiry initially had some difficulties in obtaining testimony from some officials in the Belgian government. As a result, the problem of inquiry committees was discussed in Council, which adopted a statement emphasising that, while there was no *obligation* on national authorities to attend Parliament's hearings or inquiries, they were invited nonetheless to do so on a voluntary basis, bearing in mind the duty of mutual co-operation between the Member States and the Community institutions enshrined in the Treaties. Council accepted that invitations to national authorities from the Parliament could be sent through Council.
- Committee of inquiry on hormones in meat (1988–89): this investigated another important aspect of Community policy and one which had recently sparked off a trade war with the USA. It endorsed the continuation of the Community's restrictive policy on this matter.
- Committee of inquiry on the application of the joint declaration against racism and fascism (1989–90): this committee was a follow-up to the previous committee of inquiry on the same subject attempting to investigate what progress had been made five years on, and making suggestions for further action.
- Committee of inquiry on trans-frontier crime linked to drug trafficking (1991): this committee compared the divergent legal situations and general approaches of governments to trans-frontier criminality and drug trafficking and made proposals for concerted European action, at a time when the Member States were setting up new forms of such cooperation which were ultimately included in the Treaty of Maastricht. Although a broad majority agreed on the main recommendations, the committee split almost equally on the question of whether possession of soft drugs should be de-criminalised. Thus, a minority report was also presented (and signed by the rapporteur who had been outvoted on this point).

The regular practice of setting up committees of inquiry was given formal recognition in the Treaty of Maastricht. It added a new article to the EC

Treaty (now Article 193), specifying that the Parliament has the right to set up such committees to investigate "alleged contraventions or maladministration in the implementation of Community law, except where the alleged facts are being examined before a court and while the case is still subject to legal proceedings". The text also took up the existing provision in Parliament's Rules that such committees can be requested by a quarter of Parliament's members. The Treaty article also specified that detailed provisions governing the exercise of the right of inquiry was to be determined by common accord of the Parliament, the Council and the Commission. After hard negotiations between the three institutions, a compromise was found in April 1995, paving the way for the Parliament to set up committees of inquiry governed by this new inter-institutional agreement. The agreement does not give the Parliament a general power of summons but it does provide a mechanism for it to invite Community and national officials as well as other individuals to appear before it.

After the Rules of Procedure were revised to take account of the new agreement, there was considerable discussion during 1995 concerning a subject for the first committee. A minority suggested the case of French nuclear tests in the Pacific but it was a proposal that did not win majority support. Unlike the situation in, for example, the German *Bundestag* where it is obligatory to set up a committee if a quarter of members request it, this is not the case in the Parliament. The majority is always in a position to block such a committee's establishment by blocking a decision on a proposal to plenary regarding the committee's composition.

Eventually, at the December plenary in 1995, the Conference of Presidents proposed the creation of a **committee of inquiry to examine the Community transit system**. The plenary agreed and this first committee, made up of 17 full members and 17 substitutes, came together at the beginning of 1996, under the chairmanship of the British Labour MEP, John Tomlinson and with a British Conservative MEP, Edward Kellett-Bowman as rapporteur. The Transit Committee was to meet 37 times over the following 13 months, holding 16 sessions of evidence, attended by 65 individual witnesses from 32 separate organisations. It finally adopted its report in February 1997 and presented it to the plenary the following month.

In the meantime, in July 1996, Parliament decided to set up a second **committee of inquiry on the BSE crisis**. This committee was chaired by a German Christian Democrat, Reimer Böge, with a Spanish Socialist, Manuel Medina Ortega, as rapporteur. It was originally set up for three months but its life was extended by three months, with the result that it was able to adopt its report in advance of the first committee and to present it to plenary one month earlier in February. Despite this shorter time scale it managed to organise 31 meetings with 16 formal sessions of evidence.

In both cases, unlike the practice with standing committees, the plenary was presented with a report that had already been approved but there were debates in each case, with votes on a draft recommendation addressed to the Community institutions and the Member States in the case of the transit report, and on a resolution drafted by the groups for BSE.

The success of these committees (no further committees of inquiry were set up before the fifth legislature took office in June 1999) was fourfold. First, despite the lack of any sanctions to oblige witnesses to appear, only one person, Douglas Hogg, the British Agriculture Minister, refused to attend, arguing (correctly, in strict legal terms) that he was not under any obligation to come and that his Permanent Secretary could speak on his behalf. The Transit Committee had a notable success in that it persuaded American executives of Philip Morris, Europe, based outside the EU in Switzerland, to come to Brussels, though they insisted that the meeting take place behind closed doors. Second, although there were no sanctions for perjury, both committees went to considerable lengths to ensure that the evidence given by witnesses was widely publicised, with much of the material being put on the Internet site of the Parliament. The Transit Committee sent every witness a copy of their evidence, inviting them to sign it and indicate that it was a true record: all did so, thereby contributing to the credibility of the record. Third, the work of the committees had a visible impact on the institutions investigated and in particular, the Commission. In its resolution of February 1997, Parliament warned the Commission that if the recommendations of the BSE committee were not carried out within a reasonable time and, in any case, no later than November 1997, a motion of censure would be tabled. This led directly to the reinforcement of the Directorate-General for Consumer Affairs and its taking over of responsibility from the Agriculture Directorate-General for seven scientific, veterinary and food committees advising on pubic health. Finally, and more generally, the committees served to show that the Parliament could serve as a focus for public concern on issues transcending national boundaries and could organise the obtaining of evidence from witnesses from across Europe in a way that few, if any, national institutions or parliaments could hope to match.

Despite these successes in improving the scrutiny role of Parliament, many members feel that the powers of these committees remain too weak, in particular in relation to the obligations imposed on witnesses. Hence it is likely that the Parliament elected in June 1999 will seek to activate the review clause in Article 6 of the 1995 Inter-institutional Agreement, which specifies that "at the request of the European Parliament, the Council or the Commission, the above rules may be revised as from the end of the current term of the European Parliament [i.e., June 1999] in the light of experience".

Judicial review

Parliament operates within an institutional framework where the European Court of Justice is called upon to ensure that the different institutions do not act illegally and respect the basic principle of inter-institutional balance. Hence the Parliament is able, under certain circumstances, to turn to the Court to protect its rights in the Community framework against the other institutions or to ensure the correct application of the Treaties by the other institutions and in particular, the Council. At the same time, its own actions are subject to judicial review and it can therefore be taken to Court.

Before direct elections, Parliament was a reluctant litigant. It participated in proceedings before the Court of Justice only once before 1979, and that at the request of the Court (Case 101/63, in which the Court was asked to rule on when an MEP's immunity ceased to apply, a ruling which turned on the duration of Parliament's annual session). This reluctance was perhaps because, in its original version, the EEC Treaty did not expressly mention

Parliament either as a potential applicant or defendant, other than in staff matters. In so far as it did not follow the example of the earlier Coal and Steel Treaty (Article 38), this exclusion of Parliament from the reach of the Court's jurisdiction was presumably deliberate. However, a number of Treaty provisions did allow 'institutions' to participate in certain types of legal proceedings, and as early as 1964 the Court interpreted this term to include Parliament. This limited conception of participation in legal proceedings was to change dramatically after direct elections in 1979.

The right to be consulted

A central issue for the Parliament in protecting its rights has been ensuring that the Council does not act without having taken due account of Parliament's view. Now that Parliament has the right of co-decision, this may seem less relevant but it was an essential part of the development of the institution and one in which the Court has played a major role.

In the landmark *Isoglucose* cases of 1980 (C-138/79 and 139/79), Parliament's right to be consulted on draft legislation was recognised as being part of the 'institutional balance' that the Treaty had sought to establish. Parliament, intervening in a case brought by private companies, persuaded the Court, against the views of the other institutions concerned, that this right was a fundamental procedural requirement, breach of which rendered the act null and void. The Court also rejected the rather contrived procedural argument of the Council that Parliament did not have the right to participate in this case as an institution on the ground that the term "institution" could only apply to institutions which were expressly granted the right to take annulment proceedings (i.e. Council and Commission).

However, as mentioned in chapter 7, subsequent cases have shown the limits of the *Isoglucose* judgment. In relation to Council's practice of reaching informal agreement in some cases before receiving the Parliament's opinion, the Court found in case C-417/93 that as long as the Council did not definitively adopt its position before receiving the opinion, there was nothing to stop it from using the time to search for a general approach for a common position. And in case C-65/93, the Court ruled that despite the obligation for the Council, even in urgent cases, to obtain Parliament's opinion before taking a decision, Parliament would not be able to object to Council acting without its opinion if this was the result of Parliament failing in its duty of sincere cooperation, after the Council made use of the special procedures available to deal with unforeseen circumstances.

Institutional autonomy

In 1981, Parliament was invited by the Court to explain its rules on the payment of travel and subsistence allowances to MEPs, in the framework of a preliminary ruling the Court had been requested to give by the UK tax authorities. The Court took the initiative under Article 21 of its Statute, which allows it to "require...institutions not being parties to the case to supply all information which the Court considers necessary for the proceedings". The Court allowed Parliament to submit this "information" in the form of both written and oral pleadings, which expounded the notion of

Parliament's organisational autonomy based on Article 199 (ex-142) TEC. Once again, the Court largely followed the line of argument pursued by Parliament, enjoining the Member States not to take measures, including the application of their income tax rules, which could interfere with the internal functioning of the institutions.

Illegal failure to act

A significant jurisdictional right conferred on the 'institutions' was Article 232 (ex-175) TEC, governing actions brought for illegal failure to act, or *recours en carence*. Parliament initiated Article 232 proceedings against the Council in 1983 for its failure to adopt the Common Transport Policy (C-13/83). Council pleaded for a restrictive interpretation of the term 'institution', similar to the one it had relied upon in the *Isoglucose* cases, with a similar lack of success. However, on the substantive legal questions, Parliament was only partly successful with the Court upholding its claim only as regards the Council's failure to legislate on transport services.

Parliament has subsequently brought cases for failure to act against the Council for failure to submit the draft budget on time (case 377/87) and against the Commission for failure to submit the proposals necessary to ensure the free movement of workers in the single market (case C-445/93). Both were withdrawn (removed from the register) when the institution in question acted before the case was heard.

Annulment of parliamentary acts

In the meantime, the absence of Parliament from the list of potential defendants in the EEC Treaty had not prevented a variety of parties from taking actions to annul parliamentary resolutions and other acts. First, in 1981, as we have seen in Chapter 3, it was the turn of Member States, and in particular Luxembourg and France, who objected to a Parliament resolution designating Strasbourg and Brussels as the cities where normal parliamentary meetings would be held, to the effective exclusion of Luxembourg. Parliament retorted that the Treaty of Rome did not allow annulment actions against its decisions, and that the above mentioned Article 38 ECSC Treaty, which had provided for a limited judicial review, should be only applied for the review of acts of Parliament under that Treaty. The Court, however, found that decisions taken by Parliament concerning its own functioning necessarily fell within the field of all three Treaties, and that Article 38 ECSC gave it jurisdiction to rule on the validity of such resolutions. It did, however, uphold Parliament's resolution, although it subsequently ruled against some other Parliament decisions concerning the "seat" issue.

The French ecology party, *Les Verts*, was unable to rely on Article 38 ECSC, which only benefits Member States and the Commission, in its 1983 annulment action against Parliament (C-294/83), contesting the distribution of funds amongst Political Groups and parties for an information campaign prior to the 1984 European elections. To resolve the issue, the Court noted that the Community was "based on the rule of law" and that the EEC Treaty had intended a "complete system of legal remedies". In order to maintain this completeness, the Court ruled that an annulment action could lie against any measures adopted by the European Parliament affecting third parties, the first known case of the Court's extending its own jurisdiction *ratione personae* beyond the terms of the Treaty. On the substance of the case, the Court ruled in favour of *Les Verts*, which led to Parliament discontinuing its system of assisting Political Groups with their "information" activities in the period before elections.

Six weeks later, an action against Parliament by the Council (C-34/86), similarly based on Article 173 TEC, was admitted by the Court and was also successful. In this latter case, the declaration by the President of the Parliament that the 1986 budget had been adopted was struck down and the two arms of the budgetary authority were instructed to complete the Treaty procedure, leading to the adoption of a new budget in June 1986 (see Chapter 13).

Annulment of the acts of other institutions

Parliament took the view in its resolution of 9 October 1986, that the Court's rulings on the admissibility of the cases implied that Parliament too could take proceedings for annulment (against the other institutions) under Article 230 (ex-173). A first such action was commenced in October 1987 (C-302/87), where Parliament attacked the validity of the Council's comitology decision (see page 257). Another was on the adoption of a directive based on what Parliament considered to be an incorrect legal base that avoided the co-operation procedure (*Chernobyl* case, C-70/88).

In the first of these cases, the Court ruled that Parliament did not have the right to bring cases for annulment under the then Article 173 (now 230) of the Treaty, as it was *not* specifically mentioned in the article at that time. In view of the Court's previous ruling that Parliament can be proceeded against under the same article, the ruling caused much surprise in legal circles. The Court changed its mind in the second of the above-mentioned cases, when it ruled that Parliament *could* bring such cases for the purpose of protecting its own prerogatives. The Court concluded that the fundamental interest of maintaining and observing the inter-institutional balance prevailed over the niceties of a procedural lacuna. This was later entrenched into the third paragraph of the present article 230, which was introduced in the Treaty on European Union signed at Maastricht and which came into force in November 1993. Parliament was thereby given the right to initiate annulment proceedings but only "for the purpose of protecting (its) prerogatives".

Since then, Parliament has brought a number of successful annulment cases against Council, notably for failure to consult Parliament (e.g. Lomé convention financial regulation, case C-316/91), to reconsult Parliament (e.g. harmonisation of vehicle taxes, case C-21/94) to apply the cooperation procedure (e.g. right of residence for students, case C-295/90) and for adopting an implementing measure that went beyond the terms of the original directive (on plant protection, case C-303/94). It has also brought cases that were unsuccessful (e.g. cases C-417/93 and C-65/93 mentioned above). Most annulment cases centre on the legal base (Treaty article) chosen for the proposal.

Annulment of acts of Council and Parliament acting jointly

Annulment actions are now also possible against acts of the Council and Parliament "adopted jointly" (under the co-decision procedure). In such cases, Parliament and the Council find themselves on the same side of a legal argument before the Court. The first such case was successfully defended against Germany which, when outvoted in the Council, brought annulment proceedings against a directive (94/19/EC) on the system of deposit guarantees on the ground that it violated the principle of subsidiarity. Germany has also brought a case, still pending, on similar grounds, in relation to the ban on advertising and sponsorship of tobacco products, adopted in July 1998. These cases have led to the Legal Services of Council and Parliament cooperating in defence of the Directive. Such cooperation has occurred even though the Court has surprisingly ruled that acts adopted under co-decision are in fact acts of the Council (C-239/95). This is obviously, to say the least, at odds with the practice of publishing in the Official Journal acts adopted under co-decision as acts of both institutions, signed by the Presidents of both. It is also at odds with paragraph 5 of Article 251, which requires the express approval by both institutions of the joint text proposed by the Conciliation Committee under the co-decision procedure (see p. 189).

Observations by Parliament on international agreements

A final development regarding Parliament's jurisdictional standing in the pre-Maastricht era concerned the procedure, rarely used until recent times, for requesting the opinion of the Court on the compatibility with the Treaty of international agreements to which the Community intends to become party. Though Article 309 (ex-228) TEC does not include Parliament amongst those entitled to request such an opinion, neither the Treaty nor the Statute of the Court precluded Parliament's submitting observations on requests made by others. Starting with Opinion 1/92, the Court has systematically allowed Parliament to take part in both the written and oral phase of such proceedings.

Parliament and the Court: a brief assessment

Contrary to a view held by some, Parliament is not a particularly litigious institution. In numerical terms, it has been a defendant before the Court approximately as often as it has been an applicant. Litigation commenced by Parliament has to date been concerned mainly with the choice of the correct legal basis for legislation and respect by the Council of its duty to reconsult Parliament in the case of a substantial modification of the original proposal on which the Parliament has already been consulted.

Court action has enabled Parliament to clarify certain of its prerogatives and sometimes to obtain significant progress in advancing its interpretation of the Treaties. However, now that the Parliament's powers have been substantially expanded, we can expect the kind of litigation seen in the past to decline in importance. Rather than the Parliament taking the Council to the Court or vice versa, the pattern of the future could be individual Member

States taking both institutions to the Court as a result of decisions taken in the co-decision procedure. Judicial review will therefore apply ever more to decisions to which Parliament itself has contributed.

Parliament and the application of Community law in the Member States

Another indirect way in which Parliament contributes to the correct application of Community Law is by drawing to the attention of the Commission any infringements (such as non-application or incorrect application of directives) by Member States. Under the Treaties, it is up to the Commission to initiate infringement proceedings against Member States (1105 in 1998) and, if the situation is not remedied, to bring cases before the Court of Justice (114 in 1998), many of which are settled before a Court ruling is given. These procedures are essential in ensuring the homogeneity and predominance of Community law in the Member States.

The difficulty for the Commission is in finding out about infringements; it has, after all, no police force or inspectorate at its disposal and has a relatively small staff. It has to rely on complaints from the public. In this respect, Parliament, through its members receiving complaints from constituents and from the petitions it receives, is furnishing an increasing number of complaints to the Commission. The importance of this phenomenon has been highlighted in the Commission's Annual Reports on the application of Community Law.

Overall assessment

Parliament's powers of scrutiny and control (or "oversight" as the Americans call it) have, like its legislative and budgetary powers, developed both by treaty change and by agreements reached with the other institutions. Its general powers of scrutiny are now similar to those of national parliaments but in the very particular environment of the Union, Parliament is developing its own style of control, which the other institutions can no longer ignore. As a result it has at its disposal a selection of instruments which increasingly give it the means it needs to oversee executive activity, whatever its source. This greater ability to exercise democratic control will no doubt mean that the institution will itself be subject to greater scrutiny by those outside the EU institutions.

16. A forum and channel for communication

Apart from the classical parliamentary functions it performs in the legislative and budgetary fields, in appointments and dismissal and in terms of scrutiny and control over the executive, Parliament also plays an important part as a forum and channel for communication. Thanks to its high level of autonomy, it not only undertakes the tasks that the Treaties impose upon it but can take a wide range of initiatives, many of them in response to the concerns of European citizens. In this role it enjoys more than simply formal relations with other institutions and bodies. It forms an accepted part of a network of contacts extending well beyond the European institutions. These contacts are characterised by a determination to make the European system more accessible and visible to European citizens as part of the effort to improve the legitimacy of the European Union system as a whole.

This chapter will illustrate this role by looking at the ways in which the Parliament seeks:

– to broaden the agenda of political discussion through debates, resolutions, hearings, activities in relation to human rights and in response to petitions;
– to develop contacts with other EU institutions, national governments and national parliaments; and
– to ensure a high level of openness and transparency in its work and to increase public awareness of its role in the EU.

Parliament broadening the agenda

Debates

The forum role of any Parliament is most clearly seen in its public debates. This is true for all debates, but some give members an opportunity to take a wider view that may not fit easily into the more specialised discussions that we have looked at in previous chapters.

First, there are several *set-piece debates* every year on the major issues facing the Union. Normally twice a year, the Prime Minister or President holding the chair of the European Council reports on the outcome of European Councils, a practice inaugurated by Margaret Thatcher in 1981. The report is followed by an often lively and wide-ranging debate in which many members from all Groups take part, with the Head of State or Government having an opportunity to respond at the end. Similar debates take place when the Council President, normally the Minister for Foreign

Affairs, presents the "programme" of the Presidency to Parliament at the beginning of each six-month presidency and reports on the achievements at the end of the Presidency. There are thus four annual debates on Council reports to Parliament. To complement these debates in which the Council takes centre stage, there are also separate debates when the Commission presents its annual work programme and its annual report, and an annual "state of the Union" debate introduced by the Presidents of the Parliament, the Commission and the Council.

In addition to these major debates that give members a chance to influence the main agenda of the Union, Parliament sets aside three hours per part-session for *debates on topical and urgent subjects* that are not being dealt with through other procedures (such as a Commission or Council statement followed by a debate), choosing up to five subjects under this procedure. Of the five subjects one is invariably human rights (see section below) and another, frequently, is natural disasters enabling Parliament to call for aid to be sent by the Commission to the areas affected. The Commission reports back at the next session on how it has complied with Parliament's wishes. The remaining three subjects most commonly relate to foreign affairs, allowing the Parliament to take a position on the latest events in, say, the Balkans or the Middle East. Judging by the number of diplomats who attend such debates when their country's interests are at stake, and the number of national parliaments and governments that react to such resolutions, they do not go unnoticed. Parliament's opinion is likely to carry particular clout when it concerns countries that may be affected by Parliament's power, for instance, to block the renewal of a protocol under the assent procedure or to cut off funds under the budgetary procedure.

Resolutions adopted at the Parliament's own initiative

"Own initiative" reports by parliamentary committees (see page 114) are often intended to influence specific policy issues under discussion but they can equally be used as part of Parliament's "forum" role to debate common problems facing the Member States, to discuss external issues (foreign policy, human rights, etc.) or to raise subjects in response to public concerns.

This does not always meet with universal approval. In the early 1980s, Parliament drew up a major report on Northern Ireland (rapporteur: Niels Haagerup, a Danish Liberal). The British government at that time was strongly opposed to Parliament drafting such a report, but was powerless to stop it. MEPs argued that, as the European Parliament contained members from Ireland, Northern Ireland and Great Britain, it was uniquely placed to make a constructive contribution and to investigate whether European funds spent in Northern Ireland were being used equitably and in a way that would help to make progress, a point of view that was widely acknowledged subsequently.

Motions for Resolution tabled by individual members only occasionally give rise to a report from a parliamentary committee, but do allow individual MEPs to raise issues. Such motions are translated into all the Union languages and distributed and are therefore useful, even if no follow-up takes place within Parliament, for the individual MEP concerned to demonstrate his/her activities on behalf of constituents, to place a viewpoint on record, to draw attention to a particular problem or to contribute to discussions in other frameworks (and are therefore comparable to early-day motions in the House of Commons).

Another mechanism allowing MEPs to raise issues is *Written Declarations*. If signed by a majority of members of the Parliament, they are forwarded to the institutions named therein, without debate in committee or plenary. Few such declarations obtain the requisite number of members (just six between 1989 and 1999) but again, they can serve the same purposes as those mentioned in relation to motions for resolution. Thus during the last legislature, it was an important sign to the outside world that a majority of members were willing to sign such declarations on the rights of autistic people, the designation of 1999 as European Year for the Fight Against Violence against Women and the return of the Parthenon friezes.

Hearings

Public hearings of expert witnesses or sectoral representatives provide an opportunity to seek independent expertise and advice; to enter into a dialogue with interested parties; to attract media attention to a particular issue; to obtain endorsement from third parties (such as public figures, other institutions or academic bodies) of particular points of view; and/or to provide a platform for groups that may not otherwise have easy access to decision-takers. Some hearings bring together virtually the whole range of companies, trade unions and consumers concerned with a particular industry. Committees are free, however, to invite less conventional witnesses: in October 1999 the Environment Committee invited a Swedish dog that has a unique ability to sniff for mercury, a skill it duly demonstrated at the hearing.

Hearings are a common feature of most of the world's parliaments: over 60 parliaments even have the power to summon witnesses in the manner of a court. In the Union of 15, ten national parliaments have such a power and all can invite experts to present evidence voluntarily to a parliamentary committee.

Since it became an elected body in 1979, Parliament's committees have held about 30 hearings a year. Hearings are almost always conducted in the context of drafting a report, either on behalf of a standing committee or a committee of inquiry. Committees are allowed to hold hearings with the permission of the Bureau. In practice, committees invite outside experts without reference to the Bureau if no expenses are incurred, but request the Bureau's permission beforehand if there are expenses. Since 1995, an annual programme of hearings is submitted by committees to the Bureau for approval. Each committee may invite up to 16 experts from outside Brussels.

Hearings have been organised in different ways. Some committees have experimented with an open hearing format inviting anyone interested to send in a written contribution and to present it to the committee in a speech of no more than three to five minutes. Such hearings were organised, for example, by the Economic Committee on High Definition Television (HDTV) and by the Institutional Committee on the preparations for the Amsterdam IGC. More commonly, committees establish in advance the experts they wish to invite. The selection is carried out by procedures determined within each committee. In some, it is left to the chairman, in others, the Bureau and in others again, a meeting of co-ordinators from all the Political Groups decides. Some committees then take a final vote on the choice in the full meeting. The response of invited experts has generally been good, given that there is no obligation to attend. There is widespread interest in being able to present evidence to the Parliament.

Once the participants are selected they are normally invited to present written evidence, preferably in advance. When they come before the committee, they make an official statement, which is followed by questions from MEPs. The rapporteur is normally given a predominant role in this. The Anglo-Saxon tradition of "cross-examination" of the witness is beginning to develop, with members putting questions one-by-one and having the opportunity to ask a supplementary if not satisfied with the answer.

The other institutions attend hearings in the same way as they attend the normal course of committee business. The Commission is frequently called upon to react to views expressed by expert witnesses. Most committees publish a summary of the results of their hearings in the relevant report or in a specific committee document for this purpose. It is unusual to have an *in extenso* report in the style of the House of Lords, or the US Congress, the main constraint being the multilingual nature of Parliament's hearings that normally precludes the preparation of verbatim reports on cost grounds. Occasionally a brochure or booklet has been produced, but it has been rare for evidence received to be made available in all languages, owing to the length of time required for translation and printing. One exception was the evidence received by the Committee of Inquiry into the Community Transit Regime (see p. 263) which had all sixteen sessions of evidence that it held translated into all languages, published in a separate volume and put on the Internet. Such comprehensive coverage will probably remain an exception but the availability of the Internet will certainly make it possible to make the results of hearings more widely available than they have been up to now.

Activities in the field of human rights

Parliament has put considerable effort into being a channel through which questions of human rights can be raised. Besides dealing with general human rights issues, it is one of the few parliaments that carry out casework on individual human rights violations. It has established a specific administrative unit inside the Directorate-General for Committees and Delegations (DG II) to carry out these activities.

The role of Parliament in this field has traditionally been seen as "informal", since it derived mainly from the Parliament's role as a mirror of public opinion rather than from specific legal competencies. Today this is no longer the case; revisions of the Treaties have created a solid *acquis* in this area.

As discussed in Chapter 12, the Treaties give Parliament a right of assent to many kinds of external agreement. Parliament has rarely voted to reject an agreement, but it has often purposely delayed ratification – almost always because of human rights considerations. In the early 1990s, Parliament delayed financial and technical protocols to the agreement with Israel and to an agreement with Syria. It also blocked some financial provisions relating to the Customs Union with Turkey because of reservations about democracy and human rights.

Parliament created in 1994 a chapter in the EU Commission budget entitled "The European Initiative for Democracy and Human Rights". The Parliament has successfully sought to increase human rights funding, and this chapter alone now amounts to around €90m a year. The Parliament has played an active role in establishing priorities for this expenditure, which is managed by the Commission.

Since 1983, Parliament has regularly adopted an Annual Report on Human Rights in the World. The Report includes Parliament's response to the Council's annual memorandum to Parliament on human rights activities, one of the few official communications on foreign policy that the Council submits to the Parliament. These reports have increased awareness of patterns of human rights violations across geographic boundaries and have highlighted issues such as the rights of minorities. Many of the innovations in the Commission's treatment of human rights issues have been prefigured in these reports. In 1999 the Council accepted two innovations long sought in Parliament's reports. These were the inauguration of an annual EU report on human rights, which includes material on developments inside as well as outside the Union, and the convening of a policy forum where representatives of the EU institutions can discuss human rights issues with NGO representatives and academic experts. Parliament has also pressed for the adoption of clear procedures for the implementation of the human rights clause, which is now a standard feature of the main external agreements.

Parliament's Rules of Procedure provide that human rights is one of the headings in the debate on urgent matters that takes place during plenary sessions in Strasbourg. A short-list of situations for inclusion under this heading is drawn up in the preceding week, and the Political Groups may table draft resolutions on the nominated subjects. The Human Rights Unit, operating to a very short deadline, then seeks to verify the details of each case. To do so it maintains close contacts with organisations such as Amnesty International, and also makes extensive use of Internet resources.

Many EU external agreements provide for enhanced inter-parliamentary contacts. As a result Parliament delegations meet regularly with parliamentarians from third countries, and human rights issues are frequently raised. The largest such meeting, the EU-ACP Joint Assembly, has developed a special mechanism for raising individual cases. Successive Presidents of Parliament have also intervened in individual cases, both directly with high level visitors and accredited ambassadors, and in correspondence with governments.

Every year since 1998, Parliament has awarded the Sakharov Prize for Freedom of Thought to someone, who by standing up for freedom of speech has made a notable contribution to the fight against intolerance and fanaticism. The prize was named after Andrei Sakharov because he was seen as the outstanding embodiment of these ideals. Two past winners, Nelson Mandela (1988) and Aung San Suu Kyi (1990), have since received the Nobel Peace Prize.

The impact of all these activities should not be underestimated. In September 1999, for example, two of the original candidates for the

Parliament's Sakharov Prize, Khémaïs Ksila from Tunisia and Akin Birdal from Turkey, were released from prison. The chairman of the Foreign Affairs Committee, Elmar Brok, commented: 'I cannot believe these releases are coincidental. There is increasing international recognition for the European Parliament's human rights activities and our committee will continue to raise these individual cases.'

Table 27: *Sakharov Prize winners*

Year	Winner	Country
1988	Nelson Mandela and Anatoli Marchenko	South Africa/ Soviet Union
1989	Alexander Dubcek	Czechoslovakia
1990	Aung San Suu Kyi	Burma
1991	Adem Demaci	Albania
1992	The mothers of Plaza de Mayo	Argentina
1993	The Sarajevo daily paper "Oslobodjenje"	Bosnia
1994	Taslima Nasreen	Bangladesh
1995	Leyla Zana	Turkey
1996	Wei Jingsheng	China
1997	Salima Ghezali	Algeria
1998	Ibrahim Rugova	Kosovo
1999	Xanana Gusmao	East Timor

Petitions

The Single European Act refers to the Parliament as "an indispensable means of expression" for the "democratic peoples of Europe". Thereafter the Maastricht Treaty created the specific category of European citizenship which accords specific rights to the citizens of the Union, including the right to petition the European Parliament, thereby recognising and giving treaty status to a right already provided for in Parliament's internal Rules of Procedure since 1953. It is the only rule that confers rights on persons other than MEPs.

It is a right that was little used until the mid-1970s, with only 20 petitions in 1977–78. After the first direct elections in 1979 this figure rose substantially, reaching 1,352 petitions in 1994–95; since then the figure has declined slightly, but has remained above a thousand (1,005 in 1998–99). The number of signatories to petitions, however, continues to grow: in the 1984–89 legislature, 5.5 million people signed petitions; during the 1994–99 legislature this figure increased to 10 million. This includes one petition with 3,286,647 signatures on animal welfare and in particular the huge distances travelled by horses within the Community just before being slaughtered.

The conditions for the admissibility of petitions are straightforward. They are deemed admissible if they are formally in order (are signed by a petitioner who indicates his/her name, occupation, nationality and address) and if they fall within the sphere of activities of the Union (a concept that is usually interpreted liberally). They may also be submitted electronically provided that they are confirmed in writing with a signed letter.

Since 1987, petitions have been dealt with by a special committee that Parliament set up for this purpose (having previously been dealt with initially by the Legal Affairs Committee and subsequently by the Committee on Rules of Procedure). The Committee on Petitions can draw up reports on matters referred to it, organise hearings, send MEPs to investigate on the spot, or request information or action from the Commission and, to a more limited extent, from Member States. Matters are often sent to specialised committees, occasionally for a specific opinion, more often for information only.

The Petitions Committee prepares an annual report on its work for debate in plenary. A short statement is also presented to Parliament six months after the annual report, including information on the type and number of petitions received, and is annexed to the plenary minutes rather than being the subject of debate.

The 1998–99 report showed that 693 of the 1,233 petitions considered during the calendar year were found to be admissible, i.e. to fall within the sphere of competence of the Union and to be procedurally in order. Of the others, many were referred to the relevant national authorities, such as national parliament petition committees, or Ombudsmen. In 452 cases relating to new petitions, information was requested from the Commission.

Most petitions fall into one of two categories. Some express views on a particular issue (most frequently environmental matters, human rights, foreign policy matters, animal protection and European Union). Such petitions frequently have a very large number of signatories. Generally, the Petitions Committee forwards the petition to the parliamentary committee responsible for the subject in question, and informs the first signatory of the petition of any recent Parliament standpoints on the issue.

The other common type of petition is for the redress of a particular grievance. Such petitions are usually signed by individuals. They cover a range of issues such as disputes with customs authorities at internal Community frontiers, eligibility for social security benefits in other Member States, problems with importing and registering motor vehicles from another Member State, access to employment in the public sector, civil law, double taxation and residence permits. In such cases the committee frequently turns to the Commission for help in clarifying whether there may have been a violation of Community law, in taking the matter up with the Member State and, if necessary, beginning infringement proceedings, leading possibly to a Court case.

As is the experience of petition committees in national parliaments, or of Ombudsmen, in many cases little can be done to help the petitioner. Nevertheless, Parliament can claim some important successes as the following examples cited in the 1998–99 report attest:

A. A British petitioner, a fully qualified European Mountain Leader, worked seasonally in the Val d'Aosta by bringing English clients for walking holidays in that region. However, at the request of the Aosta Mountain Guide Association, he was charged with committing an offence under regional laws for offering services for which he was not qualified.

    Following several cases concerning the provision of services by tourist guides working in a 'closed group', the Court of Justice ruled that a Member State breached the obligations of the Treaty incumbent upon it. The judgment was concerned with the conditions governing professional qualifications. The Commission took the view that the petitioner's case was similar, and in December 1997 announced that it had initiated proceedings against Italy. In April 1998 the Italian authorities confirmed that Directive 92/51/EEC had been incorporated into national law with regard to the profession concerned (No.1137/95).

B. A British petitioner wanted to travel to Bruges on Eurostar, but was detained in Brussels by the Belgian authorities on the grounds that her passport had been forged (photograph replaced). Deported from Belgium, the petitioner complained that she had been deprived of the right of freedom of movement within the European Union.

The British passport office conceded that faulty material might have been used to attach the photograph in the passport, and reimbursed the cost of her trip to Belgium (No.361/96).

C. A French petitioner complained that the Belgian authorities refused to allow her to accompany her daughter whilst driving unless she exchanged her French driving licence for a Belgian one. At the request of the Petitions Committee, the European Commission intervened with the Belgian authorities and the petitioner's problem was settled on the basis of Article 1(2) of Directive 91/439 EEC which introduced the principle of mutual and unconditional recognition of driving licences issued by the Member States. This directive is directly applicable to every citizen (No.296/97).

One particularly delicate problem for Parliament is in knowing exactly what rights it has to approach Member States for information or assistance. In April 1989, the Presidents of the Parliament, Commission and Council signed a solemn declaration concerning the rights of European citizens to petition the European Parliament and encouraging Member States to give "as clear and swift replies as possible to those questions which the Commission might decide, after due examination, to forward to the Member States concerned". They pointed to the principle enshrined, in particular, in Article 5 TEC, requiring the Member States and Community institutions to "co-operate wholeheartedly in applying the Treaties." However, progress remains limited, with the assistance of Member States being sporadic and with the Council declining to respond to the call for its officials to attend committee meetings on a regular basis.

In addition to receiving petitions directly from citizens, Parliament has very close ties with the *European Ombudsman*, who is empowered to receive complaints from any EU citizen or any natural or legal person residing in the Member States concerning instances of maladministration in the activities of the Community institutions or bodies (other than the Court in its judicial capacity). Such complaints may be forwarded directly or through an MEP. The Ombudsman has the right to conduct inquiries at his or her own initiative, except where court cases are underway.

As we have seen (Chapter 14), the Ombudsman is appointed by Parliament for a five-year term following each European election. The rules governing the performance of his or her duties are laid down by Parliament after seeking an opinion from the Commission and with the approval of the Council. Parliament's decision of 9 March 1994 on this is now contained in Annex X of the Rules.

During his first term of office from 1995 to 1999, Jakob Söderman developed close relations with Parliament, operating out of the buildings rented by Parliament in Strasbourg. He presented an annual report to the Petitions Committee and to the plenary. A cooperation agreement was reached between the Ombudsman and the Petitions Committee whereby, with the complainant's consent, cases could be passed from one to the other. The Committee on Petitions also agreed to forward to the Ombudsman any cases concerning the administration of the EU institutions and bodies. The Committee may draw up a report on cases of maladministration reported to it by the Ombudsman and did so in response to the Ombudsman's inquiry into the transparency of the EU institutions.

Finally, the Parliament secretariat has a specific service called "Correspondence with the Citizen", which responds to individual queries for information and documents.

A network of contacts

Besides the formal proceedings in Parliament itself, MEPs have a variety of ways and means of pursuing an issue with other EU institutions as well as with national governments and parliaments. Some of these involve the representation of Parliament as such, notably through its President, whereas others are open to any member. All underscore the importance of Parliament as part of a network linking the actors involved in EU policy making.

Contact channels to the other EU institutions

Since 1988 the President of Parliament attends the meetings of the European Council of Heads of State and Government. This started during Lord Plumb's presidency of Parliament in 1988. It met strong resistance from some governments but has now become an established feature of the meeting. The President does not attend the whole of the European Council meeting, but presents Parliament's views on the issues to be discussed at the opening.

The Presidents of the Commission, Parliament and Council meet together monthly, usually in Strasbourg on the Wednesday of Parliament sessions. These meetings are used as an opportunity to explore solutions to a whole range of problems where the three institutions are in disagreement. They are known familiarly as *trialogues*.

Besides the President, Group chairs regularly meet with Commissioners, ministers and Prime Ministers, especially those of their own political family. Commissioners attend some meetings of the Political Group with which they have political links. They will normally have informal contacts too with their political family. For example, socialist Commissioners have traditionally held a regular working dinner with the leaders of the Socialist Group. Group leaders or co-ordinators are in regular contact with ministers from their party, especially prior to Council meetings.

Committee chairs maintain close contact with the Commissioners responsible for their area and with the minister responsible for chairing Council meetings in his/her area. They will often meet just before Council meetings.

At the time of the 1991 intergovernmental conferences which led to the Maastricht Treaty, an "inter-institutional conference" was set up composed of all 12 ministers on Council's side, a delegation of 12 MEPs on Parliament's side and four members of the Commission. It enabled ministers to remain in touch with Parliament's views on revision of the Treaties throughout the IGCs. It was recreated after the IGCs were over, in order to negotiate agreements on issues arising out of the new Treaty. Thus, inter-institutional agreements were reached in October 1993 on the Statute of the Ombudsman, a Declaration on democracy, transparency and subsidiarity, measures to apply the principle of subsidiarity and the operation of the Conciliation Committee. Further agreements were reached in December 1994 on the rights of committees of inquiry and the question of implementing powers ("comitology") for acts adopted under the co-decision procedure. The inter-institutional conference offered a vehicle for reaching agreement on the detailed application of procedures.

For the 1996 IGC, Parliament was invited to name two MEPs to participate, along with the representatives of the foreign ministers, in a "Reflection Group" to prepare the ground for the IGC, and later, to a more limited extent, in the IGC itself, as described in the next chapter.

The most frequent contacts for day-to-day work are those between Parliament and the Commission. One Commissioner has traditionally had specific responsibility for relations with the Parliament and this link was upgraded by Romano Prodi, when he invited one of his two Vice-Presidents, Loyola de Palacio, to do this job, with the Directorate for relations with the Parliament in the Secretariat-General of the Commission reporting directly to her.

The Commission has a comprehensive internal structure for maintaining contacts with Parliament designed to ensure Commissioners and their departments are well informed as to parliamentary opinions and the state of play in Parliament. Each Commissioner has a parliamentary attaché among the members of his private office (*cabinet*), acting as a permanent link-person with Parliament and its organs. These parliamentary attachés, together with members of the Commission's legal service and Secretariat-General, constitute the Commission's "Parliamentary Affairs Group" (known as GAP). It meets every week except when Parliament is in Strasbourg to examine all aspects of relations with Parliament, and reports through the weekly meeting of heads of private offices to the College of Commissioners, enabling them to react quickly if there is a risk of political difficulties. In addition, each Commission department (DG) has a coordinator responsible for parliamentary affairs. These coordinators maintain permanent contact between their department and the relevant parliamentary committee.

It is relatively easy for meetings to be arranged between MEPs and individual officials within the Commission: most MEPs have their own individual array of contacts with Commissioners and their civil servants. Correspondence from MEPs is given priority treatment. The Commission is a relatively open bureaucracy and this structure ensures that MEPs can take full advantage of that openness.

The personal link between the two institutions is also reinforced by the fact that there are always a number of former MEPs in the Commission (see Table 28) and former Commissioners among the MEPs (currently Willy De Clercq, Jacques Santer and Emma Bonino).

Table 28: *Former MEPs in the Commission*

Commission	Year	No. of members	No. of former MEPs
Ortoli	1973–1977	13	1 (Scarascia Mugnozza)
Jenkins	1977–1981	13	1 (Vredeling)
Thorn	1981–1985	13	3 (Thorn, Dalsager, Pisani)
Delors I	1985–1989	14	3 (Delors, Ripa di Meana, Varfis)
Delors II	1989–1993	17	6 (Delors, Bangemann, Ripa di Meana, Scrivener, McSharry, Van Miert)
Delors III	1993–1995	17	5 (Delors, Bangemann, Van Miert, Scrivener, Oreja)
Santer	1995–1999	20	7 (Santer, Bangemann, Van Miert, Oreja, Papoutsis, Cresson, Bonino)
Prodi I and II	1999–2005	20	4 (Reding, Vitorino, Palacio, Busquin)

At staff level, Commissioners sometimes include in their private office ("*cabinet*") officials recruited from the Parliament, notably from the Political Groups. Even Commissioners who are not former MEPs are likely to know some Political Group staff already, through party links. More recently, Commissioners have begun to take former MEPs into their *cabinets* (in the Santer Commission, John Iversen with Ritt Bjerregard, Luis Planas with Manuel Marin and Ollie Rehn with Erkki Liikanen; in the Prodi Commission, Luis Planas and Ollie Rehn stayed on, the former with a new Commissioner, Pedro Solbes, and Raf Chanterie joined the *cabinet* of Viviane Reding). Conversely, 1999 saw the election to Parliament of former *cabinet* members (José Ignacio Salafranca, Spanish EPP and ex-deputy head of *cabinet* of Abel Matutes, Nicholas Clegg, UK Liberal, who worked with Sir Leon Brittan and Lousewies van der Laan, Dutch D66 member from the Hans van den Broek *cabinet*).

General contacts at civil servant level were long handicapped by the formal location of Parliament's secretariat in Luxembourg. However, the transfer to Brussels of most of the staff that work directly on political matters (i.e. committee and Group staff), and the presence there of members' assistants, has largely overcome that handicap. It has become much more straightforward to organise meetings such as the inter-institutional working party, generally known as the Neunreither Group after the Parliament official who established it. This brings together officials of Parliament, Commission and Council (as well as the Economic and Social Committee and the Committee of the Regions) every month to monitor progress in current legislative procedures and to try to anticipate difficulties.

Finally, Parliament sessions in Strasbourg are an opportunity for an intense round of contacts as MEPs are joined by the entire Commission (which holds its weekly meetings in Strasbourg during plenary sessions), ministers of the Council, officials, lobbyists, journalists, visiting national MPs and so on. This relatively open week-long "conclave" enables MEPs to "collar" Commissioners away from their civil servants. All concerned are virtually obliged to socialise as none of them is rushing home straight after work, all being "away from home" in a congress atmosphere. As a result, plenaries are the Union's information market where it is possible to get a picture of the latest state of play on any issue.

Contacts with individual governments

The most visible form of contact between the Parliament and national governments is the visits of Heads of State and Government. Only Heads of State of third countries or Heads of Government from European Union countries may address the plenary session. Foreign Heads of State use Parliament as a platform to address the Community. President Reagan of the USA, Pope Jean Paul II, Presidents Alfonsin and Menem of Argentina, President Herzog of Israel, King Hussein of Jordan, President Sadat of Egypt and President Havel of Czechoslovakia have all addressed Parliament. Heads of Government of EU countries address Parliament as Presidents-in-office of the European Council, though extra visits sometimes take place. For instance, Chancellor Kohl and President Mitterrand both participated in a parliamentary debate on events in Eastern Europe in the days following the fall of the Berlin Wall in November 1989.

Speeches by Heads of State in formal session have become increasingly common. Up to 1989 there were 21 such speeches but there have been more than thirty in each of the two following legislatures. Parliament has been addressed by the Head of every Member State of the Union, except the King of Sweden, including Queen Elizabeth II in May 1992. The Heads of State of Ireland and Finland have made such addresses on three occasions. And nine of the states that have applied for membership of the EU have seen their Head of State speak to Parliament in this way.

Heads of Government (as opposed to Heads of State) or foreign ministers of third countries are not entitled to address the plenary. On such occasions, usually in Brussels, a special joint meeting of the Foreign Affairs Committee, the Bureau of Parliament and the inter-parliamentary delegation for the country concerned, or some variation thereof, may be held. This procedure was first used for Foreign Minister Shevardnadze of the then Soviet Union and is known as the "Shevardnadze Procedure". The format has also been used to accommodate Heads of State visiting between sessions. Other visitors prefer to meet with particular Political Groups: Prime Minister Brundtland of Norway and Chancellor Vranitsky of Austria met with the Socialist Group and Prime Minister Bildt of Sweden with the EPP Group during the enlargement negotiations; President Yeltsin met the Socialist Group in 1991.

Plenary sessions also attract a stream of ministerial visits, with ministers generally holding a series of meetings with individual MEPs, a general meeting with those from his/her own party or country and perhaps a working dinner on a particular subject with a small group.

Day-to-day contact is through the staff of the Permanent Representations of Member States in Brussels. Each of the representations has at least one official with particular responsibility for links with the Parliament. They meet in a Council working group, the General Affairs Group (known by its unfortunate French acronym as the "GAG"), whose jobs include approving replies to parliamentary questions to the Council. Such officials also attend the more important committee meetings, where they may sit in the seats reserved for Council, and report back promptly to their ministries on what is happening. Journeys to Strasbourg have also become an integral part of the work of the permanent representations. For the UK, for instance, at least two officials from UKREP travel to Strasbourg for each session, where they are often joined by another official from the Foreign Office in London. Strasbourg provides a good opportunity for all national officials to brief MEPs, especially those of their own nationality, on particular concerns of their government as well as for MEPs to contact them for information or to ask for their own views to be passed on.

Most governments provide a written briefing on issues before Parliament, at least for MEPs from their own country. For the UK, Whitehall departments send, through the Permanent Representation, "a written briefing on all new legislative proposals" to every UK MEP and "further briefings on key dossiers at crucial stages in the Parliamentary process" as well as "briefings" on third countries for MEPs who are travelling as part of a delegation. Each Whitehall department has designated an official as "co-ordinator on EP business" to follow Parliament committee work and be available as a contact point for MEPs.

Contacts also take place, on a party or all-party basis, at the highest political levels in the Member States. In Italy, for example, there are regular working sessions of all Italian MEPs with the Prime Minister. In France, the European Affairs Minister (and former MEP) Alain Lamassoure, instituted in 1994 regular all-party monthly meetings. In the UK there are now periodic meetings for all UK MEPs with the Foreign Secretary or Minister for Europe.

The strongest political links and most regular contacts with national governments are likely to be those of MEPs from the same political parties as those in government. Chancellor Kohl met his CDU/CSU party MEPs every three months (usually in Strasbourg – allegedly for gastronomic reasons). In the UK, the Labour government agreed with the EPLP (the Labour MEPs) a "link system" whereby the MEPs designate a member in each EP committee to act as the contact point with the corresponding UK minister. The link members are regularly invited to ministerial team meetings in Whitehall, enjoying a status similar to a PPS (parliamentary private secretary to a minister) in the House of Commons. The EPLP meets regularly with the Foreign Secretary and the Minister for Europe (two recent holders of the latter office, Geoff Hoon and Joyce Quin, are both former MEPs) and a minimum of once a year with the Prime Minister. The leader of the EPLP has a weekly visit to the Cabinet Office to meet appropriate ministers according to current business. Strategic issues from a party perspective are addressed by a "European

Strategy and Liaison Committee" composed of the two key ministers, the Leader, Deputy Leader and Whip of the EPLP and the Deputy Leader and the General Secretary of the Labour Party. Such contacts ensure a flow of information and views in both directions.

One striking example of MEPs' input into national policy-making was the mechanism through which the Labour Party adopted its position on the Amsterdam Intergovernmental Conference.This was done by a working group chaired by the party leader, Tony Blair, and comprising Shadow Chancellor Gordon Brown, Foreign Secretary Robin Cook, Deputy Prime Minister John Prescott and European Minister Joyce Quin on the House of Commons side and Socialist Group leader Pauline Green, EPLP leader Wayne David and deputy leader Christine Crawley and EP Vice-President David Martin on the European Parliament side. The position drafted by this working group was endorsed unanimously by the party conference in 1995. It differed radically from the Conservative government's position on issues like the Parliament's co-decision powers, the extension of qualified majority voting, the Social Chapter and the Employment Chapter. It was implemented by the Labour government after it won power in May 1997.

Over time, MEPs have been granted equal or similar status to MPs by their national administrations. In the UK, letters sent to ministers by MEPs on behalf of constituents are treated in the same way as those of MPs, and there is equal access to government publications, government receptions and briefings from embassies abroad, for instance.

Finally, the President of Parliament also makes an official visit to each Member State during his or her term of office, which is normally used to meet the head of state and government and relevant ministers. The President normally visits the Member State holding the Presidency of Council at the beginning (or just before) its term of office, as do delegations from the larger Political Groups, holding a series of meetings with ministers.

Contact channels to national parliaments

Prior to direct elections, every MEP was also a member of his/her national parliament. Since then, the dual mandate has declined dramatically from about one-fifth of MEPs immediately after the first elections in 1979 to around 40 today. New ways have had to be found to maintain contacts with national parliaments.

The most intense and regular contacts are probably those maintained by individual MEPs with their own political parties nationally. However, there is an increasing range of more formalised parliament-to-parliament contacts. Every two years since 1981 (and from 2000 every year), there have been meetings of the President of the European Parliament with the presidents or speakers of the national parliaments of the Member States, which provide an opportunity to review the network of relations among parliaments and to suggest improvements.

At committee level, too, there has been a major growth in contacts between the European Parliament and national parliaments. These are organised in a variety of different ways. Sometimes an individual MEP gives evidence in a national parliament: this has been a particularly common link between the French National Assembly and the European

Parliament. Sometimes a delegation from a committee pays a visit: the specialised committees in European affairs in national parliaments (see Table 29 below) have been frequent visitors to the European Parliament. And sometimes a European Parliament committee invites all its counterparts in national parliaments for a roundtable: the Economic, Employment, Environment and Civil Liberties Committees have been particularly keen to make such events regular ones.

There has been scope to go further than this. In November 1990 a conference took place in Rome on the eve of the intergovernmental conferences that ultimately led to the Treaty of Maastricht. At this meeting, often referred to as the "parliamentary assizes", over 250 parliamentarians (two-thirds from the national parliaments, one-third from the European Parliament) met for a whole week to address jointly the development of the Community. They adopted a joint declaration on what they expected from the IGCs, perhaps the first time in history that the parliaments that would ultimately ratify a treaty met together to discuss its contents before their governments began the negotiations. Following this conference, some suggestions were made for it to be institutionalised, or even for a new body to be set up on a permanent basis composed of representatives from the national parliaments and the European Parliament, to be known as the "Congress". These suggestions, strongly opposed by the European Parliament, did not make any headway. Instead, at Maastricht, a Declaration (No. 14) was annexed to the Treaty, inviting national parliaments and the European Parliament to meet as necessary at a conference of parliaments of the European Union to discuss the main features of European Union. It leaves it to the parliaments to decide when they think such a meeting is necessary. So far, there has not been a consensus on holding such a meeting, and the absence of any reference to this possibility in the Amsterdam Treaty seems to imply that the Rome assizes was an experiment that will not be repeated.

The Amsterdam Treaty included a protocol (rather than a less binding declaration) on the role of national parliaments in the Union. This protocol went beyond the commitment made at Maastricht in Declaration No.13 in which governments undertook to make sure that national parliaments receive Commission proposals in good time to enable them to make their views known to their respective governments. Now six weeks must elapse between a legislative proposal being made available and the date when it is placed on a Council agenda for decision, subject to exceptions on grounds of urgency.

This same protocol gives treaty status to the Conference of European Affairs Committees (usually known by its French acronym, COSAC or *Conférence des Organes Specialisés dans les Affaires Communautaires*). The origins of this body go back to 1989 when, following a suggestion by Laurent Fabius (who was then both an MEP and President of the French *Assemblée Nationale)*, it was agreed to have regular meetings of the committees in national parliaments responsible for European affairs along with a delegation from the European Parliament. These meetings are held every six months in the country holding the Presidency of Council. They normally discuss topical issues in the Union and invite members of the Commission and the Council to appear before it. The Prime Minister and Foreign

Minister of the host country normally address the meeting. The agenda and preparations are in the hands of the parliaments of the Member States participating in the "Troika" (current, former and following Presidents of Council), together with the European Parliament (which is thus the one permanent member of the preparatory group). The European Parliament is normally represented by two Vice-Presidents who are specifically responsible for relations with national parliaments (see Chapter 6) and other members chosen according to the subjects on the agenda, making a total of six, the same size as the national delegations.

In November 1991, a set of rules of procedure was agreed according to which decisions are taken on the basis of consensus. This provision is particularly relevant given the new Amsterdam protocol on COSAC. This specifies that COSAC may make any contribution it deems appropriate for the attention of the institutions of the European Union on the legislative activities of the Union, notably in relation to the application of the principle of subsidiarity, the area of freedom, security and justice as well as questions regarding fundamental rights. Any such contribution "shall in no way bind national parliaments or prejudge their positions", but nonetheless opens the way for national parliaments to make themselves heard directly by the European institutions. It remains to be seen how easy it will be for the members of COSAC to adopt contributions, given the need for consensus imposed in its Rules of Procedure. However, these Rules were revised at the COSAC in Helsinki in October 1999 to take account of the new protocol and of certain misgivings about the role of the European Parliament. In response, Parliament agreed to abstain when voting on recommendations directed to it and all the participants accepted that abstention should not prevent the adoption of a contribution.

Almost all national parliaments have administrative units responsible for liaison with the European Parliament and the latter has a division responsible for relations with national parliaments which maintains contact with them. Officials from some national parliaments attend sessions of the European Parliament. In addition, four parliaments (the Danish *Folketing*, the Finnish *Eduskunta*, the French Senate and the British House of Commons) now have an official permanently posted in Brussels based within the premises of the Parliament and others are considering whether to follow their example.

In September 1977, the European Parliament, the Parliamentary Assembly of the Council of Europe and the national parliaments set up a joint "European Centre for Parliamentary Research and Documentation". The aims of the centre are to promote the exchange of information among parliaments, to prevent duplication of costly research, and to establish cooperation for documentation purposes between parliamentary libraries and research departments (including common access to databases). The centre is administered jointly by the Parliamentary Assembly and the European Parliament, though the latter in fact provides most of the administrative back-up. The centre comes under the authority of the Presidents of the participating parliaments to whom the Presidents of the European Parliament and the Parliamentary Assembly jointly present a report and an action programme. The centre has set up seven working parties composed of officials from the different parliaments in order to work on improved

Table 29: *List of specialist committees on European affairs in the parliaments of the Member States*

Country and Chamber	Title of Committee	Number of full members
AUSTRIA		
Nationalrat	Hauptausschuss	29
Bundesrat	EU Ausschuss	15
BELGIUM		
Chambre des représentants / *Sénat* (combined committee)	Comité d'avis fédéral chargé de Questions européennes/Federaal Adviescomité voor Europese aangelegenheden	30 (inc. 10 Belgian MEPs)
DENMARK		
Folketing	Europaudvalget	17
FINLAND		
Eduskunta	Suuri valiokunta/Stora utskottet	25
FRANCE		
Assemblée Nationale	Délégation de l'Assemblée pour l'Union européenne	36
Sénat	Délégation du Sénat pour l'Union européenne	36
GERMANY		
Bundestag	EU-Ausschuss	36 (inc. 14 German MEPs)
Bundesrat	Ausschuss für Fragen der Europäischen Union	16
GREECE		
Vouli Ton Ellinon	Epitropi Europaikon Ypotheseon	31 (inc. 12 Greek MEPs)
IRELAND		
Dail Eireann/Seanad Eireann	Joint Committee on European Affairs	19
ITALY		
Camera dei Deputati	Commissione Politiche dell'Unione Europea	42
Senato della Repubblica	Giunta per gli Affari delle Communità europee	24
LUXEMBOURG		
Chambre des Députés	Commission des Affaires étrangères et communautaires	11
NETHERLANDS		
Tweede Kamer	Algemene Commissie voor EU-zaken	25
Eerste Kamer	Vaste Commissie voor Europese Samenwerkingsorganisaties	12
PORTUGAL		
Assembleia da República	Comissão do Assuntos Europeus	27
SPAIN		
Congreso de los Diputados/ *Senado* (combined committee)	Comisión mixta para la Union europea	42
SWEDEN		
Riksdagen	EU-nämnden	17
UNITED KINGDOM		
House of Commons	European Scrutiny Committee	16
House of Lords	Select Committee on the European Communities	20

co-operation among parliament libraries, data processing departments, researchers etc. It publishes a newsletter between four and six times a year which provides information on activities in various parliaments, extensive lists of documentation and studies available upon request from each parliament, and continually updates a directory of who is responsible for what in each parliament.

Openness, transparency and public awareness

Visibility of proceedings

Parliament has consistently argued in favour of openness and contrasted its behaviour in this regard with that of the Council. The 1999 Rules revision reinforced the commitment to openness with a new chapter on openness and transparency and a statement that "Parliament shall ensure the utmost transparency of its activities ..." (Rule 171.1).

Parliament's meetings have become progressively more *open to the public*. Plenary sessions have always been open (the former provision to enable it to be closed under exceptional circumstances was never used and was abolished in the 1999 Rules revision). On the other hand, before direct elections, committee meetings were closed. After 1979 a number of committees such as Social Affairs, and later the Environment and Economic Committees, opened their doors. The Rules used to state that committee meetings were not to be held in public unless the committee decided otherwise. In January 1992, the Rules were modified to provide for neutrality on this issue, and since 1999 it is obligatory for committees to meet in public (Rule 171.3).

There are two exceptions to this rule. First, committees may decide to discuss certain designated matters behind closed doors as long as such a decision is taken at the latest when the agenda of the meeting is adopted. Second, the conciliation committee and the Parliament delegation meetings that precede the committee (see Chapter 12) are not public.

Nevertheless, Parliament's committees are more open than most of their equivalents in the national parliaments of the European Union. The parliaments of Sweden and Finland, for example, which otherwise pride themselves on their openness, provide for closed meetings for all normal business, and the Swedish *Riksdag* has only had the possibility of holding public committee hearings since 1988!

Space is provided for visitors at the back of the meeting rooms and in special rows of seats on the side. Visitors generally fall into three categories: lobbyists, the press and casual visitors. The most regular visitors are lobbyists, especially those who are Brussels-based, and who sometimes specialise in particular committees or specific subjects. Members of the press also attend but normally only for big hearings on controversial subjects rather than for routine meetings. Casual visitors are becoming more common as the number of visitors to the Parliament in Brussels grows (see below). So far there are not the same numbers as in Washington, where congressional committee meetings and their subject matter are listed in the daily press so that political "tourists" can drop in on the committee of their choice. Numbers may increase as easier access to committee agendas through the Internet grows.

The other main facet of an institution's openness is the extent of *public access to its documents*. Here the situation is more complex. Parliament's adopted resolutions are, by definition, in the public domain, but the status of "upstream" documents, such as draft reports or working documents, is less clear.

Once a document is on the agenda of a forthcoming committee meeting, it is made available at that meeting. In practice, such documents have been obtainable only by that minority of the public attending such meetings. Parliament's distribution service is not open to the public and Parliament, unlike the Commission, does not at present have an Infocentre to which people can walk in off the street, and take away the document of their choice. Documents can be requested through Parliament's information offices in the Member States (see Appendix 3), but the public may not know which documents are available.

The situation is now likely to improve. The Rules provide that "unless a committee decides otherwise its documents shall be made public" (Rule 172.2). The guidelines for implementing this decision were being prepared at the time of writing, but the basic principle is likely to be that even draft documents can be distributed, so long as their distribution has been authorised by the committee chair. Rule 172.2 also specifies that a committee document's status should be clearly indicated. It must be evident, for example, whether it represents the thinking of the rapporteur but has not been approved by the committee, or has been approved by a committee, but not yet by the full Parliament. Preliminary draft reports could thus be for internal use only until discussed in committee and could then be made public with the agreement of the rapporteur and chair. Draft reports, on the other hand, would be automatically made public unless the committee decided otherwise. Adopted reports would have the status of full public documents.

Such a system also opens up the possibility of Internet consultation, with public comments being requested by rapporteurs on draft reports, or directly on Commission proposals. An early example was when Jens-Peter Bonde (Danish member, at that time of the Europe of Nations Group), who had been appointed Institutional Affairs monitor of openness and transparency, placed a draft proposal on the Internet site of the Parliament (http://europarl.eu.int) and asked for public comments. While there was only a limited response, an important precedent was established for the future.

The position is less clear as regards purely internal documents. Until 1997 Parliament did not have a code on public access to its documents, unlike the Commission and the Council, which had developed such codes several years previously. Following on from an initiative by the Ombudsman, in which he wrote to all the Community institutions and bodies asking them how they were ensuring access to their documents, a code of public access to Parliament documents was established in July 1997. In April 1998 Parliament's Bureau took a further decision on the fees to be paid for delivery of very large documents. The Amsterdam Treaty (Article 255) provides for a right of access to documents of Parliament, Council and Commission and for the application of this right to be laid down in legislation. This legislation is likely to cause Parliament to modify its code of access to conform to the new rules laid down.

As Parliament gains greater access to confidential documents, new guidelines will have to be developed as to how they are handled within Parliament. Parliament will also have to decide how much information it should give concerning negotiations in which it is involved, such as those that form part of the co-decision and conciliation procedures.

To conclude, Parliament is generally an open institution, and more so than many national parliaments. Nevertheless, it cannot be complacent about the extent of its commitment to openness. There is no automatic access for individual visitors and a system of full document access is still being developed. Although parliamentarians from different political cultures have differing views as how far openness should go, Parliament as an institution will surely be obliged to keep its own level of openness under constant review. Only in this way will it be able to respond to the growing public demand for transparency in decision-making and thereby ensure that it can adequately play its forum role.

Lobbyists

Access to Parliament for those with a case to make for a particular sectoral, regional or public welfare interest is an important part of parliamentary life. Brussels is becoming increasingly like Washington in its variety of lobbyists. According to the *Economist* magazine, there were by the mid-1990s about 300 large companies, 150 non-profit pressure groups, 180 European law firms, 400 trade associations and 120 regional and local authority offices.

Lobbying takes many forms, from briefings in Brussels or Strasbourg for 100 or more members down to lobbying of individual MEPs in their constituencies. It can be carried out directly, or by consultants acting on behalf of clients. Some lobbyists are specialists in following the European Parliament, attending all or most of Parliament's sessions as well as those committees that meet in public. Parliament's press conferences are also open to non-journalists and are often well attended by lobbyists (and diplomats), who, however, may not ask questions.

Listening to lobbyists on various sides of an issue can be an important source of information for MEPs, but can also give rise to misgivings when a well-financed campaign is run on one side of an argument, such as when the tobacco industry tried (unsuccessfully) to prevent Parliament approving the proposal to ban tobacco advertising in 1998.

Lobbyists certainly believe that they can make a difference. One of the most high-profile and vociferous campaigns fought over European legislation in recent years, on the patenting of biotechnological inventions, set biotechnology companies and organisations against some environmental groups, notably Greenpeace. Parliament's initial rejection of the proposal (see Chapter 12) was felt by many to have been influenced by the latter, whereas its acceptance three years later was equally considered to have been affected by the former. In fact, the activity of lobbies cannot be examined in isolation. The new proposal that the Parliament approved in 1998 was very different from the one that it had rejected three years earlier, having been heavily modified to take account of Parliament's criticisms. Moreover, the nature of the argument had moved on with the lobbies eager to seek new allies (in this case, patient organisations). This has the longer-term effect of increasing still further the range of organisations that lobby Parliament on subsequent issues.

The increase in lobbying stimulated Parliament to introduce a register and code of conduct for lobbyists. The difficulty of defining a lobbyist, together with a feeling that "big" lobbies can find their way through extra procedural requirements more easily than "small" lobbies, inclined many to caution about introducing detailed requirements. A first attempt by the Bureau of Parliament to regulate lobbying failed to reach a conclusion before the 1994 elections. Parliament eventually adopted rules in 1996 on the basis of a report for the Rules Committee by Glyn Ford MEP (a first report having failed to get the necessary majority).

The rules have since been further tightened up and now (Rule 9.2) provide for all persons seeking to enter the Parliament frequently "with a view to supplying information to Members within the framework of their parliamentary mandate in their own interest or those of third parties" to be given a nominative or personal pass for up to one year on condition that they sign a public register kept by the Quaestors and respect a code of conduct. This code, annexed to Parliament's Rules of Procedure (Annex IX), specifies that lobbyists must at all times wear their (visually distinctive) pass, which displays their photo, name and the name of their employer. They must, among other things, state the interests they represent in contacts with MEPs or staff, refrain from any action designed to obtain information dishonestly, not circulate for profit any Parliament documents, satisfy themselves that any assistance provided to members is declared in the register of members' interests, and not offer any gifts. Any breach of the code may lead to the withdrawal of the pass to the persons concerned and even their firms. To deal with the possibility that members' assistants might be employed by lobbyists, the code also requires them to complete a declaration of interests. At the same time, the provisions relating to the declaration of members' interests has been strengthened. As described in Chapter 4, this includes a strict requirement to declare outside support.

As a result of these measures, Parliament now has stricter regulation of lobbyists than most of the national parliaments in Europe. All viewpoints can have access to Parliament, but such access must be transparent and above-board.

The media

Parliament devotes considerable effort to ensuring that press, television and radio journalists can have access to the institution. Both in Brussels and in Strasbourg there are pressrooms and facilities for holding press conferences. A press conference is held every Friday before the session in Strasbourg to give the latest information on the work of the Parliament in the following week, and individual members and Groups also organise meetings with the press when they think it appropriate.

The growth in the number of journalists accredited to the European Union, now around 800, the pressure on the services provided and occasional differences of opinion as to how far access should extend, has meant that some rules have had to be introduced. This is notably true for photographers and outside television crews. According to new rules drawn up in 1997, they are obliged to obtain a filming permit but can then film plenary sessions at all times and in meeting rooms with the authorisation of the chair of the meeting and of a majority of members present. Filming in restaurants and bars and the use of hidden cameras is, on the other hand, prohibited.

In the past much effort was expended to persuade the press to come to Strasbourg to attend sessions, and with some success. The average number of journalists present almost doubled between 1979 and 1994, when it reached 245 per session. More recently, this issue has become less central. Journalists still attend the major debates in the Parliament, such as the vote on the Prodi Commission in September 1999, but they are also now able to follow debates in Brussels via the Commission sponsored facility Europe by Satellite (EbS) which covers much of the Parliament's plenary sessions.

The degree of coverage of the Parliament is extremely hard to measure. Any television channel can make use of the EbS footage without asking for authorisation. Nevertheless, even on the basis of the incomplete figures that are available, and allowing for considerable variations from one year to the next, it is possible to establish that the number and length of TV reports of Strasbourg sessions has been increasing steadily. In the 1980s there were around 500 such reports annually, totalling an average of 50 hours; in the 1990s the average number of reports per year was up to about 2,500, taking up about 200 hours of air time annually.

Visitors

Although it is not possible at present to visit the Parliament in the same way that one can visit Westminster by queuing up and getting a place in the Strangers' Gallery, Parliament does receive a constant stream of visitors, particularly during sessions. Many of them come to meet members from their region, Political Group leaders, committee chairmen etc. They include lobbyists (see above) and also the general public, who can visit Parliament and sit in the public gallery.

In view of the wide geographical spread of the European electorate, Parliament makes a particular effort to help visitors who have come from far. Visitors' groups of between 15 and 40 persons may apply for a small subsidy (applications to: The Visits Service, rue Wiertz, B-1047 Brussels) and a programme of meetings with members and staff is arranged. Such groups may be, for instance, constituency party sections, students or members of professional associations, trade unions, etc.

The number of visitors has increased enormously over the years, totalling more than 200,000 in 1998. As Table 30 shows, the figure is roughly evenly spread between Brussels and Strasbourg, with two-fifths of those visiting the latter outside session periods. However, the major growth in recent years has been in visits to Brussels where in 1991 there were about 10,000 visitors per year. That figure has risen almost tenfold in a decade, whereas the number visiting Luxembourg has declined greatly.

The "European Union Visitors' Programme" (EUVP), established in 1974 on the initiative of Dutch Senator Willem Schuijt, chairman of the first EP delegation for relations with the US Congress, is jointly administered by the

Table 30: *Visitors' Groups (1998)*

COUNTRY	Brussels		Luxembourg		Strasbourg–During Session		Strasbourg–Outside Session		TOTAL	
	Groups	Visitors	Groups	Visitors	Groups	Visitors	Groups	Visitors	Groups	Visitors
BELGIUM	337	13,767	3	97	82	3,128	14	469	436	17,461
DENMARK	159	4,952	3	62	48	1,507	5	153	215	6,674
GERMANY	489	15,167	51	1,874	762	25,596	165	6,437	1,467	49,074
GREECE	83	2,801	–	–	13	432	1	45	97	3,278
SPAIN	149	4,233	–	–	98	3,284	8	359	255	7,876
FRANCE	167	5,748	6	308	189	6,094	256	13,706	618	25,856
IRELAND	56	1,675	2	75	18	579	–	–	76	2,329
ITALY	157	5,209	7	255	237	9,682	137	11,292	538	26,438
LUXEMBOURG	24	876	11	383	40	1,616	1	80	76	2,955
NETHERLANDS	230	8,276	1	30	56	1,871	6	167	293	10,344
AUSTRIA	122	3,386	–	–	44	1,238	5	202	171	4,826
PORTUGAL	41	999	1	30	42	1,230	2	90	86	2,349
FINLAND	264	5,405	2	58	14	319	2	71	282	5,853
SWEDEN	278	6,767	–	–	13	413	3	105	294	7,285
UNITED KINGDOM	342	9,718	–	–	133	4,001	7	231	482	13,950
OTHERS	359	9,385	5	120	65	1,960	43	11,001	472	22,466
TOTAL	3,257	98,364	92	3,292	1,854	62,950	655	44,408	5,858	209,014

Commission and the Parliament. Each year some 150 visitors are selected amongst young politicians, government officials, journalists, trade unionists, academics, etc. from third countries, (initially largely the USA but now world-wide). During their stay they meet leading decision-takers in the European institutions and in two or three Member States of their choice.

Public awareness of the Parliament

The Commission's "Eurobarometer" survey demonstrates that public awareness of the Parliament fluctuates: it tends to rise in election years and then slip back to a much lower level. In one sense it is hard to explain the lack of awareness of the Parliament given its increasing powers as described in this book. Yet perhaps this situation is not so surprising, if one takes into account the handicaps from which Parliament suffers. It is not, as national parliaments are in many countries, the "meeting place" of the country, the centre of national debate and the hub of public life. It is often perceived as remote and its multilingual character reduces the opportunity for cut and thrust or drama in its debates. And it operates in an institutional system that is still only dimly understood.

Should this be a source of concern? Not everybody thinks that the relative lack of public interest is important. David Curry, former MEP and later a Westminster MP, said in an interview with *EP News*: "I don't think there is any foreseeable chance of (the public) becoming passionately interested in internal market, external trade or all the things that are life and blood to European members. My recommendation is to stop worrying about it, get on with the job and recognise that 100 years ago just about the only issue which would get a full house in the House of Commons was motions to do with the status of the Church of England".

Should, then, the Parliament resign itself to being effective but unrecognised, diligent but unnoticed, interesting but ignored? Should it just get on with the job and not worry unduly about public opinion? Many would argue that Parliament should play to its strengths as a unique forum bringing together politicians from very different cultures rather than dwell on its weak relationship to the wider electorate. Others are less sure. After all, it is not just sectoral interests but every single citizen who is touched by what the European Union does. Entering and managing a common currency, for example, are not just technical issues but ones that go to the very heart of national sovereignty and identity. In these circumstances, given the Parliament's increasingly influential role, the legitimacy of the whole Union could be endangered by a severe lack of interest in its single directly elected institution.

Hence the considerable level of concern which accompanied the relatively poor turnout in the 1999 European elections in most countries. It prompted the new Parliament to expand the time available in the parliamentary calendar for members to be active in their own countries. Not only was the system of White Fridays (days without parliamentary activity) maintained but three extra weeks were marked out to be kept free of meetings in Brussels or Strasbourg. Given the volume of work which Parliament has to get through this was a clear sign of the importance accorded by the members of the fifth legislature to improving public awareness of what it does.

Overall assessment

Having examined this diverse list of instruments available to Parliament to enhance its role as a forum and channel of communication, it is perhaps worth dwelling for a moment on the purposes that they serve. It is possible to discern three directions in which Parliament serves as a transmitter and articulator of ideas.

First, and most obviously, MEPs transmit concerns "upwards". Parliament is a platform where MEPs, often in response to worries voiced in their constituencies or by national political parties, articulate concerns, express viewpoints, communicate reactions and take initiatives. Issues raised may be directed to Union institutions where the Union has a particular role to play, or outside the Union when dealing with foreign policy issues or human rights.

The second, and most distinctive direction, is "sideways". Parliament is an arena for exchanging experiences and transmitting ideas from one national political culture to another. Parliament is a meeting place for members of political parties facing similar problems, for political activists dealing with similar issues in different countries, and, often, for members having faced similar governmental difficulties. National experiences can be compared. MEPs come into regular contact with politicians from other countries more often than almost any other politicians.

Third, and perhaps not always consciously, MEPs have a role to play "downwards" in explaining the European Union to a wider public. They do this within their constituencies (where many of them have circular newsletters reporting back to party members, local industrialists and/or trade unionists, local government and others). They spend considerable time explaining their actions and therefore the Union to the local media. They are also inevitably caught up in explaining and frequently justifying policies of the Union, within their national political party. It is a difficult but essential task as Parliament takes on greater responsibility for European Union decisions.

17. Parliament and constitutional change

One feature that distinguishes the European Parliament from most national parliaments is that it does not regard itself as part of a finished institutional system, but rather as part of one requiring evolution or even transformation into something different.

Parliament's vocation to promote constitutional change was emphasised at its very first session in 1952 when Chancellor Adenauer, on behalf of the Council, invited it to draft a Treaty for a European Political Community. Parliament, designated as the "*ad hoc* Assembly" for this purpose, proceeded to do so. Although its project fell with the demise of the European Defence Community in 1954, many of the proposals prepared by Parliament were used in the negotiation of the EEC Treaty two years later.

We have already seen how Parliament has continually pressed both to develop Community policies and to improve its position within the institutional framework of the Union. It has achieved this by obtaining undertakings from Council and Commission, by taking advantage of particular interpretations of the Treaties, by negotiating inter-institutional agreements that supplement the Treaties and by getting Member States to agree to formal Treaty amendments. Parliament also had to press constantly in the early days for the implementation of the Treaty provision regarding its own direct election by universal suffrage. The achievement of this objective in 1979 was in itself a major constitutional change.

Direct elections initially had an ambiguous effect. They conferred upon the Parliament a greater "legitimacy" in that it could justly claim to be the only directly elected European institution, but at the same time they aroused public expectations that were difficult to meet. The public had, after all, been called upon to choose its representatives in an assembly that did not have a decisive say. Electors who, in the national context, were used to parliamentary elections revolving around the performance of governments and whether to change them, suddenly found themselves having to vote for a Parliament which could not elect a government. This new political animal was all too easily misunderstood by the public, and was a ready target for those opposed to the European Community, who were generally also not keen on seeing a stronger European Parliament.

Nevertheless, direct elections were a step forward. They transformed the Parliament into a full-time body and created a new class of elected representatives in Europe. Within almost every major political party, there were now a small but significant number of politicians whose career depended on making something of the European dimension. As we have seen, they acted as vital go-betweens in explaining the Union and its potential to national parties and in bringing national parties further into European discussions. This was a painstaking process. Nevertheless, it slowly helped to reshape attitudes at least in political circles, if not always in the wider public. Nowhere has this been more apparent than amongst those MEPs who were initially elected to the European Parliament on an anti-European platform, but who, over the years, changed their position and helped change that of their party.

Besides the reshaping of attitudes, the European Parliament has also set out since direct elections to press for specific institutional changes. These changes have promoted three distinct but related objectives.

First, Parliament has sought to clarify and where necessary strengthen the competencies and responsibilities of the European Union itself. Parliament has consistently argued that powers should be attributed to the Union on the basis of the "principle of subsidiarity", i.e. it should exercise those responsibilities – and only those responsibilities – that can be carried out more effectively by common policies than by the Member States acting separately. It is a measure of how far Parliament has managed to shape the political debate that this rather ungainly expression of subsidiarity has become part of the political vocabulary: it was a term virtually unknown in the English language until Parliament started to push it in the early 1980s.

Second, Parliament has argued that responsibilities exercised at European level should be carried out more effectively. Parliament has been particularly critical of the practice of unanimity in the Council, arguing that, where it has been agreed to run a policy jointly, it makes no sense to give a blocking power to each of the component States of the Union. The unanimity rule has been described as the "dictatorship of the minority". Parliament has also pleaded for a stronger role to be given to the Commission in carrying out policies once they have been agreed, as we saw in Chapter 15 on scrutiny and control.

Third, Parliament has made the case for better democratic control and accountability at European level. Those responsibilities which national parliaments, in ratifying the Treaties, have transferred to the Union should not be exercised by Council (i.e. national ministers) alone. The loss of parliamentary powers at the national level should be compensated by an increase in parliamentary power at European level.

As we have seen, Parliament has been remarkably successful in this enterprise. It sought and eventually obtained a power of co-decision with Council on legislation so that Council's decisions only enter into force with the explicit approval of a public vote in the elected assembly. It also has acquired a central role in the appointment of the Commission and its President, to complement the right of censure it had acquired when the Community was set up.

Draft Treaty on European Union and the Single European Act

The most important of Parliament's initiatives designed to promote these objectives was its proposal in 1984 for a new Treaty on European Union. Parliament took a lead from Altiero Spinelli, one of the founders of the federalist movement at the end of World War II, former resistance leader, former member of the Commission, and elected to Parliament in 1979 as an independent ally of the reformed Italian Communists. Spinelli, with colleagues from other Political Groups in the "Crocodile Club" (see Chapter 10) first persuaded Parliament to set up a special committee on institutional affairs in 1982 for this purpose.

The task of preparing the ground for a new treaty was given to the committee with Spinelli as general rapporteur and a team of six co-rapporteurs representing the main Political Groups. The committee held public hearings and its drafts were widely circulated via party political networks. In September 1983, Parliament approved a lengthy resolution specifying the contents that such a new treaty should have. The committee, with the assistance of a team of legal experts, then transformed this into a draft treaty, which was adopted on 14 February 1984 by 237 votes to 31.

This very large majority reflected the careful work of compromise and consensus building that had taken place among the main Groups. Spinelli's approach was to use Parliament to thrash out a political compromise among the main political forces in Europe on the grounds that this was more likely to lead to genuine progress than was the traditional method of preparing treaties by working parties of officials from foreign ministries.

With this broad political backing inside the Parliament, Parliament made use of four main channels to build up further support in the Member States. These were:

– Directly to governments, both individually and collectively in the European Council.
– Through national political parties, which would have to address the issue in their policy statements and manifestos for the 1984 European election, while taking account of how their MEPs had voted.
– Through national parliaments, which were invited to support the initiative and to each of which the European Parliament sent delegations to explain the draft treaty and seek support for it.
– Through interest groups, non-governmental organisations and academia, by responding to the considerable interest that the draft treaty aroused.

Generally positive reactions were immediately forthcoming from Heads of State or Government in Italy, the Netherlands, Belgium and Germany. By far the most significant reaction, however, was that of President Mitterrand, speaking as President of the European Council to the European Parliament on 24 May 1984. In a major turning point in French attitudes towards European integration, which since De Gaulle had been hostile to anything other than an intergovernmental approach, his speech culminated in an expression of support for the draft treaty, stating that "France, ladies and gentlemen, is available for such an enterprise. I on its behalf state its willingness to examine and defend your project, the inspiration behind which it approves. I therefore suggest that preparatory consultations leading up to a conference of the Member States concerned be started up". This speech, prepared after a meeting with Spinelli and Piet Dankert, President of the European Parliament, placed the draft treaty firmly on the political agenda.

At the subsequent Fontainebleau European Council, it was agreed to set up an *ad hoc* committee of personal representatives of the Heads of State and

Governments, modelled on the Spaak Committee which had paved the way to the negotiation of the EEC Treaty in the 1950s. Some Heads of Government nominated MEPs or former MEPs to represent them on the committee. These included Enrico Ferri, former chairman of Parliament's Committee on Institutional Affairs, and Fernand Herman, who was still a member (and remained one until 1999). The committee also had meetings with the President of Parliament (then Pierre Pflimlin) and Spinelli.

The *ad hoc* committee, known as the Dooge Committee after the Irish senator who chaired it, adopted a report agreeing with Parliament on the need for a new treaty establishing European Union. It recommended that this treaty be "guided by the spirit and the method of the draft treaty voted by the European Parliament". There were striking similarities between the specific proposals of the *ad hoc* committee and the European Parliament's draft treaty. However, three members – the representatives of the UK, Denmark, and Greece – did not accept the main conclusions of the committee's report.

The report was considered at the European Council meeting in Milan in June 1985. By then, several national parliaments had lent their support to the draft treaty. In Italy and Belgium, the parliaments had adopted resolutions calling for the draft treaty to be ratified as it stood. In Germany, the Netherlands and in the French Parliament more general support was forthcoming, urging their respective governments to open negotiations on the basis of the draft treaty. Even in Member States not noted for their enthusiasm, the proposals were taken seriously. In the UK, the House of Lords set up a special sub-committee that held public hearings, including one with Spinelli, concluding that some treaty changes were desirable.

The Milan European Council decided by an unprecedented majority vote to convene an intergovernmental conference (IGC) to revise the existing Treaties in accordance with the procedures set out in Article 236 of the EEC Treaty (requiring, ultimately, unanimous support from the Member States for any treaty changes). During the autumn of 1985, the Member States entered negotiations that eventually led to the Single European Act, with the three recalcitrant states (UK, Denmark, Greece) in the end willing to negotiate compromises rather than be isolated.

During the negotiations, Parliament monitored the work of the IGC carefully. Its President and Altiero Spinelli were invited to two of the ministerial level meetings of the conference, but mainly informal contacts were used to influence the discussion. The IGC had agreed to submit the results of its work to the European Parliament, and this was done in January 1986, prior to the signature of the text by the Member States. Italy indicated that it would not ratify the Act if the European Parliament rejected it. Parliament, although considering the results to be insufficient, nevertheless accepted them. The Single European Act was signed in February 1986. After national ratification (involving referenda in Denmark and Ireland) it came into force in July 1987.

The Act made only a few changes to the existing Treaties. It notably provided for the completion of the single European market by 1992; slightly wider European Community competencies as regards economic and social cohesion, the environment, research and social policy; a modest extension of majority voting and of the executive powers of the Commission; and a codification in the Treaty of the largely intergovernmental "political co-operation" on foreign policy. The capacity of the Court was increased by the creation of a Court of First Instance. As regards Parliament, it provided for the two-reading cooperation procedure and the assent procedure described in Chapter 12.

From the Single European Act to Maastricht

The European Parliament immediately began pressing for further reform. Between 1987 and the 1989 European elections, it adopted a series of reports aimed at showing the insufficiencies of the Community's constitutional system as it resulted from the Single European Act.

Initially, the Member States were not interested in reopening negotiations on the Treaty so soon. However, they were obliged to review their position: pressure built up as a direct consequence of the Single Act and the creation of a single European market. This was above all the case in the monetary field, where a majority of Member States came round to the view that a single market ultimately required a single currency and that it was time to move forward on the Community's long-standing commitment to economic and monetary union (EMU). At the time of the 1989 European elections, the European Council in Madrid agreed to the principle of a new IGC on EMU to begin at the end of 1990.

The European Parliament pressed for a wider agenda for this IGC. It adopted a resolution to this effect in November 1989 and its Institutional Committee began to prepare drafts of specific proposals for treaty amend-ments: four reports prepared by the Labour MEP David Martin were par-ticularly important in this process. At the same time, Parliament defined its strategy for enlisting broader support by proposing and securing direct dia-logue with Council in an *inter-institutional conference* and by holding a con-ference in Rome in November 1990 of all national parliaments and the European Parliament. This conference became known as the Rome *"assizes"*.

Parliament's proposals were based on the tryptic referred to earlier, of broader Community competence based on the principle of subsidiarity, a more effective decision-taking procedure, notably through extending majority voting in Council, and greater democratic accountability, notably through an increase in the powers of the European Parliament. On this last point, the Martin reports spelt out in detail the shape of a new co-decision procedure (with two readings and a conciliation committee) and a mechan-ism for involving the Parliament in the appointment of the Commission.

Parliament's proposals gradually gained widespread support. First the Italian parliament, then the Belgian government gave backing to Parliament's requests. In April 1990, Chancellor Kohl and President Mitterrand wrote jointly to the other heads of government calling for a second IGC on political union. In June 1990, the Dublin meeting of the European Council agreed to the principle of a second IGC to run parallel to that on EMU, but without defining in great detail what it should deal with. The following months were spent filling out the agenda for this IGC, and Parliament's proposals in the Martin reports were crucial in shaping the agenda.

The assizes, held the month before the IGCs opened, were particularly successful from the European Parliament's point of view. All the national parliaments participated in the week-long assizes, held in the *Camera dei Deputati* in Rome, where they provided two-thirds of the delegates with one-third coming from the European Parliament. At the end of the meeting a declaration was adopted, by 150 votes to 13, echoing all of the European Parliament's main proposals for treaty revision. It remains the only case in history of the parliaments that would have to approve a treaty meeting together to discuss its contents before their governments began negotiating.

During the IGCs, the European Parliament maintained its involvement through the inter-institutional conference, which continued in parallel with the IGCs, involving monthly meetings between the 12 ministers, 12 MEPs, and four Commissioners. Parliament's President was also able to address several ministerial level meetings of the IGCs. Parliament's delegation also toured the national capitals holding individual meetings with each head of government, pressing Parliament's case for reform.

The resulting Treaty of Maastricht was, of course, a compromise but it again included major steps forward in the direction advocated by the European Parliament. A timetable and procedure for establishing monetary union was established. European political cooperation was transformed into a "common foreign and security policy" to be run through the Community institutions, albeit with a separate legal base and largely intergovernmental procedures, described as a second "pillar" of the Union. Cooperation in Justice and Home Affairs, also outside the Community legal framework, was to be a "third pillar". New chapters and articles were added to the EC Treaty on development cooperation, education, culture, consumer protection, public health, trans-European networks, industry and European citizenship. There was a further modest extension of qualified majority voting in Council, and the Court of Justice was given the power to impose fines on Member States failing to respect its judgments. The European Parliament's powers were increased, as we have seen in previous chapters, through the introduction of the co-decision procedure, the extension of the cooperation and assent procedures, the involvement of Parliament in the appointment of the Commission, the change of the Commission's term of office to coincide with that of Parliament, and a number of smaller changes increasing Parliament's powers of scrutiny and control. Last but not least, part of the overall compromise was an agreement written into the text to re-examine some issues in a further IGC in 1996.

From Maastricht to Amsterdam

Following the entry into force of the Maastricht Treaty, Parliament once again pressed the case for further constitutional change. It secured minor changes on the occasion of the negotiation of the accession treaties with Sweden, Finland and Austria. These included a Parliament proposal both to change the order of rotation of the Council Presidency and to make it more flexible by permitting changes in the order, and the adaptation of the threshold for qualified majority voting. Furthermore, Parliament's own proposal concerning the number of MEPs for the new Member States was followed, bar an extra seat for Austria. Parliament's Institutional Affairs Committee also prepared a draft constitution in the Herman Report (A3-64/94). This was partly in response to a referendum held in Italy in 1989 in which 88 per cent of Italian citizens voted in favour of Parliament preparing such a document. Although the text was not voted on by the plenary of Parliament, which simply took note of it, it did lay down a marker for future reforms and for the consolidation of the various Treaties into a single constitutional text.

After the 1994 European elections, Parliament turned its attention to the new IGC scheduled for 1996. The Maastricht Treaty specified that this IGC should examine, *inter alia*, the extension of the co-decision procedure to other areas, and whether fully to integrate the Common Foreign and Security Policy and cooperation in the fields of justice and home affairs into the Community legal system. In practice, it also looked at the whole functioning of the European Union, particularly in respect of its potential enlargement to 25-30 Member States.

The Corfu meeting of the European Council in June 1994 agreed to set up a "Reflection Group" to prepare the IGC, composed of a representative of each foreign minister and two MEPs. Parliament therefore had an opportunity to participate directly in the preparations for the IGC. It appointed Elisabeth Guigou, former French European Affairs Minister (for the Socialists) and Elmar Brok , a German CDU member (for the Christian Democrats) as its two representatives. Parliament's Committee on Institutional Affairs prepared a set of proposals, with David Martin, Vice-President of the European Parliament (Socialist), who had prepared the proposals for the Maastricht IGC, and Jean-Louis Bourlanges (Christian Democrat) as co-rapporteurs.

The emphasis of Parliament's proposals shifted somewhat from those it made before Maastricht. It did not press for any radical extension of the field of competence of the EU, as most of its objectives in this regard had been fulfilled by the Maastricht Treaty. It restricted itself to arguing for the integration of the social protocol into the Treaty, for partial integration of the "third pillar" and Schengen into the Community legal framework, and for a new Employment Chapter designed to make policies in this area better coordinated and more visible. All these were eventually agreed by the IGC.

Instead, Parliament, aware of the controversies that had surrounded the ratification of Maastricht, emphasised the need to bring Europe closer to its citizens through measures such as greater openness and transparency, simplifying and codifying the Treaties, and giving the EU a role in protecting rights and ensuring non-discrimination.

Parliament also reaffirmed its constant commitment to making the Union more effective and more democratic. Thus it focused on extending majority voting (with a special formula for CFSP matters, such that certain joint actions could be taken without the participation of states that voted against); absorbing the WEU into the Union; strengthening the powers of the President of the Commission (to choose and reshuffle Commissioners); limiting the size of Parliament in an enlarged Union to 700 MEPs; and allowing, if necessary and under certain conditions, a majority of states to proceed further in a policy field without the others participating from the outset.

As regards democracy, the Parliament combined its call for EU decision-making to be more transparent with a call to improve the provision of information to national parliaments in good time for them to influence their governments, though it firmly resisted the idea of establishing a congress of national parliaments alongside the EP and the Council, as France proposed.

Parliament again put forward proposals to improve its own position in the Union. It called for a formal vote in Parliament on the appointment of the President of the Commission, an extension of the co-decision procedure to cover all legislation going to Council, and three crucial changes to the procedure:

- eliminating the possibility for Council to adopt a text unilaterally if there is no agreement in conciliation;
- eliminating the need for Parliament first to announce its intention to reject a text before confirming it in a second vote;
- providing that when Parliament and Council agree in first reading, there is no need for a second.

The Reflection Group, which met from June-December 1995 under the chairmanship of Spanish EU Minister Carlos Westendorp, offered Parliament a platform to press its positions. Initially, the two Parliament representatives were the only ones to have detailed proposals to put on the table and were able to play a substantial agenda-setting role. They were also two, whereas each Member State was only represented by one person. This gave them more opportunities to put the Parliament's point of view, with one speaking early on each subject discussed and the other, coming in towards the end, being able to respond to what the Member State representatives said. Not surprisingly perhaps, the Reflection Group's Report took up many of Parliament's proposals, indicating that they had broad support. However, it also showed that there were deep divisions on many subjects and that one participant (David Davies, UK representative) was unable to agree with virtually any proposal, notably those relating to the Parliament. Instead, he pressed radical suggestions of his own, such as to allow the Council to overrule European Court decisions, thereby underlining the increasing gap between the British government and other governments in the run-up to the IGC. Few thought that the IGC would be able to complete its work until after the UK general election in 1997, which opinion polls suggested that the Conservative government would lose.

This last aspect meant that it was important to keep the opposition party – and likely new government – in the UK on board. The EP's representatives in the IGC, with their access to documents, were important in this regard, and we have seen on page 283 how Labour MEPs were able to help shape their party's detailed position on the IGC.

Parliament sought to have its two representatives pursue their work in the Reflection Group, by participating in the IGC itself. This met with opposition from the then UK and French (Gaullist) governments. As a compromise, the European Council agreed that they would meet monthly with the IGC negotiating group and that the President of Parliament would have an exchange of views with the EU Foreign Ministers each time they discussed the IGC. In practice, Guigou and Brok were able to discuss every subject with the IGC negotiators, obtain every document, table their own proposals and counterproposals and join in informal dinners and conclaves.

The May 1997 election in Britain of a Labour government with views much closer to those of other EU governments, notably on the role of the Parliament, provoked an intense period of diplomatic and political activity in the six weeks before the Amsterdam Summit, due to conclude the IGC negotiations. It was further complicated by the unexpected change of government in France, with Lionel Jospin's Socialists seeking at the same time to change the emphasis of decisions concerning EMU, which were also due to be finalised in Amsterdam. Nevertheless, after negotiating until 3 a.m. on the second night of the summit, the Heads of Government again emerged with a new Treaty.

Yet again, the new Treaty did not go as far as many had hoped. On the crucial institutional changes needed to prevent an enlarged Union of more than 20 Member States from becoming paralysed, the Amsterdam Summit was unable to find a solution, agreeing instead, in time-honoured tradition, to come back to these issues in the enlargement process itself. And yet there were significant changes including:

- extension of the co-decision procedure to more than double the number of articles than it previously applied to;
- procedural changes to the co-decision procedure which coincided with those recommended by Parliament;
- turning Parliament's vote on the President-designate of the Commission from a consultative vote to a full legal confirmation;
- establishing the principle of openness, with a treaty-level obligation to publish the results of votes taken in the Council and statements made in the Council minutes, and with a right of public access to EU documents;
- giving the Union the power to adopt anti-discrimination legislation concerning gender, race, sexual orientation, disability, age and religion;
- a provision (originating from the Spinelli draft treaty) enabling the Union to suspend a Member State that ceases to be democratic or to respect human rights;
- a transfer of most of the "third pillar" issues to the Community pillar, albeit with a unanimity requirement and a limited role for the Court of Justice, and absorption of Schengen by the Union;
- the possibility of "flexibility" whereby, if a Member State or a small minority does not wish to proceed further in a policy area, the majority may, subject to a unanimous vote, proceed without it;
- the UK signing up to the Social Protocol which could now be integrated into the Treaty as a revised Social Chapter;
- stronger provisions on employment policy (new chapter), public health, consumer protection and the environment.

The new Treaty did not, however, resolve several key problems. It left untouched *inter alia* the question of the Union's legal personality, the division of the budget into "obligatory" and "non-obligatory" expenditure, the EMU provisions (including the issues of external representation and the scrapping of the cooperation procedure in this field) and the treaty revision procedure itself. Above all, it failed to settle (despite attempts to reach agreement right up to the last minute of the IGC) three particular interrelated problems generally seen as central to making the EU fit for enlargement. These were:

• the scope of majority decision making in the Council, which was only increased slightly at Amsterdam; unanimity among well over 20 Member States is felt by many to be unworkable;

- the weighting of votes per Member State in the Council with a large number of small countries poised to join, and the related issue of whether population size should be taken account of explicitly; and
- the number of European Commissioners and in particular whether each Member State should be guaranteed such a post.

It was agreed that the Union would need to return to these issues, which became known as the "Amsterdam leftovers", before enlargement could successfully take place. Many felt that a new IGC would not be restricted to these three issues above.

The Millennium IGC and enlargement

At the time of writing, the European Council has agreed to hold a further IGC during the year 2000 to deal with the three "Amsterdam leftovers". Parliament is again pushing for a wider agenda and for close involvement in the IGC, and it seems that this view is gaining ground. It is clear from the number of states that are negotiating or preparing to negotiate their entry into the Union that, even if it is limited to the institutional issues directly related to enlargement, the IGC must address crucial and difficult issues beyond the three. They include the re-allocation of seats per Member State in order to ensure that Parliament remains under the limit of 700 members, and similar questions concerning the size and working methods of the Courts. Other issues, such as the integration of the WEU, the protection of rights (with the European Council having convened a body composed of MEPs, MPs and government representatives to draft a Charter of Fundamental Rights for the Union), further codification and simplification of the Treaties into a clearer constitution, and others, may well find their way on to the agenda. This will be settled in the course of the IGC, which is scheduled to last from February to December 2000. As regards Parliament's involvement, the same formula was agreed as for the Amsterdam IGC, except that Parliament's two representatives can take part in *all* the meetings of the IGC working group.

Whatever is agreed at the IGC, enlargement will in any case pose new challenges to Parliament: new members, more languages, greater diversity and extra costs, to name but a few. The European Parliament will still not be part of a finished institutional system, but one that continues to evolve.

Table 31: *Approximate number of MEPs for applicant states under current system*

Cyprus	6	Latvia	11
Czech Republic	24	Lithuania	15
Estonia	7	Malta	6
Hungary	24	Romania	42
Poland	64	Slovakia	16
Slovenia	9	Bulgaria	22

TOTAL 246 (+626 = 872 MEPs, if current key is not reformed)

Conclusion

The three major treaty revisions since Parliament became directly elected – the Single Act, the Treaty of Maastricht and the Treaty of Amsterdam, were all strongly influenced by the European Parliament. They illustrate that, whilst Parliament is not able to secure all its wishes, it can have a major influence as a catalyst for change.

When Parliament proposed its draft treaty in 1984, it was a time of crisis in the Community, when confidence in its future was at an all-time low. Summits had broken down on the issue of budgetary contributions of Member States, the European economy was in a period of "Euro-sclerosis" and few thought that there was any realistic chance of amending the Treaties. Yet, in thrashing out an agreement among the Political Groups in Parliament and putting forward its position to governments, to national parliaments and via national political parties, Parliament was able to create sufficient political momentum for at least some national governments to press its case, and a majority of them to accept that there was a case to look at. Of course, the bottom line of unanimity among the Member States meant that there were limits as to what could be achieved, but the momentum was sufficient to enable a compromise package to get through.

Similarly, in 1989–90, Parliament was able to persuade at least the more favourably disposed Member States that there was a need for the planned treaty revision to go beyond EMU and to examine broader issues. External events, such as the radical changes in Eastern Europe, helped. But there is no doubt that the new Treaty provisions on citizenship, consumer protection, education and culture and on extending the European Parliament's own powers, would not have found their way into the Treaty of Maastricht had it not been for the constant pressure by Parliament.

By the time of the 1996 IGC, Parliament was accepted as a partner in the preparatory process, if only partly in the IGC itself, and set a large part of the agenda of the IGC. In terms of the final result, many have called Parliament the big winner of the Amsterdam Treaty, which considerably enhances its powers.

On the eve of the biggest ever enlargement of the Union and the Treaty revisions necessary for that to happen, Parliament is again poised to play a role in shaping the future of the Union.

Taking these episodes together, their cumulative results are striking. In what is historically a short period of time, the European Parliament has come a long way.

IV: APPENDICES

APPENDIX ONE

EUROPEAN PARLIAMENT ELECTIONS

The following tables show the results of elections to the European Parliament in alphabetical order by country. (Figures obtained from the European Parliament's Summary of Results.)

Austria

Party	1999 %	1999 Seats	1996 %	1996 Seats
Social Democratic Party	31.7	7	29.1	6
Austrian People's Party	30.7	7	30	7
Austrian Freedom Party	23.4	5	27.5	6
Greens	9.3	2	6.8	1
Liberal Forum	2.7	–	4.3	1
Others	2.2	–	2.6	–
TOTAL		21		21

Belgium

Party		1999 %	1999 Seats	1994 %	1994 Seats	1989 %	1989 Seats	1984 %	1984 Seats	1979 %	1979 Seats
Socialist Party	Flanders	8.8	2	10.9	3⎫	26.9	3⎫	30.4	4	12.8	3
	Wallonia	9.6	3	11.4	3⎭		5⎭		5	10.6	4
Christian People's Party	Flanders	13.5	3	16.9	4⎫	29.2	5⎫	27.4	4	29.5	7
Social Christian Party	Wallonia	4.9	1	7.0	2⎭		2⎭		2	8.2	3
Christian Social Party	German region	0.2	1	0.2	1	–	–	–	–	–	–
Liberals	Flanders	13.6	3	11.3	3⎫	17.8	2⎫	18.0	2	9.4	2
	Wallonia	10	3	9.0	3⎭		2⎭		3	6.9	2
People's Union	Flanders	7.6	2	4.3	1	5.4	1	8.5	2	6.0	1
Vlaams Blok	Flanders	9.4	2	7.7	2	4.1	1	1.3	–	0.7	–
National Front	Wallonia	1.5	–	2.9	1	–	–	–	–	–	–
Agalev	Flanders	7.5	2	6.6	1⎫	13.9	1	4.3	1	1.4	–
Ecolo	Wallonia	8.4	3	4.8	1⎭		2	3.9	1	2.0	–
Walloon Rally	Wallonia	–	–	–	–	1.5	–	2.5	–	7.6	2
Others		5	–	6.3	–	1.2	–	3.7	–	4.9	–
TOTAL			25		25		24		24		24

Denmark

Party	1999 %	1999 Seats	1994 %	1994 Seats	1989 %	1989 Seats	1984 %	1984 Seats	1979 %	1979 Seats
Social Democratic Party	16.5	3	15.8	3	23.3	4	19.5	3	21.9	3
Liberal Party (Venstre)	23.4	5	19.0	4	16.6	3	12.5	2	14.5	3
Conservative People's Party	8.5	1	17.7	3	13.3	2	20.8	4	14.1	2
Centre Democrats	–	–	0.9	–	8.0	2	6.6	1	6.2	1
Socialist People's Party	7.1	1	8.6	1	9.1	1	9.2	1[1]	4.7	1
Progress Party	–	–	2.9	–	5.3	–	3.5	–	5.8	1
People's Movement against the EU	7.3	1	10.3	2	18.9	4	20.8	4	21.0	4
June Movement (anti-Europe)	16.1	3	15.2	2	–	–	–	–	–	–
Radical Liberal Party	9.1	1	8.5	1	–	–	–	–	–	–
Christian People's Party	–	–	1.1	–	–	–	–	–	–	–
Danish People's Party	5.8	1	–	–	–	–	–	–	–	–
Others	6.2	–	–	–	5.5	–	2.1	–	11.9	–
TOTAL		16		16		16		16		16

Finland

Party	1999 %	1999 Seats	1996 %	1996 Seats
KOK (Conservatives)	25.3	4	20.2	4
Centre	21.3	4	24.4	4
Social Democrats	18	3	21.5	4
Greens	13.4	2	7.6	1
Left Alliance	9.1	1	10.5	2
Finnish Christian League	2.4	1	2.8	0
Swedish People's Party	6.8	1	5.8	1
Others	4	–	7.2	–
TOTAL		16		16

France

Party	1999 %	1999 Seats	1994 %	1994 Seats	1989 %	1989 Seats	1984 %	1984 Seats	1979 %	1979 Seats
UDF-RPR[2]	12.8	12	25.6	28	28.88	26	(43.02	41)	16.3	15
Centre Parties	9.3	9			8.42	7			27.6	25
Socialist Party	22	22	14.5	15	23.61	22	20.75	20	23.5	22
National Front[3]	5.7	5	10.5	11	11.73	10	10.95	10	1.3	–
National Movement	3.3	–								
Greens	9.7	9	4.9	–	10.59	9	3.37	–	4.4	–
Communist Party	6.8	6	6.9	7	7.71	7	11.20	10	20.5	19
Lutte Ouvrière	5.2	5								
Eurosceptic Right[4]	13	13	12.3	13	–	–	–	–	–	–
Chasse, Pêche (pro-hunting)	6.8	6								
'Energie Radicale' (Tapie List)	–	–	12.0	13	–	–	–	–	–	–
Others	5.5	–	13.3	–	9.06	–	10.65	–	6.3	–
TOTAL		87		87		81		81		81

Germany

Party	1999 %	1999 Seats	1994 %	1994 Seats	1989 %	1989 Seats	1984 %	1984 Seats	1979 %	1979 Seats
Christian Democratic Union	39.3	43	32.0	39	29.5	25	37.5	34	39.1	34
Christian Social Union	9.4	10	6.8	8	8.2	7	8.5	7	10.1	8
Social Democrat Party	30.7	33	32.2	40	37.3	31	37.4	33	40.8	35
Greens	6.4	7	10.1	12	8.4	8	8.2	7	3.2	–
Republicans	–	–	3.9	–	7.1	6	–	–	–	–
Free Democrat Party	3	–	4.1	–	5.6	4	4.8	–	6.0	–
Party of Democratic Socialists	5.8	6	4.7	–						
Others	5.4	–	6.3	–	3.7		3.6	–	0.8	–
TOTAL		99		99		81		81		81

Greece

Party	1999 %	1999 Seats	1994 %	1994 Seats	1989 %	1989 Seats	1984 %	1984 Seats	1981 %	1981 Seats
New Democracy	36	9	32.6	9	40.45	10	38.05	9	31.34	8
Socialist Party (PASOK)	32.9	9	37.6	10	35.94	9	41.58	10	40.12	10
Communist Alliance	8.7	3	6.3	2	14.30	4	11.64	3	12.84	3
Left Alliance	5.2	2	6.2	2		–	3.42	1	5.29	1
New Left (DIKKI)	6.8	2								
Centre/Right Alliance	–	–	2.7	–	1.37	1	–	–	–	–
EPEN	–	–	–	–	1.16	–	2.29	1	–	–
Political Spring (POLA)	2.3	–	8.7	2	–	–	–	–	–	–
Others	8.1	–	5.7	–	6.78	–	3.02	–	11.41	–
TOTAL		25		25		24		24		24

Ireland[5]

Party	1999 %	1999 Seats	1994 %	1994 Seats	1989 %	1989 Seats	1984 %	1984 Seats	1979 %	1979 Seats
Fianna Fail	38.6	6	35.0	7	31.5	6	39.2	8	34.7	5
Fine Gael	24.2	4	24.2	4	21.6	4	32.2	6	33.1	4
Labour Party	8.7	1	10.9	1	9.5	1	8.4	–	14.5	4
Progressive Democrats	–	–	6.4	–	11.9	1	–	–		
Independents	–	–	6.9	1	11.9	2	10.1	1	14.1	2
Workers' Party	–	–	1.9	–	7.5	1	4.3	–	3.3	–
Green Alliance	6.7	2	7.9	2	3.8	–	0.5	–	–	–
Sinn Fein	6.3	–	2.9	–	2.3	–	4.9	–	–	–
Democratic Left[6]	–	–	3.4	–	–	–	–	–	–	–
Others	15.5	2	–	–	–	–	0.5	–	0.27	–
TOTAL		15		15		15		15		15

Italy

Party	1999 %	1999 Seats	1994 %	1994 Seats	1989 %	1989 Seats	1984 %	1984 Seats	1979 %	1979 Seats
Forza Italia	25.2	22	30.6	27	–	–	–	–	–	–
Communist Parties										
(Rifondazione Comunista)	4.3	4	6.1	5	–	–	–	–	–	–
(Italian Communists)[7]	2.0	2	–	–						
Christian Democrat Parties										
(Italian Popular Party)	4.3	4	10.0	8	–	–	–	–	–	–
(Patto Segni)[8]	–	–	3.3	3	–	–	–	–	–	–
(Christian Democrats)	–	–	–	–	32.9	26	33.0	26	36.4	29
(CCD)	2.6	2								
(CDU)	2.1	2								
(UDE)	1.6	1								
Right Wing										
(National Alliance/Patto Segni)[9]	10.3	9	12.5	11	–	–	–	–	–	–
(Movimento Sociale Tricolore)[10]	1.6	1								
(Italian Social Movement -MSI)	–	–	–	–	5.5	4	6.5	5	5.4	4
Regionalist Parties										
(Northern League)	4.5	4	6.6	6	1.8	2	–	–	–	–
(South Tirol People's Party)	0.5	1	0.6	1	0.5	1	0.6	1	0.6	1
(Other Regionalists)[11]	0.7	–	1.4	–	0.6	1	0.5	1	–	–
Greens	1.8	2	3.2	3	6.2	5	–	–	–	–
Centre Parties and Lists										
(Centre List)	–	–	–	–	4.4	4	–	–	–	–
(Radical Party)[12]	8.5	7	2.1	2	–	–	3.4	3	3.7	3
(Republican/Liberal List)	0.5	1	–	–	–	–	6.1	5	–	–
(Republicans)	–	–	0.7	1	–	–	–	–	2.6	2
(Liberals)	–	–	0.2	–	–	–	–	–	3.5	3
(La Rete)	–	–	1.1	1	–	–	–	–	–	–
(The Democrats)	7.7	6								
(RI-DINI)	1.1	1								
Socialist Parties										
(Democrats of the Left-PDS)[13]	17.4	15	19.1	16	27.6	22	33.3	27	29.6	24
(Socialist Party)	–	–	1.8	2	14.8	12	11.2	9	11.0	9
(Social Democrat Party)	–	–	0.7	1	2.7	2	3.5	3	4.3	4
(Other Socialists)	2.1	2								
Others[14]	1.2	1	–	–	0.5	–	0.5	–	0.9	–
TOTAL		87		87		81		81		81

Luxembourg

Party	1999 %	1999 Seats	1994 %	1994 Seats	1989 %	1989 Seats	1984 %	1984 Seats	1979 %	1979 Seats
Christian Social People's Party	31.7	2	31.5	2	34.87	3	34.9	3	36.1	3
Luxembourg Socialist Workers'Party	23.6	2	24.8	2	25.45	2	29.9	2	21.6	1
Democratic Party (Liberals)	20	1	18.8	1	19.95	1	22.1	1	28.1	2
Green Party	10.7	1	10.9	1	–	–	–	–	–	–
Others	14	–	13.9	–	19.73	–	13.1	–	14.2	–
TOTAL		6		6		6		6		6

Netherlands

Party	1999 %	1999 Seats	1994 %	1994 Seats	1989 %	1989 Seats	1984 %	1984 Seats	1979 %	1979 Seats
Christian Democrats	26.9	9	30.8	10	34.6	10	30.02	8	35.6	10
Labour Party	20.1	6	22.9	8	30.7	8	33.72	9	30.4	9
Freedom & Democracy Party	19.7	6	17.9	6	13.6	3	18.93	5	16.2	4
Green Left	11.8	4	6.1	1	7.0	2	5.60	2	–	–
Calvinist Coalition (RPF,SGP,GPV)	8.7	3	7.8	2	5.9	1	5.21	1	–	–
Democrats 66 (Left Liberals)	5.8	2	11.7	4	6.0	1	2.28	–	9.0	2
Socialist Party	5	1								
Others	1.8	–	2.8	–	2.2	–	4.26	–	8.8	–
TOTAL		31		31		25		25		25

Portugal

Party	1999 %	1999 Seats	1994 %	1994 Seats	1989 %	1989 Seats	1987 %	1987 Seats	1979 %	1979 Seats
Socialist Party	43.1	12	34.8	10	28.52	8	22.46	6	–	–
Social Democratic Party	31.1	9	34.3	9	32.70	9	37.42	10	–	–
Popular Party (Centre Party)	8.1	2	12.4	3	14.13	3	15.4	4	–	–
United Democratic Coalition:										
(Portuguese Communist Party and Greens)	10.3	2	11.1	3	14.40	4	11.51	3	–	–
Others	7.4	–	7.1	–	10.25	–	13.16	1	–	–
TOTAL		25		25		25		24	–	–

Spain

Party	1999 %	1999 Seats	1994 %	1994 Seats	1989 %	1989 Seats	1987 %	1987 Seats	1979 %	1979 Seats
Socialist Party	35.3	24	31.1	22	40.2	27	39.1	28	–	–
Popular Party	39.7	27	40.5	28	21.7	15	24.6	17	–	–
Social Democrat Centre Party	–	–	1.0	–	7.2	5	10.3	7	–	–
United Left	5.8	4	13.6	9	6.2	4	5.2	3	–	–
Convergencia Unio (Catalan regionalist coalition)	4.4	3	4.7	3	4.3	2	4.4	3	–	–
Other regionalists	9.2	6	5.7	2	7.1	4	3.6	2	–	–
Others	5.5	–	2.9	–	13.5	3	12.8	–	–	–
TOTAL		64		64		60		60	–	–

Sweden

Party	1999 %	Seats	1995 %	Seats
Social Democrats	26	6	28.1	7
Moderate Party (Conservatives)	20.7	5	23.2	5
Left Party	15.8	3	12.9	3
Liberals	13.8	3	4.8	1
Greens	9.5	2	17.2	4
Christian Democrats	7.6	2	3.9	–
Centre Party	6	1	7.2	2
Others	0.5	–	2.7	–
TOTAL		22		22

United Kingdom

Party	1999 %	Seats	1994 %	Seats	1989 %	Seats	1984 %	Seats	1979 %	Seats
Labour	26.2	29	42.6	62	38.88	45	34.76	32	31.6	17
Conservative	33.5	36	26.8	18	33.00	32	38.76	45	48.4	60
Liberal Democrats[15]	11.9	10	16.1	2	6.23	–	18.51	–	12.6	1
Green Party	5.9	2	3.1	–	14.52	–	0.55	–	–	–
Scottish National Party	2.5	2	3.0	2	2.57	1	1.65	1	1.9	1
Plaid Cymru	1.7	2	1.0	–	0.73	–	0.74	–	0.6	–
UK Independence Party	6.5	3								
DUP	1.8	1	1.0	1	1.01	1	1.64	1	1.3	1
SDLP	1.8	1	1.0	1	0.86	1	1.08	1	1.1	1
Ulster Unionist Party	1.1	1	0.8	1	0.75	1	1.05	1	0.9	1
Pro Euro Conservative Party	1.3	–								
Others	5.8	–	4.2	–	1.45	–	1.25	–	1.6	–
TOTAL		87		87		81		81		81

[1] The Socialist People's Party were allocated a second seat when Greenland left the EC on Jan 1, 1985

[2] There was one single right/centre list in 1984 and 1994 and two (one Gaullist RPR and one Centrist UDF) in 1979 and 1989. In 1999 the mainstream RPR list (allied with Madelin's Démocratic Libérale) led by Sarkozy, obtained 12.8% and 12 seats. The Centrist list of Bayrou (remaining UDF) obtained 9.3% and 9 seats.

[3] In 1999 there was a split within the National Front and two lists were presented, Le Pen's National Front and Megret's National Movement.

[4] In 1999 this list(RPFIE) consisted of dissident RPR members led by Pasqua, as well as members from the de Villiers/Goldsmith list of 1994. In 1994 this list was called "Alternative Europe".

[5] Percentage figure is of first preference votes.

[6] Labour Party absorbed Democratic Left in 1999.

[7] Breakaway from Rifondazione Comunista.

[8] Electoral pact with National Alliance in 1999.

[9] Patto Segni had joined list with National Alliance – ex MSI in 1999.

[10] Former MSI members not accepting transformation of National Alliance into more mainstream right-wing party.

[11] Including Unione Valdostana and Sardinian Action Party.

[12] Stood as "Lista Emma Bonino" in 1999.

[13] Former Italian Communist Party.

[14] Including Italian Pensioners' Party, which won 0.7% and 1 seat in 1999.

[15] SDP-Liberal Alliance in 1984, Liberal Party in 1979.

APPENDIX TWO

WHO ARE THE MEPS?

This Appendix provides a list of MEPs from the 15 Member States where fifth direct elections in June 1999 took place. The list is divided by country, by European Parliament Political Group and by national party (with English name, short title and full name), as of October 1999. Underlining indicates re-elected MEPs from the 1994-99 Parliament.

AUSTRIA

EPP-ED GROUP: 7

Austrian People's Party (ÖVP: Österreichische Volkspartei): 7

Marilies FLEMMING
Othmar KARAS
Hubert PIRKER
Reinhard RACK

Paul RÜBIG
Agnes SCHIERHUBER
Ursula STENZEL

PES GROUP: 7

Social Democratic Party (SPÖ: Sozialdemokratische Partei Österreichs): 7

Maria BERGER
Herbert BÖSCH
Harald ETTL
Hans-Peter MARTIN

Christa PRETS
Karin SCHEELE
Hannes SWOBODA

GREENS/EFA GROUP: 2

Greens(GRÜNE: Die Grünen – Die Grüne Alternative): 2

Mercedes ECHERER
Johannes VOGGENHUBER

N.I (NON-ATTACHED): 5

Austrian Freedom Party (FPÖ: Freiheitliche Partei Österreichs): 5

Gerhard HAGER
Wolfgang ILGENFRITZ
Hans KRONBERGER

Daniela RASCHHOFER
Peter SICHROVSKY

BELGIUM

EPP-ED GROUP: 6

a. Christian People's Party (CVP: Christelijke Volkspartij): 3
Miet SMET
Marianne THYSSEN
Johan VAN HECKE

b. Social Christian Party (PSC: Parti Social chrétien): 1
Michel HANSENNE

c. Christian Social Party (CSP-EVP: Christliche Soziale Partei-Europäische Volkspartei): 1
Mathieu GRÖSCH

d. Movement of Citizens for Change (MCC: Mouvement des Citoyens pour le Changement): 1
Gérard DEPREZ

PES GROUP: 5

a. Flemish Socialists (SP: Socialistische partij): 2
Peter BOSSU
Anne VAN LANCKER

b. Francophone Socialists (PS: Parti socialiste): 3
Jean-Maurice DEHOUSSE
Claude DESAMA
Freddy THIELEMANS

ELDR GROUP: 5

a. Flemish Liberals and Democrats (VLD: Vlaamse Liberalen en Demokraten): 3
Edouard BEYSEN
Willy DE CLERCQ
Dirk STERCKX

b. Liberal Reform Party-Francophone Democratic Front (PRL-FDF: Parti Réformateur Libéral-Front Démocratique des Francophones): 2
Daniel DUCARME
Frédérique RIES

GREENS/EFA GROUP: 7

a. Flemish Greens (Agalev: Anders Gaan Leven): 2
Patsy SORENSEN
Luckas VANDER TAELEN

b. Francophone Greens (Ecolo): 3
Monica FRASSONI
Pierre JONCKHEER
Paul LANNOYE

c. Flemish People's Union (VU-ID 21: Volksunie – ID 21): 2
Nelly MAES

Bart STAES

NON-ATTACHED: 2

Flemish Block (Vlaams Blok): 2
Karel DILLEN
Frank VANHECKE

DENMARK

EPP-ED GROUP: 1

Conservative People's Party (Konservative Folkeparti): 1
Christian ROVSING

PES GROUP: 3

Social Democratic Party (Socialdemokratiet): 3
Freddy BLAK   Helle THORNING-SCHMIDT
Torben LUND

ELDR GROUP: 6

a. Liberal Party (Venstre): 5
Ole ANDREASEN   Anne E. JENSEN
Niels BUSK   *Karin RIIS-JØRGENSEN*
Bertel HAARDER

b. Radical Liberal Party (Det Radicale Venstre): 1
Lone DYBKJÆR

GUE/NGL GROUP: 1

Socialist People's Party (SF: Socialistisk Folkeparti): 1
Pernille FRAHM

UEN GROUP: 1

Danish People's Party (DF: Dansk Folkeparti): 1
Mogens CAMRE

EDD GROUP: 4

a. June Movement (JuniBevaegelsen): 3
Jens-Peter BONDE
Jens OKKING
Ulla SANDBÆK

b. People's Movement against the EU(FolkeBevaegelsen Mod EU): 1
Ole KRARUP

FINLAND

EPP-ED GROUP: 5

a. National Coalition Party (KOK: Kansallinen Kokoomus): 4
Piia-Noora KAUPPI

Marjo MATIKAINEN-KALLSTRÖM
Ilkka SUOMINEN
Ari VATANEN

b. Finnish Christian League (SKL: Suomen Kristillinen Liitto): 1
Eija-Riitta KORHOLA

PES GROUP: 3

Social Democratic Party (SDP: Suomen Sosialidemokraattinen Puolue): 3
Ulpu IIVARI
Riitta MYLLER
Reino PAASILINNA

ELDR GROUP: 5

Centre Party (KESK: Suomen Keskusta): 4
Mikko PESÄLÄ
Samuli POHJAMO
Paavo VÄYRYNEN
Kyösti VIRRANKOSKI

Swedish People's Party (SFP: Svenska Folkspartiet): 1
Astrid THORS

GREENS/EFA GROUP: 2

Greens (Vihreät): 2
Heidi HAUTALA
Matti WUORI

GUE/NGL GROUP: 1

Left-Wing Alliance (Vasemmistoliitto): 1
Eska SEPPÄNEN

FRANCE

EPP-ED GROUP: 21

a. Union for French Democracy (UDF: Union pour la Démocratie Française): 9

François BAYROU	*Nicole FONTAINE*
Jean-Louis BOURLANGES	Janelly FOURTOU
Thierry CORNILLET	Alain LAMASSOURE
Marielle de SARNEZ	Général Philippe MORILLON
Francis DECOURRIERE	

b. Rally for the Republic (RPR: Rassemblement pour la République): 6

Joseph DAUL	Hugues MARTIN
Marie-Thérèse HERMANGE	Nicolas SARKOZY (resigned 15.9.99)
Roger KAROUTCHI	Margie SUDRE

c. Liberal Democracy (DL: Démocratie Libérale): 4

Françoise GROSSETÊTE	Alain MADELIN

Thierry JEAN-PIERRE   Hervé NOVELLI

d. Civil Society (Société Civile): 1
Christine de VEYRAC

e. Ecological Generation (Génération écologie): 1
Tokia SAIFI

PES GROUP: 22

a. Socialist Party (PS: Parti Socialiste): 18

Pervenche BERES	Catherine GUY-QUINT
Marie-Arlette CARLOTTI	Adeline HAZAN
Gérard CAUDRON	François HOLLANDE
Danielle DARRAS	_Marie-Noëlle LIENEMANN_
Harlem DESIR	Bernard POIGNANT
Olivier DUHAMEL	_Michel ROCARD_
Jean-Claude FRUTEAU	Martine ROURE
Georges GAROT	Gilles SAVARY
Marie-Hélène GILLIG	François ZIMERAY

b. Left Radicals (PRG: Parti Radical de Gauche): 2
Catherine LALUMIERE
Michel DARY

c. Movement of Citizens (MDC: Mouvement des Citoyens): 2
Sami NAÏR
Béatrice PATRIE

GREENS/EFA GROUP: 9

Greens (V: Les Verts): 9

Danielle AUROI	Alain LIPIETZ
Alima BOUMEDIENNE-THIERY	Gérard ONESTA
Daniel COHN-BENDIT	Yves PIETRASANTA
Hélène FLAUTRE	Didier-Claude ROD
Marie-Anne ISLER BEGUIN	

GUE/NGL GROUP: 11

a. French Communist Party (PCF: Parti communiste français): 4

Sylviane AINARDI	Robert HUE
Yasmine BOUDJENAH	_Francis WURTZ_

b. Independents elected on the "Bouge l'Europe" ('Move Europe') list: 2
Geneviève FRAISSE
Fode SYLLA

c. Workers' Struggle/Revolutionary Communist League (LO/LCR: Lutte ouvrière / Ligue Communiste Révolutionnaire): 5

Armonia BORDES (LO)	Arlette LAGUILLER (LO)
Chantal CAUQUIL (LO)	Roseline VACHETTA (LCR)
Alain KRIVINE (LCR)	

UEN GROUP: 12

Rally for France and the Independence of Europe (RPFIE: Rassemblement pour la France et l'Indépendance de l'Europe): 12

William ABITBOL
Georges BERTHU
Isabelle CAULLERY
Paul Marie COUTEAUX
Philippe de VILLIERS
Florence KUNTZ

Thierry de LA PERRIERE
Jean-Charles MARCHIANI
Elizabeth MONTFORT
Charles PASQUA
Dominique SOUCHET
Nicole THOMAS-MAURO

EDD GROUP: 6

Hunting, Fishing, Nature, Traditions (CPNT: Chasse, Pêche, Nature, Traditions): 6
Jean-Louis BERNIE
Yves BUTEL
Alain ESCLOPE

Véronique MATHIEU
Michel RAYMOND
Jean SAINT-JOSSE

N.I (NON-ATTACHED): 6
Ind. (elected on the RPFIE list): 1
Marie-France GARAUD

National Front (FN: Front National): 5
Charles de GAULLE
Bruno GOLLNISCH
Carl LANG

Jean-Marie LE PEN
Jean-Claude MARTINEZ

GERMANY

EPP-ED GROUP: 53

a. Christian Democratic Union (CDU: Christlich-Demokratische Union): 43
Rolf BEREND
Reimer BÖGE
Christian von BOETTICHER
Elmar BROK
Karl-Heinz FLORENZ
Michael GAHLER
Anne-Karin GLASE
Lutz GOEPEL
Alfred GOMOLKA
Ruth HIERONYMI
Georg JARZEMBOWSKI
Elisabeth JEGGLE
Hedwig KEPPELHOFF-WIECHERT
Ewa KLAMT
Christa KLASS

Karsten KNOLLE
Dieter-Lebrecht KOCH
Christoph KONRAD
Werner LANGEN
Brigitte LANGENHAGEN
Armin LASCHET
Kurt LECHNER
Klaus-Heiner LEHNE
Hans-Peter LIESE
Thoma MANN
Hans-Peter MAYER
Winfried MENRAD
Peter-Michael MOMBAUR
Hartmut NASSAUER

Doris PACK
Hans-Gert POETTERING
Godelieve QUISTHOUDT-ROWOHL
Ingo SCHMITT
Horst SCHNELLHARDT
Jürgen SCHRÖDER
Konrad SCHWAIGER
Renate SOMMER
Diemut THEATO
Stanislaw TILLICH
Rainer WIELAND
Karl von WOGAU
Jürgen ZIMMERLING
Sabine ZISSENER

b. Christian Social Union (CSU: Christlich Soziale Union): 10
Markus FERBER
Ingo FRIEDRICH
Franz-Xaver MAYER
Emilia Franziska MÜLLER

Angelika Victoria NIEBLER
Bernd POSSELT
Alexander RADWAN

Ursula SCHLEICHER
Gabriele STAUNER
Joachim Johannes WUERMELING

PES GROUP: 33

Social Democratic Party (SPD: Sozialdemokratische Partei Deutschlands): 33

Udo BULLMANN	Jo LEINEN
Evelyne GEBHARDT	*Rolf LINKOHR*
Norbert GLANTE	*Günter LÜTTGE*
Willi GÖRLACH	*Erika MANN*
Lissy GRÖNER	Rosemarie MÜLLER
Klaus HÄNSCH	*Willi PIECYK*
Jutta HAUG	*Christa RANDZIO-PLATH*
Magdalene HOFF	*Bernhard RAPKAY*
Karin JÖNS	*Dagmar ROTH-BEHRENDT*
Karin JUNKER	*Willi ROTHLEY*
Margot KESSLER	*Mechtild ROTHE*
Heinz KINDERMANN	*Jannis SAKELLARIOU*
Constanze KREHL	*Gerhard SCHMID*
Wilfried KUCKELKORN	*Martin SCHULZ*
Helmut KUHNE	*Ulrich STOCKMANN*
Bernd LANGE	*Ralf WALTER*
Barbara WEILER	

GREENS/EFA GROUP: 7

Greens (GRÜNE: Bündnis 90 / Die Grünen): 7

Hiltrud BREYER	Heide RÜHLE
Ozan CEYHUN	Ilka SCHRÖDER
Friedrich Wilhelm GRAEFE zu BARINGDORF	*Elisabeth SCHROEDTER*
Wolfgang KREISSL-DÖRFLER	

GUE/NGL GROUP: 6

Party of Democratic Socialism (PDS: Partei des Demokratischen Sozialismus): 6

André BRIE	Helmuth MARKOV
Christel FIEBIGER	Hans MODROW
Sylvia-Yvonne KAUFMANN	Uca FELEKNAS

GREECE

EPP-ED GROUP: 9

New Democracy (ND: Nea Dimokratia): 9

Ioannis AVEROF	*Rodi KRATSA*
Giorgos DIMITRAKOPOULOS	*Ioannis MARINOS*
Christos FOLIAS	*Antonios TRAKATELLIS*
Marietta GIANNAKOU	Christos ZACHARAKIS
Konstantinos HATZIDAKIS	

PES GROUP: 9

Socialist Party (PASOK: Panellinio Socialistiko Kinima): 9

Alexandros BALTAS	Minerva-Melpomeni MALLIORI

Petros EFTHYMIOU
Anna KARAMANOU
Giorgos KATIFORIS
Ioannis KOUKIADIS

Emmanouil MASTORAKIS
Ioannis SOULADAKIS
Dimitris TSATSOS

GUE/NGL GROUP: 7

a. Communist Party of Greece (KKE: Kommounistiko Komma Elladas): 3
Konstantinos ALYSANDRAKIS
Efstratios KORAKAS
Ioannis THEONAS

b. Communist Alliance (SYN: Synaspismos tis aristeras kai tis proodou): 2
Alexandros ALAVANOS
Mihail PAPAYANNAKIS

c. New Left (DIKKI: Dimokratiko Kininiko Kinima): 2
Emmanouil BAKOPOULOS
Dimitrios KOULOURIANOS

IRELAND

EPP-ED GROUP: 5

a. FG (Fine Gael): 4
Mary BANOTTI (Dublin)
John CUSHNAHAN (Munster)

Avril DOYLE (Leinster)
Joe McCARTIN (Connacht-Ulster)

b. Ind: 1
Rosemary (Dana) SCALLON (Connacht-Ulster)

PES GROUP: 1

LAB (LABOUR PARTY): 1
Proinsias De ROSSA (Dublin)

ELDR GROUP: 1

IND (Independent): 1
Pat COX (Munster)

GREENS/EFA GROUP: 2

GP (Green Party): 2
Nuala AHERN (Leinster)
Patricia McKENNA (Dublin)

UEN GROUP: 6

FF (Fianna Fail): 6
Niall ANDREWS (Dublin)
Gerard COLLINS (Munster)
Brian CROWLEY (Munster)

Jim FITZSIMONS (Leinster)
Pat (The Cope) GALLAGHER
(Connacht-Ulster)
Liam HYLAND (Leinster)

ITALY

EPP-ED GROUP: 34

a. Forza Italia: 22

Silvio BERLUSCONI
Renato BRUNETTA
Luigi CESARO
Raffaele COSTA
Marcello DELL'UTRI
Enrico FERRI
Francesco FIORI
Raffaele FITTO
Giuseppe GARGANI
Jas GAWRONSKI
Giorgio LISI

Mario MANTOVANI
Mario MAURO
Francesco MUSOTTO
Guido PODESTA'
Giuseppe NISTICO
Amalia SARTORI
Umberto SCAPAGNINI
Vittorio SGARBI
Antonio TAJANI
Guido Walter Cesare VICECONTE
Stefano ZAPPALA'

b. Italian Popular Party (PPI: Partito Popolare italiano): 4

Guido BODRATO
Luigi COCILOVO

Ciriaco Luigi DE MITA
Franco MARINI

c. Union of European Democrats (UDEUR: Unione democratici Europei): 1

Mario Clemente MASTELLA

d. Christian Democratic Centre (CCD: Centro Cristiano democratico): 2

Pierferdinando CASINI
Raffaele LOMBARDO

e. Unitarian Christian Democrats (CDU: Cristiani Democratici Unitari): 2

Rocco BUTTIGLIONE
Vitaliano Nino GEMELLI

f. Italian Renewal (RI/DINI: Rinovamento Italiano / DINI): 1

Giuseppe Pino PISICCHIO

g. South Tyrol People's Party (SVP: Partito Popolare Sudtirolese): 1

Michaël EBNER

h. Pensioners Party (Partito Pensionati): 1

Carlo FATUZZO

PES GROUP: 17

a. Democrats of the Left (DS: Democratici di sinistra): 15

Massimo CARRARO
Giovanni Giuseppe Claudio FAVA
Florinda detta Fiorella GHILARDOTTI
Renzo IMBENI
Vincenzo LAVARRA
Pasqualina NAPOLETANO
Giorgio NAPOLITANO
Elena Ornella PACIOTTI

Giovanni Saverio Furio PITTELLA
Giorgio RUFFOLO
Guido SACCONI
Bruno TRENTIN
Gianterisio detto Gianni VATTIMO
Walter VELTRONI
Demetrio VOLCIC

Social Democrats (SDI: Socialisti Democratici italiani): 2

BOSELLI Enrico
MARTELLI Claudio

ELDR GROUP: 7

a. Democrats (I Democratici): 6

Massimo CACCIARI
Paolo COSTA
Antonio DI PIETRO

Pietro MENNEA
Giovanni PROCACCI
Francesco RUTELLI

b. Republicans/Liberals (PRI/LIB): 1
Luciana SBARBATI

c. Independent: 1
Marco FORMENTINI

GREENS/EFA GROUP: 2

Greens (Federazione dei Verdi): 2
Giorgio CELLI
Reinhold MESSNER

GUE/NGL GROUP: 6

a. Refounded Communist Party (RC: Rifondazione Comunista): 4

Fausto BERTINOTTI
Giuseppe DI LELLO FINUOLI

Luisa MORGANTINI
Luigi VINCI

b. Italian Communists (CI: Communisti Italiani): 2
Armando COSSUTTA
Lucio MANISCO

UEN GROUP: 9

National Alliance/Segni Pact (AN/SEGNI: Alleanza Nazionale/Patto Segni): 9

Roberta ANGELILLI
Sergio Antonio BERLATO
Gianfranco FINI
Cristiana MUSCARDINI
Sebastiano MUSUMECI

Mauro NOBILIA
Mario SEGNI
Adriana POLI in BORTONE
Franz TURCHI

NON-ATTACHED: 11

a. BONINO: 7

Emma BONINO
Marco CAPPATO
Olivier DUPUIS
Gianfranco DELL'ALBA

Benedetto DELLA VEDOVA
Giacinto Marco PANNELLA
Maurizio TURCO

b. Northern League (LN: Lega Nord): 3
Umberto BOSSI
Gian Paolo GOBBO
Francesco SPERONI

c. Revived Italian Social Movement (MSFT: Movimiento Sociale Fiamma Tricolore): 1
Roberto Felice BIGLIARDO

LUXEMBOURG

EPP-ED GROUP: 2

Christian Social Party (CSV: Chrëschtlech Sozial Vollekspartei): 2
Astrid LULLING
Jacques SANTER

PES GROUP: 2

Luxembourg Socialist Workers' Party (LSAP: Lëtzeburger Sozialistesch Aarbechterpartei): 2
Robert GOEBBELS
Jacques POOS

ELDR GROUP: 1

Democratic Party (DP: Demokratesch Partei): 1
Colette FLESCH

GREENS/EFA GROUP: 1

Greens (Dei Greng): 1
Claude TURMES

THE NETHERLANDS

EPP-ED GROUP: 9

Christian Democrats (CDA: Christen Democratisch Appel): 9

Lambert DOORN	*Arie OOSTLANDER*
Albert Jan MAAT	*Karla PEIJS*
Hanja MAIJ-WEGGEN	*Bartho PRONK*
Maria MARTENS	*Wim van VELZEN*
Ria OOMEN-RUIJTEN	

PES GROUP: 6

Labour Party (PvdA: Partij van de Arbeid): 6

Max van den BERG	Michiel HULTEN
Ieke van de BURG	Joke SWIEBEL
Dorette CORBEY	*Jan Marinus WIERSMA*

ELDR GROUP: 8

a. Liberals: People's Party for Freedom and Democracy (VVD: Volkspartij voor Vrijheid en Democratie): 6

Jules MAATEN	*Elly PLOOIJ-VAN GORSEL*
Toine MANDERS	Marieke SANDERS-TEN HOLTE
Jan MULDER	*Jan Kees WIEBENGA*

b. D 66 (Democraten 66): 2
Lousewies van der LAAN
Bob VAN DEN BOS

GREENS/EFA GROUP: 4

Green Left (GROEN LINKS): 4

Theo BOUWMAN
Kathalijne BUITENWEG

Alexander de ROO
Joost LAGENDIJK

GUE/NGL GROUP: 1

Socialist Party (SP: Socialistsche Partij): 1

Erik MEIJER

EDD GROUP: 3

Calvinist Coalition (RPF/SGP/GVP: Reformatorische Politieke Federatie / Staatkundig Gereformeerde Partij/Gereformeerde Politiek Verbond): 3

B. BELDER (SGP)
H. BLOKLAND (GPV)
R. Van DAM (RPF)

PORTUGAL

EPP-ED GROUP: 9

Social Democratic Party (PPD-PSD: Partido Social Democrata): 9

Teresa ALMEIDA GARRETT
Carlos COELHO
Carlos COSTA NEVES
Arlindo CUNHA
Vasco GRAÇA MOURA

Mario GONÇALVES MARQUES
Jorge MOREIRA DA SILVA
José PACHECO PEREIRA
Fernando REIS

PES GROUP: 12

Socialist Party (PS: Partido Socialista): 12

António CAMPOS
Carlos CANDAL
Maria CARRILHO
Elisa DAMIÃO
Carlos LAGE
Luís MARINHO

Paulo MARTiNS CASACA
António José SEGURO
Mário SOARES
Sérgio SOUSA PINTO
Helena TORRES MARQUES
Joaquim VAIRINHOS

GUE/NGL GROUP: 2

Portuguese Communist Party (PCP: Partido Communista Portugues): 2

Ilda FIGUEIREDO
Joaquim MIRANDA

UEN GROUP: 2

Centre Democratic and Social Party (CDS – PP: Centro democratico social – Partido Popular): 2

Paulo PORTAS
Luís QUEIRÓ

SPAIN

EPP-ED GROUP: 28

a. Popular Party (PP: Partido Popular): 27

Alejandro AGAG LONGO
María Antonia AVILES PEREA
Pilar AYUSO GONZALEZ
Juan Manuel FABRA VALLES
Fernando FERNANDEZ MARIN
Carmen FRAGA ESTEVEZ
Gerardo GALEOTE QUECEDO
José Manuel GARCIA-MARGALLO
Y MARFIL
Cristina GARCIA ORCOYEN TORMO
Salvador GARRIGA POLLEDO
José María GIL- ROBLES GIL-DELGADO
Cristina GUTIERREZ
Jorge HERNANDEZ MOLLAR
Iñigo MENDEZ de VIGO Y MONTOJO

Juan Andréas NARANJO ESCOBAR
Juan OJEDA SANZ
Ana de PALACIO VALLERSUNDI
Manuel PEREZ ALVAREZ
Javier POMES RUIZ
Encarnación REDONDO JIMENEZ
Mónica RIDRUEJO
Carlos RIPOLL Y MARTINEZ
BEDOYA
José Ignacio SALAFRANCA
SANCHEZ-NEYRA
Jaime VALDIVIESO DE CUE
Daniel VARELA
SUANZES-CARPEGNA
Alejo VIDAL-QUADRAS ROCA
Teresa ZABELL LUCAS

b. Democratic Union of Catalonia (CIU/UDC: Convergencia i Unió/Unió Democratica de Catalunya): 1
Concepció FERRER I CASALS

PES GROUP: 24

a. Spanish Socialist Workers' Party (PSOE: Partido Socialista Obrero Español): 22

Pedro APARICIO SANCHEZ
Enrique BARON CRESPO
Luis BERENGUER FUSTER
Alejandro CERCAS ALONSO
Carmen CERDEIRA MORTERO
Joan COLOM I NAVAL (PSC-PSOE)
Rosa DIEZ GONZALEZ
Barbara DÜHRKOP DÜHRKOP
Juan de Dios IZQUIERDO COLLADO
Maria IZQUIERDO ROJO
Miguel Angel MARTINEZ
MARTINEZ

Manuel MEDINA ORTEGA
José Maria MENDILUCE PEREIRO
Emilio MENENDEZ del VALLE
Rosa MINGUELEZ RAMOS
Raimon OBIOLS I GERMA
(PSC-PSOE)
Fernando PEREZ ROYO
Maria RODRIGUEZ RAMOS
Paquita SAUQUILLO PEREZ
DEL ARCO
Anna TERRON I CUSI (PSC-PSOE)
Elena VALENCIANO
MARTINEZ-OROZCO
Carlos WESTENDORP Y CABEZA

b. Party of the New Left (PDNI: Partido de la Nueva Izquierda): 2
Carlos CARNERO GONZALEZ (PDNI)
Maria SORNOSA MARTINEZ (PDNI)

ELDR GROUP: 3

a. Catalan Democratic Convergence (CIU/CDC: Convergencia Democratica de Catalunya): 2
Pere ESTEVE I ABAD

Carles GASÓLIBA I BOHM

b. Canary Islands Coalition (CE/CC: Coalición Canaria): 1
Isidoro SÁNCHEZ GARCIA

GREENS/EFA GROUP: 4

a. Andalusian Party (CE/PA: Coalición Europea: Partido Andalucista): 1
Carlos BAUTISTA

b. Basque Solidarity (CNEP/EA: Coalición Nacionalista Europa de los Pueblos: Eusko Alkartasuna): 1
Gorka KNÖRR

c. Galician Nationalists (BNG: Bloque Nacionalista Gallego): 1
Camilo NOGUEIRA ROMAN

d.Basque Nationalist Party (CNEP/PNV: Coalición Nacionalista Europa de los Pueblos: Partido Nacionalista Vasco): 1
Josu ORTUONDO LARREA

GUE/NGL GROUP: 4

United Left (IU: Izquierda Unida): 4
Laura GONZALEZ ALVAREZ   *Pedro MARSET CAMPOS*
Salvador JOVE PERES   *Alonso PUERTA GUTIERREZ*

N.I (NON-ATTACHED): 1

Basque Nationalists(Euskal Herritarrok): 1
Koldo GOROSTIAGA

SWEDEN

EPP-ED GROUP: 7

a. Moderate Party (Moderata samlingspartiet): 5
Per-Arne ARVIDSSON   *Charlotte CEDERSCHIÖLD*
Staffan BURENSTAM LINDER   *Per STENMARCK*
Gunilla CARLSSON

b. Christian Democrats (Kristdemokraterna): 2
Lennart SACRÉDEUS
Anders WIJKMAN

PES GROUP: 6

Social Democratic Workers' Party (Socialdemokratiska arbetarepartiet): 6
Jan ANDERSSON   *Annelie HULTHÉN*
Göran FÄRM   Pierre SCHORI
Ewa HEDKVIST PETERSEN   *Maj-Britt THEORIN*

ELDR GROUP: 4

a. Liberal People's Party (Folkpartiet Liberalerna): 3
Cecilia MALMSTRÖM

Marit PAULSEN
Olle SCHMIDT

b. Centre Party (Centerpartiet): 1
Karl-Erik OLSSON

GREENS/EFA GROUP: 2

Greens(Miljöpartiet): 2
Per GAHRTON
Inger SCHÖRLING

GUE/NGL GROUP: 3

Left Party (Vänsterpartiet): 3
Marianne ERIKSSON   *Jonas SJÖSTEDT*
Herman SCHMIDT

UNITED KINGDOM

EPP-ED GROUP: 37

a. Conservative: 36
Robert ATKINS (North West)   Roger HELMER (East Midlands)
Christopher BEAZLEY (Eastern)   Richard INGLEWOOD (North West)
Nicholas BETHELL (London)   *Caroline JACKSON* (South West)
John BOWIS (London)   Bashir KHANBHAI (Eastern)
Philip BRADBOURN (West Midlands)   Timothy KIRKHOPE (Yorkshire and
Philip BUSHILL-MATTHEWS   the Humber)
(West Midlands)   *Edward McMILLAN-SCOTT*
Martin CALLANAN (North East)   (Yorkshire/Humber)
Giles CHICHESTER (South West)   Bill NEWTON-DUNN (East Midlands)
John CORRIE (West Midlands)   Neil PARISH (South West)
Nirj DEVA (South East)   *Roy PERRY* (South East)
Densmore DOVER (North West)   *James PROVAN* (South East)
James ELLES (South East)   John PURVIS (Scotland)
Jonathan EVANS (Wales)   Struan STEVENSON (Scotland)
Jacqui FOSTER (North West)   The Earl of STOCKTON (South West)
Robert GOODWILL (Yorkshire and   *Robert STURDY* (Eastern)
the Humber)   David SUMBERG (North West)
Daniel HANNAN (South East)   Charles TANNOCK (London)
Malcolm HARBOUR (West Midlands)   Geoffrey VAN ORDEN (Eastern)
Christopher HEATON-HARRIS   Theresa VILLIERS (London)
(East Midlands)

b. UUP (Ulster Unionist Party): 1
James NICHOLSON (Northern Ireland)

PES GROUP: 30

a. LAB (Labour Party): 29
Richard BALFE (London)   *Eryl McNALLY* (Eastern)
David BOWE (Yorkshire and the Humber) *Bill MILLER* (Scotland)
Michael CASHMAN (West Midlands)   Claude MORAES (London)

Richard CORBETT (Yorkshire and the Humber)
Alan DONNELLY (North East)
Robert EVANS (London)
Glyn FORD (South West)
Neena GILL (West Midlands)
Pauline GREEN (London)
Richard HOWITT (Eastern)
Stephen HUGHES (North East)
Glenys KINNOCK (Wales)
David MARTIN (Scotland)
Linda Mc AVAN (Yorkshire and the Humber)
Arlene McCARTHY (North West)

Eluned MORGAN (Wales)
Simon MURPHY (West Midlands)
Mo O' TOOLE (North East)
Mel READ (East Midlands)
Brian SIMPSON (North West)
Peter SKINNER (South East)
Catherine TAYLOR (Scotland)
Gary TITLEY (North West)
Mark WATTS (South East)
Phillip WHITEHEAD (East Midlands)
Terry WYNN (North West)

b. SDLP (Social Democratic and Labour Party – Northern Ireland): 1
John HUME (Northern Ireland)

ELDR GROUP: 10

LD (Liberal Democrats): 10
Elspeth ATTWOOLL (Scotland)
Nicholas CLEGG (East Midlands)
Chris DAVIES (North West)
Andrew DUFF (Eastern)
Chris HUHNE (South East)

Sarah LUDFORD (London)
Liz LYNNE (West Midlands)
Emma NICHOLSON (South East)
Diana WALLIS (Yorkshire and the Humber)
Graham WATSON (South East)

GREENS/EFA GROUP: 6

a. Green P: 2
Jean LAMBERT (London)
Caroline LUCAS (South East)

b. SNP (Scottish National Party): 2
Ian HUDGHTON (Scotland)
Neil Mac CORMICK (Scotland)

c. PCYMRU (Plaid Cymru – Party of Wales): 2
Jill EVANS (Wales)
Eurig WYN (Wales)

EDD GROUP: 3

UK Ind (UK Independence Party): 3
Nigel FARAGE (South East)
Michael HOLMES (South West)
Jeffrey TITFORD (Eastern)

N.I (NON-ATTACHED)

DUP (Democratic Unionist Party – Northern Ireland): 1
Ian PAISLEY (Northern Ireland)

APPENDIX THREE

CONTACT DETAILS OF PARLIAMENT OFFICES

The following is a list of addresses, telephone and fax numbers, internet addresses and sites (where available) of the European Parliament's main offices in Luxembourg, Brussels and Strasbourg, and of its information offices in the Member States.

European Parliament

Plateau de Kirchberg, L-2929 Luxembourg, Tel: +352.4300.1
rue Wiertz (Wiertzstraat), B-1047 Bruxelles, Tel: +32.2.284.21.11
Allée du Printemps, BP 1024, F-67070 Strasbourg Cedex, Tel: +33.3.88.17.40.01

Internet site: http://europarl.eu.int

EP Information Offices in Member State capitals

ATHENS
Leof. Amalias, 8, GR-105 57 Athens
Tel: +30.1.33.11.541 to 47
Fax: +30.1.33.11.540

BERLIN
Unter den Linden 78, D-10117 Berlin
Tel: +49.30.2280.1000
Fax: +49.30.2280.1111
epberlin@europarl.eu.int

BRUSSELS
rue Wiertz 60/Wiertzstraat 60, B-1047 Bruxelles/Brussel
Tel: +32.2.284.20.05
Fax: +32.2.230.75.55
epbrussels@europarl.eu.int

Internet site: http://www.europarl.eu.int/brussels

THE HAGUE
Korte Vijverberg 6, NL-2513, AB Den Haag
Tel: +31.70.362.49.41
Fax: +31.70.364.70.01

Internet site: http://www.europarl.eu.int/denhaag

DUBLIN – 'European Union House'
43, Molesworth Street, IRL-Dublin 2
Tel: +353.1.605.79.00
Fax: +353.1.605.79.99

HELSINKI
Pohjoisesplanadi 31, FIN-00100 Helsinki (Visiting address)
Tel: +358.9.622.04.50
Fax: +358.9.622.26.10
ephelsinki@europarl.eu.int

COPENHAGEN – Kontoret i Danmark
Christian IX's Gade 2, 2, DK-1111 København K
Tel: +45.33.14.33.77
Fax: +45.33.15.08.05
epkobenhavn@europarl.eu.int

Internet site: http://www.europarl.eu.int

LISBON
Centro Europeu Jean Monnet
Largo Jean Monnet, 1–6°, P-1250 Lisboa
Tel: +351.21.357.80.31 or +351.21.357.82.98
Fax: +351.21.354.00.04
eplisboa@europarl.eu.int

LONDON
2 Queen Anne's Gate, UK-London SW1H 9AA
Tel: +44.20.7227.43.00
Fax: +44.20.7227.43.02
eplondon@europarl.eu.int

Internet site: http://www.europarl.eu.int/uk

LUXEMBOURG
Bâtiment Robert Schuman, Place de l'Europe, L-2929 Luxembourg
Tel: +352.4300.225.96
Fax: +352.4300.224.57

MADRID
Paseo de la Castellana, 46, E-28046 Madrid
Tel: +34.91.436.47.47
Fax: +34.91.577.13.65
Fax: +34.91.578.31.71 (for documentation)
epmadrid@europarl.eu.int

Internet site: http://www.europarl.es

PARIS
288, Bld St. Germain – F-75341 Paris Cedex 07
Tel: +33.(0)1.40.63.40.00
Fax: +33.(0)1.45.51.52.53
epparis@wanadoo.fr

Internet site: http://www.europarl.eu.int/paris

ROME
Via IV Novembre, 149, I-00187 Roma
Tel: +39.(0)6.699.501
Fax: +39.(0)6.699.502.00

Internet site: http://www.europarl.it

STOCKHOLM
Nybrogatan 11, 3 tr, S-114 39 Stockholm
Tel: +46.8.562.444.55
Fax: +46.8.562.444.99
info@europarl.se

Internet site: http://www.europarl.se

VIENNA
Kärntnerring 5-7, A-1010 Wien
Tel: +43.1.51.61.70
Fax: +43.1.513.25.15
epwien@europarl.eu.int

Internet site: http://www.europarl.at

EP Information Offices in regional centres
BARCELONA
Avenida Diagonal, 407bis, Planta 12, E-08008 Barcelona
Tel: +34.93.29.20.159 or +34.93.41.58.177
Fax: +34.93.21.76.682
josep-maria.ribot@espana.dg10-bur.cec.be

EDINBURGH
9, Alva Street, UK-Edinburgh EH2 4PH
Tel: +44.131.22.52.058
Fax: +44.131.22.64.105
Wscott@europarl.eu.int

MARSEILLE
2, rue Henri Barbusse, F-13241 Marseille
Tel: +33.4.91.91.91.46.00
Fax: +33.4.91.90.95.03

Internet site: http://www.europarl.eu.int/marseille

MILAN
Corso Magenta, 59, I-20123 Milano
Tel: +39.(0)2.48.18.645
Fax: +39.(0)2.48.14.619
mcavenaghi@europarl.eu.int

MUNICH
(to be set up during 2000)

STRASBOURG
Salle de Presse, LOW N00/401, BP 1024, F-67070 Strasbourg Cedex
Tel: +33.(0)3.88.17.40.01
Fax: +33.(0)3.88.17.51.84

APPENDIX FOUR

SOURCES OF INFORMATION ON THE PARLIAMENT

Primary sources

Internet

Since the third edition of this book was prepared in 1994, access to information about the European institutions has been dramatically increased by the growth of the Internet. The Parliament has developed its own site (http://europarl.eu.int) which provides a large amount of information about the workings of the institution in all the languages of the Union. As it is regularly updated, it offers a particularly good means of checking on changes in the Parliament since this book went to press.

The site contains information from the President of the Parliament, the Political Groups and the EP Information offices as well as links to the other EU institutions, national parliaments and the European Ombudsman. It is divided into four general categories entitled ABC, Activities, Press and References as follows:

ABC –   includes an overview of the Parliament, details of individual members, the newspapers of the Parliament, how to arrange a visit, how to send a petition, information on competitions for jobs in the Parliament and on traineeships;

Activities –   provides details of the work of the parliamentary committees, the plenary sessions and the conciliation committee, the texts and progress of legislative proposals (Legislative Observatory, known as "OEIL"), parliamentary questions to Council and Commission and the ACP-EU Joint Assembly;

Press –   offers information of particular interest to the press, including the satellite, TV, radio and photo services available;

References –   contains background material on EU policies as well as the Treaties, the Rules of Procedure of the Parliament, the Official Journals of the Communities and the studies prepared by the research services.

Background publications

A large number of publications are available from the Information Offices in the Member States, or direct from Brussels or Luxembourg. The following are of particular interest as basic introductory material to the work of the European Parliament:

1. The European Parliament
A basic introductory brochure

2. Parliament, *List of Members*
This regularly updated publication contains information on all MEPs, giving their name, address and telephone number, place and date of birth, national and European political party, as well as membership of parliamentary committees and delegations. It is known as the Grey List.

3. Parliament, *Vademecum*
Brief background information on MEPs plus photographs.

4. Parliament: DG III (Directorate-General for Information and Public Relations) produces the following publications, all of which are available on the Internet:
The Briefing, which gives a selective summary each month of reports coming up for debate in the plenary session;
The Week, which reports upon the results of these deliberations and includes a subject index, cumulating annually;
News Alert, which looks forward to the meetings coming up over the next week;
News Report, which reports on committee and other activities between sessions; and *EP News*, a four-page monthly newspaper.

5. Parliament: DG IV (Directorate-General for Research) prepares *Fact sheets on the European Union* which gives an introduction to all areas of Community activity with a note on progress-to-date. A new compilation appears every two or three years (latest edition published in 1999).
    For those interested in detailed coverage of the Parliament's committees and plenaries, the following publications from outside the EP are also very helpful:

Agence International d'Information pour la Presse, *Agence Europe*
Appearing daily in English, German, French and Italian, *Europe* or *Agence Europe*, as it is usually referred to, gives excellent detailed coverage of Parliament activities and includes an index. It is especially useful for committee activities. Contact: 10 Blvd St. Lazare, B-1030, Brussels, Belgium.

European Information Service, *European Report*
A bi-weekly bulletin in English and French of European political, economic and industrial news, now available with an index and an on-line computer database. Address: 46 Avenue Albert-Elizabeth, B-1040, Brussels, Belgium.

Official Documents

6. Parliament: *Rules of Procedure*, Latest edition (14th), June 1999
This contains the rules governing the detailed workings of the Parliament; it includes a full index.

7. European Parliament *Sessional Documents* are divided into three series:
- Series A, noted with the abbreviation PE Doc., contains committee reports that have been tabled for the plenary;
- Series B contain motions for resolution tabled by individual MEPs for referral to committee or material related to plenary sessions such as questions and requests for urgent and topical debate;
- Series C comprises mainly Parliament's renumbered sequence of Commission proposals for legislation (available publicly as COM Documents) and documents from other Community institutions.

For organisations and individuals wishing to monitor developments on a regular basis in more detail the following publications may prove helpful:

8. Parliament: *Agenda, Minutes* and *Debates*
Before each plenary session a draft agenda is printed and circulated. Changes to the agenda are considered by the House at the opening of the session and then each day, a daily agenda is made available.

A preliminary version of the minutes is usually available the day after adoption and must be approved by the House. It contains Parliament's official opinions on Community draft legislation, including amendments adopted, as well as resolutions voted on other topics.

The *Minutes of Proceedings* containing the positions of the Parliament (along with details of roll-call votes) are formally published within:

9. Parliament: Official Journal of the European Communities: C Series (OJ C Series)

10. Parliament: *Verbatim Report of Proceedings*
This verbatim record of debates at plenary sessions, known as the "Rainbow", gives speeches in the original language of the person speaking; it is usually made available on the next day.
A translated, definitive version of the debates appears some months later in:

11. Parliament: Official Journal of the European Communities. Annex: *Debates of the European Parliament*
A full sessional index to the debates is published annually in:

12. Parliament: Official Journal of the European Communities. Annex: Debates of the European Parliament: *Index*
This contains details of individual MEPs' activities, a subject index and a list of committee reports with dates of debates and details of amendments tabled. Answers to written questions tabled by members are also published in the Official Journal "C" Series.

Secondary Sources

In addition to the primary sources prepared by the Parliament, there has been a growing volume of books, studies and articles about the Parliament written by academics and practitioners. The following is a selection (chiefly in English) made by the authors: most were written in the 1990s but there are a few works from earlier years considered to be of particular interest.

The material is divided into six sections (General, Powers, Sessions and Activities, Members, Direct Elections and Political Parties and Groups) based on the framework provided by the Directorate-General for Research of the Parliament in its comprehensive bibliographies for the years, 1990-1996 and 1997-1999, available from the Parliamentary Documentation Centre in Brussels.

General

Books and studies
ANDERSEN, Svein and ELIASSEN, Kjell (eds.), *The European Union: How Democratic is it?*, London: Sage, 1996
BOGDANOR, Vernon, *Democratising the Community*, London: Federal Trust for Education and Research, 1990
CHRYSSOCHOOU, Dimitris, *Democracy in the European Union*, London: Tauris Academic Studies, 1998
COOMBES, David, *Seven Theorems in Search of the European Parliament*, London: Federal Trust, 1999
CORBETT, Richard, *The Treaty of Maastricht: From Conception to Ratification: A Comprehensive Reference Guide*, Harlow: Longman, 1993
CORBETT, Richard, *The European Parliament's Role in Closer EU Integration*, Basingstoke: Macmillan, 1998
DELWIT, Pascal, DE WAELE, Jean-Michel and MAGNETTE, Paul, *A quoi sert le Parlement européen?*, Bruxelles: Editions Complexe, Etudes européennes, 1999
HAYWARD, Jack, *The Crisis of Representation*, London: Frank Cass, 1995

LAURSEN, Finn and PAPPAS, Spyros (eds.), *The Changing Role of Parliaments in the European Union*, Maastricht, European Institute of Public Administration, 1995
LODGE, Juliet, *Strengthening the European Parliament and its Alternatives*, Marburg: Metropolis Verlag, 1997
LORD, Christopher, *Democracy in the European Union*, Sheffield: Sheffield Academic Press, 1998
MORGAN, Robert (ed.), *Times Guide to the European Parliament 1994*, London: Times Books, 1994
NEWMAN, Michael, *Democracy, Sovereignty and the European Union*, London: Hurst, 1996
NORTON, Philip, *National Parliaments and the European Union*, London: Frank Cass, 1996
PINDER, John (ed.), *Foundations of Democracy in the European Union: From the Genesis of Parliamentary Democracy to the European Parliament*, London: Macmillan, 1999
ROSAS, Allan and ANTOLA, Esko, *A Citizens' Europe: In Search of a New Order*, London: Sage, 1995
SMITH, Julie, *Voice of the People: the European Parliament in the 1990s*, London: Royal Institute of International Affairs, 1995
SMITH, Julie, *Europe's Elected Parliament*, Sheffield: Sheffield Academic Press for UACES, 1999
WESTLAKE, Martin, *A Modern Guide to the European Parliament*, London: Pinter, 1994
WESTLAKE, Martin, *The Parliament and the Commission: Partners and Rivals in the European Policy-Making Process*, London: Butterworths, 1994

Articles
BOND, Martyn, "The European Parliament in the 1990s", *Journal of Legislative Studies*, No. 2, 1997, pp.1–9
BOYCE, Brigitte, "The Democratic Deficit of the European Community", *Parliamentary Affairs*, Vol. 46, No. 4, pp.458–77
BROAD, Roger and GEIGER, Tim, "The British Experience of the European Parliament", *Contemporary British History*, No. 1, 1997, pp. 98–122
CORBETT, Richard, "The Intergovernmental Conference on Political Union", *Journal of Common Market Studies*, Vol. 30, No. 3, 1992, pp. 271–98
CORBETT, Richard, "Representing the People", in: *Maastricht and Beyond: Building the European Union*, edited by A. Duff, J. Pinder and R. Pryce, London: Routledge, 1994
DANKERT, Piet, "Pressure from the European Parliament", in: *The Politics of European Treaty Reform: the 1996 Intergovernmental Conference and beyond*, edited by G. Edwards and A. Pijpers, London/Washington, 1997
FEATHERSTONE, Kevin, "Jean Monnet and the 'Democratic Deficit' in the European Union", *Journal of Common Market Studies*, Vol. 32, No. 2, 1994, pp. 149–70
KOMADA, Masami, "The Role of the European Parliament in eliminating the "democratic deficit" in the European Union: its Impact on the institutional power balance of the European Union – a view from Japan", *Junshin Journal of Human Studies*, No. 3, 1997, pp. 51–66
LAPRAT, Gerard, "Réforme des Traités: le risque du Double Déficit Démocratique", *Revue du Marché Commun*, octobre 1991
LODGE, Juliet, "EC policymaking: institutional dynamics" in: *The European Community and the Challenge of the Future*, edited by J. Lodge, London: Pinter, Second edition, 1993
LODGE, Juliet, *The Democratic Deficit and the European Parliament*, Fabian Discussion Paper, No. 4, London: Fabian Society, 1991
MARTIN, David, *European Union: The Shattered Dream?*, John Wheatley Centre, West Lothian, 1993
NEUNREITHER, Karlheinz, "The Democratic Deficit of the European Union: Towards closer cooperation between the European Parliament and the national parliaments", *Government and Opposition*, Vol. 29, No. 3, pp. 299–314

NORRIS, Pippa, "Representation and the Democratic Deficit", *European Journal of Political Research*, No. 2, 1997, pp. 273–82

RAMSAY, Robert, "The Role of the European Parliament", in: *Legal Aspects of Integration in the European Union*, Deventer, 1997, pp. 207–23

SHACKLETON, Michael, "Democratic Accountability in the European Union" in: *Economic Policy Making and the European Union*, edited by F. Brouwer, V. Lintner and M. Newman, London: Federal Trust, 1994

SHACKLETON, Michael, "Interparliamentary Cooperation and the 1996 IGC" in: *The Changing Role of Parliaments in the Union*, edited by F. Laursen and S. Pappas, Maastricht: European Institute for Public Administration, 1995

SHACKLETON, Michael, "The Internal Legitimacy Crisis of the European Union" in: *Europe's Ambiguous Unity*, edited by A. W. Cafruny and C. Lankowski, Colorado: Lynne Rienner, 1997

SHEPHARD, Mark, "The European Parliament: crawling, walking and running", in: *Parliaments and Governments in Western Europe*, Vol. 1, London, 1998, pp. 167–89

SMITH, Mitchell P., "Democratic legitimacy in the European Union: fulfilling the institutional logic", *Journal of Legislative Studies*, 4, 1996, pp. 283–301

TSEBELIS, George, "Maastricht and the Democratic Deficit", *Aussenwirtschaft*, Vol. 52, No. 1, 1997, pp. 29–56

WALLACE, William and SMITH, Julie, "Democracy versus Technocracy, European Integration and the Problem of Popular Consent", *West European Politics*, Vol. 18, No. 3, 1995, pp. 137–57

WEILER, Joseph, "After Maastricht: Community Legitimacy in Post-1992 Europe" in: *Singular Europe: Economy and Polity of the European Community after 1992*, edited by W.J. Adams, Ann Arbor: University of Michigan Press, 1993

WEILER, Joseph, "The Reformation of European Constitutionalism", *Journal of Common Market Studies*, Vol. 35, No. 1, 1997, pp. 97–131

WEILER, Joseph, "Legitimacy and Democracy of Union Governance", in: *The Politics of European Treaty Reform: The 1996 Intergovernmental Conference and Beyond*, edited by G. Edwards and A. Pijpers, London and Washington: Pinter, 1997

Powers

BOYRON, Sophie, "Maastricht and the codecision procedure: a success story", *International and Comparative Law Quarterly*, 2, April 1996, pp. 293–318

BRADLEY, Kieran St. Clair, "Better Rusty Than Missing?: Institutional Reforms of the Maastricht Treaty and the European Parliament", in: *Legal Issues of the Maastricht Treaty*, edited by D. O'Keefe and P. Twomey, Macmillan, London, 1993

BRADLEY, Kieran St.Clair, "The European Parliament and Comitology: On the Road to Nowhere", *European Law Journal*, Vol. 3, No. 3, 1997, pp. 230–54

CARA, Jean–Yves De, "The Control of EC Environmental Policy by the European Parliament and the Court of Justice of the EC", in: *Legal Aspects of Integration in the European Union*, Deventer, 1997, pp. 81–92

CROMBEZ, C, "Legislative Procedures in the European Community", *British Journal of Political Science*, Vol. 26, No. 2, 1996, pp. 199–228

CROMBEZ, Christophe, "The Co-Decision Procedure in the European Union", *Aussenwirtschaft*, Nos. 1/2, 1997, pp. 63–82

DASHWOOD, Alan, "The European Parliament and Article 173 EEC: the limits of interpretation", *Current Issues in European and International Law*, 1990, pp. 73–82

EARNSHAW, David and JUDGE, David, "The European Parliament and the Sweeteners Directive: From Footnote to Interinstitutional Conflict", *Journal of Common Market Studies*, Vol. 31, No. 1, 1993, pp. 103–16

EARNSHAW, David and JUDGE, David, "Early days: the European Parliament, codecision and the European Union legislative process post-Maastricht", *Journal of European Public Policy*, 2, 1995, pp. 624–49

EARNSHAW, David and JUDGE, David, "From co-operation to co-decision: the

European Parliament's path to legislative power" in: *European Union, power and policy-making,* edited by J. Richardson, London: Routledge, 1996

EARNSHAW, David and JUDGE, David, "The Life and Times of the European Union's Cooperation Procedure", *Journal of Common Market Studies,* Vol. 35, No. 4, 1997, pp. 543–64

EARNSHAW, David and WOOD, Josephine, "The European Parliament and biotechnology patenting: Harbinger of the future?", *Journal of Commercial Biotechnology,* Vol. 5, No. 4, 1999 pp. 294–307

GARMAN, Julie and HILDITCH, Louise, "Behind the Scenes: an Examination of the Importance of the informal Processes at Work in Conciliation", *Journal of European Public Policy,* No. 2, 1998, pp. 271–84

GARRETT, G. and TSEBELIS, G., "An Institutional Critique of Intergovern-mentalism" *International Organization,* Vol. 50, 1996, pp. 269–299

GOLUB, Jonathan, "State Power and Institutional Influence in European Integration: Lessons from the Packaging Waste Directive", *Journal of Common Market Studies,* Vol. 34, No. 3, 1996, pp. 313–41

GOSALBO BONO, Ricardo, "The International powers of the European Parliament, the democratic deficit and the Treaty on European Union", in: *Yearbook of European Law,* 12–1992, Oxford, 1994, pp. 85–138

GOSALBO BONO, Ricardo, "Codecision: an appraisal of the experience of the European Parliament as co-legislator" in: *Yearbook of European Law,* 14–1994, Oxford, 1995, pp. 21–71

HERNE, Kaisa and NURMI, Hannu, "The Distribution of A Priori Voting Power in the EC Council of Ministers and the European Parliament", *Scandinavian Political Studies,* Vol. 16, No. 3, 1993, pp. 269–84

HIX, Simon and LORD, Christopher, "The making of a President: the European Parliament and the confirmation of Jacques Santer as President of the Commission", *Government and Opposition,* Vol. 31, No. 1, pp. 62–76

HUBSCHMID, Claudia and MOSER, Peter, "The Cooperation Procedure in the EU: Why was the EP Influential in the Decision on Car Emissions Standards?", *Journal of Common Market Studies,* Vol. 35, No. 2, 1997, pp. 225–42

JACKSON, Caroline, MATTERA RICIGLIANO, Alfonso and WILS, Wouter, "Consumer Law II: the role of the European Parliament in the control of foodstuffs legislation", *European Food Law Review,* 1, November 1990, pp. 53–71

JUDGE, David, EARNSHAW, David and COWAN, Ngaire, "Ripples or Waves: The European Parliament in the European Community Policy Process", *Journal of European Public Policy,* Vol. 1, No. 1, 1994, pp. 27–51

JUDGE, David and EARNSHAW, David, " Weak European Parliament Influence? A Study of the Environment Committee of the European Parliament", *Government and Opposition,* Vol. 29, No. 2, 1994, pp. 262–76

KREPPEL, Amie, "What affects the European Parliament's Legislative Influence?", *Journal of Common Market Studies,* Vol. 37, No. 3, 1999, pp. 521–35

LAVER, Michael, "Government formation in the European Parliament", *Aussenwirtschaft,* Nos.1/2, 1997, pp. 223–248

MONAR, Jörg, "Interinstitutional Agreements: The Phenomenon and its New Dynamics After Maastricht", *Common Market Law Review,* Vol. 31, 1994, pp. 693–719

MONAR, Jörg, "Democratic Control of justice and home affairs: the European Parliament and the national Parliaments" in: *Justice and home affairs in the European Union, the development of the third pillar,* edited by R. Bieber and J. Monar, Brussels, 1995, pp. 243–257

MOSER, P, "The European Parliament as a Conditional Agenda setter: What are the Conditions? A Critique of Tsebelis (1994)", *American Political Science Review,* Vol. 90, No. 4, 1996, pp. 834–838

MOSER, P, "A theory of the conditional influence of the European Parliament in the co-operation procedure", *Public Choice,* Vol. 91, 1997, pp. 333–350

MOSER, P, "The Benefits of the Conciliation Procedure for the European Parliament – Comment to George Tsebelis", *Aussenwirtschaft*, Vol. 52, No. 1, 1997, pp. 57–61

SCULLY, Roger, "The European Parliament and the Co-decision procedure: A Reassessment" *Journal of Legislative Studies*, Vol. 3, No. 3, 1997, pp. 58–73

SCULLY, Roger, "The European Parliament and Co-Decision: A Rejoinder to Tsebelis and Garrett", *Journal of Legislative Studies*, Vol. 3, No. 3, 1997, pp. 93–103

SCULLY, Roger, "Policy Influence and Participation in the European Parliament", *Legislative Studies Quarterly*, Vol. 22, No. 2, 1997, pp. 233–52

SHACKLETON, Michael, "The European Parliament's New Committees of Inquiry: Tiger or Paper Tiger?", *Journal of Common Market Studies*, Vol. 36, No. 1, 1998, pp. 115–30

TSEBELIS, George, "The Power of the European Parliament as a conditional agenda setter", *American Political Science Review*, Vol. 88, No. 1, 1994, pp. 128–42

TSEBELIS, George, "Conditional agenda-setting and decision-making inside the European Parliament", *Journal of Legislative Studies*, Vol. 1, No. 1, 1995, pp. 65–93

TSEBELIS, George, "More on the European Parlaiment as a Conditional Agenda Setter: Response to Moser", *American Political Science Review*, Vol. 90,No. 4, 1996, pp. 839–843

TSEBELIS, George and GARRETT, G, "Agenda setting, Vetoes and the European Union's Co-Decision Procedure", *Journal of Legislative Studies*, Vol. 3, No. 3, 1997, pp. 74–92

VEDEL, Georges, *Report of the Working Party examining the problem of the Enlargement of the Powers of the European Parliament* ("Vedel Report"), Bulletin of the European Communities, Supplement 4/72

WESTLAKE, Martin, "The European Parliament, the national parliaments and the 1996 Intergovernmental Conference", *Political Quarterly*, Vol. 66, No. 1, pp. 59–73

WESTLAKE, Martin, "The European Parliament's Emerging Powers of Appointment", *Journal of Common Market Studies*, Vol. 36, No. 3, 1998, pp. 431–44

WRIGHT, Elisabeth, "Can the European Parliament punish European Commission officials? Who takes the blame for the BSE mess?", *European Food Law Review*, No. 1, 1998, pp. 39–46

Members

Books and studies
ABELES, Marc, *La vie quotidienne au Parlement européen*, Paris: Hachette, 1992

BOWLER, Shaun and FARRELL, David M., *MEPs, voters and interest groups: representation at the European level*, Manchester: Manchester University Press, 1992

FONTAINE, Nicole, *Les députés européens; que sont-ils? Que font-ils?*, Neuilly-sur-Seine: CEIC, 1994

SCHÖNDUBE, Claus, *4 von 518: Blick hinter die Kulissen des Europäischen Parlements*, Bonn: Europa Union Verlag, 1993

WESTLAKE, Martin, *Britain's Emerging Euro-Elite? The British in the European Parliament, 1979–1992*, Aldershot: Dartmouth, 1994

Articles
ABELES, Marc, "Political Anthropology of a transnational Institution: the European Parliament", *French Politics and Society*, 1, winter 1993, pp. 1–19

BOWLER, Shaun and FARRELL, David M., "Legislator Shirking and Voter Monitoring: Impact of European Parliament Electoral Systems upon Legislator-Voter Relationships", *Journal of Common Market Studies*, Vol. 31, No. 1, March 1993, pp. 45–61

JACKSON, Caroline, "The first British MEPs, styles and strategies (1973–1979)", *Contemporary European History*, Vol. 2, No. 2, 1993, pp. 169–95

KAUPPI, Niilo, "European Union Institutions and French political careers: French members of the European Parliament", *Scandinavian Political Studies*, Vol. 19, No. 1, 1996, pp. 1–24

SAP, John, "The Reflection of Calvinism in the Development of the European Parliament", *Legislative Studies Quarterly*, No. 2, 1997, pp. 253–63
SCARROW, S, "Political Career Paths and the European Parliament", *Legislative Studies Quarterly*, No. 2, 1997, pp. 253–63
SCULLY, Roger, "MEPs and the Building of a`Parliamentary Europe'", *Journal of Legislative Studies*, Vol. 4, No. 3, 1998, pp. 92–108

Sessions and Activities

Books and studies
ARP, Henning A., "The European Parliament in European Community environmental policy", EUI Working Paper 92/13, European University Institute, Florence, 1992
THEATO, Diemut R. and GRAF, Rainer, *Das Europäische Parlament und der Haushalt der Europäischen Gemeinschaft*, Baden-Baden: Nomos Verlag, 1994
WESTLAKE, Martin, "The Origin and Development of the Question Time Procedure in the European Parliament", EUI Working Paper 90/4, European University Institute, Florence, 1990

Articles
BARON CRESPO, Enrique, "CFSP: the view of the European Parliament" in: *The European Union's common foreign and security policy, the challenges of the future*, edited by S.Pappas and S.Vanhoonacker, Maastricht, 1996, pp. 37–43
BOWLER, Shaun and FARRELL, David M., "The Organization of the European Parliament: Committees, Specialization and Co-ordination", *British Journal of Political Science*, Vol. 25, No. 2, pp. 219–43
CAMENEN, François-Xavier, "Administration et autorité politique au Parlement européen", *Revue française d'administration publique*, 73, janvier–mars 1995, pp. 143–55
COLLINS, K, BURNS, C and WARLEIGH, A (1998) "Policy Entrepreneurs: the role of European Parliament Committees in the Making of EU Policy", *Statute Law Review*, Vol. 19 No. 1, pp. 1–11
GRUNERT, Thomas, "The Association of the European Parliament: no longer the Underdog in EPC" in: *Foreign Policy of the European Union: from EPC to CFSP and beyond*, eds. E. Regelsberger, Ph.de Schouteete de Tervarent and W. Wessels, London, 1997, pp. 109–31
JACOBS, Francis Brendan, "The European Parliament and Economic and Monetary Union", *Common Market Law Review*, No. 2, Summer 1991, pp. 361–82
JUDGE, David, "Predestined to save the Earth: the Environment Committee of the European Parliament", *Environmental Politics*, 4, 1992, pp. 186–212
KUNSLIK, P. and JACOBSON, B. "The Enforcement of EU environmental law, art.169, the Ombudsman and the Parliament", *European Environmental Law Review*, No. 2, 1997, pp. 46–52
MARIAS, Epaminondas, "The right to petition the European Parliament after Maastricht", *European Law Review*, 2, April 1994, pp. 169–83
NEUNREITHER, Karlheinz, "The European Parliament and Enlargement 1973–2000", in: *The expanding European Union – Past, Present and Future*, Colorado, 1998, pp. 65–86
NICOLL, William, "The European Parliament's post-Maastricht rules of procedure", *Journal of Common Market Studies*, Vol. 32, No. 1, 1994, pp. 403–10
O'DONNELL, Tony, "Europe on the move: the travelling parliament roadshow" in: *Televising democracies*, edited by R. Franklin, London, 1992, pp. 254–68
RAUNIO, Tapio, "Parliamentary questions in the European Parliament: representation, information and control", *Journal of Legislative Studies*, 4, 1996, pp. 356–82
RIPA DI MEANA, Carlo and COLLINS, Ken, "Hazardous waste shipments: regulation within the EC; Action by the European Parliament", *Marine Policy*, No. 3, May 1990, pp. 271–77

Direct elections

Books and studies
BLONDEL, Jean, SINNOTT, Richard and SVENSSON, Palle, *People and Parliament in the European Union: Participation, Democracy and Legitimacy*, Oxford: Clarendon Press, 1998
BUTLER, David and WESTLAKE, Martin, *British Politics and European elections 1994*, London: Macmillan, 1995
DUFF, Andrew, *Electoral Reform of the European Parliament; proposals for a uniform electoral procedure of the European Parliament to the intergovernmental conference of the European Union 1996*, London: Federal Trust, 1996
DUNLEAVY, Patrick, HIX, Simon and MARGETTS, Helen, *Counting on Europe: Proportional Representation and the June 1999 Elections to the European Parliament*, Report prepared for Adamson Associates, Brussels, 1998
EIJK, Cees van der and FRANKLIN, Mark (eds.), *Choosing Europe? The European Electorate and National Politics in the Face of Union*, Ann Arbor: University of Michigan Press, 1996
LODGE, Juliet (ed.), *The 1994 Elections to the European Parliament*, London: Pinter, 1996
MACKIE, T. T. (ed.), *European Parliamentary Elections Results*, Aldershot: Dartmouth, 1990
SMITH, Julie, *Citizens' Europe? The European elections and the role of the European Parliament*, London: The Royal Institute of International Affairs, 1994

Articles
ANCKAR, Dag, "The Finnish European Election of 1996", *Electoral Studies*, No. 2, 1997, pp. 262–66
BARDI, Luciano, "The third elections to the European Parliament: a vote for Italy or a vote for Europe?", *Italian Politics*, No. 5, 1990, pp. 138–53
BOYCE, Brigitte, "The June 1994 elections and the politics of the European Parliament", *Parliamentary Affairs*, 1, January 1995, pp. 141–56
BLONDEL, Jean, SINNOTT, Richard and SVENSSON, Palle, "Representation and Voter Participation", *European Journal of Political Research*, No. 2, 1997, pp. 243–72
CAYROL, Roland, "European Elections and the pre-electoral period: media use and campaign evaluations", *European Journal of Political Research*, No. 1, January 1991, pp. 17–29 – all the articles in this edition of the journal are devoted to the 1989 elections
CURTICE, John, "The 1989 European Election: protest or green tide?", *Electoral Studies*, Vol. 8, No. 3, 1989, pp. 217–230
CURTICE, John and RANGE, Martin, "A Flawed Revolution? Britain's new European Parliament electoral system", *Representation*, No. 1, 1998, pp. 7–15
EIJK, C. Van der and FRANKLIN, M.N., "European Community Politics and Electoral Representation: Evidence from the 1989 European Elections Study", *European Journal of Political Research*, Vol. 19, No. 1, 1991, pp. 105–27
HEARL, David, "Notes on the Elections to the European Parliament", *Electoral Studies*, Vol. 13, No. 4, 1994, pp. 331–67
IRWIN, Galen, "Second-order or Third-rate? Issues in the Campaign for the European Parliament 1994", *Electoral Studies*, Vol. 14, No. 2, pp. 183–99
LAKEMAN, Enid, "Elections to the European Parliament 1989", *Parliamentary Affairs*, No. 1, January 1990, pp. 77–89
MARSH, Michael and NORRIS, Pippa, "Political Representation in the European Parliament", *European Journal of Political Research*, Vol. 32, No. 2, 1997, pp. 53–64
MILLAR, David, "A uniform electoral procedure for European elections", *Electoral Studies*, No. 1, March 1990, pp. 37–44
NIEDERMAYER, Oscar, "The 1989 European Elections: Campaigns and Results", *European Journal of Political Research*, Vol. 19, No. 3, 1991, pp. 3–16

OLIVER, Peter, "Electoral Rights under Article 8B of the Treaty of Rome", *Common Market Law Review*, Vol. 33, No. 3, 1996, pp. 473–98

PINDER, John, "The European elections of 1994 and the future of the European Union", *Government and Opposition*, Vol. 29, No. 1, 1994, pp. 494–514

REIF, Karlheinz and SCHMITT, Hermann, "Nine Second-Order National Elections: A Conceptual Framework for the Analysis of European Election Results", *European Journal of Political Research*, Vol. 8, No. 1, pp. 3–45

SCHMITT, Hermann, "Party Attachment and Party Choice in the European Elections of 1989", *International Journal of Public Opinion Research*, No. 2, 1990, pp. 169–84

SHEPHARD, Mark, "The European Parliament: laying the Foundations for Awareness and Support", *Parliamentary Affairs*, No. 3, 1997, pp. 438–52

SMART, Michael, "Luxembourg: The European Parliament and national elections of June 1989", *West European Politics*, No. 1, January 1990, pp. 137–58 – other articles on the elections can be found in the same edition of the journal

Political groups and parties

Books and studies

BOMBERG, Elizabeth, *Green Parties and Politics in the European Union*, London: Routledge, 1998

BOWLER, Shaun, FARRELL, David and KATZ, Richard, *Party Cohesion, Party Discipline and the Organization of Parliaments*, Colombus: Ohio State University Press, 1997

GAFFNEY, John (ed.), *Political Parties and the European Union*, London: Routledge, 1996

HANLEY, David (ed.), *Chrisitian Democracy in Europe: a comparative perspective*, London: Pinter, 1994

HIX, Simon and LORD, Christopher, *Political Parties in the European Union*, Basingstoke: Macmillan, 1997

JACOBS, Francis B., *Western Political Parties: A Comprehensive Guide*, London: Longman, 1989

JANSEN, Thomas, *The European People's Party: Origins and Developments*, New York: St.Martin's Press, 1998

JOHANSSON, Karl Magnus, *Transnational Party Alliances: Analysing the hard-won Alliance between Conservatives and Christian Democrats in the European Parliament*, Lund: Lund University Press, 1997

LEONARD, Marc, *Politics without frontiers: the role of political parties in Europe's future*, London: Demos, 1997

MORGAN, Roger, *Parliaments and parties: the European Parliament in the life of Europe*, Basingstoke: Macmillan, 1998 (2nd. edition)

RAUNIO, Tapio, *The European Perspective: transnational Party Groups in the 1989–1994 European Parliament*, Aldershot: Ashgate, 1997

Articles

ATTINA, Fulvio, "The voting behaviour of the European Parliament members and the problem of Europarties", *European Journal of Political Research*, Vol. 18, No. 3, 1990, pp. 557–79

ATTINA, Fulvio, "Parties, Party System and Democracy in the European Union", *The International Spectator*, Vol. 27, No. 3, 1992, pp. 67–86

ATTINA, Fulvio, "'Political Parties, Federalism and the European Union", in: *Federal Conceptions in EU Member States*, edited by F. Knipping, Baden Baden: Nomos, 1994

BARDI, Luciano, "Transnational Party Federations in the European Community", in: *Party Organizations: A Data Handbook on Party on Party Organizations in Western Democracies, 1960–90*, edited by R. S. Katz and P. Mair, London: Sage, 1992

BARDI, Luciano, "Transnational trends in European parties and the 1994 elections of the European Parliament", *Party Politics*, Vol. 2, No. 1, January 1996, pp. 99–114

BRZINSKI, J. Bay, "Political Group Cohesion in the European Parliament, 1989–1994" in: *The State of the European Union, Vol. 3*, edited by C. Rhodes and S. Mazey, London: Longman, 1995

COLOMER, Joseph and HOSLI, Madeleine, "Decision-making in the European Union: the Power of political parties", *Aussenwirtschaft*, Nos. 1/2, 1997, pp. 255–80

FENNEMA, M. and POLLMANN, C. "Ideology of anti-immigrant parties in the European Parliament", *Acta Politica*, No. 2, 1998, pp. 111–38

HIX, Simon, "The Emerging EC Party System? The European Party Federations in the Intergovernmental Conference", *Politics*, Vol. 13, No. 2, pp. 38–46

HIX, Simon, "Parties at the European level and the legitimacy of EU socio-economic policy", *Journal of Common Market Studies*, Vol. 33, No. 4, 1995, pp. 527–54

HIX, Simon, "Elections, Parties and institutional design: a comparative perspective on European Union Democracy", *West European Politics*, No. 3, 1998, pp. 19–52

HIX, Simon, "Parties and Elections in the European Union", *European Review*, No. 2, 1998, pp. 215–32

HOSLI, M.O, "Voting Strength in the European Parliament: The Influence of National and of Partisan Actors", *European Journal of Political Research*, No. 3, 1997, pp. 351–66

JOHANSSON, Karl Magnus, "Party Group Dynamics in the European Parliament", in: *National Interest and Integrative Politics in transnational Assemblies*, edited by E. Kuper and U. Jan, London, 1997

LADRECH, Robert, "Social Democratic Parties and European Integration", *European Journal of Political Research*, Vol. 24, No. 2, 1993, pp. 195–210

LADRECH, Robert, "Partisanship and Party Formation in European Union Politics", *Comparative Politics*, January 1997, pp. 167–85

LAHAV, Gallya, "Ideological and Party Constraints on Immigration Attitudes in Europe", *Journal of Common Market Studies*, Vol. 35, No. 3, 1997, pp. 377–406

MARSH, Michael and NORRIS, Pippa, "Political Representation in the European Parliament", *European Journal of Political Research*, No. 2, 1997, pp. 153–64

O'NEILL, Michael, "New Politics, old Predicaments: the Case of the European Greens", *Political Quarterly*, No. 1, 1997, pp. 50–67

TAGGART, Paul, "A Touchstone of Dissent: Euroscepticism in contemporary Western European Party Systems", *European Journal of Political Research*, No. 1, 1998, pp. 363–88

TSATSOS, Dimitris, "European Political Parties", *Human Rights Law Journal*, Vol. 6, No. 1–3, 1995, pp. 1–9

INDEX

The index does not contain the names of people mentioned in lists in the individual chapters or the appendices.

accession joint parliamentary committees 131, 135–6
accession treaties, assent procedure 4, 203, 204, 207
ACP-EEC Joint Assembly 130, 131, 132, 137–9, 168, 274
Adenauer, Konrad 176, 295
administrators *see* staff
AETR ruling 205, 206
Agag, Alejandro 93
Agalev (Belgium) 61, 73
age limits, in electoral systems 15, 16
agriculture 32, 191, 225–6, 256, 262
Agriculture Committee *see* Committee on Agriculture and Rural Development
Aigner, Heinrich 110
Alber, Siegbert 240
Albert, Michel 125
Albor, Fernandez 126
Alfonsin, Raul 281
Alianza Popular (Spain) 61, 62
Alleanza Nazionale (Italy) 63, 78, 79, 80
allowances 42–3, *43*, 47, 119, 265–6
amendments 151, 152, 189, 194, 195
amounts deemed necessary 230
Amsterdam IGC 88, 259, 283, 301, 302–3
Amsterdam Treaty 5, *9*
  animal welfare 163
  appointments 234, 235, 237, 241
  assent procedure 203
  co-decision procedure 188, 189, 191, 192–3, 202
  committees 105, 106
  constitutional change 160–1, 303–4, 305
  consultation procedure 183–5
  cooperation procedure 185
  electoral system 23–4
  legislative procedures *214–15*
  members' statute 46
  national parliaments 284, 285
  public access to documents 288
  seat issue 26, 30, 32–3
  transparency 202
Anastassopoulos, Giorgios 24, 240
Andreotti, Giulio 51
Andriessen report 210
animal welfare 161–3, 275
annulment proceedings 266–8
Apel, Hans 172
appointments 5, 233–4, 241–3
  Commission 234–8, 299, 303
  Court of Auditors 239–40
  European Central Bank 238–9
  Ombudsman 240
Asinello 72
assent procedure 4, 5, 203–4, *203*, 207–9, 300
assizes 279, 299–300
association agreements 4, 130, 131, 135–6, 205
  assent procedure 203, 204–5, 207–8
Audiovisual Intergroup 158
Austria
  accession *9*, 63, 207
  co-decision procedure 196, 197
  election results *25*, *308*
  electoral system 13, *13*, *14*, 15
  European affairs committees *286*
  JPC 131
  MEPs *50*, 314
  representation *12*, 22, 300
  staff 167, *167*
Autant-Lara, Claude 99
Auto-Oil package 197

Balfe, Richard 102
Ball, James 125
Balsemao, Francisco 51
Baltic States 29–30, 131
Banks, Tony 164–5
Banotti, Mary 162, 163
Barcelona process 139
Barón Crespo, Enrique 30, 70, 101, 125
Barrett, Frank 77
bars 143
Basque country 18, 75
Behrend, Hans Nikolaus (Juan) 73
Belgium
    constitutional change 298, 299
    election results 25, 308
    electoral system 13, 13, 14, 15, 16, 17,
        18
    European affairs committees 286
    MEPs 50, 315–16
    post-MEP experience 53
    representation 12, 22
    seat issue 29
    staff 167
Beobachter 21
Berlusconi, Silvio 52, 109
Bersani, Giovanni 138
Berthu, Georges 134
Bertinotti, Fausto 52
Bethell, Nicholas 50
Beumer, Anton 93
Beumer, Bouke 110
Bildt, Carl 281
Billingham, Angela 163
biotechnological inventions 196, 289
Bird, John 48
Bjerregard, Ritt 280
Blair, Tony 283
Blak, Freddy 155
Blaney, Neil 60
Blinder, Alan 239
Blokland, Hans 79
Bloque Nacionalista Gallego (Spain) 75
Bocklet, Reinhold 23
Böge, Reimer 126, 263
Boissière, Bruno 86
Bonde, Jens-Peter 79, 288
Bonino, Emma 51, 63, 72, 80, 280
Bosman case 164
Bosnia 139
Bossi, Umberto 52
Bourlanges, Jean-Louis 107, 161, 301
Boyes, Roland 48
Brandt, Willy 51
Brittan, Sir Leon 135, 280
Broek, Hans van den 280

Brok, Elmar 275, 302
Brown, Gordon 283
Brundtland, Gro Harlem 281
Brussels
    committee meetings 112, 202
    delegations 136
    Group week 86
    intergroups 158
    library 170
    MEPs' offices 41, 47, 48, 58
    open Enlarged Bureau 156
    plenaries 141, 143, 145
    press conferences 290
    seat issue 26–33, 266
    staff 35, 111, 166, 170–1, 280
    visitors 291, 292
BSE 126, 243, 263–4
budget 3–4, 6, 7
    discharge procedure 252–5
    human rights funding 274
    Parliament's objectives 225–32
    Parliament's powers 9, 211, 216–18
    Political Groups 81–2, 87
    procedures 30, 146, 181, 184, 218–25
    sport 164
budgetary authority 3–4, 216
Budgetary Control Committee see
    Committee on Budgetary Control
Budgets Committee see Committee on
    Budgets
Buitenweg, Kathalijne 48
Bulgaria 131, 304
Bureau 94, 95, 102–3, 168
    committees 121, 272
    intergroups 157
    lobbying 290
    Multilingualism Working Group 32,
        36–7
    seat issue 29, 30
    see also Enlarged Bureau; open
        Enlarged Bureau
Buttiglione, Rocci 52

cabinet 96
Cacciari, Massimo 52
Canada 134
Capanna, Mario 81, 155
car insurance 213
Carnero Gonzalez, Carlos 161
Cashman, Michael 53
Cassanmagnago Cerretti, Luisa 138
Casssola, Arnold 93
Castle, Barbara 48
Catalonia 18, 36
censure motions 243–4, 245, 254–5

Central American Parliament 10
Centre des Démocrates Sociaux (CDS)
    (France) 68, 73
Centro Democratico y Social (CDS)
    (Spain) 61–2
Centrum-Demokraterne (Denmark) 61
CFSP *see* Common Foreign and Security
    Policy
Chanterie, Raf 280
Chasse, Peche, Nature et Traditions
    (France) 63, 79
Chirac, Jacques 51
Christian Democrats *see* Group of the
    European People's Party and
    European Democrats
Christlich Demokratische Union (CDU)
    (Germany) 68
Christlich Soziale Union (CSU)
    (Germany) 68
Cicciolina 62
citizens' rights 184, 275
    European elections 14, *14*, 15, 20, 23
    see also human rights
Civil Liberties Committee *129*, 284
Clegg, Nicholas 280
Clywd, Ann 53
co-decision procedure 188, 296
    Amsterdam Treaty 183, 303
    annulment actions 268
    budget 230–1
    comitology 258–9
    committees 106
    conciliation 196–8
    Conciliation Committee 198–200
    developments resulting 200–3
    impact 193–5
    jurist linguists 35, 146, 171
    Legal Service 171
    Maastricht Treaty 4–5, 299, 300
    nature 188–9, *190*, 191
    scope 191–3
Coalición Canaria (Spain) 72, 75
Coalición Europea (Spain) 72, 75
Coalición Nacionalista Europa de los
    Pueblos (Spain) 75
Coates, Ken 126
cohesion fund 204
Cohn-Bendit, Dany 14, 53, 74, 161
College of Quaestors 102, 103, 168
    see also Quaestors
Collins, Ken 104, 110
Colombo, Emilio 51, 126, 130
comitology 255–6, 260–1, 267, 279
    1987 decision 256–7
    1999 decision 259–60

Modus Vivendi 258–9
    Plumb-Delors procedure 257–8
    related developments 259
Commission 3, 6, 7, 246
    appointment 5, 234–8, *236*, 242, 299,
        300, 303
    budget 216–30
    censure votes 150
    co-decision procedure 189, 195, 198
    comitology 255–61
    and committees 112, 113, 118, 119,
        121
    committees of inquiry 263
    conciliation procedure 181–2
    Conference of Presidents 156
    consultation procedure 177, 178, 180
    contacts with Parliament 278, 279–80
    cooperation procedure *186*, 187, 188
    discharge 253–5
    dismissal 233, 243–4, *245*
    intergroups 157, 158–9
    international agreements 204–5, 206
    judicial review 266, 269
    legislative initiative 209–11
    legislative programme 211–12
    link to election results 25
    MEPs' assistants 48
    MEPs' immunities 44
    negotiations and dialogue 201–3
    plenaries 142, 144, 145, 146, 147,
        148
    proposals 151, 200–1
    scrutiny 5–6, *9*, 32, 247–8, 249–51,
        250, 271, 296
    staff 173
Committee on Agriculture and Rural
    Development 107
    chairs 109, *126–7*
    reports 115
    subcommittees 124
    working parties 125
    see also Committee on Fisheries
Committee on Budgetary Control 106,
    107, 136–7
    chairs *128*
    confidentiality 123
    Court of Auditors 239, 240
    discharge 225, 253–4, 255
Committee on Budgets 106, 126, 135
    budgetary procedure 218–19, 220,
        221, 222
    chairs *127*
    meetings 112
    staff reform 172
    working parties 125

Committee on Civil Liberties and
   Internal Affairs *129*, 284
Committee on Constitutional Affairs 105
   see also Committee on Institutional
   Affairs; Committee on Rules
Committee on Culture, Youth,
   Education and the Media 108,
   109–10, *128*
Committee on Development and
   Cooperation *128*, 137, 138
Committee on Economic and Monetary
   Affairs 105, 284, 287
   chairs *127*
   hearings 272
   reports 115
   scrutiny 248
   subcommittees 124
Committee on Energy Policy, *see also*
   Committee on Research,
   Technological Development and
   Energy
Committee on the Environment and
   Consumer Protection 106, 187, 272,
   284, 287
   chairs *128*
   reports 115
Committee on External Economic
   Relations 105, 115, *127*
Committee on Fisheries 106, 124, *129*
Committee on Foreign Affairs 106, 115,
   281
   chairs 110, *126*
   delegations 136, 137, 139
   roll call voting 121
   scrutiny 248
   subcommittees 124
Committee on Industry, External Trade,
   Research and Energy 105
Committee of Inquiry into the
   Community Transit Regime 263, 264,
   273
Committee on Institutional Affairs 105,
   115, 160, 242, 272
   appointments 242
   chairs 109, *128–9*
   constitutional change 160, 300–1
   uniform electoral system 23, 24
   voting 121
Committee on Legal Affairs 105, 106,
   154, 201
   chairs 110, *127*
   dual mandate 19
   members' statute 46
Committee on Petitions 106, 107, 115,
   276, 277

   chairs *129*
   Ombudsman 240, 278
Committee on Political Affairs 22, 23
   see also Committee on Foreign Affairs
Committee on Regional Policy,
   Transport and Tourism 105, 106, 107,
   128
Committee on Research, Technological
   Development and Energy 105, 109,
   115, *127*
Committee on Rules 105, 115
   chairs *129*
   confidentiality 123
   lobbying 290
   see also Committee on Constitutional
   Affairs
Committee on Social Affairs and
   Employment 284, 287
   chairs 110, *127–8*
Committee on Transport and Tourism
   105, *128*
committee weeks 32, 112
Committee on Women's Rights 106,
   107, 115, 261
   chairs *129*
committees 105
   business 113–23, 146
   chairmen 41, 59, 94, 103–4, 108–10,
      126–9, 202, 279
   documents 288
   Group coordinators 110–11
   hearings 272–3
   meetings 26, 32–3, 36, 112–13, 144,
      287
   membership 81, 106–8
   national parliaments 284
   questions 249
   rapporteurs and draftsmen 117–20
   referral back 153
   scrutiny 248
   staff 31, 111–12, 168, 170
   structure and character 105–6
   subcommittees 124
   temporary 125–6
   vice-chairmen 108–10
   working parties 124–5
   see also draftsmen; rapporteurs
committees of inquiry 5, 125–6, 261–4,
   279
Common Agricultural Policy 226
Common Foreign and Security Policy
   218, 220, 246, 248, 300, 301
   High Representative 242
common position 4, 146, 151, 171, 185,
   188

Communist and Allies Group 60, 61, 62, 76, *84*
  see also Group of the United European Left; Left Unity Group
Communist Party (France) 18, 61, 62, 76, 77
Communist Party (Greece) 61
compulsory expenditure 217, 222–3
Conciliation Committee 4, 32, 188–9, 279
  composition 122, 198–200
  secretariat 170
  Vice-Presidents 97
conciliation procedure (*concertation*) 4, 181–3, 194
Confederal Group of the European United Left/Nordic Green Left 62, 63, *64–5*, 75–7
  chairs *84*
  committees 108
  see also Group of the United European Left; Left Unity Group
Conference of Committee Chairmen 103–4, 113, 114
Conference of Delegation Chairmen 104, 137
Conference of European Foreign Affairs Committees 97, 284–5
Conference of Presidents 94, 95, 102, 103
  appointments 241
  Commission 156
  committees 113, 114, 123
  ommittees of inquiry 263
  delegations 137, 139
  Group chairs 82
  intergroups 159
  non-attached members 81
  plenary agenda 146, 147
  staff 168
  see also President
Conference of the Regions 125
Conference on Security and Co-operation in Europe (CSCE) 125
confidentiality 123, 288–9
Conservative Party (Denmark) 60, 61
Conservative Party (Great Britain) 51, 88, *88*
  election results 17
  electoral system 22
  Political Groups 60, 61, 68, 69
  women MEPs 50
constituency representation 12–13, 17–18, 57
Constitutional Affairs Committee 105
constitutional change 160–1, 295–305

consultation procedure 176–81, *177*, 183–5, 200
Consumer Affairs Intergroup 158
consumer protection 213
Convergència Democràtica de Catalunya (Spain) 72
Cook, Robin 283
cooperation agreements 206
cooperation procedure 146, 185, *186*, 187–8
  developments resulting 200–3
  Maastricht Treaty 5, 300
  Single European Act 4
coordinators 110–11
Corbett, Richard 86, 172
Corrie, John 138
corruption 42, 44
COSAC 97, 284–5
Cossutta, Armando 52, 77
costs
  language 36
  travel 27, 31
Cot, Jean-Pierre 164
Council 3, 6, 246–7
  animal welfare 163
  assent procedure 4, 5, 203–4, 207
  budget 3–4, 216–32
  co-decision procedure 4–5, 188–98
  comitology 256–61
  committees 113, 122
  committees of inquiry 263
  common position 4, 146, 151, 171, 185
  Conciliation Committee 5, 32, 198–200
  conciliation procedure 4, 181–3
  consultation procedure 176–81, 183–5
  cooperation procedure 4, 5, 185, *186*, 187–8
  discharge 253
  electoral system 10–12, 14, 15, 16, 19, 23, 24
  General Affairs Group 282
  human rights 274
  international agreements 205–6, 209
  legislative programme 212
  MEPs 40, 46–7
  negotiations and dialogue 201–3
  party federations 92
  plenaries 142, 144, 147, 148
  President 95–6
  reconsultation 201
  representation 21
  scrutiny 248, 250, *250*, 251, 264–9, 270–1

seat issue 29–30
trialogues 278
voting 7, *214–15*, 296, 299, 300, 303–4
Council of Europe, Parliamentary
    Assembly 27, 139, 285, 287
Court of Auditors
    appointment 233, 239–40, 241
    information campaign accounts 87
    MEPs' allowances 42
    scrutiny 250, 251, 252–3
    seat issue 30
Court of First Instance 241, 242, 299
Court of Justice 3, 7
    AETR ruling 205
    appointment 6, 241–2
    budget 226, 227
    comitology 257
    conciliation procedure 182
    financial support for parties 20
    fines on Member States 300
    Isoglucose ruling 4, 179–81, 265
    judicial review 264–9
    languages 34
    professional qualifications 176–7
    seat issue 28, 29, 30–1
    sport 164
Cox, Pat 71, 72–3, 101, 107
Crawley, Christine 14, 283
Craxi, Bettino 51
Crocodile Club 160, 297
Crooks, Garth 164
Crosland, Tony 206
Culture Committee 108, 109–10, *128*
Curry, David 53, 109, 293
Cyprus 131, 139, *304*
Czech Republic 131, *304*

D66 (Netherlands) 72
d'Alimonte, Maria 75
Dana 53, 67, 69
d'Ancona, Hedy 54
Dankert, Piet 54, 99
Dastoli, Virgilio 160
David, Wayne 283
Davies, David 302
de Clercq, Willy 51, 110, 280
de Gucht, Karel 23
de Gucht report 21
De la Malène, Christian 82
de Mita, Ciriaco 51
de Pasquale, Pancrazio 110
de Pasquale Report 182
De Rossa, Proinsias 40
Debré, Michel 51
Dehousse report 11

delegations 130, 140, 274
    ACP-EU Joint Assembly 137–9
    ad hoc 139–40
    chairs 104
    history 130–1
    interparliamentary assemblies 139
    leadership 134
    number and composition 81, 131–2,
        132–3
    and Parliament 136–7
    role 134–6
    staff 168, 170
Dell'Alba, Gianfranco 48, 86, 161
Delors, Jacques 113, 209
Delors format of questions 249
Delors package 125, 126
democratic deficit 3
Democratic Party of the Peoples of
    Europe-European Free Alliance
    (DPPE-EFA) 75, 92, 93
Democratic Unionist Party (DUP) (UK)
    80
I Democratici (Italy) 73
Democrazia Cristiana (Italy) 68, 69
Democrazia Proletaria (Italy) 61, 76
Denmark
    accession *9*, 60
    conciliation procedure 182
    election results *25*, *309*
    electoral system 13, *13*, *14*, 15, 16
    European integration 160, 298
    Folketing 285, *286*
    language 33
    MEPs 50, *50*, 316
    representation *12*, 22
    staff *167*
Deprez, Gérard 69, 88
Desama, Claude 104, 109
Development Committee *128*, 137,
    138
d'Hondt system 108, 109
Di Pietro, Antonio 52
Di Rupo, Elio 53
direct elections *see* elections
Directorate-General for Budget and
    Finance 170
Directorate-General for Buildings and
    Administration 170–1
Directorate-General for Committees and
    Delegations 168, 170, 273
Directorate-General for Information and
    Public Relations 111, 170
Directorate-General for Personnel 170
Directorate-General of the Presidency
    142–3, 168

Directorate-General for Research 111, 119, 168, 170, 252
Directorate-General for Translation and Publishing 170, 171
Directorates-General 168
discharge 252–5
Donnelly, Alan 126
Dooge Committee 297–8
draft budget 217, 220–4
draftsmen of opinions 117, 120, 147, 148
drugs 262
dual mandate 15, 19, 50, 53, 57, 283
Duff, Andrew 161
Duhamel, Olivier 161
Duisenberg, Wim 238, 239, 248
Dury, Raymonde 86
Duverger, Maurice 14

East Germany 21, 51
  see also Germany
East Timor 140
Ecolo (Belgium) 61, 73
Economic and Monetary Affairs Committee see Committee on Economic and Monetary Affairs
economic and monetary union 185, 191, 299, 300
Economic and Social Committee 176
ECSC see European Coal and Steel Community
EDA see Group of the European Democratic Alliance
EDG see European Democratic Group
EEC see European Economic Community
ELDR see European Liberal, Democratic and Reformist Group; European Liberal, Democratic and Reformist Party
election observation delegations 139–40
elections 4, 9, 10–12, 24–5, 295
  assent procedure 204
  funding 20, 82
  national systems 12–16
  results 308–13
  turnout 8, 25, 25, 293
  uniform system 16–24
electronic voting 149, 150
Elizabeth II 281
Elliot, Michael 162
Employment Committee see Committee on Social Affairs and Employment
Energie Radicale (France) 62, 63
Energy Committee see Committee on

Research, Technological Development and Energy
Enlarged Bureau 102, 234
  see also open Enlarged Bureau
enlargement 22, 36–7, 161, 301, 304
Environment Committee see Committee on the Environment and Consumer Protection
EP News 170
EPEN (Greece) 61
EPLP 88, 282–3
EPP see European People's Party
EPP-ED see Group of the European People's Party and European Democrats
Estonia 304
EU-Latin America Conference 139, 168
EUL see Confederal Group of the European United Left
Eurathlon 164
EURATOM 9
EURATOM Treaty 176, 205
Euro-Mediterranean Parliamentary Forum 139
Eurobulletin 162
Europe by Satellite (EbS) 291
Europe of Democracies and Diversities 63, 65, 79, 142
Europe of Nations (EN) Group 62, 63, 78, 79
  see also Group of Europe of Nations
European Agency for the Evaluation of Medicinal Products 241
European Assembly 9, 27–8
European Central Bank 204, 246, 247
  appointments 5, 233, 234, 238–9, 241
  scrutiny 251
European Centre for Parliamentary Research and Documentation 252, 285, 287
European Coal and Steel Community 2
  Common Assembly 9, 27, 59–60, 105
European Coal and Steel Community Treaty 176
  censure 243
  international agreements 204
  judicial review 265, 266
European Community Treaty
  budget 216–17, 225, 229, 230
  Court of Auditors 253
  institutional autonomy 266
  legal bases 184
European Conservative Group 60, 61, 68
  see also European Democratic Group

European Constitution Intergroup 158, 160–1
European Council 11
  Berlin meeting 228
  Brussels meeting 228, 230
  Commission appointments 234, 235
  Corfu meeting 301
  Dublin meeting 299
  Edinburgh meeting 21, 26, 30, 228, 230
  Essen meeting 126
  Fontainebleau meeting 297–8
  Maastricht meeting 21, 28
  Madrid meeting 299
  Milan meeting 298
  Millennium IGC 304
  Political Groups 87
  President of Parliament 96, 278
  Rome meeting 92
  scrutiny 250, 251, 270
  Stuttgart meeting 182, 206
European Democratic Alliance see
  Group of the European Democratic
  Alliance
European Democratic Group 61, 68–9, 142
  chairs 84
  election results 17
  Presidency 99
  see also European Conservative
  Group
European Democratic Union 60, 83–4
  see also European Progressive
  Democrats; Group of the European
  Democratic Alliance
European Economic Community 9
European Economic Community Treaty
  comitology 256
  consultation procedure 176
  international agreements 204–5
  judicial review 264–5
European elections see elections
European Environment Agency 241
European Federation of Green Parties
  92, 93
European Free Alliance 61, 75
  see also Group of the
  Greens/European Free Alliance
European integration 2–3, 297
European Investment Bank 248
European Liberal, Democratic and
  Reformist Group 64
  chairs 83
  committees 108
  common manifesto 24
  election results 17
  history 60, 61, 62, 63

languages 34
political activities 87
power balances 91
Presidency 101
seating 141, 142
European Liberal, Democratic and
  Reformist Party 92, 93
European Monetary Institute 5, 234, 238
European Monitoring Centre for Drugs
  and Drug Addiction 241
European Monitoring Centre on Racism
  and Xenophobia 241
European Parliamentary Labour Party
  88, 282–3
European People's Party 24, 92, 93
  see also Group of the European
  People's Party
European Progressive Democrats 60, 61,
  62, 83–4
  see also Group of the European
  Democratic Alliance
European Radical Alliance 62, 63, 75
European Right see Group of the
  European Right
European System of Central Banks 204
European Union 2, 6–7
European Union of Christian
  Democrats 68
European Union Visitors' Programme
  (EUVP) 97, 291, 293
Eurosceptics 63, 65, 79, 142
Euskal Herritarrok (Spain) 80, 81
Eusko Alkartasuna (Spain) 75
Evrigenis Declaration 261
Ewing, Winnie 49, 61, 93
exhaust emission standards 187–8
explanations of vote 55, 150
explanatory statements 35, 119, 120
External Economic Relations Committee
  105, 115, 127

Fabius, Laurent 51, 284
Fabre-Aubrespy, Hervé 254
fascism 261, 262
federalism 6–7
Federalist Intergroup 160
Federation of Liberal, Democratic and
  Reformist Parties of the European
  Community 73
Federazione dei Verdi (Italy) 20, 74
Fernandez Marin, Fernando 52
Ferri, Enrico 298
Fianna Fáil (Ireland) 60, 61, 63, 68, 78, 79
filibustering 55–6, 60
Fine Gael (Ireland) 68

Fini, Gianfranco 52
Finland
    accession *9*, 63, 207
    Eduskunta 285, *286*, 287
    election results *25*, *309*
    electoral system 13, *13*, *14*, 15
    JPC 131
    language 36
    MEPs 42, *50*, 51, 317
    representation *12*, 22
    staff 167, *167*
Fisheries Committee 106, 124, *129*
flexibility 303
Floss, Franz 93
Folkebevaegelsen mod EF-Unionen
    (Denmark) 60, 61, 63, 79
Folkpartiet Liberalerna (Sweden) 72
Fontaine, Nicole 70, 94, 98, 101
Food Aid Regulation 183
Ford, Glyn 48, 290
Foreign Affairs Committee *see*
    Committee on Foreign Affairs
Forlani, Arnaldo 51
formal sittings 156
Formentini, Marco 52, 72
Forth, Eric 53
forum role 270–8, 294
Forza Europa 59, 62, 69
    committees 109
    and EPP Group 63
Forza Italia 59, 62, 68, 69, 72, 78
Framework Progamme for Research
    and Technology, 5th 197–8, 230–1
France
    Assemblée Nationale 141, 252, 283–4,
        286
    constitutional change 298, 303
    Court of Auditors 239–40
    election results 25, *25*, *309*
    electoral system 12, 13, *13*, *14*, 15,
        18
    legislative initiative 209
    MEPs 49, 50, *50*, 51, 52, 53, 282,
        317–19
    in plenary 55–6
    representation 11, *12*, 21
    seat issue 29, 30, 266
    Sénat 285, *286*
    staff *167*
Frassoni, Monica 86, 161
Freie Demokratische Partei (FDP)
    (Germany) 73
Freiheitliche Partei Österreichs (FPÖ) 79,
    80
Friedrich, Ingo 97, 198

Front National (Belgium) 80
Front National (France) 18, 61, 63, 79, 80

Garaud, Marie-France 79, 81
Gargani, Giuseppe 108
Gaullists *see* Rassemblement pour la
    République
Gemelli, Vitalino 108
Georgia 131
Geraghty, Des 40–1
Germany
    annulment proceedings 268
    Bundesrat 21, *286*
    Bundestag 21, 22, 141, 263, *286*
    conciliations 198
    constitutional change 298
    declaration of financial interests 45
    election results *25*, *310*
    electoral system 12–13, *13*, *14*, 15,
        17–18
    MEPs 45, 49, *50*, 51, 52, 319–20
    representation *12*, 21
    staff *167*
    unification *9*, 126
    see also West Germany
Ghilardotti, Fiorella 52
Gibbons, Sam
Gil-Robles, José Maria 70, 101, 109, 162,
    240
Gil Robles-Santer agreement 259
Giscard d'Estaing, Valéry 51, 73
Global Legislators for a Balanced
    Environment (Globe) 158
Goldsmith, James 78
Gomes procedure 114
Gomolka, Alfred 52
Goria, Giovanni 51
Greece
    accession *9*, 61
    Court of Auditors 239–40
    election results *25*, *310*
    electoral system 13, *13*, *14*, 15, 16
    European affairs committees *286*
    European integration 298
    MEPs 50, *50*, 320–1
    representation *12*, 22
    staff *167*
Green, Pauline 88, 243, 255, 283
Green Party (France) *see Les Verts*
Green Party (Great Britain) 17, 75, 155
Green Party (Ireland) 74
Green Party (Italy) 20, 74
The Greens 62, 63
    see also Group of the Greens/
        European Free Alliance

Groen-Links (Netherlands) 74–5
Groen Progressief Akkoord (Netherlands)
    61
Grogan, John 48
Grosch, Mathieu 52
Group of Europe of Nations 63, *65*,
    77–9, 142
Group of the European Democratic
    Alliance
    chairs *83–4*
    history 62, 63
    see also European Democratic Union;
        Union for Europe
Group of the European People's Party
    and European Democrats *64*, 67–70,
    281
    budget 218, 222
    chairs *83*
    committees 108, 109
    compromises 152
    history 59, 60–1, 62, 63
    political activities 87
    power balances 90, 91
    Presidency 101
    seat issue 29
    seating 141–2
    staff 85
Group of the European Progressive
    Democrats *see* European Progressive
    Democrats
Group of the European Right 61, 63, 261
    committees 109, 110
    delegations 134, 155
Group of the Greens/European Free
    Alliance *64*, 73–5
    chairs *84*
    committees 108
    common manifesto 24
    history 62, 63
    power balances 91
    protests 155
    seating 141, 142
Group of the Party of European
    Socialists 59, *64*, 70–1, 281
    appointments 239
    budget 218, 222
    censure motions 243–4, 254
    chairs *83*
    committees 108
    compromises 152
    history 17, 59, 62, 63
    information money 87
    languages 34
    political activities 87
    power balances 90, 91

Presidency 101
seating 141, 142
women 82
see also Socialist Group
Group for the Technical Co-ordination
    and Defence of Independent Groups
    and Members 60, 61, 62, 63, 80
    see also Rainbow Group
Group of the United European Left 62,
    76–7
    chairs *84*
    seating 141
    see also Communist and Allies Group;
        Confederal Group of the European
        United Left
Group weeks 32, 86
Groups *see* Political Groups
Die Grünen (Germany) 20, 61, 74
Guccione, Sergio 173
GUE Group *see* Confederal Group of
    the European United Left
Guigou, Elisabeth 301, 302
guillotine clause 197–8
Gulf States 139
Gulf War 29
Gutierrez Diaz, Antoni 81

Habsburg, Otto von 99
Haider, Jörg 80
Hänsch, Klaus 96, 101
Hansenne, Michel 51–2
Happart, José 243
Hautala, Heidi 73
Havel, Vaclav 281
Heads of Government 281
Heads of State or Government 156, 281
    Dooge Committee 297–8
    see also European Council; Summits
health and safety at work 213
hearings 272–3
hemicycles 26, 28, 29, 30, 32, 141
Herman, Fernand 298
Herzog, Chaim 281
High Speed Train Intergroup 158
Hix, Simon 5, 89, 91
Hogg, Douglas 264
Home and Judicial Affairs 262, 300
Hoon, Geoff 19, 53, 282
Hory, Jean-François
Hughes, Stephen 48
Hughes procedure 114
human rights 273–5, 303
    assent procedure 203, 204, 208
    delegations 134–5, 139
    Lomé Convention 211

subcommittees 124, 125
see also citizens' rights
Human Rights Unit 168, 170, 274
Hume, John 50, 52
Hungary 22, *304*
Hunger in the World working party 125
Hussein, King 281

IGCs *see* intergovernmental conferences
Imbeni, Renzo 52, 97, 198
immunity 44, 45, 123, 144
Independence Party (UK) 63, 79
Independents 81, 134
industry, intergroups 157–8
Industry, External Trade, Research and
    Energy Committee 105
infant formula milk 257–8
information money 82, 87, 266–7
information offices 31, 166, 170, 330–2
Inglewood, Richard 50
insider trading 213
Institutional Affairs Committee *see*
    Committee on Institutional Affairs
Inter-Institutional Agreements 220, 226,
    228–30, 231, 264, 279
inter-institutional conferences 279,
    299–300
intergovernmental conferences
    Amsterdam 88, 259, 283, 301, 302–3
    appointments 241–2
    Maastricht 279, 299, 300
    Millennium 304
    Single European Act 298
Intergroup of Elected Local and
    Regional Representatives 157, 158
Intergroup on the Welfare and
    Conservation of Animals 158, 161–3
intergroups 47, 157, *165*
    advantages and disadvantages 158–
    9
    evolution 157–8
international agreements 204–9, 268,
    273–4
    see also association agreements
Internet 45, 163, 288, 333
interparliamentary assemblies 137–9
interpretation 2, 33, 35–7
interpreters 35, 36–7, 166, 167
Ioannina Declaration 207
Iran 139
Ireland
    accession *9*, 60
    committees 107
    constitutional change 298
    election results 25, *25*, *310*

electoral system 13, *13*, *14*, 15, 16, 17,
    18, 40–1
European affairs committees *286*
MEPs 49, 50, *50*, 51, 321–2
in plenary 55–6
representation *12*, 22
staff *167*
Isoglucose ruling 4, 179–81, 185, 265
Israel 130, 134, 207–8, 273
Italy
    Camera dei Deputati 22
    constitutional change 298, 299, 301
    election results *25*, *311*
    electoral system 11, 13, *13*, 14, *14*, 15,
    17
    European affairs committees *286*
    European Constitution Intergroup
    160, 161
    legislative practice 122–3
    MEPs 41, 49, *50*, 51, 52, 53, 282, 322–4
    representation 11, *12*, 21
    staff *167*
Iversen, John 74, 280
Izquierda Unida (Spain) 76–7

Jackson, Caroline 86
Japan 130, 158
Jean-Pierre, Thierry 52
Jensen, Bo 71
Jensen, Uffe Ellerman 93
John Paul II 155, 281
Johnson, Stanley 161
joint actions 140
Joint Declarations
    against racism and xenophobia 261
    on budgetary procedure 229
    on the conciliation procedure 4,
    181–2
joint parliamentary committees (JPCs)
    130–1, *132–3*, 135–6, 139
judicial review 264–9
Junibevaegelsen (Denmark) 79
jurist linguists 35, 171, 200

Kampuchea 139
Kangaroo Group 157–8
Kellett-Bowman, Edward 263
Kick Racism out of Sport 164
Killilea, Mark 102
King, Oonagh 48
Kinnock, Glenys 48
Kinnock, Neil 173
Klepsch, Egon 30, 99, 101
Klepsch-Millan agreement 259
Kohl, Helmut 235, 281, 282, 299

Kommounistiko Komma Elladas (KKE)
71
Det Konservative Folkeparti (Denmark)
60, 61
KONVER programme 231
Korterelgessy, Niki 93
Kostopoulos, Sotiris 55
Kouchner, Bernard 53
Krivine, Alain 77
Kurds 139

Laan, Lousewies van der 280
Labour Party (Great Britain) 88, *88*, 90,
282–3
election results 17
Political Groups 60
women MEPs 50
Labour Party (Ireland) 17
Laguiller, Arlette 77
Lalumière, Catherine 51
Lamassoure, Alain 161
Lamfalussy, Alexandre 238
Lange, Erwin 104, 110
languages 7, 33–7
committees 111, 113
intergroups 162
staff 166
see also interpretation; translation
Lannoye, Paul 73
Larive, Jessie 86, 163
Latin America 139
Latvia *304*
lawyer linguists 35, 171, 200
Le Pen, Jean-Marie 44, 45, 52, 80, 261
Left Unity Group 62, 76
see also Communist and Allies Group;
Confederal Group of the European
United Left
Lega Nord (Italy) 63, 72, 80
Legal Affairs Committee *see* Committee
on Legal Affairs
Legal Service 171
legislative initiative 209–11
legislative powers 7–8, 146, 212–13,
214–15
see also assent procedure; co-decision
procedure; conciliation procedure;
consultation procedure;
cooperation procedure
legislative programme 211–12
legislative texts
quantity 200
voting order 150–1
Lehne, Klaus-Heiner 48
Leinen, Jo 161

Liberal and Democratic Group 60, 61
Liberal, Democratic and Reformist
Group 61, 62, 63
see also European Liberal, Democratic
and Reformist Group
Liberal Democrats (Great Britain) 17, 50,
72, 88, 89
Liberal Group 60
Liberales Forum (Austria) 73
libraries 170
LIFE programme 231
Liikanen, Erkki 280
Linazasoro, José Luis 93
Lithuania *304*
lobbyists 143, 289–90
intergroups 159, 162
MEPs 57
rapporteurs 119
location *see* seat issue
Lomé Conventions 125, 137–9, 211
Ludford, Sarah 50
Luns procedure 205
Luns-Westerterp procedure 205–6
Luxembourg (city)
committee meetings 112
library 170
seat issue 26–31, 96, 154, 266
staff 35, 166, 171
visitors 291, *292*
Luxembourg (country)
election results *25*, *311*
electoral system 13, *13*, 14, *14*, 15, 16,
18
European affairs committees *286*
MEPs *50*, 51, 324
representation 11, *12*, 21, 22
seat issue 29, 30
staff *167*

Maastricht Treaty 4–5, *9*
annulment proceedings 267
appointments 233–6, 240
assent procedure 203–4, 208–9
budget 230, 253
co-decision procedure 188, 189, 191,
301
committees of inquiry 262–3
conciliation procedure 194
constitutional change 300–1, 305
Court of Auditors 252
electoral system 15, 23
European Central Bank 238
European citizenship 275
legislative initiative 210
national parliaments 284

police and judicial cooperation 184,
185
political parties 92
McIntosh, Anne 86
Maes, Nelly 102
Maghreb countries 130
Maij-Weggen, Hanja 54, 154, 161–2
Malmstrom, Cecilia 161
Malta 131, *304*
Marin, Manuel 280
Marini, Franco 52
Martens, Wilfried 51, 93
Martin, David 97, 283, 299, 301
Mashreq countries 130
Matikainen-Kallstrom, Marja 53
Matutes, Abel 280
maximum rate of increase 217, 226–9
Mayor, Federigo 53
meat
    BSE 126, 243, 263–4
    hormones 213, 262
media 287, 290–1
    see also newspapers; television
Medina Ortega, Manuel 263
Megret, Bruno 80
Member States
    electoral systems 10, 12–16
    infringements 269
    representation 11, *12*, 20–2, 304, *304*
    see also European Council;
        intergovernmental conferences
Members of the European Parliament
    (MEPs) 314–29
    assistants 47–8, 111–12, 172
Commission links 279–80, 281
    communicative role 294
    declaration of financial interests 45,
        159
    dual mandate 50
    eligibility rules 14–15, 19–20, 23
    facilities, salaries and allowances 26,
        28, 41–2, *43*, 265–6
    gender 50
    immunity 44, 45, 123, 144
    incompatibilities 40, 41
    individual rights 54–6, 249
    length of service 49
    and national governments 283
    numbers 4, *9*, 11, *12*, 22, *304*
    post-MEP experience 53–4
    pre-MEP experience 50–3
    priorities 56–8
    statute 46–7
    verification of credentials 40–1
Menem, President 281

Mennea, Pietro 53
Merger Treaty 27–8
Messner, Reinhold 53
Miert, Karel van 88
Miljöpartiet (Sweden) 73, 75
milk quotas 125
mini-plenaries 32
Minority Languages Intergroup 158
Mitterand, François 281, 297, 299
Mixed Groups 80
Modrow, Hans 51
Modus Vivendi 258–9
Mol/Transnuclear scandal 262
Mongolia 139
montants estimés nécessaires 230
Morillon, Philippe 53
Morocco 208
motions for resolution 55, 114, 119, 147,
    271–2
    intergroups 163
    length limits 35, 120
    voting order 150
Motor Insurance Directive, Fourth
    210
Movimento Sociale Italiano (MSI) 61, 78,
    80
multilingualism *see* languages
Muntingh, Hemmo 161
Murphy, Simon 48

Napolitano, Giorgio 99, 108
national culture 58
national delegations 87–9
national governments 281–3
national lists 17–18, 22, 24
national parliaments 296, 297
    contact channels 170, 283–7
    dual mandate 15, 19, 57
    elections 8
    MEPs' experience 50–1, *52*, 53
    openness 287
nationality principle
    for candidates 14, *14*, 19
    for voters *14*, 15, 20
Nea Dimokratia (ND) (Greece) 61, 68
Netherlands
    Calvinist parties 79
    constitutional change 298
    election results 25, *25*, 312
    electoral system 13, *13*, *14*, 15, 16
    European affairs committees *286*
    MEPs 41, *50*, 324–5
    representation *12*, 21
    seat issue 29
    staff *167*

Neunreither Group 280–1
neutralised committees 107
New Community Instrument
    Regulation 183
News Report 111
newspapers 170
Nicholson, Emma 50
night sittings 144
noise pollution directive 135
non-attached members 81, 134
non-compulsory expenditure 217, 220,
    222, 225–9
non-legislative texts 150, 177, 200
    see also motions for resolution
Nord, Hans 45
North Atlantic Treaty Organization
    (NATO) 139
Northern Ireland 13, *13*, 18, 271
Norway 22, 131, 207
Notenboom Procedure 224
nuclear materials 262

Official Journal of the European
    Communities
    legislative procedure 195, 200
    Ombudsman appointments 240
    plenary minutes 149, 155
    verbatim reports 156
    written questions 249
O'Hagan, Lord Charles 55
OLAF 234, 241
Ombudsman 204, 277–8, 279
    appointment 5, 234, 240
    dismissal 244
omnibus transfer 221
open Enlarged Bureau 29–30, 156
openness 287–9, 303
opinions 113–15, 120
oral questions 248, 249, 250, *250*
Orlando, Leoluca 73
Österreichische Volkspartei (ÖVP)
    (Austria) 68
own-initiative reports 114–15, 271

Pacciotti, Elena 52
package holidays 213
Paisley, Ian 50, 52, 80–1, 155
Palacio, Ana 104
Palestinian Legislative Council 140
Pannella, Marco 49, 56, 60, 62, 80, 101
Papayannakis, Mihail 161
parliamentary assizes 284
parliamentary cooperation committees
    130, 131
part-sessions *see* plenaries

Parti Communiste Français 18, 61, 62, 76,
    77
Partido Andalucista (Spain) 72, 75
Partido Popular (Spain) 68–9
Partido Social Democrata (Portugal) 61,
    63, 72
Partido Socialista Obrero Español (PSOE)
    48
Partito Comunista Italiano (PCI) 61, 62,
    71, 76
Partito dei Comunisti Italiani 77
Partito Democratico Della Sinistra (PDS)
    (Italy) 62, 71, 76
Partito Liberale (Italy) 72
Partito Repubblicano Italiano 72
Partito Socialista Democratica Italiano
    (PSDI) 70–1
Partito Socialista Italiano (PSI) 70–1
partnership and cooperation
    agreements 130, 131
Party of European Socialists 24, 71, 92,
    93
    see also Group of the Party of
        European Socialists
party federations 91–3
party lists 17–18, 22, 24
PASOK (Greece) 61
PASOK (Spain) 77
Pasqua, Charles 77, 78
Patijn, Schelto 11
Patterson, Ben 172
People's Movement (Denmark) 60, 61,
    63, 79
PES *see* Group of the Party of European
    Socialists; Party of European
    Socialists
petitions 275–8
Petitions Committee *see* Committee on
    Petitions
Pflimlin, Pierre 51, 99
pharmaceuticals 213
Pintasilgo, Maria de Lourdes 51
Pitt, Terry 48
Plaid Cymru (UK) 75
Planas, Luis 280
plenaries 141
    agenda 145–7
    compromise amendments 152
    explanations of vote 55
    openness 287
    order 154–5
    procedural manoeuvres 153–4
    public debates 270–1
    question time 55, 249, 250, *250*
    records 155–6

scrutiny 248
seat issue 26, 28, 30–1
setting 141–3
speaking time 81, 147–8
timetable 32, 33, *33*, 36, 143–5
topical and urgent debates 146–7, 271
voting procedures 148–51
Plumb, Sir Henry 68, 101, 109, 125, 138, 202
Plumb-Delors procedure 257–8
Podesta, Guido 97
Poettering, Hans-Gert 67
Poher, Alain 98
points of order 144, 153
Poland 22, *304*
police and judicial cooperation 184, 185
Political Affairs Committee *see* Committee on Political Affairs
Political Groups 6, 8, 59, *64–5*
appointments 238, 239, 241
budget 219, 221–2
Bureaux 82
chairs 41, 82, *83–4*, 94, 278
changing 81
committees 106, 107, 108–11, 113
compromises 152
Conciliation Committee 198
delegations 132, 134
discipline and whipping 54, 89–90
election of Parliament's officers 99, 101–2 financial support 20, 81–2, 266–7
Heads of Government meetings 281
history 59–63, *66*
intergroups 157, 158, 159
languages 34
meetings 29, 32, 86, 143
Mixed Groups 80
national delegations 87–9
plenaries 141–2, 143, 146, 147–8, 149, 151
political activities 86–7
power balances and relationships 90–1
questions 249
rapporteurs 117–18
rights 56
staffing 26, 82, 85–6, 166, 172–3
see also individual groups
political parties 297
federations 91–3
lists 17–18, 22, 24
Pollack, Anita 14, 48, 162
polling days, European elections 11, 12, 16

Poniatowski, Michel 104, 110
Portas, Paolo 52
Portugal
accession *9*, 61
election results *25*, *312*
electoral system 13, *13*, *14*, 15
European affairs committees *286*
MEPs *50*, 51, 325–6
representation *12*, 22
staff *167*
Posselt, Bernd 48
Prag, Derek 29, 109
Prag report 154
preferential voting 18, 22, 23, 24
preliminary draft budget 217, 218–20
Prescott, John 197, 283
President 57, 94–6, *95*, 107
compromise amendments 152
declaration of MEPs' financial interests 45
election 59, 98–9, *100*, 101, 149
and national parliaments 283
offices 41
official visits 283
plenaries 142–4, 147, 153, 155
see also Conference of Presidents
press 170
press *see* newspapers
Priestley, Julian 168, 172–3
prizes 274–5, *275*
procedure without report 122
Prodi Commission 212, 233, 236–7, 247
Progress Party (Denmark) 61
Progressive Democrats *see* European Progressive Democrats
Progressive Democrats (Ireland) 72
proportional representation, European elections 12–13, *13*, 16–17, 22, 23, 24
Provan, James 97, 198
PSE *see* Group of the Party of European Socialists
public access 143, 287–9
Puerta, Alonso 77

Quaestors 94, 98, *98*, 290
election 101–2, 149
intergroups 159
offices 41
see also College of Quaestors
qualified majority voting (Council) 3, 7, 207
question time 55, 249, 250, *250*
questions *see* oral questions; written questions
Quin, Joyce 53, 282–3

quorum calls 153–4

racism 261, 262
"Rainbow" (verbatim report of plenary
    sessions) 155–6
Rainbow Group (RBW) 61, 74, 75
rapporteurs 47, 57, 90, 118–20
    committee hearings 273
    delegations 136–7
    nomination 59, 117–18
    speaking time 147, 148
Rassemblement pour la République
    (France)
    Political Groups 60, 61, 63, 69, 78, 79
    tourniquet 19–20
Raunio, Tapio 89, 91
Reagan, Ronald 281
reconsultation 201
Reding, Viviane 280
referral back 153, 180
Reflection Group 279, 301–2
regional assemblies 19
Regional Committee 105
    see also Committee on Regional
        Policy, Transport and Tourism
Rehn, Ollie 280
reports 113–15, 116, 120–2, 146, 288
    see also rapporteurs
representation 20–2, 304
Die Republikaner (Germany) 78, 134
Research Committee see Committee on
    Research, Technological
    Development and Energy
Research Framework Agreement, Fifth
    197–8, 230–1
residence principle
    for candidates 14, 19, 23
    for voters 14, 14, 15, 20, 23
Reynolds, Patrick 79
Ries, Frédérique 14, 52
Rifondazione Comunista (Italy) 76, 77
Rinsche, Günter 104
Ripa di Meana, Carlo 101
Roberts, Dame Shelagh 41
Rocard, Michel 51
Roelants de Vivier, François 101
Rogalla, Dieter 55
roll call votes 149–50
Romania 131, 304
Roo, Alexander de 86
Rosado Fernandes, Raúl Miguel 155
Roth-Behrendt, Dagmar 126
Rothley, Willi 46, 196
RPR see Rassemblement pour la
    République

Rules Committee see Committee on
    Rules
Rules of Procedure
    amendments 150
    appointments 240, 242
    assent procedure 208
    committees 113–14, 117, 122–3, 288
    committees of inquiry 263
    confidentiality 123
    consultation procedure 180
    Council 202–3
    declaration of financial interests 45,
        159
    delegations 136
    disorder 155
    individual members' rights 54–6
    legislation 200, 201, 211, 212
    lobbying 290
    non-attached members' rights 56, 81
    official languages 33–4
    openness and transparency 287
    petitions 275
    plenary topics 147
    Political Groups 59, 63, 81
    President 94, 99
    procedural manoeuvres 153–4
    replacement system 41
    speaking time 147
    terms of office 41
    urgent matters 274
    verification of credentials 41
    votes of confidence 235
    voting 149
Rumor, Mariano 51
Russia 131, 136, 140, 158
Rutelli, Francesco 52

Saby, Henri 104
Sadat, Anwar 155, 281
Saint-Josse, Jean 79
Sakharov Prize for Freedom of Thought
    102, 274–5, 275
Salafranca, José Ignacio 280
salaries
    MEPs 41–2, 43, 46
    staff 173
Samland-Williamson agreement 259
Santer, Jacques 51, 235, 280
Santer Commission 5–6, 9, 243–4
Sarajevo 139
Sartori, Amalia 52
Scallon, Rosemary 53, 67, 69
Scapagnini, Umberto 109
Schaefer, Axel 48
Scharping, Rudolf 93

Schluter, Poul 51
Schodruch, Hans Günter 110
Schuijt, Willem 291
Schuman Declaration 2
Scientific and Technical Options
    Assessment 125, 252
Scotland 18, 117
Scottish National Party 75
scrutiny 5–6, 235, 246–7, 269, 296, 300
    comitology 255–61
    committees of inquiry 261–4
    control of expenditure 252–5
    debates on statements 247–8
    judicial review 264–9
    parliamentary questions 248–50
    reports 250–2
seals 211
seat issue 2, 26–32, 266
Secretariat
    issues affecting 171–3
    languages 34
    location 26–7, 28, 29, 31
    MEPs' assistants 48
structure 168, 169, 170–1
Secretary-General 102, 142, 168
Segni, Mario 78
Seibel-Emmerling, Lieselotte 161
Seitlinger, Jean 22
Seligman, Madron 161
Seymour-Rouse, Edward 161
Shevardnadze, Eduard 281
Shevardnadze Procedure 281
Sieglerschmidt reports 20
simplified procedure 122
Single European Act 9, 305
    assent procedure 4, 203, 204, 207–8
    constitutional change 160, 298–9
    cooperation procedure 4, 185, 193
    legislative texts 119
    petitions 275
single market 2–3, 192
Slovakia 131, 304
Slovenia 131, 304
Soares, Mário 51, 99, 101
Social Affairs Committee see Committee
    on Social Affairs and Employment
Socialist Group 60, 61, 62
    see also Group of the Party of
        European Socialists
Socialistisk Folkeparti (Denmark) 61, 74
Söderman, Jacob 240, 278
Solbes, Pedro 280
SOS-Europe 160–1
Sotelo, Calvo 51
South Africa 131, 136–7, 140

South Korea 130
Spaak, Antoinette 161
Spain
    accession 9, 61–2
    election results 25, 312
    electoral system 13, 13, 14, 15, 18
    European affairs committees 286
    guillotine clause 197
    MEPs 41, 50, 52, 326–7
    representation 12, 21
    seat issue 29
    staff 167
speaking time 59, 81
special majorities 144
Spinelli, Altiero 61, 160, 295–6
Spinelli Draft Treaty 9, 241, 297
Sports Intergroup 163–5
STABEX fund 211
Staes, Paul 101
staff 166–8, 167, 171–2
    committees 31, 111–12, 168, 170
    delegations 168, 170
    inter-institutional meetings 280–1
    MEPs' assistants 47–8
    plenaries 142
    Political Groups 26, 82, 85–6, 166
    see also interpreters; Secretariat;
        translators
Staller, Ilona 62
Steel, David 14
Sterckx, Dirk 52
STOA 125, 252
Stockton, Earl of 50
Strasbourg
    committee meetings 112
    delegations 136
    Group week 86
    intergroups 158, 161, 162
    MEPs' offices 41
    plenaries 141–5, 146, 281
    press conferences 290, 291
    seat issue 26–33, 154, 266
    staff 166, 171, 282
    visitors 291, 292
structural funds 183, 204
Stuttgart Solemn Declaration on
    European Union 182, 206, 208, 234,
    248
Suárez, Adolfo 62
subcommittees 105, 124
subsidiarity 279, 296, 299
Summits
    Paris 11, 178, 206, 248
    Political Groups 92
    see also European Council

Sweden
    accession *9*, 63, 207
    election results *25, 313*
    electoral system 13, *13, 14,* 15
    JPC 131
    language 36
    MEPs 42, *50,* 51, 327–8
    representation *12,* 22
    Riksdag 286, 287
    staff 167, *167*
Switzerland 134
Synaspismos tis Aristeras Kai tis Proodou
    (Greece) 77
Syria 208, 273

TACIS programme 135
Tapie, Bernard 62
taxation
    harmonisation 191
    MEPs 46
TEC Treaty *see* European Community
    Treaty
Technical Group *see* Group for the
    Technical Co-ordination and Defence
    of Independent Groups and
    Members
television 143, 170, 291
    trans-frontier broadcasts 211, 213
temporary committees 125–6
TGV Intergroup 158
Thatcher, Margaret 92
Thorn, Gaston 51
Thorn Commission 234
thresholds, electoral systems 18, 23, 24
Tibet 134
Tindemans, Leo 51, 138
Titley, Gary 48
tobacco advertising 196, 211, 268, 289
Tomlinson, John 163, 263
Tongue, Carole 86
topical debates 146–7, 271
tourniquet system 19–20
toxic substances 261
trade unions
    leaders as MEPs 52
    MEPs' assistants 48
Trans-European Networks 231
Transatlantic Legislators' Dialogue 135
Transit Committee 263, 264, 273
translation 2, 34–5, 36, 37, 155, 156, 170
translators 35, 167
    jurist linguists 35, 146, 200
transparency 202, 279, 287–93
Transport and Tourism Committee 105,
    128

    see also Committee on Regional
        Policy, Transport and Tourism
Treaty of Amsterdam *see* Amsterdam
    Treaty
Treaty on European Union *see*
    Maastricht Treaty
Treaty of Rome *9,* 10–11
Trentin, Bruno 52
trialogues 199, 278
Tugendhat, Christopher 254
Turkey 130–1, 139, 208, 273–4
turnout, European elections 25, *25*
turnstile system 19–20

Ulster Unionist Party 61, 69
Union for Europe Group 63, 78, *83–4*
    see also Group of Europe of Nations
Union for a Europe of Nations 63, 78
    see also Group of Europe of Nations
Union Valdôtaine-Partito Sardo d'Azione
    (Italy) 61
United European Left *see* Group of the
    United European Left
United Kingdom
    accession *9,* 60
    Auto-Oil Package 197
    constitutional change 160, 298, 302,
        303
    declaration of financial interests 45
    draft treaty on European Union 298
    election results *25, 313*
    electoral system 13, *13,* 14, *14,* 15,
        16–17, *18,* 23
    House of Commons 22, 141, 157, 249,
        252, 285, *286*
    House of Lords 22, *286*
    legislative initiative 209
    MEPs *43,* 49, 50, *50,* 51, 53, 282–3,
        328–9
    in plenary 55–6
    qualified majority voting 207
    question time 55
    representation 11, *12,* 21
    seat issue 29
    staff *167*
    UKREP 282
    see also Northern Ireland
United States
    conciliations 198
    delegations 130, 135, 136
    election turnout 25
United States Congress 2, 21, 158, 213
    committees 7, 108, 124
    elections 8
    Office of Technology Assessment 252

staff 57
URBAN programme 231
urgent debates 144, 146–7, 271, 274
Uzbekistan 135

Vatanen, Ari 53
Veil, Simone 99
Veltroni, Walter 52
Venstre (Denmark) 72
Verger, Christine 70
verification of credentials 40–1
Les Verts (France) 18, 74
    financial support for parties 20, 82,
      266–7
    rotation of MEPs 20
Vice-Presidents 94, 95, 96–8, *97*, 285
    Conciliation Committee 198
    election 59, 101, 149
    offices 41, 166
    plenaries 142
Villalobos Talero, Celia 126
Villiers, Philippe de 62, 78
Viola, Vicenzo 102
visitors 291, *292*, 293
Visits' Service 291
Vlaams Blok (Belgium) 79, 80
Volksunie (Belgium) 61
Volksunie-ID 21 (Belgium) 75
voluntary consultations 176
Von Der Vring, Thomas 126
voting procedures, in plenaries 144, 145,
    147, 148–51
Vredeling, Henk 55

Wales 18

Watson, Graham 89
Weber, Jup 74
Weiss, Louise 99
Welle, Klaus 67
West Germany 11, 25
    see also Germany
Westendorp, Carlos 52, 108, 302
Western European Union (WEU) 301
    Assembly 26, 139
Wijkman, Anders 52
Wijsenbeek, Florus 86
Wilkins, David 162
Wings of Europe 158
Wogau, Karl von 125
women
    in Commission 237
    committees of inquiry 261
    as MEPs 50, *51*
Women's Rights Committee *see*
    Committee on Women's Rights
working parties 124–5
written declarations 55, 163, 272
written questions 55, 248, 249, 250, *250*
Wurtz, Francis 75, 77
Wynn, Terry 136

Year of the Environment 125
Yeltsin, Boris 281
Youth Committee, *see also* Committee
    on Culture, Youth, Education and the
    Media

Zabell, Teresa 53
Zagari, Mario 28